National Interest/National Honor

The Institute for the Study of Diplomacy concentrates on the *processes* of conducting foreign relations abroad, in the belief that studies of diplomatic operations are a useful means of teaching or improving diplomatic skills and of broadening public understanding of diplomacy. Working closely with the academic program of the Georgetown University School of Foreign Service, the Institute conducts a program of publication, teaching, research, conferences, lectures, and special awards. Its associates program enables experienced practitioners of international relations to conduct individual research while sharing their firsthand experience with the university community.

NATIONAL INTEREST/ NATIONAL HONOR

The Diplomacy of the Falklands Crisis

Douglas Kinney

Published in cooperation with the Institute
for the Study of Diplomacy,
Georgetown University

PRAEGER

New York
Westport, Connecticut
London

Library of Congress Cataloging-in-Publication Data

Kinney, Douglas.
    National interest/national honor : the diplomacy of the Falklands
  crisis / Douglas Kinney.
      p.   cm.
  Bibliography: p.
  Includes index.
   ISBN 0–275–92425–4 (alk. paper)
    1. Falkland Islands War, 1982—Diplomatic history. 2. Argentina—
Foreign relations—Great Britain. 3. Great Britain—Foreign
relations—Argentina. 4. Diplomatic negotiations in international
disputes. I. Title.
F3031.5.K55   1989
997'.11—dc19   88–29271

Library of Congress Catalog Card Number: 88–29271
ISBN: 0–275–92425–4

First published in 1989

Praeger Publishers, One Madison Avenue, New York, NY 10010
A division of Greenwood Press, Inc.

Printed in the United States of America

The paper used in this book complies with the Permanent
Paper Standard issued by the National Information Standards
Organization (Z39.48–1984).

10 9 8 7 6 5 4 3 2 1

To the Falklands War dead of Argentina and of the United Kingdom, and to those who tried to avert their sacrifice.

A High Ideal

It might seem that the ideal which I now set up for the negotiator is one too high for any man to reach. It is true that no man can ever carry out his instructions without a fault, but unless he has before him an ideal as a guide he will find himself plunged in the midst of distracting affairs without any rule for his own conduct. Therefore I place before him these considerations: that despite all disappointments and exasperations he must act with *sang-froid*; he must work with patience to remove all obstacles that lie in his path, whether they are placed there by accident or act of God or by the evil design of men; he must preserve a calm and resolute mind when the conjunctures of events seem to conspire against him; and finally, he must remember that if once he permit his own personal or outrageous feelings to guide his conduct in negotiation he is on the sure and straight road to disaster. In a word, when events and men are unkind he must never despair of being able to change them, nor again when they smile upon his efforts must he cherish the illusion that their good favour will endure forever.

—de Callières, *On the Manner of Negotiating with Princes*

CONTENTS

Preface   XV

**I. Contexts: Brushfire War, Territory, the Radicalization of
    Decolonization, Crisis Diplomacy, and Third-Party
    Mediation**   1

    Conflicting Interests Justify Conflict: Brushfire War since
      1945   1

    The Radicalization of Decolonization: Dangerous Matrix   6

    Nonaligned Resolutions on the Falklands   10

    Territory: A Question of Perception   14

    Territorial Disputes   17

    Negotiation by Any Other Name   30

    The Mediator as Negotiator: Some Basic Considerations   32

**II. Origins: The Politics of Illusion versus the Politics of
    Principle—Centuries of Dispute, Years of Bilateral
    Negotiation**   37

    Falklands Sovereignty: The Mists of Colonialism   37

    Argentine Diplomacy: The Southern Perspective,
      Otherworldliness, and Persistence   44

Signals   46

Falkland Negotiations: At the Table and on the Beach   48

1977: Unsent Signals   56

The Lobby   57

"Final" Signals, Intended and Not   60

Endgame   61

III.   **Crisis Deterrence and Management—Too Little,**
       Too Late   73

Overview   74

"Recuperacion"   74

"None for Five"   76

The Central American Connection   81

The Nonaligned and the Falklands   82

The Navy's Plan   83

Public Reaction: National Honor in the Streets   85

War by Other Means   86

Riposte   86

Resources   87

"Ungovernability"   89

Multilateral Deterrence: Confusion and Constraints in the
   Security Council   91

Bilateral Deterrence: Too Little, Too Late   92

Plan A/Plan B: Internal, Institutional, and International
   Incentives to Violence   95

IV.   **Crisis Management: Third-Country Mediation by the**
       United States   99

Overview: The Mediation Attempts   99

The Shape of the Possible Settlement   100

Differing Agendas   101

U.S. Mediation   103

The Last Plan   135

Players: The Chemistry of the Mediator as Negotiator   138

Process   143

Diplomacy and Arms, Delay and Action   144

Inhibitors: Friends, Gambits, and Timing   145

Timing: When to Negotiate, When to Mediate   145

Failure: The United States and Argentina Part Ways   147

V.   **The Peruvian Attempt**   149

Peru, Rounds One and Two   151

Torpedoed: Argentine Perceptions   156

British Perceptions   159

"Graduated" Force/Political Shock   160

The Threat: Force for Its Own Sake   163

The Deal?   167

The London Connection   171

The Phone Call   172

Closing the Loop: Risks of Multilateral Mediation   173

The Cost of High-Level Personalist Diplomacy   176

"Graduated" Use of Political-Military Pressure   177

Peru, Round Two   181

Peru-U.S. Proposal, May 5, 1982   181

Political Pressure   183

VI. **International Good Offices: The U.N. Mediation in
     New York**   195

United Nations Mediation—The Near Miss   195

Personal Good Offices   198

Method   200

Progress and Promise   201

Argentina Declines   206

Counterproposal and Collapse   209

VII. Statecraft and Force   217

Negotiations: An Overview of the Elements   218

Endgame   236

Political "Lessons" Learned and Mislearned   244

The Suez Syndrome   250

A Redefinition of the Value of Territory   251

The Rules: Power and Law   252

Timing and National Honor   253

"None for Five": "Plan B"   255

VIII. The Road to the Future   257

Argentina Creates and Reacts to "Fortress Falklands"   258

Falklands Diplomacy Becomes Falklands Foreign Policy   259

Argentina Rearms   260

Plan B Dissolves   261

Politics Resumed: The Malvinas Leitmotif   263

Britain: Fortress London/Fortress Falklands   263

Paradise Recoverable: The Kelpers, Culture, and Politics   264

Mediators: Prophets without Honor   272

Beyond Mediation   275

The Illogic of Politico-Legal Resolutions of Territorial
    Disputes   275

Solutions in Practical Politics   280

Argentine Interests, Argentine Actions   281

British Interests, British Actions   283

Joint Undertakings   287

Epilogue   291

Falklands: A Crisis for Negotiation and Mediation   291

Appendices   295

Falklands Chronology   297

Documents   339

Notes   341

Selected Bibliography   357

Index   365

About the Author   371

PREFACE

The Falklands crisis of spring 1982 offers several distinct but interrelated case studies in negotiation and third-party mediation of international conflict.[1] Attempts at averting or moderating war ran the full gamut from bilateral negotiations and General Assembly resolutions to third-party and Security Council "preventative diplomacy" via classic American shuttle diplomacy by the Secretary of State, an attempt at settlement by Peru, and, finally, the extended negotiations under the auspices of the Secretary General of the United Nations.

Each of these efforts was itself a textbook example of peacemaking. The two parties negotiated for a decade and a half. After the first use of force, the peacemakers had weeks, indeed months, to avert bloodshed—a thousand hours between the landings of Argentine and then British warriors.

Nonetheless war came, as it has more than 200 times since 1945. The roots of armed conflict lay in centuries of territorial dispute of the kind that pervades the modern world (especially the New World), leading to less and less inhibited resort to force by nation-states. The conflict was also rooted in British representational democracy, politics, defense, and worldview; the particular nature of Argentine history and the pace of her politics; in the inconsistency and unreality (abetted by the radical nonaligned states) which is the field of U.N. political activity called Decolonization; and in the mutual, longer-run failure of political and diplomatic imagination and courage on the part of both parties, their friends, and the nation-state system.

The diplomacy of the Falklands crisis includes several major stages:

—Conflicting claims and military conflict since the European discovery of the New World;

—U.N. consideration of the area under the rubric of Decolonization and dependent areas;

—Seventeen years of bilateral negotiations (accompanied by the threat and use of force and political "guerrilla warfare" by Argentina);

—Attempts at preventive diplomacy by the United Nations and the United States; and

—Three major mediations: the Haig shuttle, Peru's effort, and the New York attempt by U.N. Secretary General Perez de Cuellar (with military events proceeding in parallel).

These three major mediation attempts focused on three principal common elements:

—Military cease-fire, disengagement, and withdrawal;

—Interim Administration and governance; and

—Resolution of the sovereignty dispute.

British and Argentine diplomacy can usefully be assessed in terms of an analytical distinction between National Interest and National Honor: National Interest can be of a military, economic, or political nature, but has a concreteness to it; that is, it can be defined in terms of a scarce good or privilege that engenders conflict if contested by two nation-states. National Honor is no less a real interest of a player in the nation-state game: to a well-regarded player at the end of each important round of international negotiation or conflict. National Honor has rational, and less rational, domestic and international components and results. The distinction has explanatory power in helping one get at the issues and the negotiations in the Falklands crisis.

The Falklands War must be set in the context of the more than 220 interstate conflicts since 1945. Brushfire wars are likely to increase as a phenomenon for the rest of the century. A contributing factor will be the number of sovereignty and boundary disputes, which make up the other important context. States seem to feel less and less reticence in resorting to violence, especially over or in the name of territory.

Interstate conflicts are distinct from domestic disputes: (1) in the intangible of National Honor; and (2) in the limitations on the third party mediator imposed by the sovereignty of the two contestants. These are inherent and often unavoidable "frictions" in the international mediation process. They have led to a sad record on peaceful dispute settlement in this century.

The third important context of the Falklands dispute is the radicalization of the nonaligned nation-states in their Decolonization behavior. Argentina has framed the issue in Decolonization terms since the late 1960s. In dealing with conflicts between the principles of *self-determination of peoples* and *territorial integrity of states* (Goa, Sahara, Timor, and others), the nonaligned are currently running toward territorial integrity. This may serve their short-run interests, but their *ad hoc,* politicized behavior is destabilizing for the international order. Further, it is likely in the medium term to conflict with their own national interests.

Not all diplomacy is conducted across a table in written form. Signals, intended or not, are constantly exchanged by international adversaries. Arms and discussion, deeds and diplomacy are not mutually exclusive. The nation state uses or threatens the use of all instruments simultaneously. In the 17 years of Falklands negotiations, in parallel with the formal interaction of Argentine and British principles and politics, Argentina set out to "create new realities," establishing weather stations, stationing marines for a summer on uninhabited dependencies, resorting occasionally to gunboat diplomacy, and generally asserting sovereignty with minor gestures of "will" largely lost on the British. Britain meanwhile sent a series of political signals—some intended, some accidental—read by the Argentines as indicating longer-term acquiescence in Argentina's insistence on sovereignty over the Falklands.

Cross-cultural misperception is a constant element in the centuries of misunderstanding over the Falklands. It is epitomized in the Argentine diplomatic decision making concerning the invasion. Argentina called all five of the major questions wrong. They were none-for-five on British response, U.S. policy, Soviet veto, and nonaligned votes in the U.N. Security Council, as well as on world political reaction. Understanding the Argentine perspective and reasoning tells a lot about the subsequent Argentine diplomacy, and about the ongoing nature of the Falklands crisis.

The U.N. Security Council with its efforts to first prevent, and then undo the Argentine invasion, as well as the U.S. efforts at bilateral deterrence by high-level phone calls, lead one to a paradigm of institutional incentives for violence: that the Argentine military engaged in a rational calculus within which (given their primarily domestic orientation and the version of National Honor to which this led them) they foresaw a scenario ("Plan B") in which, even should they lose, they and their country would come out better; and particularly that their institution (the military) would retain enough control to guide the country toward a kind of transition to democracy they could live with. In that sense, Plan B was implemented. It provides a series of lessons for the Third World which have very dangerous implications for world order.

The third-party mediations each came close to avoiding war if not achieving peace. None, tragically, worked. One is struck by the common elements of each of the three major proposed settlements, and the common inhibitions to settlement. The mechanics, the specific proposals, and the real-world events proceeding in parallel with the negotiations need to be tied together. Negotiating style and other intangibles seem to explain as much as do the specifics of the proposals.

This study of the diplomacy of the Falklands crisis raises more questions than it answers. Falklands was a highly visible but little understood political crisis, which led to a war. Its mislearned lessons are unfortunately likely to lead to "more and better" resort to violence in the last quarter of the twentieth century.

Where the parties have come since the Falklands crisis gives one hope but not optimism. There are ways to harmonize or delink National Interest and National Honor, but territorial questions limit them. British confidence-building measures such as lowered force levels and a sharing of resources, and Argentine internal legislation *as though sovereign* might be some of the unilateral first steps and the best hopes for lowering Britain's costs and perceived threat level, moving Argentina toward patience and realism, and leading to a negotiating framework in which more practical solutions and new, imaginative definitions of sovereignty, National Interest and National Honor could again be discussed.

The author is deeply grateful for the opportunity afforded him for professional growth and renewal by the vision and generosity of Una Chapman Cox, whose trustees afforded him a year's sabbatical from the U.S. Foreign Service. He is indebted to Georgetown University's School of Foreign Service and the Institute for the Study of Diplomacy for the opportunity to teach and learn. Many participants in the Falklands crisis and experts on the South Atlantic were helpful in this endeavor. The author is in the debt of these colleagues—diplomatic, military, legislative, and academic—but takes full responsibility for the conclusions of this case study.

These conclusions took shape in the ministries, legislatures, universities, and "think tanks" of England and Argentina, as well as in the Falkland Islands at an antique desk in Government House and "in camp" on a sheep farm. The author has had the honor of being received in all these places as a friend and is indebted to scores of colleagues for confidential interviews and exchanges. He has been privileged to share points of view with the military officers on both sides who made the tactical and the strategic decisions. He has been warmly received in Argentine and British universities and institutes of international affairs.

Diplomatic colleagues, including the crack Argentine and British diplomats with whom I was privileged to work at the United Nations on the Falklands dispute *before* the 1982 crisis, were most generous with their time and insight. It is to their great credit that our three-way mutual respect survived the weeks of the crisis and the tense playing out of the diplomatic and then military dramas in the U.N. Security Council.

Parliamentarians of the United Kingdom and Argentina shared with me their recollections of the political processes surrounding the Falklands diplomacy, and their visions of how we might someday solve the dispute. Individual journalists deeply steeped in the unfolding of events and the contradictions in the available data were kind enough to share diligent research and firmly held convictions.

Private citizens with strong and/or informed views sought me out in England and Argentina to argue their cause—or sometimes that of the opposing nation. The people and Government of the Falkland Islands were hospitable, open, and sharply dispassionate about their then-recent experience of military occupation. (Perhaps the most poignant interviews of this effort were those in which they described their protection of Argentine enlisted men from what they viewed as excessive military discipline, or described their pride that the best-kept piece of ground on either island is the cemetery for the Argentine war dead.) Standing in the trenches on the approach to Goose Green, the white athletic socks issued to the Argentine infantry still glared against the dun-colored landscape, eloquent confirmation of the testimony of Argentine soldiers who complained that they were not given the tools to do an impossible job.

The focus of this work, however, was on those far from the trenches who lost control of and tried to moderate the Falklands crisis. Statesmen, elected or appointed, were most at risk in debriefing to an author in search of some very sensitive, elusive, and sometimes still contradictory details about the conduct of three very emotionally charged negotiations.

Overall, my interlocutors were honest about their policy views and their national predispositions. Where they were not, I credit their loyalty. I did not use their partial revelations (if uncorroborated and unavailable elsewhere) to destroy intricately derived and highly cherished positions. Where they fooled a somewhat seasoned student of negotiation and human nature, they proved their astuteness. Where they did not successfully convince or deceive, I ask that they reconsider whether the perpetuation of crisis and wartime collective myth or propaganda contributes to solution of the ongoing dispute. Conclusions based on these conversations, whether I accepted my interlocutor's views or not, remain the responsibility of the author—a judgment call and an inherent weakness in an individual analytical research effort, which is at heart only a series of case studies for others to build upon.

This assessment of the diplomacy of the Falklands crisis is a critique of the methods and not the motivations of Argentina, the United Kingdom, and those (the author included) who tried and are still trying to help them resolve their dispute. It is an attempt, much like that of U.S. diplomacy during the Falklands crisis of 1982, to find why friends went to war and to lessen the chance of it happening again.

There ought to be much to be learned here about negotiation and mediation, about peacemaking and the art of diplomacy, about the modern balance of principle and force, and about averting or moderating international conflict. This attempt to understand the tragically unsuccessful negotiations and third-party mediations surrounding the Falkland Islands, however, raises as many questions as it answers.

This is in large part because key facts about the Falklands crisis are classified for military or diplomatic reasons by various governments. Much of the author's own experience of the crisis could not be used for this reason. Other participants will find gaps covered here by speculation and hypothesis quite unsatisfactory, but must remember they declined to disclose events as they occurred. Others will be concerned with the presentation of opposing national views of events which they do not share, but these alternate perspectives serve to explain some aspect of territorial crisis and its negotiation and mediation until we have full disclosure. (Most incorrect data in a crisis was nonetheless generated or believed by a participant.) Similarly, alternative motivations and perceptions are worth exploring even if they are only likely as their development in context has explanatory power about the crisis. Those who would look further can access materials used in this case study through the Institute for the Study of Diplomacy, Georgetown University, Washington, DC 20057. Corrections would be most welcome and will eventually be incorporated into another edition.

The author looks forward to hearing from those with more, or other, answers, because the Falklands crisis is not in any real sense over. It may indeed be a paradigm for increasing interstate violence over territory or self-determination. The search for a stable and lasting solution to many territorial conflicts, and for better negotiating and mediation approaches, has to date been less than successful but the deaths in the Antarctic autumn of 1982 in the South Atlantic and those to follow over this and other territory warrant that the search continue.

I

CONTEXTS: BRUSHFIRE WAR, TERRITORY, THE RADICALIZATION OF DECOLONIZATION, CRISIS DIPLOMACY, AND THIRD-PARTY MEDIATION

> The international code of honor at this moment dictated that any set-
> tlement of a national injury other than a military one was a humiliation.
> —Julius Goebel, *The Struggle for the Falkland Islands,*
> describing the diplomatic environment of
> the 1771 Falklands settlement.

> Small wars are a heritage of extended empire, a certain epilogue to
> encroachments into lands beyond the confines of existing civilization
> inhabited by races with unconventional methods of warfare.... Out
> of the original campaign of conquest sprang further wars—all vexatious,
> desultory and harrassing.
> —British War Office manual of 1896

CONFLICTING INTERESTS JUSTIFY CONFLICT:
BRUSHFIRE WAR SINCE 1945

In the year of the Falklands crisis, the following countries were engaged directly
or informally in armed force: Argentina, Angola, Afghanistan, Burma, Chad,
Chile, Colombia, Cuba, Djibouti, Ecuador, El Salvador, Ethiopia, France,
Guatemala, Honduras, Indonesia, Iran, Iraq, Israel, Kampuchea, Kenya, Leb-
anon, Libya, Morocco, Mozambique, Nicaragua, Oman, Peru, Philippines, Poland, Seychelles, Somalia, South Africa, Spain, Syria, Thailand, Uganda, United
Kingdom, United States, USSR, Viet Nam, Yugoslavia, and Zimbabwe.

These are part of the pattern of brushfire war prevailing since 1945 and destined
to increase in the light of several trends highlighted by the South Atlantic crisis

of spring 1982. States or those who would form or take over states are resorting more and more to armed and (at least on one side) uniformed, centrally directed military violence. The causes of the quarter-thousand conflicts in the two decades following World War II are as diverse as their cultures and as old as time.

However, several trends are emerging that promise not the random and relatively infrequent continuation of old patterns but the disturbing expansion of a new one: Unless rethought and checked, the tendency toward the legitimization of violence in the name of claims for territory long separated by old injustices will expand for the foreseeable future.

A contributing condition is an increasing and more legitimated resort to arms to settle disputes generally and the concurrent weakening of the U.N. Charter and other norms proscribing the use of force to settle disputes and advocating peaceful settlement no matter how protracted and frustrating.

There is increasing attention to the resolution of territorial situations long dormant for lack of ability to influence the situation. A politics of impatience and action seems increasingly to compel states from within to be assertive about matters territorial.

Traditional legitimization of such claims in the name of territorial integrity is by appeal to raison d'état coupled with ethnic nationalism, actual or in the name of countrymen displaced. These are augmented by the politics of Decolonization and the radicalization of world normative politics.

The most legitimate form of irredentism in this view concerns territory taken by a colonial or imperialist power and forming part of a worldwide empire. The present population or real status of political development have less to do with the merits than geographical proximity. The political trend within this school of thinking about Decolonization is that the original Charter goal of self-determination is subordinate to the needs of those nation-states which acceded to independence in what they consider a less than complete form due to colonial boundaries. (There is a countervailing Third World school of thought that old boundaries are at least marked, agreed-on frontiers, whose disturbance will lead to strife.)

Making the resort to force in the name of territorial integrity more pronounced is the *radicalization* of world political questions, especially territorial ones, as a political imperative—a collective need to assert oneself, no less real because of its vagueness. The principal expression of radicalization is in anti-Western political action. Its focus is often reflective of its origins in colonialism and the succeeding multipolar, European-dominated system. Fomented by the radical nonaligned states on principle and third-party Communist patrons for more traditional political reasons, it finds one of its most consistent and often illogical political outlets in questions of territory gained if not held under older rules.

This radicalization is not in East-West terms so much as North-South, even if it is encouraged from the East. It reflects nearly universal demands for recognition and the claiming or reclaiming of national and ethnic identities. Eastern interests can suffer from the radicalization trend, even within the borders of the

Soviet Union. Many of the roots of the tendency toward the radicalization of territorial and ethnic questions lie in the West, in an old tradition running from Thomas Jefferson through Woodrow Wilson. The American Revolution, first of the modern nationalist state-formations by violent revolution, certainly pointed the way. As radical states mature, there are striking shifts in their interests from ideological purposes and poses toward pure nationalism and hence territorial offensive and even acquisitiveness. States born in violence abhor the use of force. States that abhor the use of force then begin to find it to be another form of political expression; the continuation of politics by other means. Hence, there is a strong association between the radicalization of political, especially territorial, questions, and armed violence. There also seems to be an anti-Western quality to radicalization whether or not the Western states involved are conservative or are acting conservatively in a particular situation.

The situation and even the rules may not be so much colonial (involving a dominated population) as imperial (the projection of force and even population abroad), but the distinction is subjectively blurred. Old wrongs by Europeans are favored over those by neighbors that may actually be far greater injuries to one's interests.

Providing the means to assert newly felt and newly supported grievances is a new generation of less expensive, lower-cost, smart electronic weaponry. Available in a virtual world arms bazaar, highly portable and often turn-key in their operating (if not maintenance) technology, a new generation of conventional "superweapons" scares arms-control experts as much as small nuclear devices that may be the next step in brushfire war. The superweapons are deadly in their ability to strike key targets, to make civilian populations vulnerable, and to subject leaderships to unprecedented decapitation risks. They have a tendency to make one think in ambitious terms, especially about the far-flung military resources of major and middle-size powers. With their marked abilities to defend as well as strike, they convey the illusion of power and foster robust military planning. They exaggerate civilian geopolitical thinking as much as they do military contingency planning.

Absent more realistic and constructive solutions to felt grievances, this complex of principles and realities argues for "more and better" territorial war for at least several decades. If neither claimants nor holders of territory reexamine the phenomenon of territorial violence, these wars may become so frequent as to overlap in time or causation, accelerating and worsening this deadly trend in world politics. The tradeoffs will not be between "remedying" the situations sooner by violence or later by negotiation but by resisted or unresisted violence as resorting to arms becomes the method of choice. Territorial war will become the honorable, self-assertive, "progressive" solution to territorial disputes.

National Honor versus National Interest

This analysis assumes a system of nation-states acting independently and in their own interests as they perceive them. In the last quarter of the twentieth century, these national interests as perceived by policymakers and publics are many and complex. Their broadest categories include military, economic, and political interests. Each has corresponding instruments of national policy. Certainly all three sets of major National Interests were in play in the Falklands crisis, though economics was as usual overrated, and became the subject of a gaggle of conspiracy theories. Military instruments were in the end more useful than political tools. This has unfortunate implications for an international order attuned to recent, concrete lessons.

This analysis also posits a more general and overarching National Interest of each player, which both draws on and cuts through other, more specific interests: the way in which the effectiveness of the player in the ongoing game is affected by actions in implementing more specific national interests. Broadly conceived, what might be dismissed as "image" becomes a more operational concept: an amalgam of collective civic pride; the seriousness with which one is taken in the "game"; one's own seriousness, dependability, constructive intent of other system values; the perceived legitimacy of asserted National Interests; and the cumulative record of past efforts at implementation. We shall call this complex and interrelated set of interests that bear on one's standing National Honor. It is useful, if sometimes highly artificial, to distinguish it from National Interests, a more specific and calculable set of motivations for decisions. It is distinct not only in its abstractness but also in its base in principle and consistency as a system value.

National Honor is less concrete than National Interest—political, economic or military—but no less real or important. It is the assessment and implementation of collective values for international behavior. The result is one's standing in the nation-state system based on past behaviors in securing one's interests. It is not merely group vanity, not simply image, and not purely statism. Such standing determines in large part how a country will be treated in future rounds of conflicting interests. National Honor is most interesting as a political phenomenon and most important as a factor in decision making when it tempers or contradicts concrete National Interests in favor of standing in the system. It has both domestic and international sources and results—a "toughness," or the easy resort to force. There are often significant returns to consistency, principled behavior, moderation, and reasoned compromise. While in paradigm National Honor is the realm of political principle and therefore of confrontation, it can be assessed and allowed for much as are National Interests. To fail to do so risks "more and better" brushfire war for the rest of this century in the name of territory.

This overarching interest is particularly important in territorial war and politico-military disputes because of its cumulative nature and its short "half-life." While National Honor may be well acquitted by an action perceived to have been successful, the momentum of success does not carry on well. One must continue to pile up victories or well-conducted draws to maintain status as a well-regarded player.

Territorial goals in particular tend increasingly to involve more National Honor than concrete National Interest. Successful pursuit of territorial goals can be by diplomatic means, but is increasingly conducted by threat or use of force. Force has a way of becoming widely available and effective when widely accepted as an option, but even when decisive, it gives countervailing incentive for the loser to engage in unproductive but spectacular retribution. Thus, for example, successful territorial violence leads not only to possible counterattack but to the other growing threat to world order: terrorism. The cumulative effects of National Honor in territorial questions are on the whole destabilizing for the system.

National Honor is also a tricky variable in that it has political cause and effect both within and outside the nation-state. If it can sometimes grant flexibility internationally, it is almost always a constraint in domestic political terms. However, often such a constraint can help—steeling decision-makers internally, and making one's tenacity understandable and credible externally.

While we shall define National Honor as that of the nation-state in question, this is not to ignore the internal component. A regime is conscious of its standing at home whatever the level of its direct representativeness or responsiveness. National Honor may be perceived and calculated differently at home and abroad, but it enters into the perceptions and decisions of leaders in either case.

It is precisely in the interaction between the international and domestic assessments of National Honor—of what values are to be pursued and what weight given to steadfastness versus flexibility in their pursuit—that the greatest inhibitions to dispute settlement come. Domestic components tend toward consistency as the dominant value. The international system, while rewarding consistency (tenacity), puts some weight on the strategic and constructive use of compromise (flexibility) as well.

Thus, National Honor has several interlocking and sometimes contradictory components. It is nonetheless useful for purposes of assessing international behavior to distinguish an interest based on one's status as a player from the more concrete stakes (resources, access, power, and other ''goods'' that are deemed to be in short or contested supply in the international arena). National Honor is no less an interest, and is ignored by statesmen at their peril. It is a factor and perhaps a cost in decision making about a crisis that is fully netted out only in the next crisis.

The effects of National Honor become perverse most frequently when dictated by or aimed at the domestic, rigid component. They are likely to inhibit mediation or negotiation whatever their base, however, because they are not founded on a concrete interest that can be divided, shared, or traded off for other advantage or otherwise straightforwardly bargained with. National Honor is less divisible and less subject to non–zero-sum solutions.

National Interests, in paradigm, are the stuff of solutions, and National Honor the essence of problems. Harmonizing them can often be the answer to a truly complex and apparently insoluble international conflict. A bargain that secures most if not all National Interests must do so in harmony with the expectations created by and for National Honor. Fully considered rather than dismissed,

National Honor offers solutions to the ongoing conflict of National Interests in the Falklands crisis. More than most territorial disputes, even the exceptionally numerous disputes that are so much a part of the political map of the Western Hemisphere, the Falklands has become a question of the National Honor of both Argentina and the United Kingdom. It is a paradigm of the brushfire war, which will increasingly characterize the last quarter of the twentieth century unless the international system can better deter or contain violence for, about, or merely in the name of territory.

THE RADICALIZATION OF DECOLONIZATION: DANGEROUS MATRIX

The segment of its political activities that the United Nations labels Decolonization consists in maintaining international normative political pressure on those states that administer non–self-governing territories. There are about 20 non–self-governing areas left in the current world of over 160 nation-states. Following the accession to independence and U.N. membership of Antigua and Barbuda, Belize, and St. Kitts-Nevis, it appears that there is little or no majority sentiment in favor of independence in most of the remaining territories. A few, perhaps, will accede to independence during the 1990s, but this will not be the experience of the majority of those areas that remain.

At the same time that the number of non–self-governing territories is declining in the world, the political pressure in the Decolonization process is increasing. This inverse relationship between multilateral politics and reality (as expressed by voters in the largely self-governing remaining nonindependent places) is more than politically interesting and logically perverse—it has highly dangerous connotations for international security. The paradigm of many of the value conflicts in this situation was the political-military Falklands crisis of spring 1982.

Concerned with the development and political futures of nonsovereign political entities, U.N. Decolonization activities are carried out at three levels:

—The special committee of 24 (C–24) is a year-round working group on non–self-governing territories that seeks to maintain normative pressures toward independence on the sovereign nations that control territories and colonies (administering authorities). Composed of 25 members and politically dominated by Communist and radical non-aligned states, the committee studies and reports to the General Assembly on about 20 territories registered by their administering authorities as nonsovereign. Using UNGA (United Nations General Assembly) Resolution 1514 and the Declaration on the Granting of Independence as their charter, the C–24 tacitly rejects any political future for territories except sovereignty in the form of independent statehood. It serves the Communist/radical cause well in that Western powers can be regularly criticized for their administration of and failure to grant freedom to those territories. This ignores the fact that there is little sentiment for political independence in the remaining non–self-governing territories.

—The Fourth (Decolonization) Committee of the General Assembly (GA) is one of the seven main committees of the UNGA. It meets each fall to consider a regular menu of resolutions on territories, most of them hostile to Western positions and interests. The more politically interesting resolutions concern territories in political and military disputes like the Western Sahara and East Timor, or those that are politically hot because the Communist states are politicizing the question, like Puerto Rico and the last U.N. trust, the Trust Territory of the Pacific Islands (TTPI).

—The U.N. Trusteeship Council (TC), one of the three main councils of the U.N. established by the Charter (along with the Security Council and the Economic and Social Council) is composed of the five permanent members of the Security Council: The United States, U.K., France, USSR, and China, which does not participate. The TC supervised the administration of a dozen U.N. trust territories, including the former mandated territories of the League of Nations. All have acceded to independence and U.N. membership except the TTPI. This last trust, the only strategic trust under Article 83 of the Charter, is ultimately under the control of the Security Council rather than the General Assembly, which had a role in all the other trusts. This category was established for the sole purpose of differentiating the Pacific Trust. When TTPI is dissolved in favor of a future political status to be chosen by the peoples of Micronesia, there will probably be no more U.N. trusts. The Trusteeship Council will likely be maintained as an inactive institution in case the United Nations should in the future wish to take a territory or region under its political wing.[1]

The dynamics of Decolonization at the United Nations often play out as jurisdictional disputes among these three U.N. institutions and between each of them and the administering powers. Member states of course use them to further their political interests and causes against other member states.

These three bodies interact but are not formally related. For example,the Committee of 24 has successfully asserted a role in drafting resolutions for the Fourth Committee of the GA, but the United States has to date successfully kept the Fourth Committee from involving the GA in the Trusteeship Council's handling of the TTPI.

The essence of the control of Decolonization by Warsaw Pact and radical nonaligned states has been to introduce several destabilizing presumptions into this field of U.N. politics. The most basic element is that territorial change is presumed, that is, there is no such thing as a stable status for any political unit that is not sovereign and independent. Thus, political confrontation and conflict are not only built into the system as inherent, but are, indeed, valued.

Nonetheless, neither principle nor consistency are hallmarks of this process: one working principle is that Western, northern hemisphere interests and values are not to be rewarded by any application of the basic principles of U.N. Decolonization. What is convenient for and enhances the interests of the radical nonaligned will determine any judgment calls.

This is evident in the tension between territorial integrity and self-determination. Thus, for example, in the case of the Falkland Islands, the full nonaligned Decolonization bloc could throw its support to Argentina, ignoring any possible applicability of the principles of majority rule and self-determination. Whether or not these should be controlling in all circumstances, they were utterly ignored in this case.

Since the five points of the Bandung Declaration of 1955, the nonaligned movement tried to ignore the contradictions between self-determination and territorial integrity as governing principles in territorial disputes. The contradiction can only be ignored at the peril of principle, the rule of law, and most operationally, international order.

Self-determination clearly means majority self-determination by the *resident population* in a territory. If self-determination clearly means self-determination by the majority in territorial conflicts, the Falklands is not a "regular" case for Decolonization doctrine in the sense that it was a land of recent settlement and a settler population.

Here, then, territorial integrity and self-determination are in stark contrast and conflict. The nonaligned movement in these cases has clearly come down on the side of territorial integrity. The Indian seizure of Goa evoked no condemnation from the Third World. This set the modern pattern of the nonaligned, epitomizing the inherent contradictions of the radical culture.

The international geopolitical goals and assumptions of the radical culture come up against their most telling internal contradiction in the manner of the brushfire war and questions of territorial geography. The state that today pursues a revolutionary, irredentist, or other rejectionist goal, and advocates, tolerates, or exercises violence in its pursuit, is very likely pursuing, whether it knows it or not in the very short run, internally contradictory interests.

When that goal is secured or definitively lost the interests of that state will change radically in favor of stability and the charter principles so recently seen as the unjust enforcement of the mainstream culture.[2] Today's irredentism is tomorrow's interference in the internal affairs of other states.

The principal conflicts in Decolonization define two political cultures on the subject. The Western interest is in limiting Communist and radical nonaligned attempts to increase U.N. condemnation or indeed activity concerning territories and the Trust. The radical nonaligned faction seeks to broaden its scope for political ends, such as condemning multilateral corporations and extraterritorial military bases in nonsovereign places (which they do not possess) or adding concerns not related to the remnants of colonialism such as apartheid.

Over time, however, Decolonization has had less and less to do with ending colonialism. Many states also have a very concrete interest that has a direct relationship to multilateral politics: political groups in those (usually Third World) countries who cast greedy eyes on the nonindependent regions for ethnic, military, irredentist or other reasons.

While most of the now-standard resolutions are ritually passed by the C–24 and the Fourth Committee in the General Assembly, the recent trends in Decolonization votes (e.g., the 30–70 defeat of the Cuban resolution on Puerto Rico at the 37th GA) must on balance be counted as good for the international system. While much of Western success has been in damage limitation, it could be argued that the limitation of excessive measures was so quantitatively and politically successful that years of diplomacy hostile to Western politico-legal culture were rolled back.

The current trend in Decolonization decisions by the G.A. has demonstrated a willingness on the part of a majority of U.N. members to listen to arguments of principle and consistency in territorial disputes when these are well grounded in U.N. Charter principles. Still, in the bulk of Decolonization resolutions, the GA majority is inclined to take positions favoring the interests of single, leading, radical nonaligned states often diametrically opposed to the mainstream of international law and practice, and indeed opposed to their own long-run interests. They will likely continue to do so, especially with the mislearned lessons of the Falklands fresh in mind.

The basic contradictions in Decolonization are built into U.N. Resolution 1514 itself, which recognizes in its preambular language "self-determination of all peoples" but then only the passionate yearning for freedom in all dependent peoples, and their decisive role in the attainment of their own independence. The newly independent state was becoming the final and indivisible "people" to the nonaligned and U.N. majorities. Liberation ended self-determination since the people have a right to territorial integrity. The language is explicit: with the increased weight given operative language in U.N. resolutions, the General Assembly stated that "any attempt aimed at the partial or total disruption of national unity and the territorial integrity of a country is incompatible with the purposes and principles of the Charter of the United Nations." Indeed, the very declaration is to be observed on the basis of "non-interference in the internal affairs of all States, and respect for the sovereign rights of all peoples and their territorial integrity." The declaration passed with 89 votes, including that of Argentina, in favor; none opposed; and 9 abstentions, including the United States and the U.K.

The trend there founded was reflected in General Assembly Resolution 2065 of 1965 on the Falkland Islands (Malvinas). The preambular language refers to Resolution 1514 and the ending of colonialism in all its forms, "one of which covers the case of the Falkland Islands (Malvinas)." The sovereignty dispute was noted and the parties were invited to find a peaceful solution through negotiations. The "interests of the population of the Falkland Islands" were to be borne in mind by the parties. The Resolution received 94 votes, with 14 abstentions, including the United States and the U.K.

The resolutions urging the parties to continue negotiations became a consensus process in the mid–1960s and were passed, thus, without debate or language changes. The Special Committee (C–24) and the General Assembly were to be kept informed about what the 1967 consensus called "this colonial situation, the elimination of which is of interest to the United Nations within the context of United Nations."

In 1973, the growth of the General Assembly and its nonaligned majority was reflected in a 116–0–14 recorded vote on a markedly pro-Argentine Falklands resolution (UNGA Res. 6130). The GA described itself as *"gravely concerned at the fact that eight years had elapsed"* without negotiating progress. Argentina was thanked for its efforts at Decolonization and its promotion of the "well-being of the population of the islands." The resolution declared there was a need to accelerate the negotiations "in order to put an end to the colonial situation."

In 1974, the General Assembly continued the mandate of the Committee of 24 to keep the question of the Falkland Islands (Malvinas) under review "in the discharge of the mandate entrusted to it." The C–24's annual reports and recommendations continued. In 1976, Resolution 31/49 incurred a vote of no by the United Kingdom. Abstentions increased to 32, including that of the United States, and there were 102 votes in favor. The resolution included in its preambular language reference to the 1975 Lima and 1976 Colombo declarations of the nonaligned movement, as well as the conclusions and recommendations adopted by the Committee of 24, which were approved. In addition, the resolution called upon the parties not to take "decisions that would imply introducing unilateral modifications in the situation while the islands are going through the process recommended in the above-mentioned resolutions" (Decolonization). Abstentions now included not only Western Europe, but Austria, Bahamas, Barbados, Fiji, Gambia, Guyana, Jamaica, Japan, Kenya, Malawi, Papua New Guinea, Sierra Leone, Singapore, Trinidad and Tobago, and Zaire. In 1979, the GA decided to defer consideration of the Falklands (GA decision 34/414).

Following the crisis of spring 1982, the General Assembly has passed resolutions each fall continuing the tradition of citing the Falklands as a colonial situation and thus incompatible with U.N. values. The interests of the population are reaffirmed as are now the Charter principles of nonuse of force and peaceful settlement of international disputes. In addition to the call for negotiations aimed at peaceful settlement, the Secretary General is requested to exercise his good offices to assist the parties. The voting, however, has been more split. In the voting on Resolution 37/9, for example, the United States and 89 other countries voted in favor: the United Kingdom, joined by Antigua, Belize, Dominica, Fiji, Gambia, Malawi, New Zealand, Oman, PNG, Solomon Islands, and Sri Lanka, voted no. There were 52 abstentions.

NONALIGNED RESOLUTIONS ON THE FALKLANDS

The nonaligned movement took up the question of the Falklands Islands at its Lima Conference of Foreign Ministers in 1975, demanding the elimination of colonial situations "especially in the cases of Belize, the Malvinas Islands, Puerto Rico, and Panama."

The language was strengthened in 1976 at Colombo, where the Falklands were accorded their own paragraph 119 in which the Conference firmly supported the just claim of the Argentine republic and urged the United Kingdom to actively pursue the negotiations . . . for the purpose of restoring that territory to Argentine sovereignty, thus ending that illegal situation that still prevails in the extreme southern part of the American continent.*

In New Dehli in 1977, the NAM Bureau ''urged the acceleration of negoti-ations with a view to the restoration of the territory of Malvinas to Argentine sovereignty.'' The theme was continued at Havana in 1978 to implement what was called ''the just aspiration'' of Argentina. The language remained roughly the same at the Belgrad ministerial of 1978 and the 1979 Colombo meeting of the Co-ordinating Bureau.

In Havana in 1979 under the new Cuban chairmanship, the nonaligned heads of state or government ''firmly reiterated their support for the Argentine repub-lic's right to the restitution of that territory and sovereignty over it'' and requested that the negotiations in this regard be speeded up. That language was repeated verbatim in New Dehli in 1981 by ministers and in New York in 1981 by ministers and heads of delegation.

In 1982 in Havana, the nonaligned took a major step when ministers

acknowledged that the Malvinas, South Georgia and South Sandwich Islands were an integral part of the Latin American region and that the military actions of the United Kingdom and the overt and covert actions and pressures of other developed countries harmed the entire region. In this connection, they expressed their satisfaction with the solidarity and firm support which the Latin American countries were offering Argentina in its struggle against the British attempt to reimpose a colonial regime.

The NAM denounced attempts to establish military bases on ''that Latin Amer-ican territory against the sovereign will of the Argentine republic, as a means of imposing imperialist domination in the area and as a serious threat to inter-national peace.''

They further ''deplored the military operations being undertaken in the South Atlantic'' with the asserted support and assistance of the United States. The nonaligned ''reiterated their support for and solidarity with Argentina in all its struggles to bring to an end the colonial presence in the Malvinas Islands.''

In New York in the fall of 1982, the movement returned to language unin-fluenced by the wartime climate and reiterated its support for Argentina in the ''restitution of the Malvinas Islands to its sovereignty and asked that negotiations be reinitiated.'' The good offices of the Secretary General were supported in the interests of ''a peaceful and just solution to the question.''

*Quotes showing the precise language used by the Nonaligned Movement are from its press releases giving conclusions of the meetings of the NAM Bureau, Conference (plenary), Foreign Ministers, and Heads of State.

In a meeting in Managua, however, under Sandinist tutelege in 1983, the nonaligned movement expanded its coverage of the Falklands to multiple paragraphs. While making reference to the nonuse or threat of the use of force and peaceful settlement of disputes as basic NAM principles, ministers again:

—Recognized the dependencies as well as the Falklands as part of the Latin American region;

—Applauded nonaligned efforts to "prevent the consolidation of the existing colonial situation on those islands";

—Urged negotiations under the good offices of the Secretary General in line with U.N. resolutions;

—"Considered that the massive military and naval presence and activities of the United Kingdom . . . are a cause of grave concern . . . affecting adversely stability in the area;

—"Expressed concern about persistent reports of attempts by some Latin American countries to form a so-called South Atlantic Treaty Organization (SATO) in conjunction with the racist regime of Pretoria," which would threaten the security of Africa and the independence of Namibia as well as the liberation of South Africa, and called for all Latin countries to reject the idea; and

—Noted Argentine statements in the General Assembly on the introduction of nuclear weapons by the United Kingdom" into the Falklands and Dependencies.

This expanded agenda for the nonaligned was repeated at New Delhi in 1983 by the heads of government, and will clearly form the basis for nonaligned policy. The strength of the assertions and the scope of the subject matter have grown considerably since the NAM considered it a simple colonial situation to be negotiated. The political and normative content is greater and the language stronger and more markedly one-sided.

The world political system has come to be defined territorially as a consequence of the birth of the nation-state. Geographic overlapping of sovereignty is not normally allowed and territorial jurisdiction is mainly overland and not by the people who were originally the basis of modern nationalism and the nation-state.[3] The working rule is hierarchy within and sovereign equality between those states. This leaves little room for those self-defined peoples not masters of an accepted piece of territory. Since World War II, millions have undergone the transition from subjects of foreign states to citizens of independent states. The United Nations oversaw and codified the independence movement. It did not cause or force it as a political phenomenon. That role fell to the colonizers themselves. The United States encouraged Decolonization, but like the U.N. could not make it happen. In the mid–1980s, the world finds itself nearing the end of the Decolonization process. The process, therefore, bears reexamination.

The smallest and most remote of the non–self-governing territories are not in the near future likely to be capable or desirous of self-rule or to prove economically viable. The U.N. majority feels that "viability" (size, GNP, and resources) should never be a consideration. These populations can make their own assessments. Some territories will remain non–self-governing, because they are contested by a state other than that which administers them.

In the cases of the Falkland Islands, Belize, and Gibraltar, both economic viability and conflict between an administering nation and other powers pose formidable obstacles to independence. Here the judgments of the population, indeed their very status as legitimate populations, are rejected as a valid consideration. Independence or incorporation into the administering metropol are denied them. Only incorporation into another state is a legitimate option in the view of the U.N. majority.

The assertion of territorial integrity over self-determination is a clear U.N. majority and nonaligned-movement majority trend. Section Six of Resolution 1514 states that "any attempt aimed at the partial or total disruption of the territorial integrity of a country is incompatible with the purposes and principles of the Charter of the United Nations." In its Resolution 2353 (XXII) of 19 December 1957 on Gibraltar, the General Assembly went so far as to condemn the British referendum of September 10 as a contravention of its previous resolutions. In other such Decolonization resolutions, "unilateral acts" are prohibited and can be expanded to include almost any act of the resident population or the administering power—especially those acts that make the territory more viable.

It is on this basis of territorial integrity, rather than on the basis of self-determination, that Guatemala claims Belize, Argentina claims the Falklands, China claims all of Hong Kong, and Spain claims Gibraltar. Morocco's presence in Western Sahara; Indonesian administration of East Timor; and Ethiopia's control of Eritrea demonstrate the dominance in fact of territorial integrity over self-determination. The U.N. majority, however, does itself no service by inconsistency between two principles. The U.N.'s practice of the selective nonapplication of the right to self-determination in these cases and in those pending resolution, "highlights the dangers inherent in allowing historical-ethnic claims to carve out exceptions to the hitherto universal norms of decolonization."[4]

In looking to restore territorial integrity, the claimant states have looked less to serve the peoples' interests as defined by the people of the territory. Their choices, including political status, are delegitimated in a way reminiscent of the "guidance" of conquered or subjected populations under colonialism. If true, it is said to be nonetheless irrelevant that the East Timorese prefer the Portuguese to the Indonesians, as the Falklanders seem to prefer to remain British rather than to turn Argentine; that the Eritreans want to forget Italian, British, and Ethiopian rule; that the inhabitants of Hong Kong prefer to enjoy the status quo; or that the citizens of Guyana and Belize having successfully completed the process of Decolonization wish to remain intact as peoples and sovereign as states.

The use of force is supplanting politics in settling territorial disputes. Force or the overwhelming application of power and influence need not even be military. Other charter principles are sacrificed along with self-determination, principally nonaggression, peaceful settlement, and noninterference in internal affairs. Once force is used, it tends to make the dispute less, not more, tractable. The trouble with aggression, unlike politics, is that it tends to raise the stakes and lower the commonality of interests in a peaceful settlement; in other words, the conflict takes on a life of its own.

The politics of the use of force is powerful as an example and has a tendency to be emulated. Whether violent or not, it tends to spread the unilateral"solution" of long-standing contests of will. The Indian seizure of Goa foreshadowed and in a political-legal sense helped legitimize and thus lead to the Moroccan-Mauritanian takeover of Spanish Sahara and the Indonesian takeover of East Timor. The Ethiopian "peasant march" into Eritrea demonstrates that Morocco's success in the "green march" into Western Sahara has impressed leaders of other states. In February 1976, "just as Morocco was mopping up Western Sahara and Indonesia was completing its subjugation of East Timor," President Idi Amin announced that Uganda had claims to large territories in Kenya and the Sudan because they had at one time been administered as part of (British colonial) Uganda.[5] The string of territorial seizures "legitimized" to radical nonaligned observers (and to the Argentine government) the Argentine try for the Falklands. Action, even more than U.N. and nonaligned resolutions, seems to legitimate and consolidate the predominance of territorial integrity as doctrine.[6]

TERRITORY: A QUESTION OF PERCEPTION

Contested territory is a worldwide political phenomenon. A partial list of the main areas of dispute include many which are analogous or often analogized to each other. Some are often raised in discussing the Falkland Islands. Some, indeed, bore directly on the South Atlantic crisis of spring 1982 as factors in the decision making of the parties. Not all stem from nineteenth-century imperialism, but all have one or more deeply held senses of nationalism at the heart of the matter. Together they paint a tableau of the recurrent problems and some solutions in the explosive politics of territory.

There is, of course, far more to territoriality than political geography. Questions like the Polish corridor and Bolivia's desire for an outlet to the sea; India's seizure of Goa and Argentina's seizure of the Falklands; Berlin and U.N. Headquarters in New York; the old Vatican Concordat and the Soviet war memorial in the British sector of Berlin; the West Bank and the Indo-Pakistani enclaves; the claimed Basque homeland Euzcadi, and Eritrea; all have as much political as legal content. The sources of political dispute about territory are tremendously diverse. They range from Tamil separatism in Sri Lanka, with territory undefined but clearly at the top of the agenda, to the once clearly defined Baltic states of Lithuania, Latvia, and Estonia, which were for years not noted as separate entities on Soviet maps; from unnoticed Ifni to the daily headlines concerned with or merely concerning Northern Ireland. Disputed territory is a cause or a major part of much of the world's violence. Most disputed territory is inherently and strongly conflictual, as measured by a willingness to die for these places over generations until or unless the disputes are settled.

Outlying territories such as Macao, Guantanamo Bay, Ceuta and Melilla, Gibraltar, and Hong Kong are regularly contested and protested by a state that claims them as part of its territory. Their territorial uniqueness lies in the fact that they are *of* and *in*, but not surrounded by, the claiming state: they have communications and transport access by sea and are thus not easily blockaded.[7] They may indeed have utility as outlets for the "neighboring" claimant.

Landlocked political units like Bolivia, Switzerland, Uganda, Liechtenstein, or the Vatican City are surrounded but are sovereign and therefore largely free of more than partial territorial claim or interference. In political terms, they may also enjoy a border with more than one nation-state, and these nation-states often share a common mutual border, leading to differing sets of National Interests and reducing the possibility of siege or concerted control of access. Likewise, Alaska and the former East Pakistan were not surrounded by a single foreign state.

"Surrounded" but not "contained" political units find that having multiple bordering independent states often protects their claim to separateness even in changing political environments. The independence of the Swazis was guaranteed in conventions of 1881 and 1884 between the British government and the government of the South African Republic (SAR). In 1884, the SAR was given powers of protection and administration, and from 1903 the government of Transvaal administered the territory. Swaziland's fate might have been different were it not at the edge of South Africa and fronting on Mozambique. Granted internal self-government in 1967 by the U.K., Swaziland became independent in 1968.

The territorial history of exclaves, which have neither sovereignty nor sovereign access by land or sea, is about evenly divided between agreement to maintain a foreign enclave within the host state and forcible annexation by the host state. Busingen and Campione d'Italia in Switzerland, Llivia in France, and the mutual enclaves of Baarle exchanged by Belgium and Holland represent stable territorial solutions. Portugal's foothold in Benin however was seized by force in 1961. Mount Scopus was disenclaved by the 1967 Arab-Israeli war and Portugal's holdings in India were settled by force. India and Bangladesh probably have the largest number and area of outstanding exclaved disputed territory.[8]

The exclave has been an important part in the struggles for power as well as consolidation by the nation-state as it developed along ethnic/nationalist lines in modern Europe and spread to dominate the world political system. The persistance and importance of the apparently contradictory exclaves were due to the growing nationalism they symbolized. The continual resistance of agreed enclaves indicates that there is nothing inherently conflictual about noncontiguous shared or administratively recognized exclaves, outliers, or enclaves. The fate of small territories has usually been determined by the overall interests of and relationships between the contending powers.

However, if territorial dispute need not be a source of tension, it is often a focus for tensions.[9] Those who would use an outlying or claimed territory have a political interest in obscuring the distinction. The agreed-on European exclaves, and anomalies like Point Roberts which at the extreme western end of Canada fell below the parallel agreed upon as the U.S.-Canadian border, share another quality: they are not either economically or strategically significant. Thus there was little incentive for the surrounding state to fight the "nationalism" of the inhabitants. Local heritage and pride would seem to play as much a role as any wider feeling of linguistic-cultural identification with the exo-state.

The trend toward the consolidation of national territory after the 1648 Treaty of Westphalia (which ended the Thirty Years War) has been a strong one, one of the main wellsprings and expressions of the dominant ideology: nationalism. In the first half of the twentieth century, however, nationalism seemed to have tacitly recognized outer geographic limits beyond which the nation-state could tolerate anomalies, provided questions of political principle were not violated.

The Northern Hemisphere, "mainstream" politico-legal culture is still evolving in that direction. The problems in Europe are those of access, and the trend toward reasonableness even in these questions is clear. A right of access is evolving in customary international law.[10] The very nationalism of those living in the exclave may well exceed that of the "mother country" as regards their extraterritoriality. The nation-state, accustomed to realpolitik and placing a high value on international harmony, may well be more inclined than the residents of the exclave to consider it a pawn in power relations between two states. Some of the same questions apply in matters of economic integration and trade.

The worldwide postwar trend has been the opposite. The nation-state has consistently sought to add territory. The size or economic significance of a territory has little to do with a consolidation process which is essentially political rather than territorial.

Real exclaves, a state's territory totally within the territory of another state, are less often fought over, usually representing tacitly accepted territorial/ethnic anomalies. There are over 40 exclaves in Europe alone, such as Italian and German towns within Switzerland; reciprocal settlements of Dutch and Belgians; and a strictly Spanish area within France.

Islands, however, are particularly tempting as a territorial anomaly more easily subject to both low-cost seizure and containment of the conflict. Neither military nor political factors usually lead to further or wider violence other than direct attempted reconquest.

In the 1970s, the Iranian Navy seized the Tunb Islands at the mouth of the Persian Gulf and held them. Also unanswered was China's seizure of the Paracel Islands in the South China Sea. Reconquest can, however, be equally "surgical." South Vietnam took the Spratley Islands, which were retaken two years later by the Vietnamese Liberation Navy.[11] Even military success does not always lead to peaceful enjoyment of sovereignty and exclusive use of island territory. Turkey invaded and occupied Eastern Cyprus. In 1975 Indonesia invaded and occupied

East Timor. Neither enjoys unchallenged exclusive use and possession, even though their use of force was overwhelming and rapidly consolidated.

Litoral states in particular express a view that off-lying islands are inherently or "naturally" their national patrimony. The Greek population of the Dodecanese Islands and Lesbos find such claim by the "alien" culture of Muslim Turkey unsupportable, as would the French-speaking citizens of St. Pierre/Miquelon or the culturally British nationals of the Bahamas and Bermuda. Such views based on language and culture, however, carry less weight with the immigrant societies of the lands of recent settlement like the United States, Canada, South Africa, Argentina, Australia, or New Zealand.

Size and relative power vis-à-vis neighbors have influenced British handling of very small territories. Millions of square miles of territory astride major world resources and strategic passes or passages were turned over to their native populations. Places of less value to an empire have been protected precisely because of threats to their poltico-cultural integrity. Thus a Malta can be left on its own given its natural isolation and the absence of foreign irredentist claim, while Hong Kong, the Falklands, and Belize were all coveted by powerful neighbors.

The key question in a multitude of territorial anomalies worldwide would seem to be perceptions. There are fairly clear legal, political, military and (culture-specific) moral guidelines on where to draw lines on maps, but exceptions for good-faith reasons abound. Some exceptions less clearly made in good will have also set precedents. While the Third World is still focused on what it considers remnants of colonialism, the emerging trend in territorial behavior is for states of the non-Atlantic world to seize territory against the wishes of peoples or against the wishes of other states not traditionally labeled imperialist.

TERRITORIAL DISPUTES

Several territorial disputes which were in play during the Falklands Crisis provide interesting parallels and contrasts for understanding the negotiation and mediation of contested land. They also illustrate some of the conflicts inherent between a state's perceived sovereignty and the principle of self-determination.

While political snapshots of a territorial situation are quickly overtaken by events, the core element to be watched here is the mutual interaction of the Falklands situation in the Spring of 1982 and other situations which, accurately or not, could be seen as parallel. Some were even more directly connected in the interaction of National Interest and National Honor.

Goa

The origins of the predominance of territorial integrity over self-determination in U.N. precedent can be traced to the ineffectiveness of the U.N. Security Council in handling India's takeover of the former Portuguese territories on its coast. Portugal warned the council for two weeks in a series of letters in mid-

December 1961 that Indian forces were building up on the frontiers of Goa, Damao, and Diu. Portugal reported border incidents and air space penetrations. Portugal called for the help of the Council. India replied that there had been attacks on Indian villages and that it had therefore moved military units to the area. It said that any violence in the area was caused by Goan patriots and the "alien" soldiers of Portugal, and that Indian forces massing in the area were only a response to a buildup by Portuguese troops.

The acting Secretary General U Thant appealed to both Prime Ministers not to let the situation degenerate.

India next, however, argued that there was only one possible solution to the situation consistent with the U.N. Charter and resolutions and "the irreversible course of history." This was for Portugal to leave India and allow the Goans to join their "countrymen"; that is, to be incorporated into India. The Portuguese willingness to negotiate and to give guarantees that Portuguese territory would not be used against India were ignored in the Indian frustration with 14 years of seeking sovereignty over the Portuguese zones through bilateral negotiation. Portugal had in the Indian view effectively refused to negotiate in earnest.

On December 18, 1961, India launched a simultaneous, full-scale military attack on the three territories. The Security Council voted 7–2 (Ceylon and the USSR), with Liberia and the UAR abstaining, to consider the question of the Portuguese request that the U.N. stop the aggression by India, and order an immediate cease-fire and withdrawal of all Indian troops.

The USSR argued in casting its veto that the Portuguese territories were an Indian domestic question since they were colonial in nature and formed an integral part of the state of India.

India made the case that it had sought the territories unsuccessfully for 14 years; that Goa was a question of colonialism and that as there was therefore no legal frontier between India and Goa, there could be no question of aggression against one's own frontier and one's own people. The large Indian population in Goa was claimed to be in revolt against Portugal. Appeal was made to Resolution 1541, and India said that indeed the Council should order Portugal to vacate Goa in fulfillment of resolutions 1541 and 1542.

The U.S. position was that this was not a question of colonialism but of violation of basic principles of the Charter, especially paragraph 4 of article 2. A member of the United Nations had cast aside the Charter and sought to resolve a dispute by force. This should be corrected by an immediate cease-fire, withdrawal of forces, and the resumption of negotiations.

This rejection of force as a method of solving territorial disputes was supported by the U.K., Turkey, France, Ecuador, China, and Chile. The Chilean representative noted that the wishes of the peoples of the territories should be considered. Ceylon, Liberia, and the UAR said that aggression was not in question in the light of Resolution 1542 and the fact that Goa and the others were non–self-governing territories. Portugal's failure to comply with the Decolonization requirement to submit information on the territories apparently deprived it of any right of appeal to the United Nations in their view. The Soviet representative took this a step further and sanctions should be applied to Portugal under Chapter 7 of the Charter to compel it to comply with the General Assembly's declared policy on colonialism. A resolution to this effect and with the additional element of stating that Portugal stood in the way of the territorial integrity of the Republic of India and should therefore liquidate its holdings was rejected 4–7.

A countervailing resolution submitted by France, Turkey, the U.K., and the United States was defeated 7–4 (Ceylon, Liberia, USSR, and UAR), by Russian veto. It would have emphasized article 2 principles of peaceful settlement of dispute and restraint from the threat or use of force; deplored India's use of force; included the self-determination of peoples; and in the operative text called for cease-fire, withdrawal, and negotiations with the possible assistance of the Secretary General.

The inconclusive and highly polarized nature of the Decolonization question in the context of the use of force to seize territory in dispute was put in sharp relief by the Goa crisis. U.N. General Assembly and nonaligned-movement majority opinion had the powerful example of Goa on which to build a legal and political case over generations for the predominance of territorial integrity over any question of a right to self-determination of small enclaves or islands bordering on a nonaligned state. The presumption of self-determination as the outcome for a non–self-governing territory was fatally and probably finally weakened with these majorities from 1961.

Beagle Channel

Argentina and Chile had long contested sovereignty over three islands occupied by Chile in the Beagle Channel south of Tierra del Fuego. Since 1881, Chile has controlled the Channel Islands and Argentina has laid claim to them. The dispute centered on Lennox, Picton, and Nueva Islands, located at the mouth of the channel. In 1896, the two countries called upon Queen Victoria to settle the matter, but, when she ruled in favor of Chile, the Argentines balked. That pattern of mediation or arbitration has been repeated with minor variations to this day until resolution by Vatican mediation after the Falklands War.

The two countries last nearly went to war over the Beagle Channel Islands in 1978. A former mediator, ironically the United Kingdom, had found largely in favor of Chile in 1977. On Christmas Eve 1978, however, Argentina was turning to force. Airborne forces actually crossed the border but were called back. Argentina (with the encouragement of the United States) turned to Vatican mediation. In December 1980, Pope John Paul II proposed a plan of settlement again largely favoring the Chilean view. Chile accepted, but Argentina refused. The Vatican pressed on.

Thus the Vatican mediation was ongoing during the Falklands crisis. The implications of the Falklands situation for Argentina's interest in the Beagle Channel Islands were many: a more full-time perceived enemy than the U.K.,

Chile was assumed to be waiting to move militarily. Chile prepared for similar contingencies, and a mutual spiral of fear concerning surprise attack began. No hostilities ensued but the Beagle Channel seemed as intractable as the Falklands, in part because there were two issues and therefore more than territory at stake. The projected sea frontier into the Atlantic which the islands give to Chile is symbolically more important to Argentina than the control of the channel and islands themselves. Argentina would like Chile to be a purely Pacific Ocean power.

Argentine decisionmakers clearly felt the Beagle and Falklands issues to be directly linked in 1982: in January that year the Argentine Navy's magazine *Conviccion* editorialized that seizing the Falkland Islands would aid in breaking the mediated deadlock on the Beagle Channel as it would give Argentina a stronger bargaining stance. Within months Argentina would test that proposition in the clearest linkage to another territorial dispute of any of the situations analagous to the Falklands in 1982.

Belize

Situated on the Caribbean coast of Central America and measuring 22,965 square kilometers, Belize grew out of the pirate and smuggler settlements that emerged among the bays of the uninhabited coast. It became a British colony when its inhabitants (mostly English) sought the protection of the Crown.[12] The former British Honduras gained self-government in 1964 and independence on September 21,1981. The gap of nearly 20 years in political status was due to Guatemala's outstanding claim on the territory. Guatemalan maps show the area as "Belize," Guatemala's 23d Department, yet the bulk of Guatemala's population lives in the more temperate southern region far from Belize; the northern province that adjoins Belize is largely unexplored and even less exploited. *Lebensraum* is seldom at the heart of territorial conflict.

Guatemala believes that the area was taken from it by Britain as a colonial power which therefore had no right to pass independence along to the resident population. The analogics about the non-Hispanic, "atypical" nature of the majority population and the arguments about force in enforcement of colonial territory make Guatemala's view of the situation highly analogous to the Argentine view of the Falkland Islands.

In 1859, Britain and Guatemala agreed to establish the boundaries presently under dispute. A treaty was accepted providing that Britain create a communications line by land or sea from Belize to Guatemala City. The Guatemalan government contends that Britain did not perform its stated duty and therefore has no claim to Belize. Guatemala's claim was in 1939. The 1945 constitution counted Belize as part of the national territory. A new "urgency" in the claim of Belize came with its progress toward independence, yet Belize was averse to independence without international guarantees of safety. British regiments serve there as guarantors.

Why does Guatemala claim and seek this territory? A longer and more productive coastline is less explanatory than National Honor—sovereignty over
Belize had by 1982 become the most persistent foreign policy question for
Guatemala.[13] National Honor, however, now played a role on the other side of
the border, too.[14]

Questions of self-determination, of legality and political legitimacy as applied
to an ethnic group culturally distinct from that of the surrounding region, are
similar in the Guatemalan and Argentine cases, as is British support for the
rights of those who de facto populate the territory in question. The perceived
analogy of the Belize and Falklands cases was strongly felt within Latin American. Guatemala's claim (ironically perhaps outweighed by that of, Mexico,
which does not contest the territory) was another reason for Latin solidarity in
the Spring of 1982.

East Timor

For 400 years, East Timor was a Portuguese colony: "an integral part of the
Portuguese nation" in the view of Lisbon, which refused to consider itself bound
by U.N. Decolonization Resolution 1514 on the assumption that its overseas
possessions were not "subject to decolonization."[15]

This policy, however, changed after the Portuguese revolution of April
25,1974. The reigning junta recognized the Timorese right to self-determination
and began the process of decolonization. Immediately, three political parties
organized. FRETLIN, believed to have the largest following, advocated complete
independence, and on November 28,1975 it issued a unilateral proclamation of
independence. Less than a month later, on December 7, Indonesian troops entered
the territory and repressed the "guerrillas." On December 7,1975, Indonesia
began naval bombardment and troop landings at Dili in Portuguese East Timor.

Portugal asked the U.N. Security Council to ensure the continuance of the
Decolonization process there. Indonesia said that it was not annexing the territory
and that self-determination would ultimately decide the political status of East
Timor. In Resolution 384, the council called on Indonesia to withdraw its troops
from East Timor. Indonesia crushed all resistance and proclaimed formal annexation in July 1976. Indonesia had exercised de facto incorporation of a non–
self-governing territory. The United Nations deplored Indonesian use of force
and continued to refer to Portugal as the "Administering Power" of East Timor.
Many if not most member nations felt incorporation was "tantamount to rein-
troducing colonialism in that territory."[16]

Timor's status as the 27th Province of Indonesia is still disputed by parts of
the population with the political support of a good number of countries at the
United Nations. That number seemed in 1982 to be shifting in favor of at least
tacit acceptance of de facto incorporation, in line with the trend toward the
principle of territorial integrity over self-determination. This lesson was not lost
on the Argentine Junta.

Eritrea

An indigenous Eritrean Liberation Front has been seeking the independence of its region from Ethiopia for decades. Eritrea, like so many disputed territories an "artificial" creation of European imperialism, was seized late in the colonial scramble by the Italians in 1885.[17] Eritrea (from Mare Erythraeum, Red Sea) proved more an outlet for Italian political energies and a springboard for further conquest than it did a source of wealth.

Britain ended 51 years of Italian rule in 1941. The formation of political groupings within Eritrea was encouraged but developed mainly along religious lines. The Unionist Party was made up primarily of Christians who wished reunification with Ethiopia. The Muslim League advocated independence, as did the Liberal Progressive Party. In the late 1940s, the Muslim-dominated parties and the majority of the Liberal Progressive Party formed the Independence Bloc.[18]

While Eritrea was developing political pluralism but no unified nationalist movement, Ethiopia was rapidly becoming centralized and assertive. Confident, "the only civilization and political entity in Africa and the Middle East to withstand the aggressive challenge of Europe in the late nineteenth century," Ethiopia was also becoming absolutist in its government and assertive about territory.[19]

In December 1950, the U.N. General Assembly adopted federation as a solution for the future organization of Eritrea. Ethiopian absolutism was neither able nor willing to incorporate Eritrean pluralism into its political system. Ethiopia, feeling threatened by rising Pan-Arabism, strengthened its hold on Eritrea in what it viewed as self-defense during the 1950s and 1960s. The revised 1955 constitution stated that "the Empire of Ethiopia comprises all the territory . . . under the sovereignty of the Ethiopian Crown," whose "sovereignty and territory are indivisible."[20] Christians and Muslims then joined in resistance to Ethiopia. Eritrean nationalism found political and military expression after 25 years.

Ethiopia, despite the 1974 revolution, remained unchanged in its desire to maintain Eritrea as Ethiopian soil. Indeed, territory gained by the Eritrean nationalists during the Ethiopian revolution was, by the end of 1978, back under Ethiopian control. The reversal was due to more than force of arms. The differences in political cohesion can be understood when one examines the competing slogans of the contenders: Ethiopia's "Unity or Death," and Eritrea's "Revolution before Unity." The Eritrean nationalist movement, directed toward a single goal, continues to be plagued by minimovements with different approaches to the realization of that goal. As of 1982 the central state prevailed and the primacy of national territory over ethnic decentralization was reinforced.

The Essequibo

Venezuela claims the Essequibo region of Guyana on the grounds that Britain (as successor to the Dutch) never gained title to the land west of the Essequibo

River. Venezuela asserts that the area belonged to Spain and was inherited by Venezuela after its successful struggle for independence. Venezuela rejects the border established by an English-American-Russian arbitration of 1899, an arbitration agreement that left the Essequibo region with what was then British Guiana (spelled with an "i").

Discovery of high-quality crude oil in the Essequibo region and the developments in the Falklands fueled the dispute. In 1982, Venezuela launched a $70 million program to strengthen frontier posts along the Guyanese border.[21] As in the Falklands, a Spanish-English territorial problem has held over into the twentieth century. Unlike many areas of territorial conflict, the Essequibo is mineral-rich and valuable in and of itself. It constitutes two-thirds of the territory of Guyana.

Venezuela raised active claim to the territory in a 1962 U.N. debate as a result of Guyanese movement toward independence. In February 1966, on the eve of that independence, an agreement was reached at Geneva that stipulated that representatives from Britain, Venezuela, and British Guiana were to meet periodically for the next four years to seek resolution to the dispute. In June 1970, it was agreed that for a minimum of 12 years Venezuela would not assert any claim to sovereignty over the disputed territory. Upon its expiration in 1982, Venezuela declined to renew the "agreement to disagree."

To Argentine decision-makers in 1982 the Essequibo was the arch example of why the centralizing territorial state had to at all costs deny self-determination as a valid or applicable principle: the danger lay in permanent loss of the claimed territory under independence recognized by the U.N.—a valid end to Colonialism and to any claim to colonial right of succession to title. The analogy was politically valid in Latin America, seen as parallel to Belize, and strongly enough felt in Venezuela in the Spring of 1982 that it overcame a Criollo resentment of the Argentine style in politics and made Venezuela not only a solid supporter of the seizure of the Islands but even led some to consider parallel action against independent Guyana.

While successive Venezuelan governments have favored regional stability and development over political pursuit of the Essequibo claim, the region is still marked as claimed on all Venezuelan maps. It is difficult to overestimate the power of politico-legal analogy between territorial claims cases and, indeed, as the cases of unresolved territorial dispute shrink, each solution and each festering case seems to loom larger in the minds of the parties to the remaining disputes.

Gibraltar

The natural rock fortress at the southern tip of the Iberian peninsula, which commands access to the Mediterranean from the Atlantic, was seized militarily in 1704. (Its place in British military honors is key—thus the "Gibraltar" belt buckle worn by the Royal Marines to this day.) The "Rock" has been peacefully administered by the crown and continuously occupied since. The narrow peninsula of 5.8 square kilometers on the southwest coast of Spain was ceded to Great Britain by the Treaty of Utrecht of 1713. No one purports that the act was voluntary, only sovereign. The U.K. and Spain have held talks for centuries and recently over a period of years on the future of the "Rock." Negotiations between Spain and Britain were convened in 1715, 1720, and 1721 to discuss return of Gibraltar to Spain, yet this effort seemed less and less likely as Gibraltar grew in its importance to Britain as a symbol of her growing naval supremacy and a fortress and base at the entrance to the Mediterranean. The cession was confirmed by the treaties of Paris (1763) and Versailles (1789). The 1783 Treaty of Versailles gave Spain full rights to East and West Florida and Minorca and confirmed British rule of Gibraltar, ending the protests that had arisen since Utrecht.

The 1960s saw the emergence of Gibraltar as an important issue mainly in the context of U.N. Decolonization, couched as the right of self-determination for all peoples in the "remnants of empires." Gibraltar became one of 73 places labeled a non–self-governing territory by the United Nations and thus given license to pursue self-government.

In 1964, Britain created a Government of Gibraltar. It issued Government of Gibraltar passports, which were not recognized by Spain. Spain countered this move with the argument that since the people of Gibraltar are not indigenous they have no right to determine their own future. (Spain holds that the natural population of Gibraltar fled in 1704 and now lives in the surrounding communities of San Rogue and La Linea.)

In March of 1965, Spain restricted trade in retaliation for the British refusal to negotiate the Gibraltar question.

In 1966, Britain offered to go before the International Court of Justice in efforts to negotiate, but Spain refused, preferring to keep the negotiations bilateral. About this time, prospectors in Spanish Sahara hit deposits of oil and phosphates. The Moroccan press hinted that British concessions to Spain over Gibraltar would have to be matched by a share for Morocco in the Sahara.

On September 10, 1967, a referendum was held in Gibraltar in pursuance of a U.N. resolution on the Decolonization of Gibraltar. Out of 12,762 inhabitants, 12,138 voted to retain a British connection while 44 voted to align with Spain.

In January of 1969, Britain granted a new constitution to Gibraltar which gave the colony limited autonomy and guaranteed that the Gibraltarians would not have to accept Spanish rule unless desired by the majority. On December 15, 1982, the border between Spain and Gibraltar was reopened for Spaniards and Gibraltarians who are residents of Gibraltar. While Britain must support the Gibraltarians economically as long as they maintain their wish to be British, there is a level of real-world interdependence between Spain and Gibraltar as 10,000 Spaniards travel each day to Gibraltar to work.

Conditions in and concessions by Britain about Gibraltar have often been cited as a political barometer. It is felt they will prompt other nations to seek concessions. In fact, Morocco, has not apparently modified its policies toward enclaves or the Sahara as a result of this issue. The connections or analogies may be more global and geostrategic than regional and political.

There has never been a pro-Spanish political movement with Gibraltar in the sense that Spanish nationals are not registered as voters. Because of Gibraltar's physical contiguity to Spanish soil, it is difficult to apply clear-cut rules of international law. It is a clear but contested piece of the Iberian peninsula, but so is Portugal. Treaties and wars long past clearly carry less political weight than current normative politics in multilateral and regional organizations. If NATO and its governments would clearly prefer no interruptions in the peace of southern Europe, U.N. minority opinion has so far kept pride of place for self-determination, and territorial integrity may be gaining. Spanish limitation of access by land is both a visible tactic and a stumbling block. Its precision as an instrument for expressing degrees of political pique is shown by the opening of the border to pedestrian traffic in late 1982. While asserting the principle of territorial integrity in support of its claim to Gibraltar, Spain maintains colonies on the coast of Morocco: Ceuta and Melilla. In the Lisbon Agreement of 1980, Spain stated its intention to safeguard the "interests" of the Gibraltarians, while the U.K. renewed its commitment to their "democratically expressed wishes." Both formulations proved highly analogous to the Falklands crisis, as have debates about self-determination and what constitutes a valid "population." Both NATO and European Economic Community relationships between the parties complicate the bilateral problem.

The analogies between Gibraltar and the Falklands so strongly felt in 1982 became foreign policy when in 1984 King Juan Carlos said Spain and Argentina shared with solidarity painful colonial sequels that affect their nation's integrity— their disputes with Britain over the Falklands and Gibraltar. Spanish support for the Argentine claim to the Falklands was made more explicit in a 13-point communiqué issued June 13, 1984, after Argentine President Alfonsin held several rounds of talks with Spanish Prime Minister Gonzalez. "Both victims of an anachronistic colonial situation" undertook to support each other's claims and attempts "to restore the integrity of their national territories through peaceful means."[22] The Gibraltar-Falklands analogy was perhaps the strongest for Argentina in 1982. Its political validity was measured in Spain's ferocious support at the U.N. and reinforcement of the political unity of the Spanish-speaking world.

Hong Kong

While the reversion to China of the Crown Colony has now been fixed by Treaty, and a long transition of a special economic regime guaranteed by China as receiving power, the tense negotiations were in the early 1980s a special case in regard to the Falklands as so many of the same questions were involved or invoked by one party or the other to the Hong Kong question.

Britain acquired Hong Kong proper under the Treaty of Nanking of 1842 and the Kowloon Peninsula under the Anglo-Manchu Convention of Peking of 1860. These acquisitions were without fixed term but are only 8 percent of the land area of the Crown colony. The bulk of the territory of Hong Kong is in the New Territories, which were carved out of Canton province for 99 years by the second Anglo-Manchu Treaty of 1898. They contain half the population and businesses of Hong Kong in 92 percent of the surface area.

The uncertain status of leasehold creates legal as well as political and economic uncertainties. Before 1898, the lease of territory for a specified term was "virtually unknown . . . and no precedent or doctrine in international law provides guidance in the matter of interpretations."[23]

British negotiating preferences were British administration, failing that a constitutional link to the Crown, and if that were unobtainable, autonomy for the people of Hong Kong and their way of life. China had seemed prepared to grant an autonomous constitution approved by referendum and a special administrative zone for the area of the current Crown colony.

The people of Hong Kong, of course, have some interests separate from those of either party, principally a rapid training and changeover of the administration of the colony to local personnel and the election of officials to allow them a direct and representative voice in negotiations about their political future. (This analogy to the rights of Kelper society was recognized in the Falklands.)

The greater part of the territory of the British Crown colony of Hong Kong was intended by treaty to revert to the People's Republic of China (PRC) toward the end of this century. China, culturally still stung by the "unequal treaties" of the nineteenth century, indeed claimed that all of the colony, and not just the New Territories (some 87 percent of its area) would so revert in 1997. While at the time of the Falklands crisis China and the United Kingdom seemed to have some years still to work out a solution, the effects of the political instability were already being felt and a price was being paid by each side. Secret negotiations began in 1982, following Prime Minister Thatcher's visit to the PRC. The settlement timetable was accelerated as part of the negotiation itself.

To the opening legal disagreements was added a Chinese threat to seize the colony before 1997. The interests of the parties were multivariate and complex: Hong Kong is, for example, one of China's leading trading partners and it is likely that complete Chinese "victory" (including a communist economy) in this question might kill a golden goose. Even more important than this 40 percent of the PRC's hard currency earnings is access to Western managerial and financial skills. China had nonetheless stated that, absent an agreement, it would unilaterally announce a solution in September 1984. The impending but still somewhat distant end of the lease in 1997 gave possibilities for trading time for modification of absolute sovereignty. China said it was firm about the spatial question: It would have all of Hong Kong including Victoria Island. However, China knew it was being watched by the West on investment matters and could use the market and foreign exchange benefits of a properous Hong Kong. The Hong Kong experience would be closely watched by Taiwan—with more effect on Chinese interests than the rapt attention of holders and claimants of disputed territory worldwide. However, judging by public statements, Peking would indeed assert full as well as timely control at whatever risk.

The Chinese did prefer to have their cake and eat it too: On June 15, 1982, Deputy Party Chairman Deng Xiaoping asked for suggestions for Hong Kong's future within two criteria: (1) China must take back sovereignty, (2) "but in such a way as to assure continued prosperity."[24] This implies Communist administration of a capitalist economy. A further risk was the third yet not widely recognized party to the dispute: the people of Hong Kong. Ever conscious of the fate of the Shanghai industrialists given assurances of autonomy in 1949, they would have a real if not political role. The possibility for disaster was sketched by the relocation in 1984 of the headquarters of one of the oldest Hong Kong companies, Jardine, Matheson & Co., to Bermuda.

Another institution that could be affected is the privately owned Hong Kong and Shanghai Bank. It controls 60 percent of all deposits in Hong Kong and acts as a de facto central bank.[25] Productivity and prosperity were Britain's leverage. For example, a major export like textiles (40%) was subject to separate quotas under the multifibre agreement.

Independence or home rule did not seem to be in the cards for the citizens of Hong Kong, yet the U.K. was committed to a solution acceptable to the people. Furthermore, a formerly complacent Legislative Council had demanded debate on any agreement at the draft stage. In the apparent twilight of their "colonial" status, the people were also asking for a more direct voice in governance— starting with the March 1985 district-governing-body elections. A solid if short democratic tradition would help an incorporated but autonomous trade area of Hong Kong maintain its identity beyond reversion in 1997.

In principle there was no problem with the United Kingdom acknowledging Chinese sovereignty with the approval of the people of Hong Kong and the British Parliament. Based on this interpretation of self-determination, and underpinned by guarantees from the PRC, an orderly transition that stems capital outflow and the brain drain that are now very high risks should be possible.

The PRC from its side was already investing directly and indirectly in the Hong Kong economy, an option not open to Argentina in the Falklands. The very real gains for the PRC in hard currency, the potential benefits of Hong Kong as a proving ground and a window on doing business with China, and even more important the sense in which it is a test case for the Taiwanese, give China real incentives to stick with the understanding about a special autonomous regime for Hong Kong after 1997.

The flight of major companies was the price both parties paid for continued lack of clarity in the situation. These prices were more on the Chinese side of the account than the British, as are some very unique trade relationships via Hong Kong, such as Chinese trade with Taiwan, South Africa, and Saudi Arabia, which would be difficult to arrange through other channels.

The fortunes of moderate, pragmatic leadership and foreign trade seem to be linked in recent Chinese politics (hence, concern about "reliability"). There were thus some interesting territorial options in the case of Hong Kong:

—All but formal integration;

—Autonomy as arranged for in the Chinese constitution with no exclusion of British nationals as employees;

—Total reversion on schedule, but with a transition period to avoid cultural shock to the present population; and

—Lease-back for a further period (an unlikely choice on the part of China, as it would have gone against the grain of conventional socialist thought and would risk ideological ridicule by the Soviet bloc.)

Hong Kong strongly affected decision making by both Argentina and the U.K. in 1982. The two situations cross-influenced each other both by political analogy and by legal precedent.

In the case of the Falklands, lease-back had classically been referred to as the "Hong Kong solution." This was a happier analogy back when Britain's lease on Hong Kong had decades to run, and leaseback was under active consideration in the Falklands. As time grew short for British administration of Hong Kong and political status had to be negotiated, the tensions and costs of uncertainty rose. Leaseback in this perspective began to appear to be what one Kelper called it: just passing the (sovereignty) problem along to our children.

To Argentine decision makers in the spring of 1982, British steadiness on Hong Kong was read as obduracy; concern for the rights of the inhabitants and their way of life as simple territorial greed. Hong Kong looked from Buenos Aires like good precedent for the reversion of all colonial territories to their "natural" metropoles—indeed the 200-meter depth line in the Atlantic seabed ropes the Falklands firmly to the territorial shelf, that is, to Argentina. Hong Kong, overall, reinforced not only the feeling that reincorporation was right and inevitable, part of a global pattern, but that the U.K. was incapable of seeing the pattern and needed a push.

Ironically, the two situations would continue to cross-influence one another even after Argentina had taken and lost its gamble, but the causation would be the reverse: The decisive British response in the Falklands gave Prime Minister Thatcher an excellent position in terms of National Honor and willingness to pay a price to guarantee the way of life of a population to which Britain felt responsibility. The U.K. was thus able to handle Hong Kong firmly and decisively: reversion to China but with a 50-year transition situation.

Western Sahara

Until 1974, Spanish Sahara was a colony that both Morocco and Mauritania claimed as their historical territory. The U.N. General Assembly found these claims to be invalid and had, since the 1960s, called upon Spain to implement the population's right to self-determination. The indigenous Saharawi population of 75,000 had been found by a U.N. Mission to be in favor of independence.

Morocco "settled" the former Spanish Sahara with 350,000 persons upon the departure of Spain in 1975. Moroccan troops were later sent to their defense. The Polisario Front claims sovereignty in the former colony on behalf of indigenous peoples, and is backed by Algeria. The Organization of African Unity (OAU) has tried to settle the dispute. The OAU asserts that territories must exercise the right to self-determination within established colonial boundaries.[26]

On October 18, 1975, Morocco announced a "Green March" of some 350,000 unarmed civilians to enter Sahara in order to gain what it called recognition of Morocco's right to national unity and territorial integrity.

The Security Council adopted three resolutions on Western Sahara in October and November of 1975. Spain originally called for the council to disuade Morocco from conducting a mass march. Morocco framed the intended march as its preferred means for gaining recognition of its right to national unity and territorial integrity.

Spain emphasized that its administration was ending and that it had sought to involve Algeria, Mauritania, and Morocco in the Decolonization process. Spain emphasized an International Court of Justice (ICJ) opinion that there were no legal ties of territorial sovereignty connecting Spanish Sahara to Morocco or Mauritania. U.N. visiting missions had found that the Saharan peoples wished to exercise self-determination under Resolution 1514, yet Morocco had vowed to recover its rights no later than the end of the year.

Morocco emphasized that the Sahara question was in its view a simple bilateral dispute and had been since 1957. Spain had already surrendered Tarfaya and Ifni to Morocco. Morocco had tried to obtain rights to the Sahara for a decade but faced Spanish inertia and "perversion" of the Decolonization process (i.e., toward independence not incorporation into Morocco). Morocco claimed that its citizens would simply be returning to their homelands and not invading a foreign territory, as the Sahara had legal ties with Morocco and Mauritania before it was colonized and was not *tera nullius*.

Mauritania claimed ethnic ties to the people of the Sahara as well as claiming the former legal ties. Mauritania appealed for the council to respect its rights and those of Morocco in the northern part of the territory; rights that were about to be peacefully reasserted and restored.

The Algerian representative said that Algeria had no territorial claim to Western Sahara but was interested in how decolonization was implemented, as this bore on the peace and security of the region.

The council appealed for restraint and moderation, but the Green March took place. On March 4, Spain reported to the council that Moroccan nationals, including armed forces and officials, had crossed the border in large numbers. The Green March volunteers were said to have urged by King Hassan II of

Morocco to return to their starting points, but the independence with which Morocco acted and would continue to act in assertion of territorial integrity in the face of Security Council was not lost on the world community.

An agreement was reached among Spain, Morocco, and Mauritania, which partitioned the territory and left Spain 35 percent interest in FOSBUCRAA, a successful phosphate company.

This move prompted U.N. opposition. The President-elect of the 31st General Assembly had a warning for the Third World in response to their failure to condemn the takeover, stating that they had, in fact, "condoned a trend 'to replace the old imperialism by another form of foreign control founded on territorial claims.' ''[27]

In August of 1979, Mauritania withdrew from the territory it had been granted through partition in 1976. The area was taken by Morocco and reorganized into provinces.

Algeria objects to the partition and is backing the claims of Frente Polarisario for an independent state. Saharawi guerrillas of Polisario based in Algeria continue their attempts to liberate what they see as their country, and have renamed it the Democratic Saharan Arab Republic. In 1982, it became a member of the OAU. Morocco asserts territorial integrity. Polisario and Algeria assert self-determination. The "true" or "natural" population of Western Sahara is in dispute. Rich phosphate deposits are at stake, and possibly oil as well. The U.N. was warned of, but could not prevent, a bloodless occupation of territory long cherished. Regional and world political bodies offer but cannot sell compromises on interests as Honor National becomes more and more at stake.

The United Nations, through the good offices of the Secretary General, will bring a ceasefire and hopefully a plebiscite for the Western Sahara.

There, as in the other disputed territory of the world, solutions can and will be found, whether peacefully or not. When the solution is peaceful, however, only the goodwill of the parties can make it stable and lasting. Their commitment to the solution demands that their political satisfaction be complete in their own terms, whether these are rational to the outside observer or not—it must meet their definition of National Honor. It must also satisfy each party's perception of its national interest, especially as regards defense. Only their perceived interest in geopolitical and military stability can make a territorial settlement final.

Self-determination must also in the long run be a part of such lasting settlement. Here too, the parties alone can guarantee that the sounding is valid and the results respected—in many cases, the population may not opt to join any nation state, on its borders or in its old metropole. The normative thrust of modern law and politics must be to make self-determination a component of National Honor—an element of legitimacy stemming from the will of the people, without which territory is not worth holding, that is, not in the National Interest.

NEGOTIATION BY ANY OTHER NAME

Third-party mediation of inter-state conflict by nations or international institutions has a sad track record in the twentieth century. Normative international law and a good deal of recent theory focus on the role and character of the mediator as major determinants in the outcome of a situation of mediated conflict. Unfortunately, reality seems to suggest that it is still the two or more conflicting nation-states that determine in large part the outcome of the negotiation; that mediation is, in international affairs, a variant of negotiation, not a separate and more promising form of conflict resolution.

Mediation is often negotiation via an intermediary. The two parties still determine most offers and their timing. This is not to deny the creative possibilities for their interlocuters. It only suggests the practical diplomatic limitations on their creativity.

One of the principal limitations is the constraint on the players not to hurt their standing in the ongoing nation-state game. This is one of the more perverse forms that National Honor takes in limiting nation-state behavior and inhibiting peaceful settlement.

Mediation can be seen as intervention by a disinterested third party to help resolve a disagreement or confrontation. It will appeal only to parties who at a given stage see benefit in neither legal nor military alternatives. Mediation requires that all parties to a disagreement be present or represented. The negotiators from the conflicting parties must have full authority to speak, if not decide for, their side, and the power (even by delegation and confirmation) to initiate or conclude an agreement. Public commitment to the process is important, and a deadline, expressed or implied, is helpful. There need to be incentives to produce serious bargaining. All of the issues must at least be discussable if not formally admitted to be negotiable.

Mediation requires a mediator to either transform a bilateral negotiation into a mediated negotiation or sometimes indeed to establish contact. A crisis mediator must be desired, or at least initially tolerated, and willing. It is important, of course, that the mediator's intervention be timely and that his role as interlocuter and, indeed, proposer of solutions be seen as a valid one. He must be willing to run the risks of failure associated with getting between two parties in a conflict and capable of disciplining each side in its search for total mastery and a complete "win." He needs to establish a viable form of contact with each of the parties and eventually between them, although it is entirely possible for a good mediation to be completely indirect. The mediator has at his disposal several methods:

—The shuttle in which he travels between parties, usually between their political capitals. This has the advantage of almost instantaneous implementation depending on distance and the full commitment of the personal prestige of the mediator from the beginning. It allows the mediator to serve as a buffer between the parties' more extreme statements of interests, goals, and minima. This buffer role indeed becomes quite effortless as he literally carries the message and interprets en route.

—The summons in which the parties are convened at a third point (usually the political capital of the mediator) has the advantage of putting parties in a somewhat less independent and autonomous position. By agreeing to assemble, they have made a first concession in total dignity and independence. They have tacitly admitted that a solution is desirable and have made the first step themselves in tempering National Honor in favor of National Interest if their interest lies in a mutually negotiable solution. This can then change the calculus of National Honor. Sometimes National Honor is *advanced* by the appearance of "reasonableness" resulting from a willingness to talk.

—The parties can be convened at a third point, a site having distinct (and useful) implications of its own. The mediator can attempt to set new norms and public perceptions by having them meet in an original and neutral third point, perhaps with some regional significance. He can also convene them in a neutral but recognized forum in which the place/institution itself implies norms, and the parties' concession in assembling is even greater.

THE MEDIATOR AS NEGOTIATOR: SOME BASIC CONSIDERATIONS

The parties and the mediator, when realistically seen as a literal third party, must keep a shifting and interacting array of factors in mind, including:

—What is negotiable;

—How to frame the issue;

—When to negotiate;

—Conflict and power relationships;

—Timing, atmospherics, and outside pressures;

—Felt and unstated needs, and the sensitivity to spot them;

—Relative strength of positions;

—Intelligence and the negotiations context;

—Reformulation;

—Risk taking;

—Reordering priorities;

—Trial balloons;

—Restated minima;

—Hidden agendas and the probing process;

—Real understanding;

—Trade-offs and concessions;

—Win-win and zero-sum solutions;

—Slow progress, impasse, stalemate, and failure;

—Deadlines, real and imagined, and procedural and substantive;

—The drafting process and principal options;

—Press and public affairs, domestic and foreign, informative and manipulative; and

—Ultimata.

The mediator functioning as negotiator must, whatever the nomenclature, create a process from a framework similar to the following stages of third-party mediation.

Lay up Alongside

The mediator's first challenge is to convince the parties of the credibility that he feels he has as a potential interlocuter in their dispute. For a party with whom one does not already enjoy a relationship of confidence and trust, this consists principally in demonstrating that one's national or institutional interest give one a credible reason to seek a mutually beneficial negotiated solution.

While it is tempting to try to guarantee more than that, for example; that one's potential sympathies and skill might lead to unnegotiated benefits, this can involve extreme short-run costs. It can, indeed, potentially wreck a mediation. It can lend to overconfidence, insufficient willingness to make meaningful concessions, or extreme overstatement of initial demands. One party will hold out for an advantageous but realistic position given what he assumes to be support from the interlocuter.

Conversely, it is very likely that any warnings or cautions conveyed by the intermediary concerning the other party's position will be interpreted as pro forma exercises and not a sincere desire to sketch the situation accurately in the interests of a negotiated solution.

Assess and Contrast

Having established one's credibility as a possible mediator of the conflict, it is important to work with each side in turn to assess the situation. One can then contrast for each party how its assessment differs from that of the other. This includes not only listing stated needs but searching for misstatements of perceived or real conflict.

Frame and Time

The mediator needs to sketch for the parties the process by which he would intend to interpret their differences and seek agreement. Framing the process for them may imply a time frame, though it is useful to accustom them to the idea that a renewal period may be necessary in cases where one of the parties has implied or set an unrealistic time frame. The time frame itself must remain negotiable.

Exchange/Interpret

The mediator must then begin the exchange of precise nonpolemical versions of the parties' interpretations of their own interests and needs. His interpretation should at a minimum harmonize the language and format of the two sides' presentations. The mediator must next make an interpretation of each side's position to the other with an eye to producing a clearer and, if possible, less adversarial view of the stated needs of each party. Language, of course, bears on the way a suggestion is received by the other party. Style and substance are intimately related in these initial presentations of positions.

Suggest

Should interpretation fail to produce any closing of the gap in the two positions, the mediator will have to assume a truly active role and suggest to one or both parties positions or tactics he feels will bring the two sides closer together. The degree of intervention will vary with the realism and seriousness of the parties.

Reframe

Should a strategy or text from the mediator fail to produce agreement, the mediator is left with the options of reframing the issue, pushing agreement, or disengaging.

Reframing may be promising where the parties have come to a full realization of the scope and seriousness of their disagreement. It may be, for example, that at that stage they may be willing to freeze the question as previously defined and attempt to make progress by working on subsidiary or other related issues. Sanctions or deadlines that originally appeared firm may have, by this stage, passed or been proven to be flexible. Serious consideration should be given to not attempting to immediately resolve the main dispute in the terms originally set.

Push Agreement

If it is not possible to reframe the negotiating question, the mediator may want to push agreement. This at heart is his task. The whole nonissue of "biased mediation" becomes critical in a realistic consideration of the mediator. I am not here discussing the degree of power the mediator can exercise over one party or another. Even without any such institutional or state influence over one of the parties, it is the job of the mediator in the end to convince one party or another to accept that which it states is unacceptable. A truly passive interlocuter may produce agreement where agreement was probable. To produce agreement when none is seen as likely is the challenge to the active mediator. Like the *negotiators* for the parties, the *mediator* has a variety of tactics, strategies, and gambits open to him in pushing agreement.

Disengagement

When agreement is blocked or nearly achieved but threatened by the tactics or timing of one party, the mediator should give serious consideration to disengagement. This may be necessary not only as a tactic—that is, in order to get the parties to return seriously to the negotiating table, or as a gambit to overcome serious but possibly not intentional disingenuousness or delay—but literally as a strategy in order to save both the process and the possibility of its renewal.

While it is generally assumed that any disengagement—that is, an end of the mediation by that particular mediator—represents failure, and should invoke all stated consequences, a well-timed disengagement may be the maximizing strategy for the mediator who can foresee any of the following contingencies:

1. That the stated consequences or sanctions cannot or will not be immediately invoked;
2. That an alternative process is in the offing and should, in effect, be deferred to; or
3. That disengagement, temporary or final, should be thought of as a creative option rather than the opposite of success.

Deadlock and the illusion that the negotiations are joined can be not only a dangerous political illusion but camouflage of the most effective kind for the intention to use force. The mediator is in a better position that most institutions to judge whether the parties have the possibility of agreement in a realistic time frame. If not, the most creative option is to make it clear to both parties that they will not make progress from the positions into which they have settled. It is the goal, not the process, that counts in the mediation of international conflict, and, to the extent that the mediator assumes or acquires interests of his own which prevent him from making a realistic decision about disengagement in the interest of a settlement, he does harm to his own interests and to the possibilities of a settlement.

There is a rich literature of several millenia on statecraft and negotiation, backed up by solid work in the twentieth century in the social sciences. Both science and art, mediation must in the end, however, be situation-specific. The facts of a dispute can make it objectively hard to settle. Differing perceptions of those facts can make it next to impossible. The mediator must deal with the perceptions of that situation—his own, those of each party, those of third parties who influence the mediation.

Those perceptions were quite complicated in the case of the Falklands crisis of Spring 1982. The mental checklists of the two parties included centuries of antagonism and conflict, years of mutual frustration. To get a sense of why the three principal mediations of the Falklands crisis failed—why this was not a simple tradeoff in territorial/economic National Interests—one must look at the history of that seldom noticed slice of the South Atlantic. The recent years of negotiation, with words and with gestures, help one to understand why force was used and why National Honor was so much tied up in the situation for each party. One then has a better perception than was possible for most in 1982 why more violence had in the end to be employed—how stacked the diplomatic deck was against peaceful settlement by mediation.

II

ORIGINS: THE POLITICS OF ILLUSION
VERSUS THE POLITICS OF PRINCIPLE—
CENTURIES OF DISPUTE, YEARS OF
BILATERAL NEGOTIATION

> The antiquity of the dispute is one of its illuminating peculiarities. It is
> neither important enough to solve nor unimportant enough to forget.
> —H. S. Ferns
> *Britain and Argentina in the 19th Century*

FALKLANDS SOVEREIGNTY: THE MISTS OF
COLONIALISM

Sovereignty over the Falkland Islands has been the subject of claim and counterclaim, assertion and acts of war, since their discovery. Territorial claims are based variously on discovery, domination or governance, and settlement or effective occupation.

The *discovery* of the Falkland Islands is one of the origins of disputed sovereignty. Four major European powers laid claim to right of sovereignty by discovery.[1] Claims based on sightings were cloudy at best, and those based on the presence or naming of bodies of land in the South Atlantic by cartographers even less dependable. Papal decisions (the Bulls *Enter Coetara* and *Dudum si Quidem*) dividing the New World between Spain and Portugal in its southern latitudes were not accepted by Protestant European states. Pope Alexander VI in 1494 sought to defuse the potential conflict between Spain and Portugal in their maritime and colonial expeditions. He set a meridian 100 leagues west of the Azores. West of the line all discoveries would be Spanish, and east of it they would belong to Portugal. Non-parties also rejected the Spanish-Portuguese Treaty of Tordesillas of 1494 which realigned the division. Players other than the British and the Spanish abound in the history of the Falkland Islands: Venetians, Portuguese, Dutch, and other navigators and seamen plied the area as Europe searched for the short route to the Indies and then began to realize the strategic importance of controlling the straits and the passage around the Horn. Much of the attention given to the era of discovery came later and was done specifically in support of modern sovereignty claims in the nineteenth century. This still applies to most works on the history of the islands.

Europeans reached Brazil by 1499, and in 1502 Portuguese ships with Amerigo Vespucci as geographer may have sighted the Falklands for the first time. Spanish claims of discovery by Magellan (1520) and Camargo (1540) predate those of Great Britain. Maps and globes of the Hispanic world had shown land in the area for a century when, in 1592, Captain John Davis of the British vessel *Desire* is claimed to have discovered the Falkland Islands, also said to have been seen by the Englishman Hawkins in 1594. The best documented claim is that of Sebald van Weert, who captained a Dutch vessel in 1600. The first landing was by Captain John Strong in 1690, a full century later. He named the sound between the two major islands in honor of Viscount Falkland of the British Admiralty.

Major claims in the South Atlantic in the period of discovery are thus separated by decades, indeed centuries. Interest in the area was in inverse proportion to its distance from continental Europe. They are further clouded by a 1604 Anglo-Spanish peace treaty which voided rights based on discovery.

Argentine inheritance of the islands from Spain is a two-part case based on (1) recognition of the Spanish claim and (2) recognition of the "transfer" of title to these islands to the former Vice Royalty of Buenos Aires, later the Argentine Republic. Argentina asserts that the rights of Spain to the islands passed to it. There was no formal or direct transfer by Spain. Great Britain has never recognized any right of Argentina to the islands. This is important because a 1604 Treaty of Peace between Spain and England returned the situation to prewar status, nullifying any rights to the Falkland Islands based on discovery.

Britain certainly recognized that there were Spanish areas of the New World which were not open to it. Under the Treaty of Madrid of 1670 which eliminated British trade or navigation in the Spanish seas and the Spanish Indies, Britain confirmed this "spheres" approach. These provisions of the Treaty of Madrid were firmed up in the 1713 Treaty of Utrecht. Sovereignty by inheritance from Spain as agreed sovereign of the southern New World is most firmly bedded in the Treaty of Utrecht. In the Spanish and, later, the Argentine view, article eight of the treaty is seen as protecting Spanish claims to the New World against British claims of discovery, settlement, or military action. Britain decided after the Seven Years War to practice the "containment" of the Spanish New World, ringing the mainland with strategic naval bases.

Great Britain could be said to have tacitly recognized the competing existence of Spanish claims in the 1771 declarations restoring to Great Britain its settlement of Port Egmont. The Spanish declaration stated that restoration did not affect prior sovereign rights of Spain over the islands, yet the practical effect was

Spanish recognition of the British settlement. Britain did not comment on the Spanish reservation about sovereignty, but silence is not acknowledgment of sovereign rights, only apparently part of a deal. If the deal was a pure return to the status quo ante, it was the last agreement to disagree on the islands. There may have been more to the deal: Britain was said (but cannot be proven) to have agreed clandestinely not to pursue the claim. Whether by tacit or secret negotiation, or the all-powerful hand of public expense, in 1774 the British left. Britain further loosened its grip when it signed the Treaty of Peace of Versailles in 1783. The Versailles agreement repeated the provisions of 1670 and 1713 regarding New World territories.

The trend of tacitly accepting Spanish de facto hegemony in the South Atlantic continued through the eighteenth century. The Saint Lawrence Convention of 1790 restrained British and Spanish subjects from establishing *new* colonies in the South Atlantic or settling territory occupied by Spain. The Falklands were occupied by Spain in 1790. The proscription of new colonies on the South American mainland was clear. Whether Britain would consider as "new" a future Falklands colony in the absence of Spain is ambiguous, as may have been its intent in negotiating the agreed-on language. The British claim to sovereignty over the Falklands would seem to have survived the 1790 Nootka Sound/St. Lawrence accord which lapsed between 1795–1814.

The British view firmed up in the nineteenth century. Certainly from the time of the Spanish abandonment of the Falklands in 1811, Britain viewed the pact of 1790 as inapplicable by official cessation of governance by the Governor of Montevideo acting for and still loyal to the Spanish crown. Spanish rights exercised between 1774 and 1811 were viewed by the U.K. as having lapsed. England neither placed reservations on nor allowed mention of Argentine claims to the islands in the 1825 Treaty of Friendship, Commerce and Navigation by which Britain recognized Argentine (mainland) independence and de jure sovereignty.

Acts of Domination or governance, as distinct from settlement, depend on declared or formal government of the islands. In 1765, Commodore John Byron "took possession" of Saunders Island off West Falkland and all surrounding islands in the name of George III. Strong had not done so upon his 1690 landing. France was also in the process of declaring formal possession, but sold its claim to Spain. Spain named numerous and successive governors between 1774 and 1811, who exercised authority over the islands without British protests. It made official decisions such as the 1766 Royal Bill declaring the islands to be dependencies of the Captaincy General of Buenos Aires. In the first decades of the 1800s, neither Britain nor Argentina really ruled, controlled, taxed, or protected the growing whaling industry in the harbors of the Falklands, but Argentina continued the line of Acts of Domination. On behalf of the new republic of Buenos Aires as heir of Spain, David Jewett took (purely) formal possession of the islands in 1820. Nine years later, the Government of Buenos Aires created the political and military commandancy of the Malvinas Islands. Then and later, in 1832, the U.K. protested Argentine domination as infringing on British rights. Conflicting claims based on governance thus reverted to the contest begun in the discovery phase.

Colonization, or *settlement,* began with the French. In 1764, French colonists from Saint Malo, who had hunted seals in the area for some time, established the first settlement in the Falkland Islands. (Saint Malo is the origin of the Spanish *Malvinas* from the French *Malouines.*) Settlement continued the next year, as the British took formal possession of the Falklands for George III. In 1766, the first British population was established at Port Egmont on Saunder's Island near West Falkland. Spain moved quickly in 1767 to purchase the French settlement and buy out France's claim (which was never recognized by England). A Spanish governor was appointed, dependent on Buenos Aires, and a Spanish garrison was established at the former French settlement of Port Louis, which was renamed Puerto Soledad. Direct Anglo-Argentine confrontation began in 1769 as warnings were exchanged with Port Egmont. After consolidating their garrison, in 1770 the Spanish expelled the British by force (14,500 soldiers: Argentines recall that overwhelming numbers made the Spanish victory bloodless), thus beginning a series of military and "effective possession" claims. Spain and Britain almost engaged in the first Falklands war, but the British crown was able in 1771 to negotiate repossession and reoccupation of Port Egmont. Spain made a reservation, however, on sovereignty: Restoration could not and ought not in any way to affect the question of the prior right to sovereignty over the Malouine Islands, otherwise called Falkland's Islands.

The returning British settlers were withdrawn three years later in 1774. Their occupation, it was said, was economically unviable (and perhaps politically pre-agreed). In the manner of the day, they left a plaque "maintaining" sovereignty over the Falklands and politically nullifying their evacuation.

From 1774 to 1811, a Spanish Governor-General under the Viceroy of Rio de la Plata in Buenos Aires governed a Spanish-speaking population in the Falkland Islands. The Port Louis/Puerto Soledad settlement was continuous for almost half a century. France and Spain, discovery aside, annexed and effectively occupied East Falkland. In parallel, the U.K. also did so at Port Egmont off West Falkland from 1766 to 1774. The British case asserted discovery as the basis of sovereignty. Alternatively, it posited discovery followed by *prompt* real possession. The discovery claim is contested and flawed for either party. British discovery and occupation were separated by over 70 years: discovery by Davis (1592) or Hawkins (1594), until claim by Byron (1765) and possession by McBride (1766). That settlement only lasted an interrupted eight years, and was abandoned in 1774. The Spanish then destroyed Egmont.

The British-Spanish relationship took its conflict to shore in 1806, as British troops invaded the mainland at Buenos Aires. Taking and then losing the city, the British unintentionally discredited Spanish rule and produced a surrender of military and civil power by the Viceroy to the leader of the indigenous volunteer troops who had defeated the British.

The Vice Royalty of La Plata revolted in 1810 and fragmented eventually into Argentina, Uruguay, Paraguay, and Bolivia. Its grip on the Falklands was equally tenuous as it fought for autonomy, then from 1816 on for independence, and later territorial integrity.

As Buenos Aires moved toward full sovereignty and independence in stages, Spanish authorities removed the Falklands garrison in 1811 because it was too expensive, and left a plaque like that of the departed British in order to maintain sovereignty. Following independence in 1816, the United Provinces of the Rio de la Plata claimed the islands in 1820 and tried to settle the unpopulated Malvinas in the late 1820s. The legal basis was both right of inheritance from the colonial metropole (Spain) and the purported secret eighteenth-century Hispano-British negotiation and agreement on British departure after a decent interval. Britain had recognized Argentina in 1825 without reservations regarding the islands. Buenos Aires designated a governor and then a military commandancy of the Falkland Islands. Great Britain, the last of whose citizens had given up living in the Falklands over 50 years earlier, protested in 1829. Buenos Aires at this point had little more than a garrison, and the islands could not be considered populated by Argentines. The first civilian population in this era, Luis Vernet's settlers, consisted roughly of 30 blacks, 34 residents of Buenos Aires, 28 English-speaking people, and 7 Germans. Vernet's deputy was British, and Vernet's own loyalties are called into question by his overtures to the British on several occasions. The islands were serving as fishing, whaling, and sealing bases for many nations. They were principally a penal colony and military outpost of the new Argentina.

In 1831, in the first U.S. armed action against a Latin power, the frigate U.S.S. *Lexington* took and destroyed Puerto Soledad, spiked its guns, and routed the Argentine settlers, fishermen, and whalers from the Falkland Islands. The intervention was launched in reaction to the failure of the Argentine government to deal with a seizure of two U.S. schooners and their cargo in the Falklands during 1831 by the Argentine governor Luis Vernet. U.S. fishermen had fished Falkland waters for half a century without Spanish interference. Vernet claimed powers never exercised by Spain, whether in the island or off Patagonia or Tierra del Fuego. Off to a brilliant start, U.S.-Argentine relations were suspended for a decade and focused on the *Lexington* incident for half a century. The U.S. Secretary of State had stated in 1830 that Buenos Aires had "no good title to these islands." The U.S. Supreme Court ruling on the seizures of U.S. vessels again evoked a U.S. Executive Branch position that the Falklands were not Argentine territory. This was reversed, however, as the United States began a general policy in the nineteenth century of neutrality in New World territorial disputes. That would remain U.S. policy at and through the Falklands crisis of spring 1982.

A year after the U.S. intervention, and Argentine resettlement, the British reestablished British occupation and settlement. On January 2, 1833, a landing party from H.M.S. *Clio* expelled the 25-man Argentine garrison. The British evicted the Argentine settlement at Puerto Soledad. As in the Spanish takeover of 1771, the whole action was bloodless. Some settlers (including Antonio "the Gaucho" Rivero), farm laborers, and ex-convicts were allowed to stay. This first reported contravention of the Monroe Doctrine of 1823 was said to have been assisted by the United States. It may be more than chance that this followed on the heels of the U.S. intervention. The United States certainly felt its interests and citizens in the area threatened by Buenos Aires. The United States certainly did not object to, probably supported, and may have instigated the U.K. landing as bringing "order" to the area. Argentine Minister to the Court of Saint James Manuel Moreno became the first of many Argentines to reject and protest the British seizure of 1833. Britain replied through its Chargé d'Affaires (relations were not broken) that its rights to the islands had never been relinquished, and included the right to garrison them, which it had just exercised.

A century and a half of legal, political, diplomatic, and military debate began with the British occupation of 1833. Formal civil government was established for the Falkland Islands by the United Kingdom in 1843. A decade later, the Royal Falklands Company (or Falkland Islands Company) was granted a charter for the economic development and exploitation of the islands.

Argentina, having protested the British 1833 seizure at length, continued to maintain that it held sovereignty over the Falkland Islands. This was formally reasserted in 1841 with the Argentine case resting principally on proximity to the Argentine mainland. It was the view of the Rosas government from 1850 on that relations with Britain had been normalized. In debt and fragmenting, the Argentine confederation dropped its claim until 1884–88 when British occupation of the islands was again actively protested. While the claim to the Malvinas became a regular bell to be rung in public political discourse, a gap of 35 years indicates the marginal economic and even strategic value of the islands to the nineteenth century, at least compared to the immense global power and reach of 19th century imperial England. Britain declined an offer of sale in exchange for cancellation of a major loan. The Rosas regime in Argentina focused on the capital and the Pampa, not the frontiers; on ranching, not trade and the seas. Britain's interest was expressed for years by a token Royal Navy presence about equal to the 18 Argentines they had replaced.[2]

In the twentieth century, the resources of the area made South Atlantic exploitation more appealing. Its strategic importance grew with the number of bluewater navies and the prospect of global war. In 1904, Argentines constructed a whaling station at Grytviken on the island of South Georgia, one of the Falklands dependencies. They also operated a meteorological station from 1905 to 1943, and held a U.K. lease for 500 acres to be used by the Argentine Fishing Company. Argentina's claims and assertiveness grew with its real interest in the South Atlantic.

In 1908, Argentina raised its claim, dormant for 20 years, at the Rome Postal Convention. This formal interest followed several years of activity in the islands south of the Falklands.

In 1908, the following were designated by the U.K. as *Falklands* dependencies: South Georgia, the South Orkneys, the South Shetlands, the Sandwich Islands, and Grahamland in Antarctica. The South Orkneys were the subject of sovereignty negotiations in 1913, but the talks deadlocked. The Dependencies (today limited to the South Georgia and South Sandwich Islands, with the British Antarctic Territory separated) are Dependent Territories of the United Kingdom whose administration was formalized by Letters Patent of the Crown. They are legally distinct regimes, administered from Stanley by the Crown, not by the Falkland Islands government. Their history of discovery, exploration, and settlement is separate from that of the distant, inhabited Falklands. They might better be called the South Atlantic Dependencies. The punctuation is instructive: "Falklands," not "Falkland's" Dependencies. The name reflects their administration from the Falklands, but they are Dependencies of the Crown, and not of the Falklands.

In World War I, the British and Germans clashed at sea off the Falklands in a historic example of British strategic foresight. The British Navy intercepted and utterly destroyed the Imperial German Navy's Pacific squadron as it steamed to join the sea war off Europe.

In a miniature of the struggle for the Falkland Islands, Argentina unilaterally established a wireless station in 1925 on Lourie Island in the South Orkneys. In 1927 and 1928, negotiations again failed, but Argentina applied for an international call sign and frequency for her radio station.

It was not until 1927 that Argentina first claimed sovereignty over South Georgia and its outlying islands, yet by various acts undertaken with British approval, permission, license, or lease, it tacitly acknowledged British sovereignty. In 1945, the United Kingdom repossessed the Argentine meteorological station at Grytviken and returned all equipment to the Argentina Fishing Company. This would be the last U.K. dislodging of Argentine presence in the Dependencies. British responses would become primarily diplomatic and naval.

In 1947–48, Argentina first claimed the South Sandwich Islands. Thus, not until after World War II did the Argentine claim to the South Atlantic assume its present dimensions: not only the Falklands, but South Georgia and South Sandwich Islands discovered by Cook in 1775 and never occupied or settled by Argentina, and the Antarctic zone below 60°. From 1947, Argentina began to pursue a strategy of parallel diplomatic and military pressures for sovereignty over the Falklands. At the Rio Treaty Conference in 1947, for example, Argentina made a reservation of its position on the Falklands. Noting that colonies or possessions of European countries might fall within the security zone to be established by the Rio treaty, Argentina reserved its position of sovereignty over the Falklands and Dependencies including the Argentine Antarctic sector. (The U.S. position was that the Rio Treaty does not affect questions of sovereignty.)

The Argentine claim now formally included the misnamed Dependencies governed from Stanley, though not claimed as discovered, settled, or previously administered from Buenos Aires. Argentina continued to operate its radio station and to make other effective exercises of sovereignty or civil government in the Dependencies, especially at Grytviken. The postwar scope and strength of the claim grew together. In 1947, Argentine cruisers and six destroyers conducted maneuvers off the Falklands themselves. A British naval task force was sent to the area in reaction, and the Argentine navy subsided. The principal diplomatic focus for Argentine diplomacy became the United Nations.

ARGENTINE DIPLOMACY: THE SOUTHERN PERSPECTIVE, OTHERWORLDLINESS, AND PERSISTENCE

A world map centered on the South Atlantic gives one a very different view of geopolitical reality. The world is mainly empty and desolate. Only about one-tenth of the surface is land. Except for that sliver in the center, the east and west are water and the south is ice. Resources beyond the Southern Cone of Latin America are under water or under ice. The seasons, reversed of course from those of the northern world, grow rapidly harsh as one moves south from a center at Comodoro Rivadavia. By the latitude of Rio Gallegos and Stanley, snow already falls on the sea in each month of the year, and there are no frostless seasons.

The little of this world that is land lessens from there. Southward there is only Tierra del Fuego, which is strategic, they say, but also desolate. To the southeast lie the chains of islands of the Scotia Sea: Falklands, Georgias, and Sandwich, increasingly small and desolate. They end near 60° south latitude, south of which the United States recognizes no territorial claims, contested or not: the effective beginning of the Antarctic.

To the north, the northern coast of South America lies on the horizon, its mass diminished by polar convergence of projection lines like a north pole. Central and North America are out of sight over the northern horizon, irrelevant to the South Atlantic world. Washington is 5,500 nautical miles away—no closer or more related to the southern ocean than to Cairo.

The world to the left consists of empty Pacific Ocean. To the right, Africa is over the horizon, with Ascension Island lying 3,380 nautical miles from Stanley, the last regular population on the edge of the land world.

The eye gravitates naturally southward to the widest and most significant surface area in the southern world: Antarctica, resource-rich and the land of the future. The polar region does not suffer the same cartographic fate as the north coast, since it wraps well around the horizon and is as large as the land mass to the north from this perspective. The projection shows all of the Antarctic icecap—well into what Australia and New Zealand consider their part of the world. Such is the sweep of a southern view of the world.

The Antarctic Peninsula reaches up toward Tierra del Fuego, defining the average reach of sea ice, making Drake Passage seem a minor and geologically insignificant interruption much the same as the Strait of Magellan. Likewise,

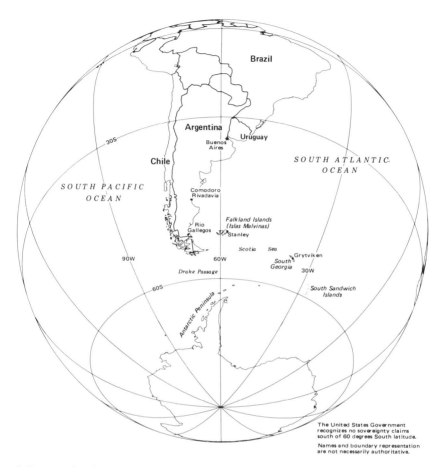

A Perspective Map of the World Centered on the Falkland Islands

the island chains seem an extension of the continent. It is all central land tied by surrounding oceans, which limit and negatively define it as one region.

The South Shetlands and Orknies lie within the 60° circle, but in the southern continental perspective they are Antarctic stepping stones respectively to Cape Horn and South Georgia, and seem more on a line with the Sandwiches—a southern tier below a parallel Falklands-Georgias tier.

Geology takes one beyond the surface of our map. The mountains and the parallel fault define the backbone of the New World. Like the rocks themselves, they wrap south and east from the continent to the islands. Geological structures are contiguous if not all continuous—they seem to the Argentine eye a continuous belt of national resources.

Internal distances within the South Atlantic world are great. Stanley is 1,000 nautical miles (nm) from Buenos Aires. It is another 1,000 miles from there to

Southern Thule in the South Sandwiches. The next land at Tristan de Cunha is over another 1,000 miles.

Thus, in the South Atlantic worldview, the Falklands begin to seem relatively near to the little central sliver of continent: 380 nm from Rio Grande in Tierra del Fuego, 390 nm from Puerto Descade, 423 nm from Rio Gallegos—the focus of a small arc of coastal mainland in the extreme south. This "cradle" perspective on the islands is exaggerated in the mental map of the Argentine people, who learn from the second grade on that this claim in the Scotia Sea is part of their patrimony. Seen as national territory, the islands are even closer. Their inherent or natural relationship to the mainland (fatherland) is as obvious to Argentines as it is irrelevant to the British, who on average lie 30 miles from France, Belgium, or Holland. It was more apparent to their Norman forebears. To Argentines, the contrast with the 8,000-mile distance to the U.K. is also telling. To the British, used to reciprocal loyalty with far-flung places, it is far less telling—culture, politics, and other factors carrying much more weight than geography and geology. Vegetation, topology, and climate, which remind English-speakers of the Scottish moors and bogs, and are functions of being closer to a pole, bespeak Patagonia to Argentines. Even the eye says to them that the Falklands are inherently part of the Southern world.

SIGNALS

In the postwar era, Argentina has repeatedly stated and demonstrated the political will and military capabilities to occupy the islands of the South Atlantic. In the period of bilateral negotiations, Britain for 17 years sent tacit diplomatic and defense signals to the effect that it desired to be done with the Falklands question despite the wishes of the majority of the islanders and the Parliament. However, from 1967, if not 1947, Whitehall acknowledged that self-determination would be a preponderant principle. The Falklanders, for all practical purposes, were given the veto in questions of political status. The postwar British governments were consistent in these two conflicting policy lines through several roles of the electoral dice.

Each British Foreign Minister was willing to consider the legitimacy of the Argentine claim. Each British Cabinet lent increasing support to the idea that compromise might be possible. The Wilson government ("round 1") refused to dismiss the Argentine claim. The Heath government signed the communications agreement giving Argentina control of civilian air traffic and oil supply. The Nationality Act was seen by many as tantamount to making the Falklanders Argentine passport-holders. Argentina was encouraged to build a temporary airstrip; to supply petroleum, oil, and lubricants; and to provide access to additional schooling and medical care in Argentina.

Over this period, Argentine irredentist feeling grew stronger. Frustration with the negotiating process increased with the emergence of the strength of the Falklands lobby, and what the Argentines regarded as near tranference of sovereignty. The acceptance of the wishes rather than the interests of the Islanders also rankled.

The Argentine territorial claim is a constant in its policy, and worldwide claims on continental shelves and exclusive resource zones increased Argentina's confidence. An anticolonial zeitgeist and the radicalization of Decolonization both encouraged and pressured Argentina.

Argentina made the assumption that a mechanism could be found to translate real-world supplies and services into sovereignty, while the British assumption was that the real-world benefits to the Kelpers of increased Argentine supplies and services could be kept separate from the question of sovereignty until such time as the population was willing to consider it.

The principle of self-determination had underlain the whole of the British postwar experience with Decolonization. Argentina saw Decolonization as an irredentist, territorial process of undoing imperial rather than colonial conquest. The right of peoples to self-determination under Article 1(2) of the U.N. Charter clearly depends on the exercise and implementation of the wishes of the people involved. Article 73 of the Charter refers to the interests, not the wishes, of the peoples of dependent territories as being paramount. The U.N. majority grew more and more inclined to the Argentine view.

The U.K. adopted a new tactic in response to the increasing Argentine emphasis on Decolonization: to increasingly insist on direct decision by vote or plebiscite of the Kelpers, arguing that their *interests* must be reflected in their *express wishes*. (Argentina attributes the formulation to the "Lobby.") The British included representatives of the Falklanders in discussions, and increasingly insisted that the U.K. Government was a spokesman only for their wishes and not for any third-party interest. Only during the preconflict stage of the Falklands crisis did Her Majesty's Government begin to qualify in ministerial pronouncements the insistence on wishes over interests.

While Argentina pursued political goals in the U.N. context in the postwar years, it began building and pursuing its case with actions rather than words in the South Atlantic world. In 1948, the Argentine Foreign Ministry established a separate department to both assert and embody its claim to the South Atlantic islands. The Argentine navy paralleled diplomatic action with major maneuvers in the Antarctic area to flex Argentine political muscle in the regional context. Britain responded smartly, dispatching H.M.S. *Nigeria* to the area, but in the diplomatic context Britain registered its non–self-governing territories, including the Falklands, with the United Nations in its new Decolonization structure.

In the early 1950s, Argentina took legislative action in both the Senate and Chamber of Deputies to formally declare the Falklands Argentine possessions. Again, equal attention was paid to tacit bargaining and real-world assertion. As in 1953, the Argentine Government decided on a naval landing at Deception Island. The Royal Navy dispatched H.M.S. *Snipe* to counter the Argentine gesture.

In 1955, Argentine somewhat undercut its claim by rejecting ICJ jurisdiction, the opinions of other international courts, or mediative or arbitrational panels. Argentina stated its case purely in politics and force of arms. This left them only the political bodies of the United Nations, the regional organization OAS (Organization of American States), or the nonaligned or other less formal gatherings as fora in which to shore up the legitimacy of their claim. All these fora had the advantage that while they might not yet be ready to rule in Argentina's favor and might not be politically binding, they were also unlikely ever to rule in favor of Great Britain and in any case could not give force to such ruling. Argentina was thus securing a longer-term open and safe political field in which to play, while undercutting any possible final or definitive juridical or mediative ruling that might in any way diminish its advantage in proximity and ready applicability of national resort to force.

FALKLANDS NEGOTIATIONS: AT THE TABLE AND ON THE BEACH

The elected administration gave the next impetus to the Argentine claim, moving the dispute to the United Nations. Argentina raised the question of the Malvinas Islands in the Subcommittee on Small Territories of the Committee of the Twenty-Four (C–24) in 1964. Both Britain and the United States were then members of the C–24. The British position was that sovereignty was not negotiable but that questions of welfare of the islanders and contacts with Argentina should indeed be discussed. The report of the special committee resulted in General Assembly Resolution 2065 of December 16, 1965, citing the Falklands as an instance of colonialism. The resolution called for bilateral negotiations toward a peaceful settlement of the territorial dispute. Both the Charter and Resolution 1514 (XV) were referred to. Bilateral discussions were not new. Britain was not assertive about sovereignty when Argentina raised the question between 1910 and 1936. Prescription became the main argument after the centennial of British occupation. Lord Willingdon had led talks in Buenos Aires in 1940 which discussed the future sovereignty of the islands. There had been increasing public interest in the traditional claim to the Malvinas for over two years. Under the elected Illia regime, the cause gained political momentum within and beyond Argentina. A national holiday, Malvinas Day, had been established, and official contacts with the U.K. had been made on the subject.

U.K. Foreign Secretary Michael Stewart discussed Falklands in Buenos Aires in January of 1966, and six months later a meeting was held in London. The agenda in the British view was the lessening of friction, and the aim was to limit the scale of the dispute. The Argentine view was that the agenda was the return of the sovereignty of the Falkland Islands to Argentina.

Argentine Ambassador Ortiz de Rosas was involved in the 1966 talks and also worked on the Falklands for his seven years at the Argentine mission to the U.N. He considered the 1966 talks too formal and lacking in any serious results. The Argentines made a four-page statement. Ortiz de Rosas was told that some watching and waiting was in order, but that the British representative would eventually tell them informally when the U.K. meant business, and quiet, serious discussions would ensue. Following the 1966 coup which brought General Ongania to power and made Ortiz de Rosas the Chargé d'Affaires following the resignation of his ambassador, the British Under Secretary of State for the Americas called from the Foreign Ministry and proposed lunch. He suggested that the political counsellor, the embassy's expert on the Malvinas, also attend. Over lunch, an unofficial, deniable scenario complete with official disclaimers was offered. Its essence was that the United Kingdom had no strategic, political, or economic interests to pursue in the Falklands. The Islands were in balance in funding terms, in the sense that they were almost self-sufficient. The idea was suggested for consideration that they would eventually become Argentine territory and the question was the timing and method of Argentina's assertion of sovereignty. "If you want to conquer the hearts and souls of the islanders, you must prove yourself a friend and demonstrate that they will be better off with you."[3] Communication and understanding would be needed. Ortiz de Rosas reported this exchange, cautioning that it would be a long process but arguing that the method was sound and that Argentina should try it the British way.

Unofficial incidents raised Argentine public consciousness about the Falklands as much as official policy. In September 1964, Argentine civilians landed a light plane at Port Stanley, planted a flag, and took off without being apprehended. In September 1966, 20 Argentines ("Condor Commandos") hijacked an Argentine airline's DC–4 and forced it to land at Port Stanley. The Argentine government denied responsibility for or association with each incident, but the costs of political guerrilla warfare began to emerge: The first incident led to the establishment of the contingent of Royal Marines on East Falklands and the second incident to its being raised to platoon strength. Also, HMS *Puma* went to the Falklands in the penultimate U.K. naval response—the last would be in 1977. This third quick gunboat response told Argentina that its gestures would be countered. However, this led many to conclude that only the ultimate military "gesture" would secure justice: "The Argentine people must realise that one day they will have to employ the argument of force in place of the force of reason."

A mixed military signal was also conveyed by the general British retrenchment of 1966. Of three postwar cutbacks this had the widest implications for Argentine planning on the Falklands. The British Ministry of Defense renounced carriers and "landing . . . of troops against sophisticated opposition outside the range of land-based air cover."[4] From 1966, the U.K. demonstrated an increasing willingness to compromise on the Falklands (in contrast to Argentine military government belligerency) and an increasing reluctance to make naval shows of force in response. However, its concessions were always on issues other than sovereignty, while no government stated or showed willingness to defend sovereignty.

In diplomatic parallel to the military and political signals of 1966, in November

1966, Britain proposed a freeze on the question of sovereignty, which would last 30 years. During the freeze, no actions in normalization of relations, trade, and other contacts would be taken as affecting either party's position. At the end of the freeze, the Falklands would choose between British and Argentine sovereignty. Argentina rejected the freeze proposal.

In March 1967, the British informed Argentina that under certain conditions the United Kingdom would cede sovereignty of the Falkland Islands to Argentina. The situation changed the next year: the primary condition was that the wishes of the islanders were now to be a determining factor. It was made clear in 1968 parliamentary and public statements that the United Kingdom would not cede sovereignty without the express consent of the Kelpers.[5] To Argentina, this just advanced by 19 years the inevitable vote by "colonists" to remain British.

Indeed, as the negotiations turned to producing a Preliminary Understanding, the islanders objected to this very concrete diplomatic work and began lobbying Parliament and the British public through the Falkland Islands Emergency Committee against any discussion of sovereignty transfer. British Members of Parliament and other ranking figures made up the spearhead of the Falklands lobby, which is now called the United Kingdom–Falkland Islands Committee. In direct touch with members of the Falkland Islands Executive Council, the committee sent an open letter to all British MPs in February 1968 creating a scare about the momentary transfer of sovereignty to Argentina. The government made clear that there would be no such transfer without the consent of the Islanders, but declined to go into details of the negotiations in public debate. Only from the March 1968 questioning of Lord Chalfont was there widespread parliamentary interest in the Falklands question. Even then there was no consensus for settlement.

The discussion of the wishes of the islanders proceeded in parallel with the discussion of safeguarding their interests. Language was agreed on in August 1968 under which the United Kingdom would recognize Argentine sovereignty as of a date to be agreed on as soon as possible following a settlement of how the interests of the islanders could be secured by safeguards and guarantees to be offered by the Argentine government.

The U.K. had taken the Argentine/U.N. formulation of "interests" and turned it effectively into the potential equivalent of "wishes" : a package of benefits so convincing that the Kelpers would accept it. In a unilateral statement to be published in parallel, the British government would state that the transfer of sovereignty would have to be acceptable to the people on the Islands. This was the high-water mark of concrete discussion of the transfer of sovereignty, but it was turned back by the reaction of the Islanders, Parliament, and the British press. The Cabinet decided in 1968 to abandon the attempt to reach a settlement on the basis of transfer of sovereignty with approval of the Islanders as sketched out in the memorandum of understanding. The Argentine Government stated that it could accept neither the contingency on the wishes of the Islanders nor the U.K. unilateral statements on the subject being linked to the memorandum.

Starting in December 1968, the principal course of British policy on negotiations was set: to negotiate with Argentina, yet make it clear that the transfer of sovereignty without the Kelpers was not negotiable. The wishes of the Islanders (self-determination) were enshrined as the basis of British negotiation policy.

Argentina was willing to reopen talks in 1969, which it took up again in June 1970. A military coup in Argentina affected the negotiations in two ways: The acceptability of the Argentine regime to the Kelpers declined (were that possible), yet the decisiveness of the government of Argentina and its ability to implement increased. Sovereignty was not on the agenda, but Argentina read the request to provide services as license to court the Islanders and move forward to transfer of sovereignty. Improved communications and transport were successfully negotiated and, in July 1971, air and sea services between the Falkland Islands and Argentina were agreed to. Argentina offered the Islanders a travel document allowing them freedom of movement in Argentina. (Argentines were to have freedom of movement in the Falklands but not in the Dependencies.) A package of inducements to the Islanders was included: reciprocity on taxes, exemption from Argentine military service, scholarships, domestic-level mail, and telegram and telephone service.

Several aspects of the arrangement backfired. Three particularly poignant cases indicate the potential for cross-cultural failures of communication. Scholarships for the best British school in Buenos Aires were accepted by about a dozen students from the Falklands. The rarefied world of the Anglo-Argentines, however, led to a high incidence of alienation and failure, and the experiment, founded on the best of intentions and what the Argentines viewed as a high-quality serious effort, failed for that reason. Likewise, the British hospital in Buenos Aires was judged distant and unfamiliar, but a more familiar environment was found with the Argentine state oil company Hospital in Commodoro Rivadavia with Canadian nuns providing translation. Delegations of Falklanders were brought to the mainland for familiarization with Buenos Aires, but many found themselves highly uncomfortable. The Kelper experience with Argentina was not a culturally happy one. It did not mirror that of the settled foreign populations such as the Anglo-Argentine and the Welsh communities, which were to have been the main object lessons: Their adjustment has been long and mutual.

Argentina felt that with the communications agreement it had made major concessions. It had abandoned years of principled consistency on subjects such as rejecting postage and passports, and had in its view received no reciprocal concession from the U.K. (The British White Card travel document could be seen as blanket permission for Argentines to visit the Falklands, especially as they controlled transportation.)

Its precedents about economics, contacts, and communications firmly set, Argentina pressed for a return to the discussion of the question of sovereignty. In January of 1972 this was framed as a resumption of the 1966 and 1968 talks, and was made a condition for further talks on communication. Argentina slack-

ened this position to allow agreement in May 1972 for Argentina to build a temporary air strip so as to switch their seaplane service over to regular aircraft. The U.K. maintained its position that any further political talks would not constitute negotiations on sovereignty, and 1972 marked a first clear impasse. Argentina again went to the U.N., securing Resolution 3160.

In January 1974, the British government began to assess the possibility of condominium rather than transfer of sovereignty. After consultations with the Islands Executive Council, the new government of Sir Harold Wilson raised the question of condominium with the Argentines without approval or participation of the islanders. It was clear by August 1974 that the Kelpers were balking, and the U.K. informed the Argentine government that the discussions would not therefore be practical. The ''Andorra'' solution of joint sovereignty was little debated and not seriously considered.

Communications negotiations nonetheless continued, and resulted in an agreement on the supply of petroleum products in September 1974. Two supplementary agreements of June 1974 on Argentine depots at the Stanley airfield aborted, but a Treaty of Communications, including the abolition of passports and the Argentine construction of a temporary airstrip as well as certain Argentine education and fuel services, was implemented.

Taking a cue from the apparent Argentine willingness to pursue the mutual benefit approach, in July 1975 the United Kingdom proposed discussions of joint development of the southwest Atlantic. Argentine Foreign Minister Vignes accepted the possibility and linked it to transfer of sovereignty with lease-back for fixed term. The Argentine proposal included immediate occupancy of South Georgia and the South Sandwich Islands with British acquiescence. In his address of November 8, 1975, to the UNGA, the Argentine representative introduced the idea of unilateral action: Describing the present state of affairs as a breaking-off of negotiations, he said Argentina would not fail to assert its rights in the form it deemed most appropriate, and tacitly accepted unilateral action. (Roughly, the same formulation would be used before the 1982 invasion.)

If issues with cooperative potential dominated Falklands discussions in the first half of the 1970s, elsewhere Argentina watched as Iran (in 1971) and Turkey (in 1974) seized island territory long claimed, and the world (in particular, a once-dominant Great Britain) did nothing.

References to invasion had been a regular part of pressure by Argentina. By the mid–1970s, the opposition began to be more vocal than the government. In denying the press campaign mounted in December 1974 by *Cronica,* Argentine Foreign Minister Vignes had said to the Congress that he *preferred* negotiation to invasion. He hinted at invasion again to the press in March 1975. He even phrased his July 1975 counterproposal for lease-back in terms of a unilateral occupation of South Georgia and the South Sandwich Islands rather than a British turnover, with the occupation to be accepted by the U.K. Argentines were upset by what they saw as the unilateral quality of the Shackleton economic mission.

An attempted military coup in 1975 raised the temperature of nationalism—the military had been recommending invasion. The naval incident with HMS Shackleton fueled the flames.

The new Argentine Foreign Minister, Manuel Arauz Castex, in a January 2, 1976, reply to U.K. Foreign Minister James Callaghan, said that the two parties "were rapidly moving towards a head-on collision" with only one course open to Argentina whatever government might be in power and with the backing of the whole nation as well as "all the other nations of the world assembled in New York."[6] Arauz Castex may have been exaggerating for effect about the inevitability of the collision course, but January 1976 was certainly a low point in bilateral relations: Argentina denied transit to the islands to the mission of the Labor Peer Lord Shackleton, then sent a destroyer to fire across the bow of a research vessel, believing him to be on board. Five years of relatively successful diplomacy crumbled as Argentina withdrew its ambassador.

The hardening of the Argentine position, underway for some two years already, was cemented by the announcement in October 1975 of the Shackleton survey to assess in a comprehensive way the long-term economic possibilities for the development of the Falkland Islands and the Dependencies. Argentine objections were virulent and constant right through the publication of the *Shackleton Report* in May of 1976. If economics had until now provided the Argentines with a lever on the sovereignty question and a real as well as propaganda leverage on the Islanders, the Shackleton survey and the renewed, vigorous, and systematic U.K. effort at increasing the population and economy implied by the survey were anathema to Argentine interests. Every aspect of the Shackleton survey process served to heighten Argentine sensitivity, and coincided with an increased effort by a new and zealous Argentine foreign minister, Arauz Castex, who, for example, noted that the Shackleton team arrived in the islands on the anniversary of the 1833 occupation. He began to refer more specifically to the U.K. having unilaterally broken off negotiations, and continued the rhetoric of the implied threat of invasion. In only 24 hours he rejected the British Foreign Minister's offer of January 2, 1976 to send a senior British official for confidential discussions, and withheld the return of his ambassador to London as well as issuing a press communiqué suggesting that the U.K. withdraw its ambassador from Buenos Aires.

This official attention fueled the already hostile press environment in which references to the use of force were becoming less and less veiled. The Argentine Foreign Ministry was obviously briefing the papers in some depth, and went so far as to discuss Argentine contingency planning.

However, the campaign did not reach the levels of specificity attained by the Argentine daily paper *Cronica* the year before and the government did not encourage any action or demonstrations against the British embassy. As the fervor in Buenos Aires subsided, London reiterated that, while a solution was possible and the area could indeed be one of cooperation rather than confrontation between the two governments, both the wishes and the interests of the Falkland Islanders would determine the acceptability of any solution. Met halfway, Argentina chose diplomacy over war, stabilizing its inclination to negotiate.

One inhibiting factor on military action in early 1976 was probably the military's judgment that a successful recuperation of the Falklands would be credited to their own civilian government headed by Isabel Peron. The airstrip was extended as planned. Communications were not interfered with, and air service continued. The armed forces commanders had apparently ruled out invasion as the solution to the 1975–76 impasse. They had also ruled out direct measures against the Islands and the Islanders as likely to be counterproductive in their ongoing public relations campaign with the Kelpers.

The commanders chose instead to concentrate on the scientific research vessel R.R.S. *Shackleton*. On February 5,1976, the Argentine destroyer *Almirante Storni* fired on and attempted to board the *Shackleton* 78 miles south of the Falklands. On orders of the British Governor, she declined to proceed to Ushuaia and continued on to Stanley. The military, though apparently not the Argentine Government, had been planning the action since before the first of the year, with the intention of making a no-casualties gesture and reinforcing the Argentine claim to a 200-mile limit to include the continental shelf and islands as well as the coast. The ship as hostage would also have served as further pressure on the British government to negotiate sovereignty if the issue of the ship's ''innocent passage'' were framed as a condition of its release. The military had shown one thing very clearly: It preferred political-military gestures to outright invasion with the attendant risks for itself and benefits for civilian government.

The U.K. lodged a strong protest, but parliamentary debate brought out the weakness of Britain's position in the islands: her main assets were 37 marines, the *Endurance*, and a dependence on Argentine desire for good relations. However, British Under-Secretary Ted Rowlands was cheered in the Commons when he said that the position of the government was clear: to respect the wishes of the Falkland Islanders.

Despite (or perhaps because of) the attempt to seize the *Shackleton*, there was agreement in New York in February 1976 between the new Argentine Foreign Minister and Minister of State Ted Rowlands that the British-Argentine dialogue should be resumed.

Private talks were begun in July and August 1976 with the Argentine military government that had taken power in the coup of March 23. The new Callaghan government in Britain had reviewed its policy and decided in March that a fresh dialogue on the full range of issues in the dispute *including future constitutional relationships* (sovereignty) was in order: New government, new negotiation, and new possible terms.

This potential renewal of British flexibility was matched by a new Argentine government with increased determination to regain the Falklands. They saw the U.K. as defeated in the fishing war with Iceland; being reasonable out of necessity and lack of will. Certainly the inhibition of not wanting to add to the luster of a civilian government was removed along with that form of government. Both the risks and the benefits of an invasion were now a clear, consistant, and institutionally *internal* calculus for the military government of Argentina.

However, the first instinct of Argentine President General Jorge Videla's Junta was to turn not to the force of arms but to the United Nations. In Resolution 31/49, Argentina secured approval of the view of the C–24 that Argentina had made continuous efforts to facilitate decolonization and to promote the well being of the Kelpers. The Resolution passed 102–1 (U.K.) with 32 abstentions.

The military was also pursuing a parallel track along the lines of the *Shackleton* incident. On December 20,1976, the patrol helicopter of HMS *Endurance,* the icebreaker on station each Antarctic summer, discovered an Argentine military presence on the South Sandwich island of Southern Thule, at the furthest tip of the Falkland Dependencies. The Argentines had gone ahead with unilateral occupation. The British Foreign Minister requested a military response.

The Argentines were unilaterally implementing the suggestion made and rejected in 1975 that Argentina should occupy the uninhabited Dependencies and that occupation be accepted by the British government. The Argentine government obviously placed a high value on unilateral action in that they accrued considerably more prestige than actions agreed to by the U.K. This symbolism is especially important to Argentine National Honor in domestic terms.

In response to the January 5, 1977, British query, the Argentine Foreign Ministry replied on January 14 that the operation was intended to establish a scientific station. This was said to be within "the scope of Argentine sovereignty." The reply hinted at the nonobjection formula by expressing the hope that nothing would be done that would endanger negotiations in order to attempt to provide the British government a way out. The note hinted broadly that the station might not be permanent.

The exchange through chargés d'affaires continued with a formal U.K. protest on January 19 which called the establishment of the station a violation of British sovereignty in the South Sandwich Islands. The U.K. presented no ultimatum, however, simply expressing the hope that Her Majesty's Government (HMG) would learn that the scientific program had been terminated. This left the Argentines the opportunity to either retain their presence or gracefully retreat, confident that the effort and the precedent were worthwhile for their cause. The British made no public announcement and the existence of the station remained closely held for almost five years—a sharp contrast in Argentine eyes to the handling of events in 1982. Over that period, the station was reinforced. Indeed, the intention had been to reinforce the station to considerable size until mid-or late March when weather would prevent British ships from entering South Atlantic waters.[7]

A proportionately stronger British reaction had been planned for, and the Argentines had made contingency plans to take reprisals against the British Antarctic survey party on South Georgia when Argentine personnel on Southern Thule were removed by the U.K. This was to have provided the proper diplomatic

moment for a joint Navy–Air Force operation against the Falkland Islands themselves in conjunction with a special emergency session of either the U.N. Security
Council or perhaps the General Assembly.

Here the outlines emerge of the junta's equally cautious handling of the military
and multilateral diplomatic aspects of the Falklands crisis. There was clear
recognition in Argentine planning that the battle would be won at the U.N. as
well as at Stanley: The Southern Thule occupation was to be a symbol of
Argentine presence and thus of Argentina's continuing claim to sovereignty.
Any reaction that had been evoked from the British government would have the
value (1) of putting the U.K. in a reactive diplomatic and military mode, (2)
assessing the strength not only of its political will but of its political base in
dealing with this far outpost, and (3) of establishing a physical Argentine presence
to counter somewhat the inherent U.K. advantage of physical possession of the
Falklands proper. Thus, it would set the negotiations in a new framework: Small
as it might be, an Argentine presence eventually backed by a more substantial
civilian operation (perhaps summer whaling) might provide a real counterweight
to the Kelpers and their historical and continuity arguments before the Committee
of Twenty-Four.

Ironically, the scope of Argentine actions were again limited by the character
of the government. Having just installed itself as a military junta by a military
coup, it was not at all clear that Argentina could count on widespread diplomatic
support at Turtle Bay in New York. The Falklands Plan was again not implemented. A "new reality" was however established, and Argentina could refer
to and judge the British non-reaction to its occupation of Southern Thule. (That
occupation would only end on June 20,1982, when British forces from the
Falklands Task Force retook the island.) The timing and contrast with parallel
events also formed Argentine opinion: In the same year that Argentina fired on
a civilian vessel and withdrew its Ambassador over Shackleton's visit, Britain
merely protested an occupation and "downgraded" diplomatic representation.

If any one factor would make succeeding Argentine decision-makers doubt
the political will and/or military capability of the British government, it had to
be the continuing militarily unchallenged presence on Southern Thule. Distinct,
minor, distant, and token as that presence might be, the United Kingdom had
labeled it a violation of its sovereignty, and it clearly was. The fact that it was
tolerated from 1977 to 1982 spoke well for British restraint in the Falklands
negotiations, but augured poorly as a demonstration for the Argentines. One
man's minor provocation is another man's *beau geste*. "Secret" talks took place
in Rome in July 1977. British Foreign and Commonwealth Office (FCO) Deputy
Under-Secretary Hugh Cortazzi met for three days with Argentine Under-Secretary Gualter Allara. Argentina's claim was firm. British rejection of it in favor
of the wishes of the 1,750, islanders was equally firm.

1977: UNSENT SIGNALS

In November of 1977, the British government *secretly* dispatched a hunter-
killer submarine and supporting surface ships to the Falklands in response to the

1976 firing on HMS *Shackelton* and the Argentine landing on Southern Thule. The diplomatic climate was bad. The Argentine press was rife with invasion rumors, and the Argentines had interrupted the fuel supply monopoly they had been given. New York talks were scheduled for December with Ted Rowlands leading the British delegation, but Argentine press and public opinion held out little hope of their being productive. Belize again bordered on crisis, and reinforced the feeling that Argentina might resort to force in the Falklands. The Argentine Navy seized a half-dozen Soviet fishing ships. Britain found for Chile's case in the Beagle Channel dispute. Invasion was again the watchword in Argentina's lively political culture.

The level of bilateral tension decreased because the New York talks were smooth if not highly productive, resulting in ongoing subcommissions to discuss sovereignty and the parallel economic/social conditions and programs. HMS *Dreadnought, Phoebe,* and *Alacrity,* with two escorts, remained on station during December as these negotiations proceeded in New York. The British Cabinet decided that the dispatch of the submarine should be kept secret lest it prompt the Argentines to invade. Wisely, it was later kept secret to avoid wounding Argentine pride, calling into question the good faith of either side in negotiations, or reminding the Argentines that British intelligence and military capabilities were fairly well honed and would require lightening strikes without any preliminary intelligence indicators were an Argentine invasion to succeed.

There were, however, several costs to the secret dispatch of an increased British presence in the Falklands area. Argentina not being informed, it was neither militarily deterred nor made increasingly aware of the potential cost of an invasion. Neither public nor elite opinion was affected. Aggressiveness and even the use of force not only had no costs, they literally gained ground. The attack on a British vessel, occupation of British-claimed soil, threat of invasion of the Falklands proper, and other hostile measures were not met with any known British response other than returning to the negotiating table.

Argentina would test the two-part formula in 1978. Falklands negotiations would be dropped. A massive naval/land show of force would be mounted against Chile over the Beagle Channel dispute, and abandoned in favor of Papal mediation only under heavy pressure. In 1979, Anglo-Argentine relations grew better with the return of the British ambassador, but talks remained suspended until sovereignty was again seen by Argentina as on the table along with the interesting option of leaseback.

THE LOBBY

The population of the Falkland Islands declined from 2,400 persons in 1965 to only 1,800, by the outbreak of hostilities. The lobby for the 1965 status quo in the Falkland Islands became, in several senses, like the umbrella organization of the Palestinian people: diffuse, personalist, and, in acquiring a manipulative character, subject itself to manipulation. Whether the PLO is using Arab governments or vice versa is often very unclear in Middle East politics; so it became with the Falklands lobby in the United Kingdom, and so too the strength and organization of the lobby became an end in itself. Worse, it became a polarizing, focusing force tending to prevent any evolution toward accommodation or change in original group goals. British governments and indeed elected or appointed Falkland Islands representatives came and went, but the lobby in London was a consistent, one-issue advocacy group whose goals included the suppression of discussion of alternatives to the status quo in the Falkland Islands.

Under the territorial compromise called lease-back, formal sovereignty would be transferred to Argentina but administration of the Islands would remain with Great Britain for a limited period (to be negotiated; likely somewhere between 20 and 50 years). The high-water mark of the lease-back came in the winter of 1979–80. A Falklands referendum finally rejected lease-back or association with Argentina after a decade of wooing the population. However, it was not a full and fair hearing for this potential solution to the Falklands dispute.

Long seen in the British Foreign Office as a likely and mutually advantageous solution, lease-back had never enjoyed political popularity either in the Falklands or with their lobby or parliamentary supporters. It was specifically suggested by Neville Henderson in the 1930s, and Lord Willingdon likely discussed lease-back with the Argentine government in the 1940s as the Foreign Office had drafted a ''Proposed Offer by His Majesty's Government to Reunite the Falkland Islands with Argentina and Acceptance of Lease.'' The idea needed a politician to push it, and found him in the person of a junior Minister of Foreign Affairs in the 1979 Tory government, Nicholas Ridley. The lease-back concept would seem to mesh very nicely the requirements of National Honor and National Interest. It called for compromise on the areas given high priority by Argentine National Interests (energy, marine resources, and military/strategic) and compromise on British National Honor priorities (interests/wishes of the Kelpers, divestiture, and orderly decolonization). As regards its value as a precedent, Hong Kong, Gibraltar, and Belize had to be taken into account in 1979. The British intention to retain Gibraltar and parts of Hong Kong leased in perpetuity could be seen as compromised by Falklands lease-back. The Guatemalan government was certainly looking for any precedent or concession that might offer an alternative to a transition to independence in British Honduras/Belize.

Lease-back as a concept antedated the Tory government of 1979, but, while it was favored by those concerned with relations with Argentina and Latin America in general, it was vitriolically opposed by the Falklands lobby and its supporters in Parliament. Indeed, it became a political symbol for the remnants not of empire but of overseas British citizens.[8]

Ridley nonetheless pursued what he saw as the only rational, viable policy alternative for settling, as opposed to delaying, the Falklands crisis. Lord Peter Carrington saw its policy merits, but also its political unviability. Prime Minister Margaret Thatcher opposed any concessions to the Argentines. The overseas and defense committee of the British Cabinet passed the idea to the Cabinet itself, which gave Ridley little or no support. He was instructed to put a range of options to the Falkland Islanders in consultations, which predictably resulted in their choosing the status quo. The House of Commons supported that choice at the end of 1980, and those who knew the Falklands issue and understood its political limits to include both the wishes of the islanders and of Parliament recognized that lease-back was politically dead as a British policy option.

In February 1981, another round of the New York talks was begun. Ridley had no viable negotiating strategy, given political constraints on British diplomacy concerning Falklands; nor did this leave him even a clever means of delay. He did succeed in having the Argentine delegate deal directly with Kelper members of the British delegation, setting a healthy precedent in support of the principle of self-determination. Argentina took the risk in the service of its established method of demonstrating that it could maximize the economic and social conditions on the islands. Cavandolle discussed concessions bordering on apartheid: distinct and continuous administration, law, social life, and education systems for the Kelpers into the forseeable future. The Argentines were clear and self-restrained in seeking their long-term goal: formal, de jure sovereignty. The British had nothing to offer on sovereignty or even an ongoing discussion of the topic. (*The Economist* reported that internal British discussions included options like the offer of a 99-year lease. A date might have been agreed on for somewhere between the years 2000 and 2081.)[9]

Before the negotiations were resumed, Ridley left the British Foreign Office to be replaced by Richard Luce (whom Argentines saw as representing the Lobby) and, in November 1981, a new Falkland Islands Council was seated with two moderate members replaced by what many (and especially Argentines) considered opponents of compromise. Islanders formally joined the negotiations in March 1981, over Argentine protests.

Ortiz de Rosas asked Island representatives to list the guarantees that would satisfy their doubts about Argentine administration. He was never given such a list. He volunteered to incorporate safeguards into a U.N. treaty and public declarations about the nature of Argentine administration of the English-speaking population. In the February 1982 negotiations, the list was still not forthcoming.

General Robert Eduardo Viola was replaced as head of the Argentine Junta by General Leopoldo Galtieri. Nicanor Costa Mendez again became Argentina's Foreign Minister. To complete the cast of characters, Enrique Ros was named Argentine negotiator in New York for the resumption of negotiations in February 1982.

At a critical moment, which might indeed be called complete stalemate, and after 17 years of negotiation, both negotiators were again switched by their governments. In the February 1982 negotiations, the Argentines were fully aware of extensive discussion of the lease-back option—some may indeed have decided that it was their best option.

Costa Mendez's instructions to Ros were to obtain a regular schedule of meetings, inclusion of sovereignty in the list of negotiable items, and a firm commitment to reach agreement within the calendar year. The compromise reached on February 26,1982, in New York largely met the Argentine demands: A negotiating commission would meet on an open agenda and aim for settlement in 1982. Each side would seek political agreement as rapidly as possible. The closing communiqué was positive. Ros, however, found no support in Buenos Aires for what he had initialled. On the morning of March 3, the Argentine Junta stated its total dissatisfaction with the outcome of the February New York talks, and implied that it would no longer feel bound to pursue its national interests by peaceful means.

The Junta's stated agenda had been discussed in New York and progress made. It's unstated goal, however, was sovereignty by year's end. The appropriate national means was to be Argentine naval infantry. The contingency planning had begun in December 1981 or very early in 1982. The question now was when.

"FINAL" SIGNALS, INTENDED AND NOT

By the summer of 1981, the United Kingdom had decided to withdraw H.M.S. *Endurance,* not to build a new Marine barracks in the Falklands, to remove the British Antarctic Survey scientific team (the only U.K. presence) from South Georgia, and to declare all but 400 of the Kelpers not to be British nationals.[10] Each decision was arrived at in separate channels, for differing reasons, which were mainly valid in the terms in which they were framed. The combined effect, however, sent a fatal confirmation of a trend Argentina *wanted* to perceive: lack of British National Interest and means in the South Atlantic.

Lord Carrington confessed to Ortiz de Rosas in this period that the Falkland Islands problem was not a priority in British foreign policy as Zimbabwe was and India had been. In other words, it was not enough of a problem to receive the intensive high-level political and diplomatic attention required for solution. (This proved to be a self-fulfilling prophecy.) Ridley set out to correct that, telling Ortiz de Rosas that he would like to solve the problems of Belize, the Malvinas, and Gibraltar. His personal approach to eventual Argentine sovereignty was a lease-back for a specified period of years, with two flags flying over the Islands, a U.K. Governor as well as an Argentine High Commissioner, and both languages in use. This proposal could not, of course, be expressed, much less expressed as a commitment.

Ortiz de Rosas feels that in his trip to the Falklands, Ridley presented the case in such a way that there were few alternatives for the Kelpers. He assured the Islanders that the U.K. would meet its responsibilities to them, but emphasized that Argentina and the world were pressing and that the status quo could not be maintained. He concluded that the Islanders could tell the government to freeze negotiations or seek condominium (per a U.K. suggestion made one month before the death of Peron). In answer to a question from the audience, he said that the period of transition could be from 9 to 999 years.

The Argentine recollection is that the British suggested 99 years to Argentina and were refused. The Argentines suggested thinking in terms of generations, that is, that transition should be accomplished within one lifetime or before the end of the century. Ortiz de Rosas insisted that the issue, if not necessarily the outcome, must be Argentine sovereignty. The diplomats had used up their time. Their government was considering other means, as it had on occasion for decades.

ENDGAME

The invasion was seen as an option by its architect Argentine Admiral Jorge Anaya, but depended on the critical foreign policy assessment that a nonviolent invasion would provoke little or no U.K. reaction, and on the British answers to a *bout de papier* of January 27 demanding intensified talks.

There are two major views of the time constraints or deadlines perceived by the Junta. One is that recuperation had to be completed by calendar year 1983 or the 150th anniversary of British occupation. The other is the thesis that Argentine Junta leader General Leopoldo Galtieri was told by his economics minister that the politico-economic lid must be kept on until summer 1982, when the economy would begin to turn around. The reality was likely that these judgments came in series, moving D-day further and further back. The economics/bread-and-circuses factor was secondary if at at all causal: Galtieri himself has pointed out that invasions and occupations (risk of war apart) are harder on a population and harder to manage than price riots. Far more prominent in the Junta's thinking were the 1983 anniversary and a general determination to recover the islands before then. Events in South Georgia may have determined the final setting of D-day.

The timing of the Argentine decision must be seen in the perspective of decades of planning for such an option as invading the Falklands. Within that context of standing and constantly updated contingency planning, there were pressures in each direction in the spring of 1982: The New York talks had agreed in principle, between February 26 and March 1 that a Negotiating Commission would meet regularly with an open agenda and attempt to achieve a settlement within a year. Ambassador Ros stated very clearly that he needed British political affirmation of this initialled agreement within one month; that is to say by March 26. However, within 24 hours of the New York communiqué and before Ros could reach Buenos Aires to brief the Junta on what he had initialled, the Junta issued a statement in Buenos Aires regarding "other mechanisms" for regaining the Falklands. Such a statement would not likely have been issued had a definitive decision to invade in the immediate future been taken—indeed, all government statements would have been soothing in content and tone—unless the political proprieties were adjudged more important than surprise.

The United Kingdom convinced Ros that his 30-day reply deadline could not be met. The U.K. would not rush consultations with the Islanders. The Argentine press campaign reached fever pitch, and war was in the air in Buenos Aires.

Why Ros conceded the one-month deadline is not clear, but the concession was, in retrospect, only a temporary stay.

The February compromise on a Negotiating Commission with an open agenda and regular meetings and the tacit goal of resolving the Falklands territorial conflict in the calendar year 1982 had been real progress. Its rejection before Ros's return to Buenos Aires was a clear signal of the junta's attitudes, if not intentions, but crisis would come to the South Atlantic in March in the South Georgias before April in the Falklands.

The Argentine Navy had decided on a future South Georgia occupation to be called Plan Alpha on August 10,1981. If implemented, and if it succeeded without British armed response, Alpha would with the Thule Station in the South Sandwich Islands constitute an Argentine presence moving ever upward toward the Falklands and another politico-legal precedent.

A new Junta at the end of 1981 thought bigger: Army General Leopoldo Galtieri and Admiral Jorge Anaya discussed an invasion of the Falklands (Plan Blue) in December. In January 1982 they brought the third Junta member Air Force Brigadier Basilio Lami Dozo in on their thinking. On January 12 they fixed a July 1982 D-day and established a very tightly-held planning cell. One of its jobs was not only to hold the plan closely but also to disseminate false clues and signals. The principal false leads were reassurance to even military officers that nothing was planned, and later that the target was South Georgia or an outlying island off the Falklands. Bellicose statements in public were sufficient only to maintain the aura of "diplomatic" pressure consistent with a show of force—the ultimate diversion.

As always the Argentine military had contingency plans in place regarding the South Atlantic, whether Georgias or Falklands. A key and difficult question in its implications for risk assessment, crisis management, and negotiation/mediation is whether those plans were implemented in a controlled way or whether they were forced upon their masters. The possible relationships between an incident on South Georgia (involving Argentine scrap steel workers) and the Falklands invasion are each instructive, whichever you conclude to be the case, because they illustrate policy options and mechanisms in crisis escalation. At heart the probability is that, as history often warns, the plans and military capabilities were there and were therefore used under pressure. That pressure is hard for non-Argentines to relate to and requires the immediate background to help one form a view of whether when the Davidoff scrap metal crew landed in the South Georgias they were on business, being used for long-run intelligence, actually sheltering an advance team for an occupation party, or themselves forming the spearhead of a plan to provoke British armed action to justify the seizure of the Falklands to the north.

There is an Argentine school of thought to the effect that there is no connection between the Falklands crisis and the Davidoff scrap operation on South Georgia until the British menaced innocent workers with armed force and thereby Argentina with national humiliation:

Operation Alpha was the codename for a demonstration occupation similar to the "Thule Base" in the South Sandwich Islands since 1976—a bloodless occupation to demonstrate seriousness, interest and constructive intent to explore and maximize the potential of a piece of the Southern World. It is contended in this perspective that Alpha, designed by the Argentine Navy under the administration of Robert Eduardo Viola, Galtieri's predecessor, was never implemented. (One must allow as for any operations plan that it may have served as an operational response to perceived crisis.)

The Viola administration had approved Davidoff's plan to salvage the metal in old whaling stations, authorized transport (the Argentine Navy utility vessel *Buen Suceso*), and closed out the matter at the decision-making level—which, lest we ever forget, is where all South Atlantic and Antarctic matters are handled in Argentina.

The trip, when begun on March 9,1982, was so low key and commercial in nature that neither Navy head Admiral Anaya nor Foreign Minister Costa Mendez were aware that Davidoff was on South Georgia until the situation was stirred up by the British Governor.

The Argentine Marines were on Antarctic maneuvers with the *Bahia Paraiso,* as they had been the two previous years. The vessel was thus available with Argentine Marines when Davidoff's workers were "menaced" with forceful eviction by the *Endurance* with British Royal Marines embarked.

Here was the most palpable Argentine fear—humiliation and a step backward from a little toehold they had realized for commercial activity in the Dependencies and thus more Argentine presence and precedent. Instead there would be further exercise of British sovereignty, even after obtaining general permission and then notifying the British Embassy of the trip to the islands, followed by more years of endless negotiation. Here one sees a politico-military crisis which is generated by political fear. Argentine leaders were focused on the hardening of Islander attitudes and what they saw as the increasing strength of the Falklands Lobby and the distinct possibility of an end to negotiations of any kind.

This fear in combination with the South Georgia developments, whatever their origin, was too much of an opportunity to pass up if one had the plan and the tools at hand. Argentina chose under what it considered intolerable threat to defend both its citizens and its geopolitical entitlement—its National Honor and National Interest—in what is claimed in this scenario to be a sudden unanticipated, much less induced, crisis. General Galtieri, testifying years afterward, is said to have told the Rattenbach Commission investigating Argentina's conduct of the war that the South Georgias incident began the South Atlantic crisis: the British were going to remove the 40 scrap workers with the *Endurance.* "This," explained General Galtieri, "affected the national honor and dignity and thus, in connection with events elsewhere, obliged one to take the decision of March 26."[11] The decision of March 26 was to land in the Falklands. To Galtieri it was perfectly natural that the threat to his citizens assessed on March 23 was not answered overnight March 24/25 by removing them from harm's way but by landing Argentine forces to defend them. It also struck him as natural that the forces to then proceed to the Falklands were readied and dispatched within days as Plan Blue became Operation Rosario—the occupation of the Falklands.

Beyond the thesis that these events were totally unrelated and spontaneous, there is the mildly more conspiratorial possibility (not necessarily contradictory) that within the Navy there was a cell of operational planners helping to move events toward a situation where Alpha would be seen as needed. Captain Nicholas Barker of the *Endurance* had warned that the Davidoff operation seemed linked very tightly with the Argentine Navy. The Argentine Chief of Naval Operations at the time, Admiral Juan Jose Lombardo, has since speculated that there were naval or marine personnel with Davidoff's people and takes a very conspiratorial view of the scrap operation as do the journalists of the Buenos Aires daily *Clarin* Raul Cardozo, Ricardo Kirschbaum and Eduardo Van der Kooy in their *Malvinas, La Trama Secreta* (Buenos Aires: Editorial Planeta Argentina, 1983). Such a cell could maintain readiness on its own, or with Junta-level orders. Readiness could be action-oriented, ready to seize or even force events, or it could mean little in Argentine terms as regards active conspiracy to use force: as regards the South Atlantic, there is no activity, commercial or otherwise, which is without interest to the government taken in the wide context of National Interest. As with the few Argentines on the Falklands through the years who were probably of intelligence value, there is no spot where the government would not like to know more, be present, project and protect Argentine presence.

Finally, there is the possibility that indeed there were Argentine Marines with the Davidoff party from when it left Argentina, and that they were scouts to undertake an armed reconaissance of the island, and especially of the British Antarctic Survey station—pathfinders for a main force of marines aboard the *Bahia Paraiso* whose mission would be to occupy South Georgia and remove the British. Were this the case, the venerable Alpha, so long coveted as another presence operation, had evolved into both pretext and trigger for *the invasion of the Falklands—Plan Blue*. The crack commandos of the Buzo Tactico had been training for Blue since February—the constant readying of options is the soldier's job—but their use was probably foreseen for the Antarctic winter toward June 1982. Galtieri almost unleashed them three times, but the timing was far less than ideal. This leads one to some doubts about the relationship between Alpha (if it was being implemented) and Blue:

1. Assuming Alpha and Blue were being implemented in series, the British response to Alpha would be key.

2. Depending on the success of of the Alpha (A) landing and the reaction of the U.K. government, the Blue (B) landing would follow at an advantageous time.

3. Alpha, however, followed Blue: the Argentine commandos on South Georgia did not actually overcome the British Royal Marines landed by *Endurance* until the day after the Falklands landings.

4. Thus it would appear that if Alpha was premeditated it had the purpose of prevoking an intensified situation. The only deadline after that initiation would have been well met: like the Falklands occupation, it was done without killing defenders and was

complete such that there were no hostilities and the landings were *faits accomplis* as the Security Council passed Resolution 502.

With the addition of combat troops overnight (March 24/25) the precise degree of planning or spontaneity of the South Georgia incident ceased to matter. Great Britain faced hostilities on soil it administered. Argentina was prepared for all options. Its perspective was that it had no option in the face of the dispatch of *Endurance* because the embarked Marines were to remove Argentine citizens which would be tantamount to hostilities if one considered that they were on their own soil—which is what Argentina claimed in the Security Council. One way or another, contingency planning had led Argentina to war. A good plan is flexible and Alpha was precisely that. Argentina's options were open on March 26: Alpha, whatever it was before, was now open ended. It could be played, depending on further British response, as a ceremonial or lasting occupation if unopposed. If opposed, it became the prelude to the Falklands. If not opposed, it could still be read as British acquiescence in territorial seizure and trigger the Falklands then or later.

Whether protest, provocation, or pretext, the scrap-metal salvage party put ashore on March 19 on the South Georgia was a major factor in the Falklands conflict. The long-standing planning of the Argentine Navy made it highly probable that any such incident of whatever intent had the effect intended by the Viola-regime authors of Plan Alpha: stimulating the British to an armed reaction sufficient for Argentine diplomatic purposes but insufficient to counter Argentine arms. The contingency planning gave ready options. Almost any U.K. reaction would have served Argentina's purposes. There had been a long history of deliberate provocation and probing by the Argentine Navy and nonmilitary parties of all kinds in the South Atlantic with subsequent diplomatic effect.

The British reaction is characterized by Argentines as overreaction. Britain saw itself as restrained in handling the incident. *Endurance* was ordered not to arrest the workers as originally intended. She landed her marines at Grytviken and headed back. On Sunday, March 28, the U.K. requested U.S. mediation of the South Georgia incident, which Argentina declined on March 30 as not dealing with the whole archipelago.

On March 30 (three days before the invasion), Britain stated in a press release from its mission to the United Nations that "the unauthorized presence of Argentine citizens" on South Georgia was unacceptable and that, "it comes to the point, it would be our duty to defend and support the [Falkland] Islanders to the best of our ability." The new element in the Foreign Office press statement was a direct connection between the crisis in the Dependencies and possible Argentine invasion of the Falklands.

The warning may have rung a little hollow in Buenos Aires.[12] A full week earlier, Richard Luce, minister at the FCO and formerly head of the New York negotiations concerning the Falklands had told the Commons that it was the duty of any British government to "defend and support the Islanders to the best of their ability."[13] The British Ambassador made the identical warning about South Georgia to the Argentine Foreign Minister on March 25. That same message that territory would be defended with force was the essence of the call that the Prime Minister asked the U.S. President to make to the Argentine Head of Government on March 31.[14] The message was clear in both public and diplomatic channels. The operative question in Buenos Aires was whether London meant it. If an armed ice-patrol vessel was the only real presence, the hunter-killer submarine *Superb* had reportedly been dispatched from Gibraltar on March 25.

The British reaction to the scrap-workers was thus split: firm on the strategic plane (in the U.K.) and less so on the tactical plan (in the South Atlantic). To Argentine decision-makers the South Atlantic is reality and the Northern Hemisphere is theory. The March 23, commitment in Parliament for the government to defend the South Atlantic islands did not seem to the Junta to be translated into completed action in South Georgia: *Endurance* was dispatched with marines. She was to arrest the workers, then put on hold. Parliament met. *Endurance* was again to arrest, but left the Argentine scrap party alone. The Argentines were declared to be in violation of British sovereignty, yet that sovereignty was not enforced. From London, not removing the Argentines seemed prudent and restrained. In Buenos Aires it was seen both as vascillating and menacing. Either argued for military action.

The opportunity foregone by restraint was in not arresting the Argentine scrap-workers on March 24 before the overnight military landing. An interesting hypothetical scenario flows from that road not taken: With their polite removal to Montevideo for immigration violations, Argentina would have been deprived of the political need and the diplomatic cover of "rescuing endangered and humiliated" Argentine citizens.

With Davidoff's workers evacuated (and any pathfinders removed with them, and thus a probable plan Alpha foreclosed by swift British action,) wiser heads might have prevailed in Buenos Aires on March 26 when the Falklands landing was moved forward to April 1,2, or 3. *Endurance* might indeed have interposed herself between the amphibious task force and the Falklands, denying the "peaceful" takeover so prominent in the Argentine decision making on the invasion. British decision making (in this scenario) had put too much emphasis on tactical/local restraint (not ruffling the feathers of Argentine citizens) and too little on the strategic (moves or reported/rumored moves to bring British power to bear in the South Atlantic). Risky as it might have been, having chosen to put all its chips on *Endurance,* it could be argued that England should have stuck with her. As an armed vessel but clearly not a ship of the line, she had good credentials for light "enforcement." Her captain was in the best tradition of the sailor-diplomat, well familiar with and well thought of by the Argentines. *Endurance* (assuming any possible Alpha units with the workers were not heavily armed), acting in her armed cutter role, might have served her deterrent purpose to the fullest in a bluff exercise of consular prerogative, out of the reach of Argentine air power and ahead of her Exocet-armed destroyers and crack troops.

British strategic firmness was too little and too late to deter. It was only enough to inflame and support those who said diplomacy had run its course. It firmed up or speeded up the Falklands invasion. If planned or ''sold'' to the Junta as a probe, Plan Alpha may have become an accidental *casus belli* when Argentina realized it might lead to British naval reinforcement of the area as in the past. The scrap-workers who had lowered their flag when ordered to do so were next joined by Argentine troops landed in darkness. The invasion planners had been promised ten days' notice. They got two days. Argentine diplomats beyond the Foreign Minister and the U.N. Ambassador received no notice. Washington Ambassador Steve Takacs was telephoned at H-hour and noted that the invasion would not be welcomed by the United States.

The British system of parliamentary government by Ministers grouped in a Cabinet dates in its present staffing and decision-making structure from a reorganization by Lloyd George during World War I. Supporting the Ministers with their specific portfolios of national responsibilities is the Cabinet Office and a series of specialized Cabinet Committees. The Cabinet Office is headed by a Cabinet Secretary who provides ongoing expertise and continuity (there have only been four incumbents since Sir Maurice Hankey in 1916) in the conduct of the business of Her Majesty's Government. Broad policy review is performed by the Think Tank, the Central Policy Review Staff, yet the work of assessing the questions and likely answers to them in British public life still falls principally to Ministers.

The Joint Intelligence Organization in the Cabinet Office scans Britain's foreign and defense interests for early warning signs of threats. Its current intelligence groups or CIGs (while there is an annual assessment, the Latin American CIG never discussed Falklands in 18 meetings in the last half of 1981 and the opening months of 1982) report to the Joint Intelligence Committee on items to be considered for the senior Joint Intelligence Committee's Red Book, which summarizes upcoming events for Ministers on Thursdays.[15] Falklands never made it into the red book.

On 24 January, *La Prensa* had reported (p. 1) that ''The possibility that the islands will be recovered by military means is virtually certain.''[16] On 12 January, the working party had been appointed by the Government to plan the invasion of the Falkland Islands. On February 18, *La Prensa* spoke of the total defenselessness of the islands. On the 2 March, Argentina issued its post-negotiation New York communiqué stating that it reserved the right to choose the procedure for settling the dispute which best accorded with her interests. However, British intelligence readings were that military action was not under consideration as an immediate option. Over the month of March, those readings evolved from diplomatic offensive, to occupation of an outlying island, to the 30 March judgment that failure to resolve the South Georgia situation peacefully might lead to invasion.[17]

Prime Ministers rely more on Cabinets than do U.S. Presidents. They do not necessarily have as much trust for the departments that serve their ministers. If the Foreign and Commonwealth Office saw the Falklands crisis coming over a period of years, then Prime Ministers had little respect for the professionals and the procedures of their Ministries. Whitehall (broadly, the executive "branch," including defense, as distinct from Westminister, the legislative) was unable to get the Falklands item before the Foreign and Defense Committee of the Cabinet. It was eclipsed by subjects like the Cabinet battle over the size and composition of the Royal Navy. Defense was too costly. Retrenchment was politically impossible. Politicians and foreign affairs professionals opted for deterrence, yet it was really a trip wire, meant, in the appropriate wording of a prewar officer of the landing party in the islands, to invoke the full might, awe, and majesty of the British Government. Such deterrence, however, required regular, clear signals of interest, and early, clear knowledge of the opponent's intent. In the real world, neither politics nor intelligence gathering admit of such precision. Britain was unwilling to liquidate, undisciplined in its "signals," oblivious to open-source intelligence on "intentions," and unable to get into place the backup force of submarines and frigates that had been used previously. Two aspects of the decision making need to be looked at separately: strategy (deterrence while negotiating and unwillingness to either defend or surrender territory), and tactics (intelligence readings in the final months before the invasion). The Cabinet system, which should give the chief executive a wider command of issues, instead became a filter of information that kept important decisions and later important developments from Cabinet-level attention.[18]

By Monday, March 29, both the British Cabinet Office and the Office of Prime Minister were seriously concerned with the possibility of invasion. On this Monday before the Friday invasion (April 2), the Cabinet dispatched a submarine to the Falklands from the Mediterranean. The Junta was judged to be weighing a decision to invade. (The decision had in fact been made on the 26th and the Argentine Navy put to sea on the 28th). The first crisis meeting of the British Cabinet was on the evening of Wednesday, March 31, yet its first Falklands Crisis Management Session was too late to manage the crisis in any real sense. The Argentine Navy had been en route to Falklands for three days. Royal Navy steaming time to the South Atlantic was assessed as three weeks. Reseizure was being assessed as impossible when the Deputy Chief of the Defense staff joined the meeting and volunteered that the Navy could do the job. By then, only high-level intervention (individual or multilateral) or surrender were left as diplomatic options.

The United States and Argentina were alive with rumors of war. Newspapers, embassies, and business were alerted to the possibility of a Falklands invasion. The government of Uruguay was (inaccurately but widely) rumored to have offered evacuation from the islands for any Kelpers who so wished.[19] Demonstrations against the military regime orchestrated principally by the Peronist party were reaching a crescendo in the streets of Buenos Aires. The only British naval unit in the South Atlantic was away from Port Stanley with a good part of the garrison in response to the South Georgia gambit. The Argentine fleet was already known to be at sea. By Tuesday, invasion rumors were rife in Uruguay.

On or about Tuesday, March 30, General Galtieri made the final decision to go ashore (the jump-off order), but weather delayed the landings two more days. The Navy turned the fleet on its final leg toward the Falklands, setting in motion the years of planning for their recapture. This final decision was likely taken long after circumstantial evidence of all kinds pointed to an invasion, and it may indeed be that the rumor of war was one of the causes of war.

A British submarine was said to have been dispatched from the Mediterranean. Such a possibility must certainly have placed further pressure on the Argentine Navy to proceed with the Falklands option while the invasion task group was already at sea.

The British Embassy in Washington informed the United States of the U.K. assessment that the Argentines were going ashore in a full-scale amphibious invasion. President Reagan was asked to intervene. Galtieri was giving an address to the Feria del Libro (the major national book fair—a nice touch of normalcy) and was not available. Galtieri returned the call two hours later. Rather than stating a firm U.S. policy if forced to choose, Reagan pleaded that the invasion be stopped. With interpretation halving the one-hour conversation, the two heads of government could accomplish little. The Argentine SEALS (special forces frogmen) and beachmasters (who direct landing craft) were probably already studying the Falklands shoreline and marking the landing zones from a submarine. The Buzo Tactico shock troops would be ashore at 10:00 p.m. Atlantic/Buenos Aires time on April 1.

The scrap workers incident on South Georgia, the removal of Royal Marines from their position at Stanley to South Georgia in response to that incident, the pre-positioning of units of the Argentine fleet at sea in the joint maneuvers with Uruguay, and perhaps the feeling that the iron would never be as hot again, led the junta to decide to proceed with its gamble.

The Argentine Junta could not resist. There was no significant British trip wire. That is to say, neither all the Royal Marines nor, more significantly, the British patrol vessel stood in the way of occupation of the Falkland Islands without combat deaths. Given that the Argentine diplomatic requirement of *no casualties* could probably be met, the gamble seemed worth it to Buenos Aires. This was the main precondition for the five principal assumptions in the diplomatic area, and most specifically for the calculation that there would be no British military reaction.

Father Colin Campbell has called the Cuban missile crisis "one of the most dramatic triumphs of personal judgment over institutional reflex."[20] In the Falklands crisis, reflex predominated. Inured by years of invasion scare and rumor, the U.K. government did not *as a whole* pick up on the signals.

Warning signs noted by captain Barker of the *Endurance* included:

—Highly irregular behavior was shown by the Argentine navy toward Royal Navy presence in the area, HMS *Endurance;*

—Regular crew exchanges and soccer matches were broken;

—Rendezvous and even courtesy receptions were not carried out;

—Appointments with ranking officers were broken on short notice with the explanation that commanders had been summoned to Buenos Aires from the distant naval outposts of the south;

—Normally chatty colleagues declined to acknowledge hailings even when they knew they were on British radar; and

—Units began to drift toward the string of British-occupied islands.

On March 11, a plane had made a landing at Stanley purportedly for emergency reasons. (Oil was seen leaking from the plane.) While the Argentine Air Force had been flying into Stanley for years under the Communications Agreement, Argentina might have wanted to test the security response to an unscheduled set-down of a troop-carrying aircraft.

Press speculation on the invasion option was widespread and denied only by the Foreign Ministry press spokesman. Political as well as press "reporters" in Buenos Aires discussed the possibility openly. The Junta seemed in its political and diplomatic remarks to be laying the legal framework to support such action. The scrap-steel worker incident was handled most assertively and with no apparent concern for its escalation.

Many of these actions seemed, however, the opposite of the behavior of a state intent on waging a surprise attack. Actually, as seasoned practitioners of psycho-political guerrilla warfare in the South Atlantic, the Argentine military would likely have maintained normalcy. It would not have been credible to have drawn the British Embassy and patrol ship into excessive confidence with friendly actions and statements; rather, normalcy in the South Atlantic consisted of the usual statements and shows of Argentine determination, to be misread as negotiating pressure.

Argentina not only seized but indeed may have created the moment: No British naval presence, a reduced British Marine garrison, the onset of Antarctic winter, the diplomatic cover of recent "unsuccessful" negotiations, and finally the British "menace" to Argentines on South Georgia determined the timing.[21] These were proximate and permissive factors, not causes. The Argentine grievance was centuries old, the motivations as deep as culture, the reasons of convenience many, and the military planning polished for years and updated for months. At its heart, however, the invasion was a diplomatic inevitability. It had loomed several times over several decades. Seventeen years of British diplomacy unsupported by either military force or the political leeway to settle a territorial question had inevitably and definitively failed.

The policy failure was more critical than the intelligence failure. Consistent follow-through, a tough use of *Endurance* and the marines, might have validated deterrence for a breathing space in which to move to a strategy of defense. British officials were not caught off guard. There was no failure to foresee the Falklands landings in the long run, as they had not been set in motion earlier; and no failure in the short run to predict them, but only the place and purpose. Politico-military surprise is still possible in the last quarter of the twentieth century.

The question was one of ability to apply power. As the U.K. Defense Attaché in Buenos Aires had warned in early March, intelligence indicators would not be firm enough in time to deter Argentine military action. That is a failure of deterrence policy, only mildly abetted by intelligence failure. The immediate inapplicability of a great deal of Great Britain's residual military and industrial might was a major element in the Argentine decision.

British officials had expected escalation in the traditional manner. Along with a crescendo of "cause," they expected a standard escalation of the application of sanctions and then force. Argentina, in such a scenario, would be expected first to cut off critical supplies and services such as oil and transportation rather than proceeding immediately to military action.

What this did not allow for was the well-planned military surprise attack. If the Argentine plan had indeed been to recuperate the Malvinas within the calendar year 1982, this did not mean that its planning was *ad hoc*. D-Day was a moveable feast. Argentine anger rose in a calculated way. It did not drive Argentine planning or advance the date. Flexible planning determined the occasions about which one could manifest public anger and therefore invoke National Honor. National Interests were coldly and calculatingly determined in advance, and one way was perceived of maximizing those interests. This lay precisely in framing the question as invoking National Honor so as to rally the country and international support to Argentina's cause. For this reason, few real and many false signals were sent; no increasing tide of anger was evident; no preliminary or lower-grade actions such as interruption of services and supplies, economic sanctions, or even hostile diplomatic behavior or withdrawal of missions were used as part of the building of a case.

This may well, however, be the essence of territorial war for the rest of the century, whether irredentist or not. The taking of the territory is the real war aim rather than the righting of any immediate or invoked cause. Rising tension is more likely to be created than to be a driving force in the crisis. Indeed, in order to achieve tactical surprise, force is used before political tension peaks or is in any predictable way becoming "unbearable." While some tension is needed to rally both domestic and international support, and indeed some tension is better than a pure but obviously disingenuous appearance of political calm, war does not come as the result of the political tension, but is rather an expression of a well-thought-out, longer-run calculation of National Interest and National Honor.

III

CRISIS DETERRENCE AND MANAGEMENT—TOO LITTLE, TOO LATE

For the first time in its history, Argentina is the protagonist of a situation that is shaking the international order.
—Navy commander and ruling junta member, Jorge Anaya

Each and every tongue is a distinct window into the world. Looking through it, the native speaker enters an emotional and spiritual space, a framework of memory, a promontory on tomorrow, which no other window in the great house of Babel quite matches. Thus every language mirrors and generates a possible world, an alternate reality.
—George Steiner

Y los derechos se toman, no se piden; se arrancan, no se mendigan.
—Jose Martí

Where cross the crowded ways of life,
Where sound the cries of race and clan,
Above the ways of selfish strife,
We here thy voice, O Son of Man.

—Anglican hymn

The invasion of the Falkland Islands has been a humiliating affront to this country.
—Lord Carrington in his letter of resignation

I have to say that I could have done with more wholehearted support from the United States throughout the exercise.
—Sir Anthony Parsons

OVERVIEW

The political reasons for undertaking military reaction to seize territory, and the factors that go into operational decisions such as when and how, are complex and interrelated. The net effect of the two equations is such as to make crisis deterrence (last-minute intervention by a third party, national or international) difficult if not impossible. The reasons have a grounding as much in National Honor as in National Interest. They often therefore find their explanation as much in domestic (indeed nationally idiosyncratic) values and decision processes as in internationally understood classic motivations for war by the nation-state.

"RECUPERACION"

The Argentine seizure of the Falkland Islands on April 2,1982, was seen by the Argentine government (as it was indeed seen by many expert analysts and observers) as a politico-military *fait accompli*. Whatever the strength of British political will (witness its "toughing out" the suicide by starvation of IRA terrorists), the political intentions and military capabilities of the British government were in doubt.

Beyond the Argentine readings of tacit signals in the South Atlantic, the Royal Navy was in a centuries-long decline. The two aging carriers, 60 ships of the line, 32 submarines, and 9 amphibious vessels, were heavily committed to NATO or spread worldwide and not available for the South Atlantic.

The Argentine Navy had a carrier, ten major surface combatants, four submarines, and two amphibious ships which could be totally devoted to its national goals in the area. They had the advantage of operating from the long Argentine Atlantic coastline with a series of major naval bases. In addition, Argentina's naval air and air force arms had the Islands within their operating ranges. Argentina's minor surface warships had a bearing on the equation that those of the United Kingdom did not. Argentina's applicable force seemed very well balanced against the resources the U.K. would be able to field in any Falklands conflict. If there is a lesson here about forces and geopolitics, it is clearly that one must factor in the flexibility and depth of the industrial base of the other country and, when calculating its "other" commitments, must assess their relative strength and importance in the decision making of the other party. Britain was quick to both adapt other national resources for the Falklands campaign and to draw down on units engaged in fulfilling other commitments in order to make sure that its South Atlantic Task Force was viable.[1]

The Falkland Islands themselves were, for all practical purposes, undefended. Naval Party 8901 was a detachment of Royal Marines whose mission was to deter adventurism such as the Condor Commando landing on the islands. Their resistance at Government House and in falling back from the airport at Stanley was an effective if largely political answer to the initial pre-dawn attack by Argentine special forces, followed by a main force hundreds of times their size, supported by the aircraft carrier *Veinticinco de Mayo,* her escort of destroyers, a loading ship, and three transports off the Falklands. Surrounded by Argentine armor, with Government House riddled with bullet holes, Governor Rex Hunt ordered the marines to surrender.

British military catch-up options were few and extreme: Strike strategically at the landing forces by air and hope to land and surrender, refuel for the return in the face of the fresh air resources of the *Veinticinco de Mayo,* or fly in for the token defender's sufficient smart rocketry to make the invasion a costly one. (Indeed, several truck-mounted antiaircraft and antiship cruise missile batteries might well have been the best investment the British Ministry of Defense had ever made.)

There was indeed some doubt as to whether Britain's reduced, distant naval power was available and applicable in this situation. British forces were not viewed with awe by the Argentine military. British combat efficiency was matched by some elite Argentine units like the 601 Commando Company. Argentine forces on the ground had first-rate equipment such as U.S. armored personnel carriers. A serious air force was spearheaded by the Israeli Dagger, Douglas A–4, and the French Super-Etendard armed with the Exocet cruise missile. The end of the opening round would lead most observers to agree that a British counterattack would be what the ground commander of U.K. forces General Jeremy Moore would later, quoting Wellington, call a "near-run thing."

However, within three days of the invasion, the Royal Navy left Portsmouth, the skeleton of a carrier battle group taking a salute from Lord Nelson's flagship *Victory* and pointing out, if it were needed, the serious underestimation of the Thatcher government's political will and the strength of the British military tradition. Ill-equipped and hastily assembled, understrength units and ships nothwithstanding, the United Kingdom in short order assembled a carrier battle group embarking the Royal Marine commando units, Two and Three Para, the Scots and Welsh Guards, Gurkha units, the Special Air Service, and the Special Boat Service.

If a winter war at the end of a long supply line with poor air cover and difficult amphibious landing conditions were a daunting prospect, this was precisely the United Kingdom's job in its reinforcement of NATO's northern flank in Norway. The possible scope of this political will should have been assessed by the Argentine government. It should have been decoupled from military capability and certainly distinguished from the negative cultural and economic assessments many Argentines would make of the United Kingdom in the 1980s.

No Argentine government should have assumed that it would face in the Falklands seizure only the initial British presence in the area of a platoon of Royal Marines at Stanley and the patrol vessel *Endurance,* yet that seems to have been the working assumption since no serious planning for holding as opposed to seizing the islands was prepared. The doubling of the Marine contingent by holding over the outgoing rotational platoon was not a deterrent late in the invasion planning.

The decision to invade already taken, what of the second-order Argentine assumptions? What further defense was anticipated? Certainly there must have been knowledge of the lack of British nuclear subs in the South Atlantic from other national sources, or the invasion fleet could not have been launched in good conscience. With that knowledge, the British reaction becomes a question of political will, of reaction rather than response, as the U.K. resources would be at such distance that the Islands could be garrisoned and stockpiled by Argentina. However, with that logistics advantage came the incremental cost of increased British will—the determination bred of outrage, of surprise but not incapacitating shock.

Both the population and, indeed, the bulk of the Argentine military were surprised by the Argentine actions of April 2. If they would later assess the decision as an internal political maneuver and a failed experiment that proved the incapability of the military to perform its one constitutional role, there were few such thoughts in the broad spread of Argentine opinion immediately following the invasion.

"NONE FOR FIVE"

The decision of the Argentina Junta to invade the Falkland Islands, or, from the Argentine perspective, to recapture the national territory of the Malvinas, was a critical political-military decision in the history of the Argentine Republic. Pending detailed knowledge of that decision-making process, one must assess it by its results rather than by its intentions. Five diplomatic questions were key in a rational decision to invade. That decision was conscious and rational, based on internally consistent Argentine perspectives on those five key questions:

1. What will be the reaction of the United Kingdom Government?
2. What about the United Nations Security Council and its role in maintaining the peace?
3. What would be the reaction and role of the nonaligned caucus in the U.N. Security Council?
4. Can Argentina count on "world opinion"?
5. What about the United States, that is to say, the Reagan Administration?

If, indeed, the critical five questions were asked, they were answered incorrectly, and from such miscalculation came the most crucial mistake in Argentine statecraft.[2]

U.K. Reaction

There must have been underlying assumptions about the limitations on the U.K.'s freedom of action, and on the character and capabilities of the government. Some credit must have been given to the widespread misapprehension that the lion was effete; that the United Kingdom was afflicted by general social and economic malaise if not decline, and that, for this reason, its political and military capabilities were inhibited. Any student of NATO affairs would question that judgment. Indeed, ironically, the Thatcher government had shown remarkable political will in decisions such as allowing the IRA hunger-strikers to starve themselves to death. Equally firm was U.K. participation in the North Atlantic Alliance,and especially in its specialized role in the defense of the northern flank. Ironically indeed, the very ships and same troop units used for the Falklands campaign were those earmarked for the defense of Norway. A further irony is that several of the principal ships involved were to have been sold or scrapped within a short time, and a delay in the decision to retake the Falklands might have yielded major benefits to the Argentines. The question of timing (see below) must have been domestically critical since political-military factors argued for the delay.

Since it seized the Falkland Islands, Britain had spent over 400 months of its national life engaged in about 20 wars, winning all but a few of them decisively. In the twentieth century, the U.K. has fought several dozen small wars, two world wars, and a U.N. peace action. Its staying power is demonstrated by the half-century of conflict on the Northwest Frontier and two centuries in Northern Ireland, and is not purely a function of empire.[3] This track record is of serious concern to modern Soviet planners for the European theater, yet seemed to evoke little respect in Buenos Aires. With two wars in its martial tradition, it was difficult for the Argentine military to have any perspective on the combat effectiveness of a military with this solid and institutionalized tradition of combat.

The Security Council

There must have been a very heavy presumption that the Soviet Union would veto any negative action against Argentina's decision. Whatever the Russians may have promised or implied, were they indeed consulted, they did not in the end veto Resolution 502 calling for Argentine withdrawal. Certainly, the USSR was not comfortable with the Argentine Junta. A traditional trade partner since Argentina's revolution, it nonetheless would also have had little interest in defusing a split in the West, especially the wider split of Spanish-and English-speakers.

The Nonaligned

The crucial working majority of nine votes needed to pass a Security Council Resolution hinges on the nonaligned caucus (the Group of Eight). Should it achieve unanimity, it can pass or block any security resolutions subject only to one other nation's approval or veto. The Group of Eight did not go with Argentina on the question of how it chose to recuperate the Falklands. Indeed, they did not even abstain. Panama cast the only vote against Resolution 502. Communist states and Spain abstained. The Third World recognized its interest in a world order in which there is narrow room for justifying armed invasion.

World Opinion

Argentina perceived the nonaligned movement and the General Assembly as key elements in a crucial political judgment that the good opinion of mankind could be rallied to the cause of recuperation. This was at heart a failure to distinguish ends (the sovereignty case) from means (military invasion). The nonaligned majority in the U.N. had indeed passed multiple Decolonization resolutions increasingly favoring the Argentine position. Argentina was to discover during the playing out of the diplomatic side of the Falklands crisis how meaningless such mass statements of solidarity are. Indeed, the whole Decolonization phenomenon was to prove to be a double-edged sword providing both legitimacy and political ammunition for each party in U.N. debate. The Nonaligned (which Costa Mendez did not believe in) had been courted for decades but are not a true element of Argentina's self-definition. It is interesting to speculate on how the General Assembly majority would have voted on the question if framed as breach of the peace rather than sovereignty, but Argentina's diplomacy was not able to assemble the forum.

The United States and Argentina

Characterizations of the U.S.-Argentine relationship ever since Peron tend to be general in nature and extreme in character. There is something about the relations between major states that necessitates categorization that is often inaccurate, unhelpful to real understanding, and destructive of the rational assessments of international relationships that preserve order. Argentina is incorrectly referred to either as an ally or as a natural enemy. Without consideration of the complexity or the regular change in the character of its government, it received blanket labels such as "fellow democracy" or "dictatorship." Unnecessary and even incorrect deductions about the U.S. long-term relationship with Argentina stem from such labels. If Argentina gave too much weight in its Falklands decision making to expressions of friendship and solidarity by U.S. policymakers, the U.S. public and press during the crisis distanced themselves from Argentina and its then-current form of government in an equally unthinking and categorical way.

Argentina is not an ally of the United States.[4] We lack, as indeed we lack with all Latin republics, a mutual defense commitment in which an attack on one is an attack on the other which automatically institutes collective hostilities.[5] The Argentine reaction to the U.S. April declaration that its mediation was at an end and it intended to support Great Britain in the South Atlantic conflict was one of, first, stark disbelief, and then a feeling of betrayal. Like the Argentine decision-makers' consensus that the United States would support Argentina's recuperation of its national soil, the feeling of betrayal was based on their assessment of the Reagan Administration's interests in the Southern Cone of South America (Argentina, Chile, Paraguay, Uruguay); on statements that indicated "understanding" of the problems of the military government; and certainly in part on the Argentine Army's very helpful presence in combating subversion in Central America. The three led to an impression that the basis of an alliance was forming.

If there are "inherent" relationships or dynamics between the United States and Argentina, they are many and multivariate. Both, of course, are major regional actors, grain exporters, and active political cultures, implying an inherently competitive and contentious relationship. They are also both New World states with New World outlooks, and, on occasion, both democratic polities with a shared interest in preserving a kind of freedom in politics and trade that has made the lands of recent settlement prosper.

The Argentine government was neutral in World War I. Argentina evinced a desire to be included at the Paris peace conference ending World War I and, in the 1921 opening meeting of the Assembly of the League of Nations in Geneva, Argentina proposed the admission of the defeated powers. Formally neutral until the last, large segments of Argentine opinion were openly sympathetic with the Axis in World War II.

Argentina and the United States do perhaps share a common interest in a free-trade environment. They are not important trading partners for each other. They have light but not always conflicting ties, and differing world views, especially in their self-image vis-à-vis the USSR which tends to define so much of U.S. policy. Most Argentines would look on their country's activities in Central America in 1981–82 as creating at most the illusion of an identity of interests with the United States about East-West matters. The long tradition of foreign policy independence in Argentina makes territory much more important than far-off foreign policy concerns which are not assessed as national interests.

Thus, the U.S.-Argentine relationship is not inherently a strong or warm one. With skewed perspectives about each other, minimal economic ties, conflicting trade interests, and no real security relationship, the lack of internal coherence in Argentine politics and the varying persistent U.S. pressures for Argentina to define itself in terms favorable to U.S. policies lead the two to a pragmatic, shifting relationship. The important element here is how to limit the damage of misperceptions and to add an element of mutually supportive behavior to the interest in each other's policies which is the only consistent hallmark of the relationship. Lacking the common external "colonialist enemy" of the nineteenth-century American republics' relationship, Argentina and the United States must precisely define the common ground that they regularly but perhaps mistakenly assume they possess.

As one might surmise from its diplomatic history, Argentina has seldom, if ever, looked to the United States as a model, yet its international behavior has been congruent with norms that the United States recognizes or espouses. A nation of immigrants, with both industrial and agricultural economies, Argentina benefitted from both the progress and the freedom that the New World offered to immigrants under the guarantees of democratic constitutionalism and liberal, free-trade economics. Ironically, in the boom that followed, Great Britain financed and principally benefitted from that economic growth.

Free trade implied, of course, maintaining the largest number of constructive international relationships possible. Argentina thus avoided "entangling alliances" much as the United States did in its early diplomacy. It chose market-oriented rather than abstract political associations when forced to choose.

Choice, of course, seemed inevitable as World War II loomed. Great Britain was no longer the source of capital or the marketer of grain that it had once been. The United States was reluctant either to lend for arms or spend for grain. Bad crops, the success of rival Brazil in securing defense loans and markets for its not quite so competitive goods, and a more vocal and virulent political behavior by those of the political elite favoring the Axis, secured Argentine neutrality in World War II.[6] The caustic U.S. rejection of the Argentine idea of New World nonbelligerency further changed that elite in favor of those who were absolutely open in their admiration of Mussolini and Hitler.

Neutralism in the name of maximized grain exports, however, is a consistent thread in Argentine foreign policy and meshed very nicely with the foreign policy of the military leaders following their 1943 coup. Juan Peron found no inconsistency (indeed a good deal of interlocking) between neutralism and his longtime admiration for the foreign policy of Mussolini, to whom he had been accredited as Argentine military attaché.

The Argentine concern with strategic balance with Brazil was unfortunately ignored by the United States during this period. It sought to have Argentina break relations with the Axis in the name of regional security, yet the United States not only would not recognize, but indeed chastised, Argentine concern with subregional security. The break with the Axis came rather more in spite of than because of U.S. pressure. By emphasizing Juan Peron's links with the Axis, the United States managed not only to increase his hostility but in part to secure his election.

In the 1960s, the Frondizi government achieved rapproachment with Brazil and indeed went beyond the emphasis of regional geopolitical concerns to a startling statement by the Under Secretary for Foreign Relations that Argentina's "lesser strategic significance" was cause for solidarity with the rest of the continent.

Argentina is alternately generalized about as the keystone of the Southern Cone, a gateway or control point for transit of southern oceans, a key alternative route around a Panama Canal in time of crisis, and "a dagger pointed at the heart of Antarctica." While it does, of course, control any sea lines jointly with Chile (in the negative sense of a naval, naval air, and maritime cruise-missile base against shipping), Argentina's size, location, resources, and political culture make it a significant regional or middle player in world affairs. Any further generalization should be very carefully made.

As Argentina's pretentions waned, however, U.S. claims on its foreign policy increased: The pressure in the 1960s was to break relations with Cuba, and again this was done at extreme cost to friends of the United States within Argentine politics.[7] When the Frondizi government finally did break relations with Cuba in February 1962, it lasted little more than a month following its violation of the national consensus about independence, trade, even-handedness, and neutrality in world affairs as the core of Argentine diplomacy.

Even Argentines concerned with human rights abuses under the military government of General Jorge Videla resented the heavy-handedness of the Carter Administration's prescription for Argentine behavior. Moderates, the natural allies of the United States in outlook and interests, again suffered.

The pattern of U.S. public moral prescription weakening those Argentines who were most in agreement with the United States was repeated during the Falklands crisis, this time with the greatest long-run cost. In the United States, anger was the most universal public reaction to the Argentine invasion. It was certainly the most widely shared initial reaction in the U.S. Government. To the credit of U.S. diplomacy, however, U.S. prescriptions were presented in terms of Argentine interests.

Only in the context of the difficult bilateral history of the United States and Argentina can one appreciate the limits on U.S. diplomacy in the Falklands crisis.

THE CENTRAL AMERICAN CONNECTION

The Argentine role in Central American counterinsurgency was in lieu of rather than in support of U.S. actions. In the month preceding the Falklands crisis, Argentina is said to have financed and trained the anti-Sandinista forces operating to interdict the flow of military supplies from Nicaragua to El Salvador and Guatemala through Honduras. The Galtieri government had agreed with the Reagan Administration that Argentina, with financial and intelligence support from the United States would organize the arms interdiction effort.[8] According to this scenario, the United States retained the role of protecting Honduras, funding political opposition groups in Nicaragua, and maintaining a liason with Nicaraguan exiles. The Galtieri government had indeed a longer-term commitment predating the Reagan Administration to induce Eden Pastora Gomez (Commandante Zero) to spearhead the overthrow of the Sandinista regime. The Reagan Administration reaffirmed on March 9, 1981, the Carter Administration's covert programs of increased intelligence gathering and support for democratic opposition groups in Central America. Covert military operations to intercept arms supplies were added with a budget of 19.5 million dollars.

On November 16, 1981, the Reagan Administration adopted a ten-point program resulting in National Security Decision Document 17. NSDD 17 included contingency plans to deal with Cuban military action, notify Congress of plans to step up covert intelligence activities, and increase military assistance to Central America. The CIA is said to have been offered blanket authority for political and paramilitary activities to strike at the Cuban arms supply line through Nicaragua. The initial 500-man force was to be paid for by the United States and to be supplemented by a 1,000-man force then being trained in Honduras by Argentine army officers. This was to be done primarily through third parties. It was this participation in training the larger field force that was threatened by the U.S. decision in the Falklands crisis. General Galtieri is said to have been completely clear on the subject: any cooperation with Great Britain would end his assistance in Central America.

THE NONALIGNED AND THE FALKLANDS

The commonwealth tie often cut across nonaligned solidarity on the Falklands as in the Security Council Resolution which Britain and the United States vetoed on June 4. The six nonaligned countries on the Council were split down the middle in their voting on this last Security Council consideration of the Falklands crisis.

Nonaligned membership has become a great help in seeking a Security Council seat. Given that the nonaligned almost universally share a colonial experience in their past, they tend to react as a group to any invocation of anticolonialism in political questions. They tend, however, to forget or ignore the principles of independence and self-determination which were the basis of their national struggles. Within the Latin American countries that form so large a part of the Third World but not normally of the nonaligned movement, Argentina held a special place. Recognized by many as developed, it was also exempted from U.N. human rights resolutions in the U.N. Third Committee which handles human rights in that it was an "anti-imperialist" power.

Nonaligned political views can be expressed in any form in which the NAM enjoys a majority. For example, at the May 1982 World Health Organization meeting, the nonaligned caucus chose a particularly unrelated forum to state on May 6 that the position of the British government was stubborn and insensate. The nonaligned's backing for Argentina's claim was, of course, inconsistent with the principle of self-determination.

Cuba very effectively manages the nonaligned group for Latin America. The senior Latin country, Cuba, has also of course served recently as chairman of the movement. Many of the nonaligned Latin states are new to the movement, and no group can so far match the radical initiative shown by the phalanx of Cuba and Nicaragua. They defined territorial issues in particular in Decolonization terms, making the other Latin states even less likely to protest any extreme formulations.[9] Regional solidarity, galvanized by Cuban leadership, united the

Latin group and then the majority of the nonaligned as a whole behind the Argentine cause in the Falklands crisis.

Ironically, Guyana, with long-standing membership and good radical credentials within the NAM, was able to block Venezuela's candidacy for NAM membership under the Cuban aegis. Guyana asserted that it was precisely the Venezuelan claim to the Essequibo that motivated Venezuela. Indeed, by October 1982, Latin American issues were so prominant that they would dominate the New York ministerial meeting of the NAM for the first time. The only strong caucus within the group along with Africa, the U.N. Latin American Group (GRULA) has reflected to an inordinate degree the territorial disputes that are the focuses of so much of the foreign policy of its members.

On the U.N. Security Council, the Non-Aligned Group has become an organized force in the 1980s. Caucusing for the important decisions, they reflect a broader nonaligned consensus on most occasions. Consulted by NAM regional groups and by the Non-Aligned Coordinating Bureau (NACB), they have become an important force in Security Council consideration. The NAM clearly intends to increase its influence on the Council. The nonaligned can by themselves provide the best part of the nine votes needed to pass a Security Council resolution. While no NAM member has a veto, they do have the power to move events with only a few adherents from among the rest of the Council.

Their discipline, however, is another question. On Resolution 502, one saw the bulk of the nonaligned vote with the mainstream politico-legal culture. The 36 members of the Non-Aligned Coordinating Bureau might well have voted quite differently, and the NAM as a whole would probably have been inclined to follow the (not directly related) long-standing nonaligned position on the sovereignty question.

At the August 1975 Lima NAM ministerial, Argentina secured strong support for its claim to the Falklands Islands. Self-determination was specifically set aside as unrelated. Vigorously reinforced over the years, such nonaligned support was very much a part of Argentina's planning for and defense of its recuperation of the Islands.[10] With 100 of the then 157 members of the United Nations formally on record as favoring the Argentine case for sovereignty, British diplomacy faced an uphill battle as regarded the nonaligned and the General Assembly majority. The United Nations Charter cites self-determination twice as one of the general goals of the United Nations organization. Its sense was that movement toward self-government, usually resulting in independence but in any case clearly dependent on the electorally expressed wishes of the peoples concerned, was desirable under U.N. plebiscite supervision. The continuing emphasis on Decolonization in a largely noncolonial world warps the politics of the United Nations and makes it both less sought after and less effective as a peacemaker.

THE NAVY'S PLAN

The Argentine Navy has had operational plans for decades for the most realistic of its possible battle scenarios. Argentine strategic planning has included operations against the Andean passes of Chile, the Beagle Channel Islands, and, perhaps third in order of likelihood of implementation, the Falkland Islands. Falklands would nonetheless be the most naval of the three contingencies, and seems to have been that politically most dear to the heart of the naval leadership.

Indeed, Argentine journalists have posited a scenario in which Admiral Anaya supported General Galtieri's selection as head of the junta and president in exchange for his commitment to implement the Malvinas operation.[11] Anaya saw Galtieri as the ideal man to carry out the plan Anaya had supported for years. Former Navy Commander Emilio Eduardo Massera had presented one version of the Malvinas plan in 1977, of which Anaya was the author, but it was not implemented. Vice-Admiral Juan Jose Lombardo, Operations Commander in the 1982 invasion, had submitted his own plan to President Peron in 1974, and, later, to his widow and successor, Isabel Peron.[12]

The senior war school (Command and General Staff College) of the Argentine armed forces consists of a very rigorous three-year course. (Only 50 percent of the students continue through the second year, and only 25 percent make it into the third-year cut.) The final exercise during the third year usually contains four scenarios for Army officers: attack and defend against Brazil, and attack and defend against Chile. In some years there are exercises involving internal subversion. For naval officers there is only one exercise. That exercise is to seize the Falkland Islands. Junta member Admiral Jorge Anaya played that game as a student, rewrote it as an instructor, and refined it as Chief of Operations for the Argentine Navy.

It is instructive that the Army and Navy play separate games. Among the lessons the services learned in their "hot wash-up" assessing the 1978 Argentine incursion that almost came to war with Chile, was that their military strike would have failed due to the inability of the services to conduct joint operations.

They also concluded that longer readiness times were necessary to bring Argentine units to their maximum efficiency. In the two weeks before the Falklands recuperation, the Army was looking westward and preparing for action with Chile. The 25,8,3, and 7 regiments (battalion-size) of the Argentine Army had less than a week's warning at the battalion level to prepare for the operation. General Manuel Jorge Garcia of Five Corps may have had as much as two weeks.

Many Argentine foreign affairs experts and analysts considered an Argentine strike against South Georgia highly likely. Around March 25, a week into the crisis over the scrap-steel workers, such a scenario became highly probable as there were clearly heightened states of readiness among Argentine forces.

It seems likely that the incident concerning the South Georgia scrap steel party began years before as a legitimate commercial enterprise. That the delayed preparations were sloppy on the consular side cannot be attributed to inexperience nor to the fact that the area was not populated or directly administered by resident British officials. It was likely by design for politico-military reasons and out of residual Argentine resentment of any assertion of British sovereignty. Certainly the hoisting of the Argentine flag by the scrap steel party seems to have been the kind of spontaneous gesture in which Argentines have consistently engaged in the Falklands and the Dependencies.

It is equally possible that the role of the Argentine Government went from being that of an observer to a participant and fomenter in these events. The Foreign Ministry certainly began to see the potential for political gain in the incident. The Navy's normal"frontier" role was providing open ocean transport to exploratory, scientific, commercial, and other Argentine ventures. The Navy changed first to asserting in national councils that there should be no positive response to the British request for proper documentation of the workers, given that this was territory claimed by Argentina, then to advocating a mini-invasion. The Foreign Ministry and the Navy vied for the role of champion of Argentine nationalism over the South Georgia incident. Each institution would begin to see the accelerating tie-in with the Falklands invasion plan and the possibility of advancing the date correspondingly. Just as Anaya had played, changed, and supervised the Falklands game of the war school, Foreign Minister Costa Mendez had written his thesis on the Argentine claim to the Malvinas Islands. The plan found informed support on all quarters in the Argentine Government, although it appears the decision was made at the top. Even Ministers were informed *post facto* and even then only on a "need to know" basis.

The military plan depended on three major military assumptions by Argentine decision-makers, paralleling somewhat the political questions: no British use of counterforce, and no Security Council or U.S. sanctions concerning the recuperation of the Islands. When the operational orders were cut for the Malvinas plan, those assumptions were built in. When the assumptions did not play out, however, Argentine military doctrine of adaptation and update was abandoned in that the orders were not changed.

The game, as played at the war school, consisted principally in an armed Argentine recuperation of the Falkland Islands, which would then be turned over to (depending on various assumptions) the United Nations or a token Argentine garrison roughly the size of that which had been emplaced by the British; that is less than 100 troops. In this sense, the most common scenario was a bloodless recuperation of the Falklands and a situation of *fait accompli* in which there was no need for defense of the Islands. Such a scenario evolved from the December/January broadbrush planning by the Junta, through the Plan Blue meetings of January and February into an initial reinforcement of the landing force to shock Britain into not reacting. The reinforcement approved in Plan Blue was still a light reinforcement. That was hastily increased in numbers of troops, but not sophistication of concept, when England answered by dispatching all the ships and troops it could assemble.

PUBLIC REACTION: NATIONAL HONOR IN THE STREETS

In the traditional scenarios for the plan, Argentina would turn over the recuperated Islands to the U.N. or would leave only a token garrison behind in hopes that this would would forestall or, at worst, throw a bad light on any British retaking of the Falklands.

Such options, if ever realistic or planned, were eliminated from official thinking by the British dispatch of the Task Force on April 3 in combination with the demonstrations of April 4 in the Plaza de Mayo. While it is highly likely that the government had a role in assembling crowds, the Argentine tradition of expressing political opinions in mass demonstrations took over. A largely spontaneous wave of patriotism washed over Argentina. A liberating sense of accomplishment and political/juridical rather than military victory swept up all but the most thoughtful of Argentines. The propaganda machinery of the armed forces was not yet fully geared up, yet the nation was fixated on the Malvinas. The size and fervor of the demonstrations far surpassed those of the previous month against the economic policies of the government. They were comparable only with the year Argentina won the World Cup in soccer (and the support for Raul Alfonsin who would replace the military government in 1983).

When debate within the Government began on how to consolidate Argentina's recuperation of the islands, two voices began to be regularly heard in opposition to any withdrawal, whether down to a token force or in favor of the United Nations or other nonnational placeholders for Argentine sovereignty: those of Admiral Anaya and the Jefe de la Casa Rosada.

WAR BY OTHER MEANS

The degree of diplomatic planning was evident in the smooth response of Argentina to the accusation in the U.N. Security Council on April 1 that it planned to invade the Falkland Islands the following day.

Ambassador Eduardo Roca claimed that it was Britain that was about to use force against Argentine territory (the South Georgia scrap site) and that Argentina therefore had to attack in self-defense. A bluff offer was made to negotiate differences provided that Argentine sovereignty was conceded in advance. The offer was never, of course, tested; nor at the time of the call by the Council President to refrain from the threat or use of force did Argentina say that it would comply. The invasion began 12 hours later.

Just as blithely, Argentina completed its occupation of South Georgia at 11:30 A.M. April 3 as the U.N. debated passage of Security Council Resolution 502.

RIPOSTE

Prime Minister Thatcher told the House of Commons that same day that the United Kingdom would free the islands from occupation and return them to British administration as soon as possible. She reminded the Commons that for a decade and a half British governments of both parties had clearly told the government of Argentina that the Islanders' wishes rather than just their interests were the deciding factor for the United Kingdom, and no change in sovereignty was possible without their consent.

Foreign Secretary Francis Pym told the Commons on April 7 that the departure of the first elements of the South Atlantic task force on April 5 was only one element of a wider British policy of increased pressure on Argentina in order to secure withdrawal of the invading troops from the island and make it possible to continue negotiation in search of a peaceful settlement. He was very clear, however, that force would be used in self-defense if diplomacy failed.

RESOURCES

Natural resources are largely potential or latent in the South Atlantic. Politically, they are at most passively, secondarily, or "manipulatively" motivating— even more appealed to than appealing; more than often used to question rather than analyze the other party's motivation; as often a rationale for geopolitics as a distinct basis for national positions and actions.

Although rarely the real basis for national policy, resources were or were said to be considered by each side in the Falklands conflict to be a key motivating policy influence of *the other* party. Both sides indeed appreciate the potential of the area, but neither was directly motivated in its diplomacy by resource considerations.

Scope and Potential

The South Atlantic and the Antarctic are potentially resource rich. Even should large resources be present, however, there is doubt as to their exploitability and their viability at forseeable market prices.

Oil and coal would seem to be the most promising mineral resources, yet at present, without agreed regimes in either the South Atlantic or the Antarctic, exploration does not even seem to interest many potential exploiters: A Russian station in the Antarctic is sitting on a coal seam 25-feet thick at the surface but is burning oil; U.S. oil companies declined the use of a research vessel already in the Antarctic.

The geological and other indirect evidence of potential is contradictory. The petroleum potential of the Falklands was originally posited from their being the "trailing margin" of a tectonic plate, a geology like that of the U.S. East Coast. That promising coast has yet to produce a first-rate oil field. The rich oil fields of Argentina added to the promise . . . perhaps the Malvinas basin is related to the Magallenes Basin which makes Argentina self-sufficient in oil and lubricants. However, an analogy for the U.S. east coast would be to Pennsylvania, and the two do not seem to hold equal deposits. Years of seismic soundings and exploratory drilling will be required in order to map the location and volume of South Atlantic oil reserves.

Exploration may not lead to exploitation. At 100-foot drilling depths a million barrels justifies a well; at 800 feet, a billion barrels are needed. Even geologically conducive structures do not mean that the hydrocarbons were deposited or deposited in sufficient quantities.

Marine resources are equally promising but presently underexplored and underexploited. They depend less on an agreed-on regime, but could still benefit from joint exploration and exploitation. The miniature shrimp-like krill, food source for whales, may be exploitable human protein in a decade should other sources and fisheries decline through mismanagement. Krill will likely, however, suffer the fate of other nontraditional proteins, which must be made into appetizing form and usually fail in the marketplace. Marine mammals, like krill, are potentially infinite renewable resources. It is in the management of renewability that the need for political accord becomes crucial. Krill may already be overfished as regards their own replenishment and the needs of whales in the South Atlantic.

Nonfuel minerals abound in Argentina. Rose of the Andes is indeed a mineral unique to the country. Few such minerals, however, are sufficiently scarce or strategic. Fewer would pay if mined underseas.

Thus, resources are only a long-term, potential National Interest in the South Atlantic for either Argentina or the United Kingdom.

The Antarctic Connection

As in geopolitics, it is in combination with the Antarctic that the potential of Falklands resources becomes so large as to not be ignored. The pure scale of the areas claimed territorially by both parties promises potentially large amounts of twenty-first century resources. As the geographic spread of the Falklands and Dependencies give scope to Antarctic territorial claims, the resources potential of the Islands is multiplied in the oceans and land to the south.

In immediate terms, both geological and marine resources could best be explored and exploited on a regional scale. This is currently blocked by political conflict—bilateral in the Falklands, multilateral in the Antarctic. Ironically, cooperation in the Falklands may become the basis for an alliance of the two "territorial" states on the Antarctic.

Resources as a Factor in the Crisis

The two parties each share a long-run interest in the resources of the region. They have explored and approached their interests differently, and are guided thus by different immediate influences in the crisis.

The United Kingdom is already exploiting natural resources in the Falklands but only to a minimal degree, by raising sheep for wool. The largely self-supporting economy is focused on wool, with about half the acreage and sheep under the Falklands Islands Company. (Fishing is viable if not then of local interest.) To the British government, however, resources in the area are less a promise of national wealth than a patrimony for Kelper self-sufficiency. Distance (transportation costs) and politics (insurance risks in the face of enduring Argentine hostility) rob any resources in this century of at least direct benefit to the "metropole." With North Sea gas and oil, and Atlantic fisheries, Britain looks closer to home for a resources base in medium-future terms. Into the next century, the U.K. recognizes that Antarctica may well become viable but will likely be the subject of an international regime sharing exploitation profits if not products. Thus, at the margin, resources are a secondary consideration to the U.K. in the Falklands. While the wealth of the Falkland Islands Company (FIC), and its purchase by the fuel company Coalite, which deals in solid fuels and has bought the parent company of FIC to diversify into brewing, are the stuff of great conspiracy theories of decision making in Western elites, Britain's political and geopolitical interests dominate in her decision making.

Argentina treats resources as a more integral part of her national security decision making about the South Atlantic and the Antarctic. The national territory, natural riches, resident nationals, and borders are all of a piece in Argentine geopolitics. The State has supported the exploration and population of the frontier and the use of the resources not only in the interest of the local population but of the nation as a whole. In return for such subsidy and encouragement, the Argentine nation secures its claimed area and exercises effective sovereignty and occupation. In conceptual terms, the process is the same whether it is dish antennae for villages on the Andean border with Chile, a naval support vessel for a scrap-steel crew in South Georgia, schools for families to live at Antarctic stations, or the resident Argentines supporting the former oil and aviation services provided the Falkland Islanders.

Argentina feels no sense, thus, of remoteness in distance or time about resources in the Southern World. The national territory, felt to include the Scotia chain and the claimed slice of the southern continent, is to be developed where possible for its real (medium-term) resources potential but in any case is to be developed as an assertion and proof of sovereignty. The Argentine civilization is, while not usually put into words this way, destined to civilize and utilize its allotted piece of the globe. It is as much a mission as a quest for usable material goods.

Neither party was thus directly motivated during the Falklands crisis by resources considerations. Both have long-run interests in resources, if for differing uses. Each shares an interest in the wider Antarctic region, but neither is prepared to spill blood for it. The motivations for high-risk diplomacy and eventual expenditure of lives lay elsewhere. If resources are indeed a long-run, previously crucial or "underlying" motivation for war, they may yet prove a potential basis for solution. Widely thought of as a cause, resources may yet be a cure.

"UNGOVERNABILITY"

A few of the insights of a rich literature on leadership and mass influence on governance cast an interesting light on whether Argentina was "falling apart" and could only look for an external enemy. Advanced in the context of the crisis of political will and legitimacy in Western democracies, the notion of ungovernability offers insight into some of the strengths and weaknesses of the argument that the Argentine Junta had no choice but external adventure. As interpreted by R. Rose and G. Peters, the notion of ungovernability focuses on *political bankruptcy,* which "is the fate that faces a government that so mismanages its economy that it loses popular consent as well as economic effectiveness."[13] Political overload defines a situation of national product growing more slowly than the costs of public policy and the claims of take-home pay. Overload results from scarce resources, inadequate governmental institutions, insufficient output with less payoff than expected, bureaucratic inertia leading to increasing costs of implementing public policy, and the effects of rising expectations.

If most of these conditions were present in Argentina in the spring of 1982, they were indeed prevalent in much of the non-Communist world. (The United States economy is one of the worst managed if the public debt is used as a yardstick of long-term viability.)

There may be a parallel in Argentina to Samuel Huntington's argument that in the U.S. political culture there is a permanent gap between high expectations concerning public institutions and *low* de facto regard of government.[14] In such a situation, public opinion is more bitterly disappointed and proportionately more critical as the discrepancy between creed and reality increases. If this gap is unique to the United States among Western (Northern) nations, as Huntington argues, it may nonetheless have found an ironic mirror image in Argentine public life.

Added clarity about the *timing* of public reaction to government effort is provided by Albert Hirschman's insight that there are cycles of increased public engagement followed by private retreat resulting from frustrations experienced through public engagement.[15] If (as the Junta hoped) the Falklands crisis would bring the Argentine people back into identification with and indeed into participation in their public life, after a long freeze of politics and political enthusiasm, under military government, the military defeat in the Falklands would certainly encourage the down side of such a cyclical trend.

Huntington posits increased political participation leading to increased policy polarization; the polarization then leads to the increasing distrust and a sense of decreasing political efficacy among individuals; and this sense of declining efficacy leads in turn to decreased political participation.[16]

The same pattern is seen at the other end of the political spectrum as represented in the Hoover Institution Report, "The United States in the 1980's": "We do not want to turn our country into a puritanical garrison state; but we will not survive unless we save more than we spend, work more than we play, and spend more on defense and less on welfare."

D. Sanders, in his *Patterns of Political Instability,* posits a sophisticated approach in which political instability is defined in terms of:

1. Regime change: changes in regime norms, changes in type of party system, changes in military-civilian status;

2. Government change: changes in the effective executive, Cabinet changes; and

3. Community change: successful acts of secession.

These forms of change are related to two types of political challenge:

1. Violent challenges: assassinations, acts of guerrilla warfare and political terrorism, deaths from political violence, riots, attempted coups d'état; or

2. Peaceful challenges: political strikes or strike threats, protests and demonstrations, opposition motions of censure, antigovernment speeches by opinion leaders (or, obviously, electoral campaigns).[17]

Sanders posits that in the Atlantic area, peaceful challenges tend to precede regime changes and violent challenges tend to precede governmental changes. The Argentine "riots" preceding the Falklands invasion must be put down as peaceful challenges, especially in the context of Argentine political expression. Effective responses could have been found in the spectrum of fiscal and monetary instruments. Neo-Marxist writings on governability and crisis in government, of course, come to very different recommendations.[18]

Thus, the literature on the breakdown of governing systems and regimes points one in no certain directions. Argentina and many other Latin states failed to create democratic regimes during the 1950s. The current collapse of authoritarian regimes in Latin America as the continent moves towards liberal democracies seems to be a trend for the remainder of this century. The consolidation of democratic politics in Venezuela has been in progress since 1958. Other factors such as voter turnout, executive durability, and the sensitivity to political violence within the society are seen as affected by a variety of local conditions, socioeconomic variables, and constitutional limits.[19]

Although many are oriented toward democratic states, the studies certainly point out how complex and hard to manage is a "crisis of governability." If, however, Argentina faced such a low point on a scale of governability, one must bear in mind that this was not a new or particularly imposing experience to the Argentines, nor were some of the normal indicators such as mass demonstrations to be read in the same way as in other political systems. Price riots in particular would not provide the motivation for the Falklands invasion. At most, the hope of correcting impending ungovernability provided a possible fringe benefit.

MULTILATERAL DETERRENCE: CONFUSION AND CONSTRAINTS IN THE SECURITY COUNCIL

The U.N. Security Council warned Argentina against invasion, and, after the invasion, recognized a breach of the peace. The Secretary General later offered his good offices and conducted indirect negotiations at U.N. Headquarters under

Security Council auspices. Both were, in many senses, textbook workings of the U.N. peace and security machinery, yet they failed to restore the peace. The small successes and the overall failure can both be profitably examined in the light of the many constructive ideas about reform of the U.N. peacekeeping mechanism. We can learn not only from what was done, but from what might have been done.

The U.N. Charter envisions the Security Council as maintaining world peace. The collective security system envisioned in the Charter works through the mechanism principally of the 15-member Security Council, which is intended to maintain international peace and security; develop friendly (that is, nonbelligerent) relations among nations; and to search for international cooperation on global issues, whether political, social, or economic. If it does not attain the first two goals, its successes on areas of agreement have been spectacular, ranging from peacekeeping to the elimination of smallpox. The U.N. is not simply a world debating legislature. If it is not a world government, few wish it to be. Member states are as much sovereign as they are equal while participating in the U.N., which is perhaps best thought of as a framework rather than a system or a super-government. The Falklands crisis demonstrated that the United Nations can be both definer and sometimes enforcer or reinstitutor of normative international law. To the extent that modern international law has as much political as legal content, this is only reflected in the United Nations. The U.N. Army was eliminated in the first drafts of the charter in San Francisco in 1945. What remained of U.N. power to contravene the sovereignty of member states is in the area of action by the Security Council to maintain or restore international peace and order.

The Security Council process is by nature adversarial. Resolutions are not only resisted but are the subject to counter resolutions. On April 2, the United Kingdom introduced draft resolution S/14947 which would have the Council call on "the Governments of Argentina and the United Kingdom of Great Britain and Northern Ireland to seek diplomatic solution to their differences and to respect fully the purposes and principles of the Charter of the United Nations." That draft became Security Council Resolution 502 on April 3, but not before Panama introduced draft resolution S/14950 calling upon the United Kingdom to cease hostilities and refrain from any threat or use of force, and to "duly" respect Argentine sovereignty. The Panamanian resolution garnered seven votes in favor, three opposed (United States, United Kingdom, France) and four abstentions (Guyana, Jordan, Togo, and Zaire, who all voted in favor of Resolution 502). The U.N. system did its job as nation-states currently wish that job defined.

BILATERAL DETERRENCE: TOO LITTLE, TOO LATE

Nations too can intervene to attempt to keep the peace. However, the President of the United States was no more successful than the U.N. Security Council at deterring the Argentine invasion of the Falkland Islands. President Ronald Reagan's calls of March 30 and April 1 to General Leopoldo Galtieri were designed to convince the head of government not to use force. His second call was specifically to halt the invasion planned for that midnight. Galtieri refused.

At this juncture, the intervenor had no real mediating role. Indeed despite concilliatory language he was intervening against one party in its perception. Neither time nor the intervenor's position allowed him to generate compromise solutions.

Beyond the military timetable and the inherent momentum of a medium-size operation such as the Falklands invasion, Galtieri had the advantage of tactical, if not strategic, surprise.[20] He was challenged too late: the fail-safe point at which ships could be recalled was past. Argentine scouts were ashore.

The lead elements of the main force would land only five hours later, at 4:30 A.M. Falklands time.

Informed of Reagan's call, Galtieri returned from opening the major annual book fair to the Casa Rosada and phoned Reagan following delivery of his speech. He likely knew what a call at this juncture would concern, and certainly had no desire to test the working thesis of tacit U.S. acceptance at that late hour. The Argentine fleet had been at sea for days, but the majority opinion in Buenos Aires at this stage was that this activity was related to the South Georgia confrontation. He could still achieve tactical surprise.

The deterrence attempt lasted an hour, which must be halved to allow for translation. Galtieri declined the good offices of the United States Government, as he had concerning South Georgia. He expressed as much by silence and mood as in words the impatience of the Argentine Government and its exasperation with diplomacy. From the Argentine perspective, the talks had been about the cession of sovereignty to Argentina, and, in those terms, had failed utterly. The only hope Galtieri would offer was that it was not too late for Britain to cede that sovereignty.

President Reagan warned Galtieri firmly "that the British would certainly fight in case of an Argentine landing on the Falklands."[21] He asked for but did not receive Galtieri's assurance that there would be no invasion. The U.S. President was in no position to either dictate or, indeed, mediate. Galtieri's offer of holding the invasion force should Britain that very night make a political capitulation (to be effective within months) was already ruled out by the British Prime Minister's clear statement that Great Britain would defend the islands against any use of force. The President's call confirmed what U.S. Ambassador to Argentina Harry Schlaudeman had found earlier in the day: that Galtieri was absolutely determined to follow through with the invasion that was in preparation.

In the words of then U.S. Assistant Secretary of State for Latin America Thomas Enders: Our ties with Argentina proved too weak to promote effective cooperation in support of common interests. Repeated efforts were made . . . to explain to Argentine leaders what would happen if they did what they proposed to do. Although our predictions consistently proved accurate, they were not believed. Communications failed utterly.[22] The exchanges of Galtieri with Schlaudeman and Reagan were both too late and too early; too late to deter, too early to open mediation. While Ambassador Enders's estimation also applies to Secretary Haig's mediation when it contained elements of warning, and indeed to U.S. counsel to the Argentine Government up until the surrender of Argentine forces in the Islands, there does not seem to have been any increase in Argentine credence given to U.S. assessments. If anything, U.S. judgments about the consequences of Argentine actions seemed to decline at the same time that the judgments were being put forward as real indicators of bad faith on the part of the United States. Itself the instigator of the use of force in the crisis in the twentieth-century round, Argentina was unable to deal with or accept at face values assessments of the relative weight of military force in the Falklands crisis.

By 2:00 A.M. on April 2, Buenos Aires time, rumor of the invasion of the Falkland Islands would be as far abroad as the Swiss press. However, most of the Argentine military staffs did not know that the invasion was to be launched at dawn on April 2. For those officers who did, the orders were business as usual. On the evening of the 31st, the British military attaché had dinner with Menendez and two other Argentine Army officers. On the evening of April 1, the outgoing U.S. Chief of Naval Operations, Admiral Thomas Hayward, was in Buenos Aires to bid farewell to his Argentine colleagues and was offering a reception for Admiral Anaya at the residence of the U.S. Ambassador. Around 10:00 A.M., Anaya took a phone call, after which his officers at the reception appeared to relax considerably. This call may have been to tell Anaya that his SEALS were ashore. (Argentine special forces did not go ashore until 0430 hours.)

If Galtieri told Reagan by his ultimatum (Argentine sovereignty that evening or else) that his call came too late, there could have been military support for a political decision. There would have been a sound military basis for the inability to recall: the lack of secure cryptographic communications capability, without which the Argentine Fleet Commander could not have assured himself that any orders to postpone or cancel the invasion were genuine. He does not claim a "green light" from the United States. Ambassador Schlandeman's demarche and President Reagan's call were decidedly "red." The working assumption, however, would have to be that it was strategic British disinformation.

More tellingly, there was a major institutional factor to be considered: In 1978, the near invasion of the Beagle Channel area by the Argentine Army was cancelled when U.S. Ambassador Raoul Castro convinced Washington to arrange Vatican mediation of the Beagle dispute. The Argentine Army was reined in and recalled its units, which had indeed *already* crossed the Chilean border. The succeeding years of mediation by the Vatican and others, resulting in decisions which they considered to have favored Chile's position, were taken as an object lesson by the Argentine Army about using and being talked out of using force, as well as about peaceful "settlement" of disputes. The lesson for the Malvinas operation was, "Don't be dissuaded at the last minute."

PLAN A/PLAN B: INTERNAL, INSTITUTIONAL, AND INTERNATIONAL INCENTIVES TO VIOLENCE

Did Argentina "lose" the Falklands conflict? Argentine decision making before the Falklands invasion must certainly have included the possibility of military and diplomatic failure. The costs, however, may not be accountable in the same terms if seen from the Argentine military perspective. Herein lie dangerous implications for territorial violence: There are incentives militating against the systemic politico-legal norms, internal and institutional pressures that are motivating and very immediate, and multilateral political institutions and pressures that are at best permissive.

The Argentine military knew before the Falklands invasion that it could not hold onto power indefinitely. That had been its plan, in departure from a long tradition of interim rule. The Argentine military was not only an accepted, regular intervenor in the country's politics, it was indeed often the preferred instrument of some of the civilian political groups. Against the wishes of other parties and indeed of many in the military, a political group would seek military intervention when it was going to lose or could not obtain political power. While viewing itself as a separate institution, the army was willing to make temporary alliances with other institutions in Argentine national life. Other services and branches sometimes took opposing or competing roles—one had to check whose battle dress was in evidence in which public buildings. If the last military government was qualitatively different in its decision to govern the country for an extended period, it was part of the pattern in that it went into power to defend not only its view of national security but its own institutional well-being as one of the major targets of terrorist activity. The military viewed civilian politics as bankrupt and the economy as not far from it. Social and political collapse for lack of political will seemed imminent. The military determined to supply that political will for national and institutional reasons.

The real problem was that the military had taken power this time to change the nature of government in Argentina. They intended to make it proactive, action-oriented, autocratic, and capable of transforming Argentine national life. If their view of government was modern, their institutional structure was feudal. The three services—Army, Navy and Air Force—had as much trouble governing in tandem as they would have had they ever tried combined operations in the field. If there was great enthusiasm in 1978–79 for the economic accomplishments of the military government, this had completely faded by the beginning of Galtieri's term. If there had been hope for political unity through the crushing of terrorism, the accomplishment was limited in negative consensus. If the Argentine majority was glad that there was no more terrorism, they were neither rallied nor inspired by the prospect of politics guided by the military. This was where the Falklands recuperation became key to the military vision of national life. What was needed was not taking peoples' minds off their problems. What was needed was a sense of lift, of national consensus and vision.

Argentines accuse their politicians of having rallied behind the military government in the hour of victory and then deserted them when the reality and the dimensions of the Argentine military defeat emerged. Argentine politicians had really deserted the Government, however, by 1980. By then they would no longer ignore or even deny the possibility of a return of the parties to political power. This constituted a breach of the passive support that the military government had enjoyed until 1980, and signalled the real beginning of the political process.

In this sense, the military government came to recognize that its time in office was finite. That they planned on ruling, either by sheer power or on a wave of popular opinion via a Falklands operation, did not obscure the fact that they could not count on as long a military rule as they might have originally envisioned.

The original scenario had been for orderly terms of office for each member of the Junta. It proved to be the very process of transition from the administration of Robert Eduardo Viola that caused the politicians to begin thinking about democratic rule. The transition led to the first open dissent and there was a whiff of political opening and consequent opportunity in the political climate in Buenos Aires. Viola had begun talks with major institutions in national political life. Such talks may indeed have led many to believe that there was a form of proto-politics already in operation; in other words, that there was advantage to be had, and one had to compete to obtain a share in whatever the new game would be.

With rekindling of politics came economic disaster. The overvalued currency appeared to many to be due for devaluation at about the time of the transition. Tremendous capital flight ensued, then 10 percent devaluation, then a series of devaluations that gutted the Argentine peso. Viola was stung by charges of incompetence from the business community. The military saw itself as leading the development of the nation, and especially the business recovery.

The reemergence of the political parties proved their resilience. Said by many during the 1970s to be dead, Peronism manifested considerable strength. The Radicals showed their flexibility with new people and new ideas following the death of Balbin in September 1981, while Raul Alfonsin emerged as the new power at the center of the Radical movement. The essence of his appeal was his challenge to the relationship between government and the military in Argentina.

If there had been great civilian support for victory, there was also in the five years preceding the war widespread public support for order and the suppression of terrorism. Civilian supremacy was not a strong tradition in Argentina. Argentines counted on the military as one more institution to be factored into political questions and decisions. Argentine politicians have traditionally recognized that they had to live with the military as an institution and respect its major concerns. Almost the whole society had acquiesced in the Argentine military's response to a challenge to the integrity of the state and the military institution, but governance had robbed the military of its influence and prestige to a degree few could have anticipated. It was also taxing the military's self-esteem and indeed its will to govern.

Measures for the redemocratization of Argentine political life were announced on March 4, 1982, a month before the military undertook the gamble that would call into question its very competence in things military and seal its demise as a major institution in Argentine politics. In several senses, however, it had already recognized that its days were numbered: that it had no vocation or gift for governance. Dramatic military success well might not have reversed years of managerial failure. One heard little of the Malvinas during the year preceding Galtieri's accession to power, while one heard much about the Beagle Channel. *Desaparecidos* (the victims of disappearances) and economic ruin dominated debate about Argentine public life. Thus the political stage was set for decisions far more sophisticated than military adventurism to erase economic failure, and more complicated than the normal analysis of decision making about invasion. Such decision theory is usually held to be based on assessment of the international system. Argentine decision making was as much internally based as externally, and the decisions had a military/institutional perspective difficult for Argentine civilians, much less the wider world, to appreciate. Nowhere else would a full-color, oversize history of the Officers' Club be displayed in a downtown book-store and sell. The Argentine military is a world apart, within a country which is also a world apart.

A separate political-cultural world, Argentina has looked north not to the United States but primarily to Europe, particularly Berlin, Paris, and Rome, for external models, to the extent that it desired any. Culture, language, government, and public life in general are no more New World in character than are the constellations at night similar to those of the Northern Hemisphere. Political development and institutions have come along separate paths from the other major (and themselves variegated) Western Hemisphere models. There is no polar star, astronomical or political, in the separate world that is Argentina.

In that world, the Argentine military is a major, largely autonomous player. Set apart, it is traditionally in its own view the *defender* rather than purely the servant of the Constitution and thus of civilian governments. Having decided, perhaps for the first time, to rule rather than be a caretaker after assuming political power, the Argentine military had by 1982 taken the mantle of defender *and* government. It drew incentives for the Falklands invasion from each role.

In immediate terms, the Argentine decision must have taken some account of rioting and other anomic responses to food shortages and immediate critical economic problems which were reaching violent levels in the weeks preceding the decision to invade the Falklands. More telling, however, was their general discredit as an institution in managing the nation's affairs. One would not reverse that with a military victory, but even a defeat would buy some time.

What then was Plan B if indeed Argentina failed to recuperate the Falklands? Argentina was nonetheless likely to achieve a level of national unity unobtainable by the military government before the invasion. While the occupants of the Casa

Rosada, Argentina's "White House," might still be seen as military men, after the invasion they could no longer be seen as marionettes. An honorable attempt to recover national soil would "validate" the institutions of the Argentine military and give them a new lease on political power. Whether that new lease was a strong one leading to continued direct governing of Argentine public life, or, under this working hypothesis, a weaker mandate conveyed by honorable failure with a very short half-life, the military would still be able to lead Argentina toward the kind of return to democracy with which the military would be comfortable. The leadership would be changed but the institution would prosper. In that sense, it appears that Plan B has been implemented. The military retained control of its society and, indeed, control of the process of moving toward democratization. It maintained that control for two years. It might well not have been accorded those years had it been simply in the institutional position of mismanager of the nation's affairs. Self-critical as ever, a bloodied and beaten Argentina was nonetheless a more united society than before the attempt to recover the Falkland Islands.

IV

CRISIS MANAGEMENT: THIRD-COUNTRY MEDIATION BY THE UNITED STATES

Britain does not appease dictators.
                    —British Foreign Secretary Francis Pym to the Commons

There is no doubt of the paramount influence of the United States. After all, Argentina does not have many friends in the world.
                    —Nicholas Henderson

There should be no mystery about American purposes abroad. They should be hospitable to our society and to our ideals.
                    —Alexander Haig

We shall consider any attempt to extend their system to any portion of our hemisphere as dangerous to our peace and safety.
                    —James Monroe on the European powers

OVERVIEW: THE MEDIATION ATTEMPTS

There were major diplomatic efforts to mediate the Falklands dispute by American Secretary of State Alexander Haig, President Belaunde Terry of Peru, and U.N. Secretary General Javier Perez de Cuellar.

Their approaches and working methods were radically different. They worked by shuttle flight, telephone, and alternating sessions with the parties. Their efforts spanned the military stages of the crisis from standoff to full-scale war.

However, the striking thing about the major attempts to mediate the Falklands crisis was the high degree of participation of the mediators in both the process and the proposals. Each included a mechanism involving the third party actively, both to implement the interim military and administrative arrangements, and to turn them into an ongoing search for a more definitive settlement of the question of sovereignty over the Falkland Islands.

It is helpful in assessing the three mediation attempts of the Falklands crisis to view the mediators not as the ideal disinterested facilitators of the second-track theory of negotiation but as yet another element in a negotiation: a third party to the dispute.

One must remember that such a third party approaches a mediation differently. That is to say, he has different stakes and points of emphasis. This can extend even to the question of what is to be mediated. One of the problems in the Falklands conflict was that the mediators all proceeded from the natural goal of the mediator to make or find a settlement. This is not always (or sometimes ultimately) the goal of one or both parties.

Toward the absolute end of the settlement, mediators also tend to be too rational about the questions involved. In this sense, they are off base; they are not communicating completely with the parties. If the mediators could be absolutely rational and frank about the inherent worth of the Falkland Islands and prefer a settlement involving considerable sacrifice by each side of its positions, the parties were more likely to view the question in its broadest and most political terms.

Thus, to the United Kingdom this was not a question solely of territory, but of high principle. Following the invasion by Argentina, the Falklands question became a question of the most abstract order, invoking the powerful imagery of the full political mythology of English-speaking cultures. Response to Argentine invasion, occupation, and military governance of the Falkland Islanders evoked St. George rescuing the innocent maiden from the dragon. More tellingly, the full imagery of dictatorship and aggression from World War II was evoked not only by but for British leadership, as was the vivid memory of British response from an "underdog" position as victim to victor.[1] Similarly, to Argentines, the Falkland crisis became a question of defending the fatherland, invoking a political panoply from El Cid expelling the Moors; through the liberator tradition of Marti, Bolivar, Artigas, Sarmiento, and San Martin; to the successful expulsion of British troops by the population of nascent Buenos Ayres in the early nineteenth century.

THE SHAPE OF THE POSSIBLE SETTLEMENT

The principal efforts at mediation also had several elements in common, stemming from the combination of the military and territorial nature of the crisis: military disengagement, interim administration of the territory, and negotiations to solve the ongoing dispute.

Military disengagement involved the end of military hostilities, the guarantee of its finality by mutual withdrawal of armed forces, and an implicit or explicit concrete commitment not to reintroduce those forces. Arrangements were to be supervised and verified by a third party, but each side wanted to be in a position to act unilaterally if it felt it necessary.

Interim administration of the islands also involved a third party, be it national, multinational, or international. Proposed third-party administrators were essentially independent of, or underpinned or assisted by, the traditional organs of local self-government. Local autonomy, however, was balanced in most proposals by the possibility of increased Argentine access to the Falkland Islands (and dependencies) during the period of interim administration. In other words, proposals suggesting a large degree of local autonomy (suitable to the British/ Kelpers) included provisions for a large degree of Argentine access (suitable to the Argentines). Conversely, proposals for less autonomy were accompanied by less access.

The question of resumption of the 17 years of bilateral negotiations to solve the ongoing territorial dispute centered on the conflict between emphasizing process and emphasizing purpose. As before the invasion, Argentina insisted that the negotiations were about establishing Argentine sovereignty. The United Kingdom insisted that they were about the future of the Falklands.

DIFFERING AGENDAS

Thus the parties had differing agendas and ideas as to what was indeed negotiable. The common view of the elements of a solution disguised fundamental disagreement about the heart of the dispute. Territoriality seemed to continue, as it had throughout most of the 17 years of bilateral negotiations, to make the Falklands a zero-sum game. Only consequences changed in the mediation phase of the dispute; the use of force had only raised the stakes. Indeed, too much weight would be put by mediators on avoiding further violence. The mediators assumed this was perceived as a significant benefit by each party.

The United Kingdom sought:

—A cease-fire and withdrawal of Argentine forces, with non-reintroduction to be guaranteed;

—Restoration of British authority, in whole or in part;

—Basic guarantees of local rights and institutions;

—Third-party assistance in implementation;

—Control of Argentine access and communication at preconflict levels as governed by the 1971 bilateral agreements (i.e., in the Argentine view, excluding sovereignty talks); and

—An agreement that would not prejudice the final outcome of sovereignty negotiations (to include a formula on future negotiations on the question of sovereignty).

British strategy was to apply increasing and coordinated pressure toward these ends. That pressure could be diplomatic, economic, and, if necessary, military.

The coordinated and balanced use of persuasion and force can be seen in this strategic view as a continuum; the two are self-reinforcing and are used in tandem. Indeed, at times they are inseparable. The continuum can be visualized as an arrow stretching from Portsmouth to Stanley. With the progress of the fleet in implementation of force, the trade-offs between the use of the two instruments change. The closer one gets to the capability or the need to make an amphibious landing in the Falklands themselves, the less diplomacy is to be depended upon or tactical sacrifices made to succeed via pure diplomacy.

Argentine goals in implementation of its search for sovereignty were:

—Interruption of British rule;

—Effective interim control of administration of the Islands;

—Freedom of access;

—Involvement of third parties principally to limit British use of force and help secure Argentine gains;

—Immediate military withdrawal to home bases, preserving and indeed reserving Argentina's geopolitical advantage and ability to use force again with minimum warning time; and

—Widened recognition that Decolonization applied and that the controlling norm was territorial integrity.

These steps were to lead to:

—Negotiations leading to effective Argentine sovereignty in the near or medium term; and

—A settlement formula that would result in permanent Argentine sovereignty at a near (and fixed) future date.

Were this unobtainable, Argentine strategy was to seize the islands by force but defend them diplomatically, garnering world political support to defer British political and possibly military countermeasures. Very limited in scope initially, the defensive strategy began to unravel almost before it was implemented. In the U.N. Security Council debates in New York, many of Argentina's working premises dissolved in the face of some very apt British diplomacy.

The Argentine strategy can be visualized as an arrow, spiraling outward from the Falklands. As much would be done as was necessary to hold the islands. This was seen first as a mere question of deterrence, of putting so many troops on the Islands that there would be no question of any British military response, then withdrawing some of them. It would prove necessary, however, for Argentina to go further and further, both militarily and politically, legally and financially, in order to maintain a successful defensive posture. The Falklands would eventually come to consume the nation, the government, and Argentine diplomacy.

Each side realized that the arrangements for administration and negotiation were related, and tradeoffs could in principle be made between the two. Argentina, for example, stated openly in Costa Mendez's letter of April 2 to Secretary Haig that if negotiations were less restricted in aim (Argentine sovereignty) or deadline, concessions on interim administration would be needed in compensation: in other words; Argentina would need more control of the Islands and/ or more access (e.g., to be able to send settlers to the Falklands to change the nature of the society).

U.S. MEDIATION

Following the Argentine announcement of April 2 that it had captured the Falklands, South Georgia, and the Sandwich Islands, the politico-military temperature rose rapidly. The United States government used feelers from both sides seeking what it could do to interpose itself as a mediator. In the sense that the mediator seeks compromise, this was more of a U.S. role than either party originally intended. Given the firmness of each of these positions, a most unlikely climate for any effort at mediation evolved: Since the civilian landings of March 19 on South Georgia, Argentina had forcefully reasserted its claim that Britain had illegally seized the Falkland Islands in 1832. Britain had stated a determination to defend the Islands.[2]

The mediator was as surprised as anyone by the events taking place in the South Atlantic. British Ambassador to the United States Nicholas Henderson concludes that U.S. Assistant Secretary of State for Inter-American Affairs Thomas Enders "had derived no inkling of any Argentine intention to move to military confrontation"[3] during his visit to Buenos Aires in March. Indeed, he cites Enders as telling Haig in his presence on March 31 that "the United States Government had had an assurance from the Argentine Foreign Minister that the Argentines were not contemplating any action, a promise that had been just confirmed."[4] The Junta's security and indeed their dissemblance on their plans was brilliant.

On April 2, the British U.N. delegate charged Argentina with aggression, and asked the Security Council to demand that Argentine forces withdraw from the Islands immediately. The Argentine representative denied the charge, stating that Argentina had recovered for its sovereignty islands that properly belonged to it. Argentina, he said, would negotiate any issue with Britain except sovereignty.

London broke off diplomatic relations with Buenos Aires, condemning the invasion as unprovoked aggression in disregard of the appeal by the Secretary General of the United Nations and the president of the Security Council.

H.M.G. warned before the Security Council meeting that appropriate military measures were being taken to ensure British rights under international law. The Government announced the formation of a carrier task force (not yet given orders to sail) and the Defense Minister, John Nott, reported that a substantial number of ships had been ordered to the area several days earlier.

On April 4, the British made clear that the Falklands Islands and dependencies remained British territory, inhabited by British people, and announced that if the islands could not be regained through diplomacy, force would be used instead. While insisting that they preferred peaceful settlement, they noted that this did not look likely. The government then announced the dispatch of the 36-ship naval force to the Islands.

The Argentines responded that "if the Argentine people are attacked by military, naval, land or air means, the Argentine nation in arms, with all means at its disposal, will present battle." Further the Foreign Minister said, any change or disturbance in the peace would be the sole responsibility of the United Kingdom. The Argentine Navy was on alert, and it was reported that two of its three submarines left for the Islands on April 3. (Argentine officers deny this report.) Military supplies were arriving hourly by plane at Port Stanley (the Falklands capital). A naval transport ship had brought dozens of heavily armored amphibious vehicles to the harbor there.

Such was the diplomatic climate in which the United States volunteered to mediate. That climate would affect the mediation before the mediation could begin to affect relations between the parties.[5]

The new British Foreign Minister, Francis Pym, stated in a message to U.S. Secretary of State Alexander Haig H.M.G.'s determination to secure Argentine withdrawal and a return of British administration to the Falklands. This was conveyed to Haig on April 6. Haig mentioned to the British Ambassador, Sir Nicholas Henderson, an idea of negotiating with the British and the Argentines a mixed administration of the islands[6] following mutual withdrawal of military and naval forces and the emplacement of a peacekeeping force drawn from two Latin American countries, Canada and the United States.[7] Negotiations would then follow.

Haig met separately with the Argentine and British ambassadors. The two adversaries suddenly represented major but competing U.S. interests, in that the United States maintained or sought the full range of constructive bilateral relationships with each. The Argentine Ambassador told the Secretary that the U.S. plan for a four-nation peacekeeping force was at the outer edges of what the Junta could accept; the U.K. preferred the United States *alone* as administrator.[8] Bidding high, Argentine Foreign Minister Costa Mendez asked on April 6 that Haig secure reversion of the Islands to Argentina or at least a presumption of reversion in new negotiations with a halting of the U.K. task force. His unstated backup position was administration by a small group of mutually acceptable countries, or better still, mixed British-Argentine administration under U.S. guarantee.

However, the United States did not "rush" into the decision to mediate the dispute. It had clearly offered to help in March with the South Georgia scrapworkers incident. (Argentina sought more on the grounds that this was only part of the wider question of the South Atlantic islands problem—somewhat of a signal in itself.) The United States was asked by each side what it could do to help. Haig had been formally asked by Lord Carrington to help with the South Georgia incident on March 28. The Argentine government had been warned in diplomatic and military channels in Washington, as well as by the embassy in Buenos Aires, that a military solution would do grave damage to the bilateral relationships. U.S. Ambassador Harry Shlaudeman had detected dissembling and delay on his request first for assurances of nonbelligerent intent and then for a meeting with the head of state. President Reagan had called Galtieri to try to head off military conflict on April 1.[9]

In the U.S. Department of State, a week is an almost drawn-out decision-making time-frame, and there were both substantive and procedural reasons for decisive and timely intervention: The bilateral conflict among friends was a given—that "interest" was not in play. The question was whether it would become armed conflict. Still in play, then, was the U.S. "systemic" interest in peace, order (especially in the Western Hemisphere), in not seeing conflict escalate, and hence in avoiding or undoing breaches of the peace.

In Haig's view, the crisis

involved the credibility of the already strained Western alliance, the survival or failure of a British government that was a staunch friend to the United States, the future of American policy and relations in the Western Hemisphere as well as in Europe, the possibility of yet another dangerous strategic incursion by the Soviet Union into South America, and most important of all, an unambiguous test of America's belief in the rule of law. Moreover, in Latin America, the rule of law as the basis for change is more than a theoretical imperative. The map of the continent displays many territorial disputes that under the rule of might-makes-rights, could inflame the region.[10]

A negotiated Argentine withdrawal would serve U.S. interests and might salvage the bilateral relationship with Argentina. Stepping aside would serve none—the U.S.-U.K.-NATO relationship was not seriously at risk given the number and specificity of bilateral commitments as well as the overriding special relationship. The North Atlantic Treaty is just that: It does not cover out-of-area conflicts south of the Tropic of Cancer. It is only part of the special relationship, which is overriding in security terms but would not necessarily determine a situation not involving the survival or a *mutually recognized* vital interest of the other partner.

The United States had traditionally sidestepped the legal stage of territorial disputes in Latin America in order to protect its interests. It was more likely to intervene if not take a side when the peace was threatened: Of the many territorial disputes of Latin American countries, only a few since 1945 have reached the level of armed conflict. When they have, the United States within the OAS, has played an active role in resolving the dispute (e.g., Nicaragua-Honduras in 1957) or in putting out the fire (e.g., El Salvador–Honduras in 1969.)

As military events and national pride narrowed Argentine room for maneuver, it was judged that a negotiated settlement could not be arranged later without increasing risk to the stability of the Argentine government if not the country. Whether it could yet be arranged, with neither party yet really chastened nor blooded, was open to considerable debate. This was not lost on the U.S. Secretary of State or the U.S. Government as a whole. This was high-risk, high-gain strategy.

Similarly, it was felt in Washington that a settlement could not be arranged at lower levels, by more quiet channels, or by another mediator:[11]

The United Nations, with its vociferous anticolonialist coalition of Third World and Marxist members, would probably not be able to act quickly enough to be effective, and the debate was certain to digress into issues that would exacerbate a situation that could only be resolved by quiet diplomacy. The OAS was unsatisfactory for similar reasons. There was no time to form a consortium of European and American states, and besides, this was not a problem ideally suited to the methods of a committee.[12]

That majority is in the U.N. General Assembly, which sits in the fall. The debate would no doubt digress, but the good offices of the "executive branch" of the United Nations, the Secretariat under the Secretary General, is as skilled and swift at quiet diplomacy as any nation-state. The problem might have come in the U.N. obtaining British agreement to its mediation—the United States had already secured that role. The OAS was unsatisfactory for an additional reason: One party of the dispute is not a member of the OAS. Multilateral diplomacy—a coalition of mediators—held more promise but certainly lacked speed. The United States may not have been the ideal mediator, but its experience put it forward on pragmatic grounds: It could be on the job in hours. Whether a mediator should move into place rapidly is a debatable question, but is distinct from the criticism that the United States preempted other, perhaps better, mediators.

How the United States came to mediate formally and who was to make up the U.S. mission is also worth further attention. Secretary Haig recalls that the "President had offered the good offices of the United States in finding a basis to negotiate a resolution of the dispute."[13] Others speak of the two parties asking what the United States could do. Still others feel the United States was pursuing its own interests. That would imply the United States volunteering to "solve" problems the parties did not perceive. The inquiries as to what the United States could do were open-ended. They focused on interests and goals of the respective parties and could be seen as requests for U.S. help in securing those interests.

Consciously or not, the U.S. Government read them as requests for formal, public help in avoiding war by making concessions. Each party accepted the resulting U.S. offer of assistance. Rather like Nikita Khrushchev when John Kennedy replied only to his *first* letter (offering a way out of the Cuban missile crisis and not his second (positing withdrawal of Soviet missiles on U.S. pullout of missiles from Turkey), the parties agreed to something perhaps rather different from what they had proposed. Instead, they were talked into asking for mediation by the mediators: ''In a series of conversations with the British and the Argentinians, [perhaps the U.S.-initiated talks 1–6 April in Washington] it became clear that both sides hoped that I [Secretary Haig] would serve as intermediary.''[14]

The conviction that only the U.S. Government would be acceptable to the parties and could therefore make peace was a self-fulfilling prophecy only in its first half: acceptability. A large component of the National Honor of the United States is its self-image as defender of order and world peace. Making peace was harder.

The decision was made that the U.S. Secretary of State must himself ask the Argentine Junta to reverse its actions; must convince them before the two sides joined battle in a major way, at which point U.S. support for the British would become inevitable; and must secure not only a military withdrawal but a basis for solving as opposed to deferring the underlying dispute; and thus had to avoid rewarding aggression but neither punish nor completely frustrate Argentina's policy of seeking Falklands sovereignty.

Thus, this was a decision to encourage the U.K. to do more than simply recover the Islands—to set limited war aims and concede something to Argentina despite rather than because of its aggression, and to seek a longer-run solution, which implied concessions by a party (other than the Islanders) that felt aggrieved and saw itself as still holding military cards—the United Kingdom. As regards its relationships with Argentina, it was a move from a neutrality that had tacitly aided the power holding disputed territory to a mediation that implied concessions by the new holder of the same territory. Thus each party got more intervention by the mediator than it may initially have had in mind by asking what the United States could do to moderate the behavior of the other party. It was a decision not just to mediate but to put the United States in a place it had always avoided—in the middle of a territorial dispute.

On April 6, President Reagan agreed to Secretary Haig's suggestion that he mediate the crisis in order to avoid futher bloodshed and remove a potential threat to U.S. interests in Latin America.

Francis Pym's message to the Reagan Administration on April 6 that the British goal was Argentine withdrawal and the return of British administration to the Falkland Islands made clear the British view that the U.S. role would be crucial.

Secretary of State Haig's reaction to the British demarche was that he had indeed been thinking of U.S. mediation of the crisis aimed at possibly securing a mixed or multilateral administration of the Falklands. The British Ambassador clarified to Haig that H.M.G. could not enter negotiations about the future of the Falklands until Argentine troops were withdrawn.[15] Further, he said that it was inopportune to think in terms of multilateral administration. He stressed that Argentine withdrawal and the reimposition of British administration were preconditions for negotiations; that the United Kingdom was not concerned with Galtieri's future; and that the political situation in Great Britain was analagous to the U.S. approach to its 52 hostages in Iran. The principles of peaceful settlement and self-determination were in play. Accepting the British precondition of Argentine withdrawal, Haig suggested a mixed commission both to mediate and to function as an interim administration, or the possibility of involving the Organization of American States. The British Ambassador expressed doubt as to whether either would be constructive and further spoke against involving the United Nations Secretary General, painting Resolution 502 as a sole and sound basis for action.

Haig emphasized to Ambassador Henderson that a public U.S. tilt toward Great Britain would lose the only leverage anyone had on Buenos Aires. Henderson attributed Galtieri's failure to heed Reagan's entreaty (not to carry through with the invasion) to Reagan's having gotten in touch with Galtieri only shortly before the landings and thus too late to stop them. He felt (from a uniquely British perspective) that Argentina's sad economic situation would make it vulnerable to a broad spectrum of possible U.S. influence.

Henderson reported to London that Haig was not tabling a clear-cut plan of action but rather testing British attitudes. If indeed he was testing British attitudes, he was finding them very firm and, at least in the tone of his conversations, accommodating them no less firmly. He stated that he was fully aware of the strength of British public opinion on the Falklands. He was determined to do everything possible to help the British government. He was conscious of the (political) problems and views of the Prime Minister herself. He accepted as an initial premise that Argentine withdrawal must be a precondition to future negotiations. (He was no less clear in his own mind that British concessions would be needed.)

British strategy throughout the diplomatic efforts was that with the British task force underway, the threat of force should lead to successful diplomacy, or unsuccessful diplomacy would lead to violence (hopefully, successful violence).[16] The initial British impression was, nonetheless, that Argentina did not believe that the United Kingdom was prepared to use force to retake the Falklands. The British also believed that this might become a self-fulfilling prophecy as the Antarctic winter, the length of the supply line, and the expenditure of fuel and other scarce resources progressed.

The British Ambassador to Washington, Sir Nicholas Henderson, believed that Haig operated from two premises:

—Argentina was guilty of aggression and should not be allowed to get away with it lest it set an example with dire consequences for world peace; and
—A military solution would harm not only both parties but also the United States.[17]

Henderson characterizes Haig's approach as one of taking sides while giving the impression of complete impartiality. This neutral posture, maintained until the end of April, ''was difficult for people to understand on the other side of the Atlantic"[18] since the British saw themselves as an ally who had been the victim of aggression. Haig was worried that any tilt toward Britain prepared fertile ground for the Soviets in Argentina and in Latin America at large.

Haig was fully conscious of a wider U.S. interest in vindication of "mainstream" Western rules of the game. "I felt the interests of the free world were better served by my taking those risks [mediating], even though I anticipated the outcome."[19] Henderson emphasizes that Haig assured him of the Administration's sympathy for the British cause despite the press spokesman's characterizing the U.S. course as "down the middle" and Reagan's statements that the United States was a friend of both of these countries. Haig indeed assured the ambassador several times that there would be no repeat of Suez. Henderson very insightfully captured some of the U.S. doubts about the case of the Falklands that made the Suez analogy very applicable: "A recessive feeling about colonialism, concern that Britain would eventually expect the United States to pick up the check, worry about the Russians and the fear that what Britain was doing would rally other countries in the area against Western interests."[20]

The United States was indeed, as Haig assured the Ambassador, not at heart impartial. It was partial in two directions: Strong currents of support were running for both the British and Argentine causes. The traditional U.S. neutrality on territorial disputes had tacitly favored the status quo and thus Great Britain. Neutrality now favored the Argentine status quo in occupation of the Falkland Islands. Friends of Argentina in the U.S. Government urged caution and a mediating role. The concept of the "Latino lobby" dear to the hearts of British journalists is first-rate political phrase-making but conveys little understanding of the point of view of those argued for the primacy in the Falklands crisis of U.S. interests in Latin America.

There was no support within the United States Government from any quarter for Argentina's act of recovering the Islands by armed force. There was little widespread or profound understanding of Argentina's territorial case, either on the traditional bilateral basis or in its rather newer decolonization argumentation.

Argentina was, of course, playing a particularly vital role in support of the Reagan Administration's perception of its interests in Central America. New possibilities were firming up for a very strategic improvement of U.S.-Argentine cooperation in the South Atlantic area. Placed against the broad interests in the subregion and Latin America as a whole, Britain's stake in the Falkland Islands did not measure up for many observers. Indeed, to many, the lingering U.S. political distaste for what was seen as a remnant of colonialism called into question the framing of the issue as one of aggression. Most Latin American governments and much of the nonaligned world were to conclude that there was an argument to be made that Britain's case was fatally flawed by the colonial origin and commercial nature of its settler population in the Falklands.

Perhaps unconsciously, many observers merged the sovereignty debate and the question of how Argentina proposed to settle that debate. Tacitly, they abandoned U.S. neutrality on the sovereignty question. They then gave more weight to one view of the merits on sovereignty than to the questions of principle (and vital U.S. interest) involved in the breach of the peace.[21]

Argentina's initial military tactics in support of the strategy of holding the islands long enough to secure recognition of her sovereignty over the Falklands was to discourage the U.K. militarily with the semblance of massive occupation and defensive preparations.[22] Deterrence of British reaction was to lead to a gradual acceptance by international opinion of their occupation. The Argentine estimate of British political will and politico-military position was that such a stunning and effective strike would leave the U.K. down on one knee and ready to formalize its loss. Such a scenario was certainly to be considered. The Junta, however, gave it a probability bordering on certainty, and acted accordingly.

There was no major Argentine military preparation to defend the retaken islands—no second half of the Malvinas plan; nor was there a creative, flexible diplomatic strategy—only tactics. If the old war game for recuperation relied on U.S. or U.N. intervention leading to resumed bilateral negotiations, the new plan seemed to rely on military bluff. Diplomacy would only be a tool to legitimize what was maintained by military *fait accompli*. When the bluff was called by the dispatch of a task force, Argentina would turn to reinforcement under the cover of the series of third-party mediations. The problem with this was that the tactics betrayed the strategy: Using the mediators as cover for military reinforcement and political recruitment abroad (in search of majority political opinion on sovereignty) limited their chance of avoiding violence precisely by too obviously counting on them to stall.

Argentine diplomacy thus held little room for concessions, rather taking an all-or-nothing approach. Holding out for guaranteed sovereignty by a date certain, Argentina abandoned the most creative aspect of the traditional "just war" plan: the return to the bargaining table without absolute insistence on the fruits of military victory. Such insistence led first to diplomatic and then to military failure.

The British and, to some extent, the U.S. delegation would view the Argentine diplomatic effort as intransigent and, at times, irrational. Henderson was told by Haig on April 21 that the Argentine leadership's style was irrational and chaotic.[23] Haig told him that there seemed to be 50 people involved in decisions. If he reached agreement on one of the points at issue with a member of the Junta, this was invariably countermanded by a corps commander entering the room an hour or so later. One British perception was that the Argentine government was not guided by a coherent or consistent strategy, but neither was it necessarily committed to a military solution given its lack of confidence.

The Mediator's Interests and Honor

Seen as literally a third party to a dispute, the mediator is as subject as the parties to his National Interests and National Honor. While there were competing U.S. interests, certainly a dominant consideration was the U.S. worldwide sys-

temic interest in a stable and peaceful world order. This tended to a large extent
to influence U.S. thinking. The United States could not any more than Great
Britain see a breach of the peace rewarded. In this sense, the mediator's institutional values and, hence, National Honor, were invoked and began to determine
strategy: If there was risk to the Galtieri government, it would grow rather than
lessen were the crisis allowed to worsen and proceed to military events and an
escalation of the stake of National Honor involved.

What would seem, however, to be a congruence of British and U.S. National
Interests, began rapidly to diverge as discussion between the two countries moved
from the strategic to the tactical period. On a tactical level, the United Kingdom
would seek to use the congruence of values with the mediator. However, from
the mediator's perspective, the most fruitful and immediately applicable tactic
would be a partial reward for Argentina; some concession that Argentina had at
the moment achieved a considerably stronger hand by its possession of the
islands. Here the difference in the mediator's strategy would emerge: Peace by
a compromise was very different from the British tactic of peace by a reinstitution
of British authority so as to deter future breaches of the peace.

London, Round One

President Reagan directed Haig to actively sound out the U.K. and Argentina
on ways of avoiding a military confrontation. Haig began that sounding process
on April 8 in London with a meeting with the senior British officials including
Prime Minister Thatcher.

The mediator's strategy depended on compromise, and his tactic was to ask
the party to concede something to make this possible. The British strategy was
founded in firmness and principle, with the advantages they convey in negotiation. Haig argued that the combination of diplomacy and force required that
something be conceded at this stage to start talks, so as to both advance discussion
and allow applicable force to be positioned.

What Haig had undertaken, in the view of the British Ambassador, was the
mission of bridging a gap between the British and Argentine positions.[24] The
British were prepared to back up with force their insistence on Argentine withdrawal, British sovereignty, British administration, and self-determination for
the Islanders.[25] Diplomacy was preferable but not in any absolute sense, and
force could and would be used. The Thatcher government pictured itself in a
political corner in which National Honor would not permit either appeasing "a
dictator" or appeasing invasion, much less the two combined. National Honor
on several planes was involved: politico-military standing, bargaining reputation,
the analogies to the historical experience of Thatcher's predecessor with an
expansionist National Socialist Germany. If Haig was thinking Waterloo,
Thatcher had Munich firmly in mind. If she was also very conscious of Gibraltar
and Hong Kong, she shared with Haig a concern for the credibility of a NATO
country.

Haig was caught between that British outlook and an Argentine administration that insisted either on:

—A time-specific negotiated solution yielding Argentine sovereignty, or

—A system of interim administration that would give Argentina a dominant role in the interim period leading inevitably to sovereignty.

Secretary Haig had said on his arrival in London that he had no American-approved solution in his kit bag. However, the British feared he had. Haig's State Department had been using as some elements of a possible solution *mutual* withdrawal and third-party peacekeeping forces, followed by negotiations presumably about the now unnegotiable: sovereignty. Haig also stated on his arrival at Heathrow Airport that the situation was very tense and very difficult. After more than six hours in meetings with Prime Minister Thatcher and senior British officials, he told the press that he was impressed by the determination of the British Government. James Reston said that Secretary Haig was concerned for the wider implications of the crisis, and was insisting that Argentina accept the principle of self-determination and withdrawal of Argentine troops before the resumption of negotiations.[26] Argentine leaders were said to have told Haig that everything relating to the crisis was negotiable except Argentina's claim of Falklands sovereignty.[27]

At this point, Haig was firm with the British Government. He did not pretend to proceed from identical interests, only parallel ones. His tactic was to insist to the British that Argentina needed a way to withdraw with its National Honor intact. He put cross-cultural emphasis on the Argentine outlook and argued the risk of an enhanced Soviet presence or role. He emphasized the "great hazards to the British of a military landing" and realistically pointed out that a solution other than a negotiated one would have public opinion costs, especially in the United States.[28] He urged Britain to be less unequivocal in asserting sovereignty and suggested an international or multinational solution as he had originally discussed with Henderson in Washington. Asked by Thatcher about his plan, Haig said he sought constructive ambiguities—a sign of a sophistication not widely attributed to his mediation.

The British Cabinet and Foreign Office felt Haig did not understand their position. Many of his April 8 themes were old material to Falklands experts and seemed to amount to a plan—a plan they found overtaken by events. Its balance seemed to them to ignore the new element in an old equation: aggression. In meetings at the Foreign Office, 10 Downing Street, and over dinner, the British Government became disillusioned at higher and higher levels. Haig's emphasis on something to give the Argentines and on avoiding war seemed to the U.K. players to limit both their options and the legitimacy of their cause.

Hence, the Prime Minister and, later, her Cabinet seemed perhaps more stern and purposeful than even they intended in response to their chosen mediator. The emphasis was on self-defense—war.

This was war as the last option, war as the consequence of aggression by others, but war nonetheless. Determined that Argentina must withdraw from the Islands and that the reimposition of British administration was a *sine qua non* of National Honor on several levels, Prime Minister Thatcher struck the U.S. Chargé d'Affaires in London as heading a government that was bellicose, high-strung, and more unpredictable than in any recent U.S. experience with the U.K.[29] Prime Minister Thatcher's thinking drew the analogies not only to dictatorship and aggression in Europe in 1930s but to the British diplomatic handling of that expansionism and the danger of appeasement. Neither as international relations nor domestic politics would Britain's definition of its own values tolerate any thought that the Falklanders were parallels to the Czechs whom Neville Chamberlain described in 1938 as a faraway people with little relevance to Great Britain.[30]

The British leadership and nation, however, were not unanimous on the subject of how to respond to that aggression. Indeed, the Falkland Islanders themselves were not, and many harbored—one town actually expressed—some of the thoughts of the new U.K. Foreign Secretary Francis Pym who expressed doubts about war as a solution during the talks. It was less a question of whether or not the Prime Minister enjoyed "the full support of the other members of her government" than of the consideration of the full range of options and their costs and benefits that was still underway when the mediator came to London.[31] The fact that the task force was en route did not mean that Britain had only one option, only that it had deployed another option. It may be that indeed the sense of continuing debate and the risk of the external appearance of confusion added to the need for the Prime Minister to express resolve in extreme terms to the mediator.

Assuring her that the United States was on Britain's side, Haig still put forward to the British the U.S. plan for a multinational but not international force on the islands to provide interim administration. The Prime Minister declined it as politically unacceptable to Britain in that it did not restore British authority, and probably unacceptable to Argentina in that it envisioned self-determination:

I pressed on the question of interposing an international force on the islands and setting up some sort of interim administration and providing for self-determination. The notion was too woolly, Mrs. Thatcher said. The House of Commons would never accept it because she was pledged to restoration of British administration, which meant the courts, public services, and all the normal apparatus of government. No vague international presence could substitute for this essential authority. She feared that we were talking about negotiations under conditions of duress, which would be a terrible insult to Britain. In any case, she felt that Argentina would never accept self-determination because all the islanders wanted to remain British. As for sovereignty: British sovereignty was a fact. It continued no matter what the Argentines had done or may do.[32]

Buenos Aires, Round One

It was Haig's judgment that either government would fall unless it could obtain its initial position: "Unless some way could be found to alter British authority and provide for an Argentinian role in the government of the Falklands, Mrs. Thatcher's terms ruled out Argentinian acceptance. If Galtieri accepted her terms, it would be the end of him."[33] Thus, the Secretary approached his first trip to Buenos Aires with the question framed as "Could I bring enough back from Buenos Aires to satisfy Mrs. Thatcher."[34]

To the British government, self-determination was nonnegotiable, and self-determination as expressed by the Kelpers meant reimposition of British rule in the Falkland Islands. There was little for the mediator to take to Buenos Aires.

Huge crowds turned out for Haig's arrival (a little tacit bargaining with the *yanqui* Foreign Minister who had just stated how impressed he was with British resolve) and even larger ones the next morning (a classic, full-scale Plaza de Mayo official turnout of over one-quarter million, and the first increase in bargaining intensity). The talks had not yet started, but the first signals had been sent and misread. The Government was transmitting popular will and its force; the mediator was reading authoritarianism and recalling National Socialism in interwar Axis Europe.

Haig met in Buenos Aires on Saturday, April 10, with Argentine Foreign Minister Costa Mendez for four hours and held two short meetings with President Leopoldo Galtieri. The mediator had two parallel tactics to emphasize: normative pressure based on Resolution 502 and a request for concessions based on the possibility of avoiding war.

The opening points for the Argentine side were references to the crowds, regime survival, destabilization of the South and West, and Soviet bloc aid in defense of continued Argentine occupation of the Islands. They supported Argentine solutions by addressing Argentine problems. Insofar as these bargaining points solved no British problems, they were not germane. Compromise and negotiation, British government needs and survival, were reviewed and substantively ignored. The bottom line was that Argentina had seized and would maintain control, terming it sovereignty. Sovereignty might be negotiated, reasoned over, and even surrendered ceremonially and militarily *if* guaranteed politically following a decent interval; but regardless, Argentina must have it. This was all the more so, Galtieri argued, given the tumult outside in the Plaza de Mayo.

The principal operational question was: In the event that Argentine withdrawal and a halting of the British Task Force could be arranged, on what basis and by whom would the islands be governed *ad interim*?

Discussion began, according to Argentine diplomats, with the Costa Mendez Washington proposal of May 6: A joint interim government with participation by Britain, Argentina, and a third party—possibly the United States. (One does not find much note of Argentine proposals or plans in the historical literature of the Falklands.) The Argentine government still had doubts about the proposal as not guaranteeing Argentine sovereignty as the outcome of negotiation. At a minimum, the Argentine flag must fly until its sovereignty was formalized by negotiations. Argentina's public position was that it did not "reconquer" the Falkland Islands simply to return to the status quo ante. Argentina was insisting that its occupation merited a British concession; that the situation had changed because of the use of force. Argentina had earned major British concessions. (The British Cabinet saw the use of force as changing the situation in an opposite way: making major concessions to Argentina impossible.) Like the British Cabinet, the Junta did not share the mediator's priority of avoiding large-scale hostilities.

Again, several facets of National Honor were key to a party's concerns: Galtieri spoke of National Honor, heavily tied to military honor; that is, holding ground taken by force of arms, or securing guaranteed if delayed de jure sovereignty via "negotiations." He also had clearly in mind both the domestic and international image of the regime itself: "You will understand that the Argentine government has to look good too."[35] British honor was considered. Any solution had to be honorable, but it had also to be an Argentine win. Galtieri, if not the whole Junta, saw the conflict as having been honorably resolved by force: Britain could stand down because of a military *fait accompli*. If one were powerless, there was no shame.

Each side had now expressed distaste for the mediator's device of joint interim administration. Any idea rejected by both sides can't be all bad. The mediator persisted. The two teams agreed to try to edit the U.S. proposal along the lines discussed and reassemble at 6:00 P.M.

A major problem was that the Junta still believed the British task force to be political rather than military in nature. They failed to perceive the "continuum" nature of such an operation: Should gunboat diplomacy fail, one uses the guns. Haig pointed out that the task force was en route, was a real military threat, and would likely prevail militarily. The Junta did not concur.

The Junta was equally unimpressed with political warnings by Haig and U.S. General Vernon Walters that if it came to war, the United States would have to take the British side and the consequences for the Argentine government would be disastrous. Through long sessions on Saturday and Sunday, the Argentines clung to Galtieri's belief that all they had to discuss was an end to sanctions, Argentine settlement during interim administration, and the date by which resumed talks would lead to Argentine sovereignty.

The U.S. redraft of late afternoon, Saturday, April 10 (the Gompert Draft) proposed:

—Mutual withdrawal in accord with Resolution 502 within two weeks under the observation of the United States, Canada, and two Latin states;

—Communications and (of key import to Argentina) *movement to the Islands* to be reopened; and

—Sovereignty to be negotiated by year's end.

At the scheduled 6:00 P.M. Saturday session, the Argentine side rejected this version also as not preserving what Argentina had won. They informed U.S. Assistant Secretary of State Enders that Argentina had not taken the islands simply to hand them back.

Foreign Minister Costa Mendez proposed later that evening the first of the guaranteed sovereignty tradeoffs: Open transportation would have to permit Argentine immigration or the talks would have to be designed to arrange the manner and date of the formal turnover of the islands. The Argentine side was told by the mediator that this would never be accepted by the Thatcher government.

Haig started over with Costa Mendez and his military and civilian advisors (rather than with Galtieri) late on the night of Saturday, April 10. And for "eleven hours of intensive and often tumultuous negotiation," there were only occasional breaks and periodic steak sandwiches and coffee during the marathon session. Until the early morning of Easter Sunday, April 11, the mediator sought something that would have value and persuasiveness in London. The session was helped by the imposition of sanctions by the EEC. Haig also feels that Galtieri was beginning to get a sense that time was running out militarily.[36] In the early morning, Galtieri gave the mediator a new set of minima: "He could not withdraw both his military and administrative presence from the Malvinas and last a week."[37] On that basis, the U.S. redraft went back to the original text with two changes: "Argentinian troops would leave the islands and the British administration would be restored. But economic and financial measures against Argentina would be terminated within two weeks, the flags of the six nations would be flown at the headquarters of the consortium and finally national flags could be displayed at the residences and on the official automobiles of all countries represented on the islands."[38] The two teams had decided at one o'clock in the morning on Easter Sunday that Argentina's presence could be honorably preserved by the liberal use of flags by the Argentine representatives on the island.

The next morning, however, as Haig was departing for London, Costa Mendez reintroduced guaranteed sovereignty, that is, either freedom of Argentine immigration or a guaranteed transfer at the end of the negotiating period. This "proposal" of April 11 was a nonstarter.

Haig, nonetheless, found the Argentine Junta a little more flexible than the Thatcher government after one round with each. The U.K. was seen as not afraid of military engagement, especially as it might help "save face" and politically nullify the Argentine surprise invasion. In an unscrambled radio-telephone conversation with President Reagan from his plane, Haig's strategy options were said to have been spelled out as including heavy pressure on each side to avoid further hostilities. (Reagan: "Don't hold back on making me the bad guy and insisting on restraint if that's necessary.")[39]

Sadly, Argentina would mistake such U.S. requests for British restraint as a *solution* rather than a device to permit them time to research mutual compromise. Urging restraint on Argentina was viewed in Buenos Aires first as lip service[40] and then a stab in the back. If the idea of compromise enjoyed only sporadic vogue at 10 Downing Street, it was seen only as an export commodity in the Casa Rosada.

Public Diplomacy, Public Pressure

If both Argentina and Great Britain expressed themselves to the United States as agreeable to the idea of discussing a peaceful solution, neither foreswore the right to pursue its maximum demands in public.

Argentine Foreign Minister Nicanor Costa Mendez, after his first meeting with Haig, said that he was sure that an honorable and just peace could be achieved. However, by Sunday, April 11, Argentine officials in Buenos Aires were expressing their pessimism and their doubts about peaceful settlement to the press. As Haig returned to London from Buenos Aires, indeed as early as April 8, Argentine sources had hinted that they might shift their policies in favor of the USSR and Cuba should the United States oppose their occupation of the Falklands. They cited their good trade ties in proof of that possibility and as a way of countering a presumption of continuing cooperation such as in Central America. The Argentines let Haig know what they thought of his using Resolution 502 as an argument in their letter to the Security Council the day after he left Buenos Aires: 502's call for withdrawal was invalid unless its call for case-fire was also observed—that is, the British Task Force was stopped.

Great Britain likewise maintained public pressure in support of its position: Defense Minister John Nott said that the U.K. would "shoot first" in the Total Exclusion Zone. Political determination would be increasingly stressed to and through the press by the Thatcher government. Well might President Reagan ask his Secretary of State on April 9, "Did you get any idea as to whether the emotion that you met in your meetings goes beyond the Parliament to the people as well?"[41]

Even the mediator was seen as exercising pressure through the press. Secretary Haig's statement of April 8 about not having an American-approved solution in his "kit bag" was read cynically in Buenos Aires. The Argentine reaction was that he was therefore in London to get his instructions. He also stated on his arrival at Heathrow Airport that the situation was very tense and very difficult. After more than six hours of meetings with Prime Minister Thatcher and senior British officials, he told the press that he was "highly impressed" by the "firm determination" of the British Government. In Buenos Aires, he would cite as a basis for thinking a settlement was possible not only the Reagan Administration's improved relations with Argentina but Resolution 502 and its call for

Argentine withdrawal. James Reston said that Secretary Haig was concerned for the wider implications of the crisis and was insisting that Argentina accept the principle of self-determination and withdrawal of Argentine troops before the resumption of negotiations.[42] Argentine leaders were said to have told Haig that everything relating to the crisis was negotiable except Argentina's claim of Falklands sovereignty.[43] All this translated in Buenos Aires as public pressure for Argentine withdrawal.

The press began to back-influence the manipulators. Thatcher was toughened by media polls showing a majority of Britons in agreement with her "hard line" on the Falklands before her government had firmly adopted it. Not only did over three-quarters favor recuperation, but more than one-half preferred force to diplomacy as the means. Haig was undercut in U.S. policy-making by a leak overstating U.S. help to the U.K. and White House reaction to media coverage of Haig's personal involvement in the crisis. With the United States attempting to mediate, the U.S. press was urging the commitment of a U.S. carrier and listing British options in a prescriptive way: Newsweek editorialized on April 26 that torpedoing a ship would not win the battle of the Falklands but might persuade Argentina to negotiate more seriously.

Public speculation on negotiating options became very creative. Haig was believed to have carried an Argentine proposal for replacing Argentine troops with peacekeepers, joint administration of the islands, and *dual citizenship* for the Kelpers. There was also said to be a "loose package of negotiations including simultaneous pullback of British and Argentine forces after Great Britain recognizes Argentine sovereignty."[44] "Mr. Haig returns to London with a three-point proposal for a simultaneous pullback of the British Navy and withdrawal of Argentine forces, British recognition of Argentine sovereignty, and interim administration of the islands by the United States, Britain and Argentina."[45] There was little British interest in such Argentine ultimatums.

London, Round Two

On Monday, April 12, Haig returned to London as the British blockade took effect, and Peru proposed a 72-hour truce.[46]

The mediator now believed that British firmness was not having the intended effect of producing compliance with Resolution 502. Some sort of compromise in the British position would be needed. The Cabinet met with the U.S. delegation at 10 Downing Street and reviewed the U.S. draft. The review, however, was overtaken by the Argentine "walk-back" presaged a *bout de papier* given by Costa Mendez to Haig as he had boarded his plane. Costa Mendez talked to the press, asked for time in a conversation with Haig, and only then confirmed the walk-back. While Haig was in London, the Argentine position hardened as Costa Mendez conferred with his military government.

Haig had U.S. suggestions to offer, prepared by the U.S. team during the parallel talks in Buenos Aires. There was more British interest in the most novel of these: tripartite interim administration until the end of the year while discussion of sovereignty proceeded (or in the British view, began); this certainly evoked more interest than in the quadrilateral guarantees with both parties present.

Haig called Buenos Aires in the afternoon but it was not until after midnight in London and he had spent 11 hours with the British that Costa Mendez rejected the multiparty idea as leaving sovereignty open—the Argentine maximum demand was that sovereignty was settled and needed only ratification. Nothing that resembled the "colonial" *status quo ante bellum,* even leaseback, could be discussed. Argentina would, he said, withdraw militarily only if the symbols of sovereignty—flag, governor, administration, communications, currency, and police—remained in place under U.S. guarantee. The almost casual Argentine reintroduction of Argentine civil administration and freedom to settle the islands cancelled all the apparent progress made to date.

The Argentine rejection of three-way administration left the British on good ground with the mediator. They in turn insisted that both Argentine troops and Argentine flag must go—any solution other than the withdrawal of those Argentine symbols would topple Prime Minister Thatcher's government.

Haig's mission nearly collapsed on April 13. The Argentines had in effect reneged on the whole understanding with Haig about the possible terms of settlement. The new article from the Monday evening Junta meeting would have the effect not only of prejudicing negotiations in favor of full Argentine sovereignty but also of setting the date in advance. (Haig had thought their agenda for the meeting was limited to ratification of the U.S. idea of interim administration.) If the withdrawal of concession was deliberate, it was badly timed.[47]

The U.K. had implied some flexibility on Monday: It might be possible to consider joint administration while discussing sovereignty. Britain had caught up with Argentina, but Argentina then backed off with its timetable and *governor* demand.

On Tuesday at an extra session the Prime Minister made it plain to Secretary Haig that Argentine troop withdrawal was a precondition for negotiations, and that the wishes of the Falklanders would govern British positions in any negotiations. Raising the political-military temperature slightly, she not only warned against any Argentine testing of the TEZ (Total Exclusion Zone) but said that any such challenge would be taken as evidence that diplomacy had been abandoned in favor of force. The stated British priorities were:

—Implementation of Resolution 502;

—Self determination; and

—No Argentine access or pressure (i.e., no fixed deadline) during negotiations.

The Prime Minister conceded only that the interests of the islanders might be considered as well as their wishes, and that the islands' administration must at least be "recognizably British."[48] Upon leaving London, Haig said he had received new ideas that indicated British willingness to pay some diplomatic price to avoid the necessity of using force.

He also had produced an Argentine stand-down on continued civil administration. He had both offered to Costa Mendez to return to Buenos Aires and tacitly threatened to break off the mediation. 'The results will be felt within hours if I do not continue with this process.''[49] He made it quite clear that the governor was not a workable element, and that were that withdrawn, a workable solution might be at hand. Costa Mendez called back within 12 hours, by noon on Tuesday, April 13, which would have made it very early in the morning in Buenos Aires. The Argentine government dropped the idea of an Argentine governor. It was informally suggested that if London gave indications of flexibility, Argentina would propose dropping the governor in favor of a British agreement to comply with the 1964 U.N. declaration on Decolonization, that is, to decolonize the islands. The British fleet was to confine its movements and the United States was not to assist Britain militarily in any way. Haig assured Costa Mendez that on the latter point the United States would not go beyond "customary patterns of cooperation" but that any military limits on Britain without a withdrawal agreement would be unrealistic.[50]

Haig consulted with the British government and was able to tell Costa Mendez that there seemed to be a sense that the negotiation could continue. Haig would go next to Buenos Aires.

Washington, Round One

The mediation seemed to the press and public to have stalled. As Secretary Haig returned to the United States, British officials were being openly confident about U.S. backing and pessimistic about a diplomatic solution before the arrival of the British Task Force. Haig briefed the President, describing the situation as increasingly dangerous since neither side showed flexibility. They decided to sharpen the point to be made to Argentina. On April 14, Reagan urged Galtieri by phone to show flexibility and to exercise restraint. (Galtieri had called to ask Reagan to ask him to stop the British fleet.)

Editorial opinion in the United States began to express doubt about the effectiveness or even the desirability of the U.S. mediating role. *The New York Times,* in its editorial of April 15, took the position that U.S. shuttle diplomacy was overdoing U.S. evenhandedness and failing to promote U.S. interests, as well as averting the attention of the Secretary of State from the Middle East, Central America, and arms control.

Britain publicly sketched out its political, politico-military, and military posture toward the crisis. On April 14, Prime Minister Margaret Thatcher, in a speech to the House of Commons, stated publicly that a prerequisite for settlement was the withdrawal of Argentine troops from the Islands. She further insisted that, first, the sovereignty of the Falklands was not affected by the act of invasion and that, second, what mattered most in future negotiations was the wishes of

the Falkland Islanders themselves. Britain had set her political goal: self-determination, and thus the status quo desired by the Kelper majority.

Thatcher reaffirmed Britain's desire for a peaceful solution, but warned that
if the 200-mile blockade zone around the islands were tested, the British
would conclude that "the search for a peaceful solution has been abandoned."
Any such challenge to the TEZ would be taken as evidence that diplomacy
had been abandoned in favor of force. Penetration would meet with "the necessary action."[51] Britain had set the limit of its preference for diplomacy over
force—engagement at sea or in the air. Argentina was not to consolidate what
it held.

Britain meanwhile moved to strengthen naval and air forces. This included
not only the 24-hour ship Royal Fleet Auxiliary recommissioning and chartering
tankers and extra cargo and passenger ships, one of which would carry over 20
Harrier jump jets to the area in addition to the approximately 20 already enroute.
The Navy requisitioned four trawlers to be used as mine sweepers. The Air
Force announced that its Nimrod reconnaisance aircraft were flying scouting
missions from Ascension Island (3,500 miles from the Falklands). C–130 aircraft
were sent to Ascension. The task force now outnumbered the 17-ship Argentine
Navy. There was public discussion of the task group reaching the Falklands by
April 20. The threat of force was now fully credible.

The Argentines, for their part, stated that the British fleet must halt before
Argentine forces would withdraw. The Argentine government staked out its
minimum political condition: that the Argentines retain some element of sovereignty—for instance, the continued presence of the Argentine flag over the
islands—during discussions on the area's future. This was a potentially useful
minimum demand. It reflected the failure of the tactic of halting the British at
Ascension.

Argentina continued airlifting troops and equipment to the Islands. The Ninth
Infantry joined the 2,500 Marines, bringing total forces there to about 9,000.
Armor, artillery, antiaircraft units, and tactical aviation were added.

The 180,000-man Argentine Army was beefed up by retaining the 80,500
trained 1981 draftees. Another 450,000 reservists were available. (The United
Kingdom had about 320,000 men under arms.) Most of the Argentine fleet
remained at Puerto Belgrano, but there seemed to be little doubt that the Navy
would be deployed to the Islands—about 375 miles south—in the event of
hostilities.

European diplomats noted to the press that while Prime Minister Thatcher's
resolve should not be doubted, some degree of tough posturing by both Argentine
and British leadership was primarily intended for domestic consumption. Undoubtedly true, but the escalation of political firmness and military capability
was most clearly and principally aimed across the bargaining table. Furthermore,
to the extent that populations need to be rallied, the domestic invocation of
National Honor is also an "input" to the negotiation/mediation as well as preparation for the threat or use of force.

Customary Patterns of Cooperation

One classic dilemma of the nation-state as a mediator was exemplified in the Falklands crisis by the problem of ongoing relationships with the two parties. The mediator would of course maintain normal diplomatic and trade ties with the parties; however, normally one would not enter upon new or expanded relationships that were not evenly applicable to both parties. Indeed, Haig had so assured Costa Mendez from London.[52] Nonetheless, the United States, during its mediation, expanded military supply under these relationships considerably more with the United Kingdom than with Argentina.

To say that the U.S.-British relationship had a lot of this expansion built into it in advance was of little comfort to the Argentine Government. Whether or not Argentina sought a neutral mediator, as it publicly professed, its internal and public decision making was made more difficult by a gradually emerging perception of a tilt by the mediator, not only in public normative statements and private menaces but in a growing supplies and services relationship with the United Kingdom.

Much was made of satellites in the press during the crisis. The United States and the Soviet Union are known to never confirm or deny questions such as whether they maintain intelligence satellites that can when so directed cover the South Atlantic.[53] Great Britain and Argentina do not, yet both parties received information on weather and ship movements and we do not know the sources. The United States and the U.K. have an ongoing, routinized sharing of intelligence information which is more developed than the exchanges with Argentina, but the Argentines received both weather and movements information. They may have had Soviet help. The U.S. may have wanted Argentina specifically to know when their navy was in danger of encountering Royal Navy units so as to avoid armed conflict, which it was felt would be the end of any negotiation. Argentina may have received other data from the Soviets as well, confirming the findings of its commercial aircraft tracking the British and of the aircraft quickly provided by Brazil. At heart, the fuss over satellites was political as each side operated ships, submarines and aircraft in the South Atlantic by this stage.

The following list of material supplied to Great Britain by the United States has not been repudiated by either government because each wisely neither confirms nor denies speculations on sensitive matters: 200 Sidewinder AIM–9L air-to-air missiles; Harrier-Sidewinder adaptor plates; eight Stinger antiaircraft systems; Vulcan Phalanx air-defense gun system; Harpoon antiship missiles; Snake air-to-ground radar-seeking missiles; 18 CTU–2A air drop containers; 4,700 tons airfield matting; one C–47 helicopter engine; 350 torpedo exhaust valves; 12 1/2 million gallons aviation fuel; satellite dishes and encrypting facilities; submarine detection equipment; flare cartridges and M130 dispensing systems; 60mm illuminating mortar rounds; 40mm high-explosive ammunition; other assorted ammunition; night vision goggles; special mess heaters; and long-range patrol ration packs ("America's Falklands War" *The Economist*, March 3, 1984,

p. 31.) The list strikes logistics specialists as reasonable. It constitutes a solid logistics backup, but is nothing near the fantasies of those Argentines who delude themselves that they were defeated by the United States not the United Kingdom.

The military cooperation grew rapidly. One critical question in judging the appropriateness of the mediator's role as arms supplier is when key items were *delivered*. A related question is whether Argentina was denied any ongoing supplies, services, or cooperation. The wider question is whether a mediator, often chosen not for his disinterest and remoteness but precisely because he is a partner, can then carry on customary patterns of cooperation.

By mid-April, each side had doubts about this pattern: The Argentine Junta felt that the United States was aligning itself with the U.K.; the U.K., with better information but not much more perspective, thought the United States was entirely too evenhanded.

Britain needed strong support from its closest ally in the face of an invasion of what it views as territory for which it is responsible. The U.S.-U.K. debate was about the most effective form that support could take. It was the U.S. view that negotiating neutrality was to be exhausted before military options.

Argentina laid claim to the new-found friendship, which General Galtieri was fond of calling an alliance. After a difficult half-century of political standoff, Argentina felt her new attitude warranted U.S. support for her just claims. The United States should be entirely neutral in word and deed, not just during mediation but beyond any failure of the mediation. Argentina first sought to neutralize the United States as mediator, and then turned to the mediator to deter British military reaction.

That was an unobtainable maximum demand. Beyond the special relationship, with its significant presumptions about political, military, and intelligence consultation and cooperation, much of U.S.-U.K. political-military cooperation was by prearrangement and even contract precisely so as to depoliticize it and allow for very rapid calculations in crisis. In a significant sense, the special relationship compromises the sovereignty of each party mutually. Argentina had never sought or secured such a relationship. (If it received any help along these lines from the Soviet Union, it did so *ad hoc* and apparently with a clever arms-length refusal to pay a price.)

The special relationship was one factor that Argentina should have considered before it created the spring 1982 crisis. They factored it in as a permissive contingency (United States to restrain U.K.) but ignored its reciprocal obligations (United States obliged to help U.K., limited in its ability to restrain U.K.).

That such relationships could not be engineered or undone in the midst of a politico-military crisis was recognized tacitly by the Junta in requesting *and then retaining* the United States as mediator.

Buenos Aires, Round Two

Haig followed with talks in Buenos Aires from April 15 to April 19. He impressed on the Argentines the long-standing nature of U.S. obligations to the

United Kingdom. He warned that when the first major armed clash took place, the United States would have to stand at the side of the U.K.

At the opening of this second round of talks in Buenos Aires, the British fleet was nearing Ascension Island, then a week's estimated steaming time from the Falklands. (Haig let the Junta know via an open phone call that "British military action was imminent.")[54] Diplomatically, the fleet was seen as steaming at half-speed. It was more likely consolidating supplies in the order they would be needed, cross-decking troops and their materiel between ships to assemble landing waves, and refitting before the final leg south. The Junta began to focus on using diplomacy to hold the British fleet, which they now saw as a possible military threat, at Ascension. From the disbelief shown during Haig's first visit at the idea that the U.K. would use force, the Junta progressed to incredulity. Costa Mendez told Haig: "I am truly surprised that the British will go to war for such a small problem as these few rocky islands."[55] By the end of Buenos Aires Round Two, lead elements of the Task Force were two days from South Georgia.

On arrival on April 15, Haig presented the counterdraft worked out in London to the Argentines: "Argentinian withdrawal from the islands, a halt by the British fleet at a distance of 1,000 miles from the Falklands, an interim administration by Britain and Argentina with the United States also present in the islands, an immediate end to economic and financial sanctions and guaranteed completion of negotiations on the question of sovereignty by the last day of 1982. It seemed inconceivable to me that any rational government could reject these terms."[56] There were six hours of talks leading to an optimistic air on the fringes of the negotiation.

The Junta rejected the terms and made a counterproposal before midnight: The plan shifted the Argentine emphasis from guaranteed sovereignty to control of and a key administrative role in the interim administration. The Argentine proposal posited mutual withdrawal over 14 days; the Royal Navy pulling back roughly 3,000 miles to Ascension Island and the Argentines 300 miles to their home ports and bases. Drawdown was to be half in the first week and half in the second. The plan was intended to guarantee effective Argentine possession that would itself lead to sovereignty. The governor was in effect back in, but a British governor would be there also.[57] Immigration was still envisioned, and the talks were still weighted toward Argentine sovereignty. The proposal was in written form and was to date the most complete document in the negotiation.

It was also almost the end of the negotiation. At this third switchback in the circuitous course of Argentine decision making, Haig told Costa Mendez, "I am sure the British will shoot when they see this message."[58] The mediator began to pack his bags, pending a change in the Argentine position:

It would be fruitless to carry these latest proposals to London. To do so, moreover, would be unfair to the British government because it would shift the onus for ending the negotiations onto it, when in truth the fault lay in Buenos Aires.[59]

On Friday, April 16, Haig met at the Casa Rosada with Galtieri. Galtieri was concentrating on a problem of image: U.S. Embassy contingency evacuations of nonessential personnel to Montevideo. He might better have thought through what the perceived need to evacuate said about the Argentine government stirring up demonstrations and the real judgment of the U.S. government about his strategy and tactics. Haig had trouble getting him to focus on substance: the advantages of the last-agreed-on draft. Haig asked for and got a meeting with the full Junta the next day at 10:00 A.M.

On Saturday, April 17, the Costa Mendez counterproposal presented to the U.S. Secretary Thursday evening in Buenos Aires became the focus for further negotiation between the mediator and the full Junta. The mood of the talks was bad on Saturday morning. The mediator had his bags very obviously loaded onto his plane, and flight plans were filed for London. Haig was indeed expected in London over the weekend but he had nothing to bring to the British by way of lowered Argentine demands, which had been the condition of his return. The British government even sniped "on background" to the press at tripartite administration while Haig was trying to sell the idea to the Junta.[60] Haig was finally face-to-face with the two Junta members whom he considered the roadblocks— the shadowy figures of Admiral Jorge Anaya and Air Force Brigadier Basilio Lami-Dozo he envisioned as countermanding and retracting agreed progress.

The costs of the mediating role were becoming clearer to them and to Haig. U.S. officials began to express themselves as concerned about the U.S. interests involved in what they insisted were likely to be successful efforts of Secretary of State Haig to find a diplomatic solution. Either the British or Argentine government or both might fall from power over most imaginable outcomes. The U.S. diplomatic effort might, in a seldom considered cost, drive further wedges between the United States and its European allies who were unhappy with U.S. formal and public neutrality on the issue of the Falklands. The possible cost to the improving U.S.-Argentine relationship was becoming more sharply defined as Secretary Haig found it increasingly necessary to point out to the Junta the likely results of maintaining its current attitudes and positions.

Prime Minister Thatcher cut short a weekend in the country to return to London, fueling speculation that the mediation was going badly and she might soon meet with Haig.

Haig was not, however, in any position to return to London. He needed further sessions with senior Argentine officials; he was still trying to avert war and he was pushing his original Five Points:

—Argentine withdrawal;

—Diversion of the British fleet;

—An end to sanctions;

—The establishment of provisional administration under Argentine-U.K.-U.S. supervision (until December 1982); and then

—Negotiations over the final status of the Islands to *begin* December 1982. The mediator's
view was that sovereignty was best left aside during the crisis and negotiated later.
(How the islands were to be administered after December 1982 was left open-ended.)

London would not get open-ended talks; Buenos Aires would not get a set
deadline or guaranteed possession.

The Argentine military committees considered the plan beginning the evening
of the 17th. The Army General Officers met twice. The consensus was that the
mediator was attempting to gloss over the key issue of sovereignty with his
proposals of Friday and Saturday; sovereignty was indivisible and both parties
could not claim to have won it. The transition/administration focus was a ruse
to secure Argentina's concession of the advantages. Haig's new ideas looked to
the Junta like cession of these advantages of occupation, and merely a recycling
of Buenos Aires Round One. His concentration on avoiding hostilities was not
the top priority of the flag officers. His talks would begin (in December 1982)
when they wished them to *end*. The wishes of the Islanders might lead to
independence, a loss of the "colonization" argumentation, and their irrevocable
loss to the Argentine nation.

Argentina rejected the proposal by indirection. Argentine officials were clear,
at least in public, at this point on their position: There was not going to be a
peaceful settlement unless Britain conceded the sovereignty issue. Anaya's navy
was prepared (they believed) to defend the islands. Lami Dozo was hesitant
about war, but his service decided to hold out. (An Argentine official put the
Argentine reaction at the time succinctly: Haig "still [didn't] believe that we
[were] willing to go to war over the principle, as he [thought] the English [were].
Today we hope he is learning."[61]) Galtieri led the 54 Army Generals toward
war. The three services were unanimous. Haig met far into Saturday night with
Galtieri.

U.S. leverage was apparently slipping. The press took this up as a theme.
Roger Fisher of Harvard and others began calling for U.N. mediation. The British
battle fleet was said to have passed Ascension Island, the symbolic halfway
point. Fifteen days after their initial landing, Argentine troops totalled over 9,000.

Realizing his "Five Points" were not selling, Haig reworked the Argentine
proposals with Foreign Minister Costa Mendez. Haig secured agreement on April
17 from each of the three members of the Junta that the two drafts could be
merged: that agreement was possible. The teams broke up into drafting groups
again but the drafts did not converge following the subsequent round of drafting.

Haig pressured the Argentines with the special relationship. The Argentines
pressured Haig with their estimate that they had 11 of the 14 votes needed for
the two-thirds majority to convene the 21 parties to the Rio Treaty of Hemispheric
Defense to consider an extra-hemispheric threat to the peace.

New Argentine proposals were delivered to the U.S. delegation in the early
morning of April 18, and the Foreign Ministers and their teams were reconvened
for a session at the Casa Rosada at 2:00 P.M. on April 18. Around 8:30 P.M.,

Haig met with Galtieri. Haig told the Junta two new elements of his "determination" points: The Thatcher government, the closest NATO ally of the United States, was not to fall. Either Argentina stopped inflating reports of its ability to defend the Islands and negotiated on the basis of Resolution 502, or the United States sided with the U.K. The first 10 of almost 12 hours of continuous negotiation produced little change. (Secretary Haig attributes this to a consensus process the Junta was conducting with Corps Commanders and equivalents in all three services. He also attributes the Argentine walk-back on withdrawal of forces to this government by committee.)

The Argentines thought they were doing rather well at this point. Their perspective on April 18 was that their draft (the third of three in the 16–19 April talks) was worked by the two sides and in the end met all the conditions the U.S. had suggested. They recollect that Haig termed it miraculous, and that this was essentially what he sent to London (minus point eight) for consideration.

When the Junta reconvened near midnight, the proposal first boiled down to:

—Joint administration with U.S. or other international supervision for periods ranging from eight months to five years;

—Argentine representation on the Island Council; and

—U.N. resolution of the sovereignty question as a variant on guaranteed sovereignty.

Agreement was reached by early Monday morning:

By 2:40 A.M. on April 19, we had produced a draft, acceptable to the Argentinians, providing for an immediate cessation of hostilities and the withdrawal of forces, an Argentinian presence on the island under a U.S. guarantee, and negotiations leading to a resolution of the question by December 31, 1982. I believed that Mrs. Thatcher would have great difficulty in accepting this text.[62]

Haig met again with the Argentine negotiators on Monday morning from 9:30 until 10:00, "to clear up a number of unresolved points. This, too, was a strenuous session, but by 1:00 P.M., we had in hand a modified text that anticipated some of the British objections."[63]

This text was conveyed to the British telegraphically at 9:00 P.M. on the evening of Monday, April 19. The British had considerable reservations about the Argentine peace proposals that Haig forwarded.[64] The Junta, however, reneged on these simple terms via another of Costa Mendez's airport notes—a sad and losing negotiating gambit. A "new" condition was imposed on Haig, after he had telegraphed the previous terms to London and was in fact en route London, to the effect that Argentine sovereignty had to be guaranteed as the outcome of the close-ended talks. The further last-minute insistence on guaranteed Argentine sovereignty would have been completely unacceptable to the U.K. and was therefore withheld by Haig as unproductive. The essential elements of settlement in the British view were:

—Return to British authority in the islands, including the return of the Governor-General, as well as

—Self-determination for the Kelpers.

In their view, the aggression had to be completely undone and the prewar situation restored as a vital element of principle.

The British would not confirm reports that the Argentine proposals included referring the sovereignty issue to the United Nations. Great Britain, of course, perceived the U.N. as favorable to the Argentine position on sovereignty. The General Assembly had in the past voted this way overwhelmingly. The Security Council had passed Resolution 502 but was seen as slipping, becoming as concerned with counterforce as with first use of force. In this, the Argentine strategy of holding and legitimizing was working.

Argentina seemed to the world not to be taking advantage of the Haig mediation, except to dig in on West Falkland Island. The perception of the Argentine negotiating team was different. They did not feel at one end of a line of communication but more shut off from the U.K. than when they had direct talks. They could recollect no statement to them of British demands or minima—even in response to specific questions—only Haig plans and Haig interpretations. (In this view, the first concrete demands they saw from the U.K. were to be on May 17 during the Perez de Cuellar mediation.) Further, the Argentines felt that their five proposals, or plans, given to the mediator in April, had not been answered and might not have even been shown to the United Kingdom as integral proposals. He had not held the British Task Force at Ascension, nor was he reining in Chile—the traditional enemy now felt to be menacing the Argentine rear. Haig clearly meant to block invocation of the Rio Treaty on Hemispheric Defense by Argentina.

In these internal Argentine perceptions one forsees the breakdown not just of the Haig shuttle after Buenos Aires Round Two, but indeed of the mediation itself on April 30: The mediator was pursuing peace and the reinstitution of international law and order, while Argentina was pursuing the Falklands Islands. Argentina was not responding to the mediator's articulation of norms and risks because it did not perceive them. They saw the dynamic as quite different: The mediator was not meeting their needs.

The Argentine government was still adamant about the guarantee of Argentine sovereignty. This being met by an equally firm British stance that open-ended negotiations would be the only negotiations upon which the U.K. would enter, Argentina began pursuing other tracks. It was moving out on the spiral, already in the process of requesting a convocation of the Organ of Consultation of the Rio Treaty and mentioning to foreign offices and diplomatic missions that Argentina fully intended to invoke the "attack on one, an attack on all" clause in the 1947 document. Not all moves out on the spiral, however, had as much political impact as they generated confusion and contradictions. Any change of venue or entry into new fora must be coordinated with ongoing diplomatic and military efforts.

The concessions Argentina was willing to make were in the area of interim administration. Its position on the return of a British presence was softening in direct proportion to absolute firmness on the eventual guarantee of Argentine sovereignty (now via the U.N. decision ploy).

Argentine negotiators felt too that they had made real concessions de facto in the islands (no major changes in customs or life-style) and were willing to consider more: an elected Islander council, English-language education, full compensation for property if desired, and return of the British flag and officials to make the governmental transition.

Argentina offered to withdraw its troops in favor of joint administration and full Argentine sovereignty by the end of 1982. There seemed no way around Argentine insistence on guaranteed sovereignty. There had been hope until wheels-ups that Galtieri might settle for Territorial Integrity of Argentina as the stated agenda of the proposed talks (as he could interpret this as implying unification of the Falklands with Argentina) rather than sovereignty which was unacceptable to Great Britain.

Haig judged that not only could Costa Mendez not deliver that compromise, but he raised the stakes as Haig's departure approached with the announcement that Argentina was assembling the OAS and then added a new demand, such that nothing could be agreed in Buenos Aires.

As Haig departed, however, the Argentine Foreign Minister believed Haig should be able to make peace with the Argentine "Gray Text" of April 18/19, as these were the best terms Argentina was prepared to offer. In Buenos Aires Round One, they had offered flexibility on *either* sovereignty *or* administration of the islands, and felt they had been even more flexible in Round Two. This was Argentina's third proposal of Round Two and the Junta felt they had gone some way to compromise, including the new element of admitting reintroduction of (largely) British civil administration and of referring not to the interests or wishes of the Islanders, but to their rights.

In fact, from the Argentine perspective it was *they* who were being undercut. A key flaw was already developing in what had been agreed with the mediator: they put great weight on what they believed was an understanding that the U.S. would tacitly guarantee eventual sovereignty even though it was not in the text offered to London. This allowed them to be forthcoming in the Grey Text of April 18/19. However, in discussion they heard the mediator refer to there being little possibility of the application of the U.S. tacit guarantee. As the tacit guarantee seemed to fade, the Argentine team turned to the device of Point Eight: explicit guarantee of eventual sovereignty. The subtleties of the tacit bargain evaporated, and the Gray Text suddenly lost the deftness which had made it highly viable in Argentine eyes.

The mediator still saw enough promise in the formula to send it to London, but only without Article Eight. He would later describe this omission to Galtieri as his first active intervention as a mediator. Even without Article Eight—and Argentine sovereignty was the most widely accepted Argentine claim in the international community—the United Kingdom did not accept the Gray Text.

The United Nations was standing by, but being discreet. On April 15, U.N. Secretary General Perez de Cueller said that he did not wish to take any steps that would undermine the mediation by Secretary Haig.

Despite the Argentine press manipulation by the Government, the mood in Buenos Aires began to evolve from one of jubilation about the seizure of the Islands to the recognition of the serious prospect of war and destruction. The popular conception of the Haig mission was still that the essence would be to soften the British position and thereby produce both peace and continued Argentine occupation. This was probably the major distortion by the Junta of the diplomacy of the Falklands crisis, both avoiding the consequences of and, indeed, misdirecting and thereby "changing" public opinion. It was done to make sure that National Honor dictated only one clear course: continued occupation of the Malvinas. It was announced that President Galtieri would fly to the islands on April 22 while Pym would be in the U.S. meeting with Haig after his return to Buenos Aires. Both U.S. and British officials were making it quite clear in the public domain that the Argentine offer, which Haig had taken back to the British, was unviable.

Impasse

The British tacitly rejected the Haig reformulation of the Argentine offer, as the Argentines had rejected Haig's proposal to them. Her Majesty's Government told him en route London not to bother. He diverted from a Caracas stop to Washington. Haig, however, still told the Argentines that their text should be considered the basis for a settlement. (Presumably, he meant with the exclusion of the eighth article.)

Worse than diplomatic deadlock resulted from the second round of U.S. mediation in Buenos Aires. The Junta and the United States seemed to decrease their mutual confidence.

The concentration of military backgrounds at the top of the U.S. and Argentine delegations does not seem to have produced the ease of communication that many of the players apparently expected. States team seemed not only to decrease their mutual confidence in this Round but indeed to come very close to seeing the real problems of perceptions and values which might make a solution impossible via this mediator. Those value differences were not a question simply of personal chemistry as they went to the substantive heart of the political questions in play in the crisis.

The world seemed surprised at first that these two teams so heavy on career military experience did not agree quickly and easily. This was, of course, because the universality of military organization belied an immense cultural-political gap. Much was made of the concentration of military backgrounds without considering the value systems of those militaries. The Army which formed Walters and Haig is inarguably constitutional; the Argentine services had written their own and not even observed that. If Haig attended the model military academy, many speculated that he shared a bond with Anaya and Galtieri who had been together at both grade school and the Liceo Militar. The reality is that Haig's values formed at West Point were closer to those of their Liceo Militar classmate Raul Alfonsin who as civilian President would see the Junta tried for high crimes. Haig's Army is meritocratic, decisive, long on combat experience, action-oriented. The mediator's experience with leaders with the habit of command spanned working with Douglas MacArthur through Henry Kissinger and Richard Nixon, and ultimately included serving not only as Supreme Allied Commander, Europe, but de facto administering the United States from the White House. Thus Haig found the Argentine decision-making structure not only slow and bloated (the Argentines considered the Military Committee of eight officers, including the three Junta members, streamlined), but utterly focused on retaining a power they considered their duty and which his value system saw as having been usurped by them.

Haig held that he was telling the Argentines the cold, hard facts. The Argentines considered themselves the players who were being direct, while finding the mediator evasive. They judged that he did not answer their questions; did not present them with, or inform them on, the British position; often returned to a session with his own position changed.

More substantively, the Argentines expected far more from the mediator than he ever promised, or his government would ever consider. If he implied guarantees, certainly it was nothing approaching the basic expectation of the United States which helped persuade the Junta to take the invasion gamble in the first place: formal, sympathetic (biased) and perpetual mediation of the dispute until resolved in favor of Argentine sovereignty. If Argentina had geopolitical anxieties in March and April of 1982, they were that the bilateral negotiating process which they could not speed up or control might simply continue. What Haig needed to offer to secure their withdrawal from the Islands, in Argentine eyes, was standing mediation of the dispute couched in 1965 U.N. Decolonization terms.

That was an expectation that could not be met—the claiming State has soaked itself for too long in its own perspective and its own propaganda. Argentina fervently felt the injustice of a world in which the British would not cede and the United Nations could not make them, but the United States felt there were far graver problems facing mankind. Indeed the West had grave doubts that Decolonization was still a valid concept. The Third World seemed to be applying against rather than in support of self-determination this ideology which the United States all but invented when most of the world was not self-governing, and then all but forced on its wartime allies. Decolonization, which seemed to occupy so much nonaligned rhetoric and paper so long after the populations which sought

independence were granted it, was de facto over. It was certainly not to be
applied where the population objected, and especially not as framed by a so-
called nonaligned U.N. majority which regularly villified the United States as a
matter of collective policy when it believed itself to be the shield and sword of
democracy and human rights. Given the kind of mediation Argentina had expected, the Junta came slowly to the realization that they had chosen the wrong
mediator in the United States.

From the beginning, Secretary Haig had posited a clear set of values which
would guide the mediator. He had left no room for the politics of illusion, only
a little empathy and a refusal to condemn in order to try to contribute to avoiding
further bloodshed. He had defined his own mission in very precise (and from
the Argentine perspective, narrow) terms: the implementation of U.N. Security
Council Resolution 502; that is, Argentine withdrawal. The Argentine military
told General Walters that their one precondition was to obtain mention of Argentine sovereignty in a final solution. From the Argentine perspective, Haig,
was unwilling to address sovereignty, and his mediation was doomed. Less
menacing but more ominous was Argentina's turn to the Rio Treaty mechanism—
a move that put more diplomatic pressure on the mediator than on the opponent.

The British Fleet had been underway for two weeks. Most of the Argentine
Fleet had been at Puerto Belgrano, but now several major combatants sailed for
an unknown destination. The whereabouts of the two "mystery fleets" added
to the tension. They would soon contribute directly.

The mediator had been moving toward the outline of a settlement. That settlement seemed more agreeable and advantageous to one party (Argentina) daily;
yet they would not close the deal by dropping guaranteed sovereignty. Haig's
understandings with London, tacit and explicit, were threatened by the shape of
his proposal, and even more by the Argentine proposal. According to Haig,
these terms were:

The British must either give Argentina sovereignty over the Falklands, or approve an
arrangement for governing the island that amounted to de facto Argentinian sovereignty.
This Mrs. Thatcher would never give them because it rewarded aggression and betrayed
the islanders.[65]

Secretary Haig dated the inevitability of war from Costa Mendez's letter to
him at plane-side on April 19: "Once again, in an exercise of bad faith unique
in my experience as a negotiator, the Argentines had gone back on their word
and returned to their original, impossible terms. War was now inevitable."[66]

Washington, Round Two

Argentina went on the offensive. The Junta (beginning during B.A. Round
Two) pursued a Rio Treaty meeting, as much to discipline Chile as to garner
support against the U.K. and the mediator. The OAS decided on April 21 to
convene as the Organ of Consultation of the Rio Treaty on the 26th. Galtieri

went from his sessions with Haig to the Falklands, and stated during his visit to Stanley that Argentina would continue to insist on a guarantee of its sovereignty. He restated the Junta's rejection of the British proposal for compromise, but dispatched his Foreign Minister to Washington to meet again with Haig. It was unclear whether Costa Mendez was simply balancing the Washington visit of Pym or might be bringing new Argentine proposals in the light of each side's rejection of the other's main elements of a solution.

In Washington, U.S. policy was crystalizing around Argentina's firmness that there would be no withdrawal from the islands without guarantee of sovereignty.[67] It was decided that, should the Haig mediation fail, the United States would support Great Britain over Argentina. Indeed, this might be done even in the event of any failure to make any real progress. The President, however, had made no formal decision. There was no date for deciding that the mediation had failed, but a background statement was made conveying the assessment that further stalemate would "cost us in Britain" without gaining the United States anything in its relations with Argentina. The United States was putting itself on the record in an off the record manner.

It was also making a little-noted change in course, abandoning a mediating role for a more forceful stance, bordering on imposing a solution, which had been seen by many as its role all along:

In the face of the latest Argentinian refusal, the United States could either abandon the negotiations or make one final attempt to resolve the situation. President Reagan approved my suggestion that we abandon good offices, discard the earlier draft agreements, and present an American proposal to Argentina and Britain. . . . [This] called for an eventual negotiated transfer of sovereignty, but preserved the basic British position by providing for free choice by the islanders as to whether they would be associated with one or the other of the parties, opt for independence, or even accept compensation for leaving the Falklands.[68]

Both Foreign Ministers came to town for Washington Round Two. Francis Pym received the first look at the U.S. plan informally from Judge William Clark on April 22 at the NSC (National Security Council), an end run on the mediator that, he implies, resulted in, the plan being sent in raw form to the British Cabinet.[69]

Britain could not accept that the transfer of sovereignty was compatible with self-determination. Several of the options seemed tantamount to a Kelper right to exile within or beyond their islands. From the British perspective, it was too late in the process of deploying applicable force to consider again the full transfer of sovereignty, no matter how far in the future. The British government would allow the U.S. plan to be put to the Argentines, but would not itself commit to it, even in principle.

Great Britain reciprocated the Argentine diplomatic escalation at the OAS. On April 24, Pym termed the latest Argentine proposals unacceptable and returned to London; the next day, British forces recaptured South Georgia. The Argentine Foreign Minister announced somewhat belatedly that Argentina and the U.K. were at war. However, neither party declared war during the South Atlantic crisis of spring 1982. Actions speaking as loudly as words, it was less than accurate of the mediator to characterize the chance to avoid bloodshed as "in the hands of the Argentines." All the players, including the mediator, were setting the pace and direction of events in choosing the timing and strength of pressure and concessions. "It was my plan to present this draft to Pym, negotiate down to the British bottom line, and then pass the proposal on to the Argentinians."[70]

Costa Mendez arrived in Washington on April 25 and, in addition to his offensive at the OAS, planned to discuss the U.S. plan. With the British retaking of South Georgia, the Foreign Minister postponed his meeting with Secretary Haig. Costa Mendez indignantly cited the attack on South Georgia as having led the Argentine Government to believe that "negotiations with Britain had terminated."[71] Costa Mendez declined to meet with Haig because of the British recuperation of South Georgia, and concentrated rather on the OAS meeting. Diplomatic messages were nonetheless exchanged with both London and Buenos Aires by Washington. The United States would not agree that U.S. mediation effort was ended.

Haig told the OAS session that U.N. Security Council Resolution 502 was the proper basis for a peaceful settlement. He said that the Rio Treaty did not provide such a basis, and was not an appropriate or effective way to solve the Falklands crisis.

Britain's increase in military pressure in South Georgia was backed up by a Thatcher statement to the Commons that implied that military action in the Falklands might follow very soon: The time for diplomacy, she said, was growing short. She pointed out parallels in the British recapture of South Georgia to Argentina's taking the Falklands. She emphasized that the action was completed by 10:00 A.M. on April 25; and stressed that there were no British casualties and serious injury to only one Argentine soldier. Britain, she said, did not fire the first shots, and the nearly 200 Argentine prisoners would be repatriated quickly. She asked that peace talks be resumed, especially since Foreign Minister Costa Mendez had Secretary Haig at hand in Washington.

As the Haig mission slowed, however, political Washington began to circle over the failure. Columnists Robert Evans and Charles Novak contended that the White House Chief of Staff had undertaken a campaign to oust Haig.[72] That this did not hurt Haig's negotiating effectiveness is difficult to believe. Haig dates the firm campaign to remove him from office as originating after the failure of his Falklands mediation.[73]

Haig did indeed take up his efforts again, meeting with Costa Mendez on April 26 and asking to return to Buenos Aires for a third round. He warned as well that the U.S. proposal would become a matter of public record. The Junta rejected that request, and only later said that Haig should be in touch with Costa

Mendez in Washington on the fringes of the OAS meeting. The Junta was probably making a procedural point in response to Haig's private but published complaint that Costa Mendez was not empowered to negotiate since the Argentine Junta made all its own major decisions. On April 25, Ambassador Shlaudeman saw Galtieri in Buenos Aires to ensure that the U.S. Plan had been transmitted by Costa Mendez.

We asked that the Argentinian government inform the United States government by midnight April 27, Buenos Aires time, whether it could accept the agreement. Galtieri, receiving this message, seemed to Shlaudeman to be tired but composed. He remarked that no one wanted war, but if Britain attacked, Argentina would resist with all her means. "I do not understand," he said wearily, "why the United States government, with all its resources, cannot stop Mrs. Thatcher from launching this attack."[74]

Basically, the party still only wanted one thing of the mediator: to freeze the situation so there would be no military reaction to military action.

THE LAST PLAN

In the face of this Argentine tactic, the United States made an urgent final appeal to the parties to accept a final, formal U.S. proposal as the basis for settlement to avoid major military engagement.

Major elements of the detailed proposed U.S. memorandum of agreement were:

—Cessation of hostilities;

—A 50 percent drawdown of forces within several days;

—Total Argentine withdrawal within 15 days;

—The end of economic and financial sanctions;

—A tripartite U.S.-U.K.-Argentine special interim authority, each member staffed by not more than ten persons and, accompanied by his country's flag;

—Two Argentine representatives of the Argentine population with at least one Argentine on each council;

—Restoration of movement, travel, and transport; and, finally;

—Negotiations on a definitive status and removal from the U.N. List of Non–Self-Governing Territories by December 31, 1982.

Had the parties been unable to reach agreement by the end of the year, the United States would have undertaken a six-month mediation.

An interesting element of the U.S. proposal was that the agreed goal of the negotiations should be the Decolonization of the Falkland Islands. Specifically, the parties would undertake to negotiate the removal of the islands from the list of non–self-governing territories. There are three ways recognized under international law by which a territory can (and in the view of the U.N. majority *must*) become self-governing: incorporation into a metropol as in the case of Hawaii and Alaska; sovereign independence, the route chosen by the two-thirds of the U.N. member states who have become independent since the U.N. was founded; and the achievement of self-governance and free association with another state, the choice of the people of Puerto Rico and one option open to the peoples of Micronesia.

The U.S. proposal was open-ended on the sovereignty question and thus consistent with both long-standing U.S. policy and the U.S. mediating role. It offered the advantage of an apparently definitive settlement in the sense that any solution would no longer be subject to political review by the United Nations. The proposal might, however, have had the unfortunate effect of leading each side to believe that its policy goals could be implemented in the name of the agreed-on objective. In a sense, it brought the dispute full circle to the basic disagreements of the parties as to whether the Falklands would be administered in implementation of territorial integrity or self-determination. Indeed, both positions were referred to, and the U.N. resolutions were also referred to but left unnamed under the collective of "relevant" U.N. General Assembly Resolutions.

Thus, while a stated purpose of Decolonization might at first glance seem to favor Argentina and thus be primarily designed to secure her agreement, the real meaning of the provision was simply to ensure that any solution to the ongoing Falklands dispute would be a definitive one both as regards Decolonization and territory. The special interim authority (representatives of the United States, the U.K., and Argentina) was charged not only with an interim administration of the islands but with recommendations to both parties on the essence of the primary British goal: how to take into account the expressed wishes of the Kelpers. Argentina's ongoing interest (expressed as territorial integrity) was in making itself the de facto metropole for the Falklands. This was incorporated in the principle of nondiscriminatory communications, commercial, and travel links, but balanced by the countervailing respect for the traditional rights and guarantees of the Kelpers (self-determination).

Time appeared short. An NSC staff member was quoted as saying that a more generalized armed conflict was in the offing. The Argentines sought the fleet that they believed was about to land. The United States made public its judgment that the crisis had reached a critical point. Haig met again with Costa Mendez on April 28 at the State Department. A favorable formal response from Argentina was still possible.

The British probably saw the last plan before the Argentines, or so the Argentines believe. By April 27, Haig had formally put the last plan, the tenth major draft of the mediation, to both Governments, and had requested a firm and rapid reply. The British perception is that the Junta referred the plan to Corps Commanders and that their reply was construed by Haig as a rejection.

The U.K. increased the political-military pressure on April 28 by announcing the imposition of a 200-mile total sea and air blockade around the Falklands as of April 30 to apply to all traffic of all nations. Both sides were in the process of official consideration of the Haig plan, but the plan was widely noted to contain neither of the party's stated preconditions; that is, it had no guarantee of ultimate Argentine sovereignty nor a firm commitment to self-determination by the Kelpers as sought by Great Britain. British commandos were known to be ashore in the Falklands and attention turned to the possibility of full-scale amphibious landings. Prime Minister Thatcher told the Commons in emergency session that the issue of war and peace was up to Argentina. She had concluded, she said, that *diplomacy was not going to produce Argentine withdrawal*. She discounted the usefulness of U.N. or ICJ intervention, but was not yet willing to pronounce in a final way on the Haig proposals.[75]

Secretary Haig told the U.S. House Foreign Affairs Committee that it was unlikely that war could still be avoided, that the United States agreed with Great Britain that aggression should not be rewarded, and that his diplomatic shuttle had apparently failed to produce a solution to the Falklands crisis.[76]

Not to be left out of the slide toward violence, Argentina declared its own blockade of 200 miles around the Falklands as a free-fire zone effective immediately. Elements of the British fleet were widely known to be within the 200-mile zone, and the declaration seemed directly aimed at them.

Argentina asked for clarification of some elements of the U.S. plan. This was widely seen as a simple delay and one more effort at avoiding British landings.

On April 29, the Argentine Foreign Minister brought his nation's reply to the U.S. Secretary of State: Argentina's objective, it was said, was the recognition of its sovereignty over the Malvinas. "For us, [this] is an unrenounceable goal. . . . The document that you sent falls short of Argentinian demands and does not satisfy its minimum aspirations."[77] Neither could Argentina accept a "binding referendum" among the inhabitants of the Falklands on future political status. The Argentine reply of April 29 was taken as a rejection of the finality condition of the draft. Thus, Britain never had to take a position. Costa Mendez informed Haig that Argentina had not rejected the U.S. proposals. Costa Mendez seemed to imply that the impending hostilities were leading to some flexibility in the Junta's position and some preference for diplomatic over military solutions. Chief among these areas for flexibility would have been the removal of Argentine troops in exchange for the lifting of the British threat, but Argentine thinking at its most *"posibilista"* was still focused on a brief period of British administration, followed by a formula like joint rule of the Islands. Argentine sovereignty was still assumed as the outcome. From the Argentine perspective, it was impossible to accept the referendum on the wishes of the Islanders proposed by the United States or an interim tripartite government operating by majority rather than unanimity. It felt either would negate all it had achieved with the gesture of military occupation, leading back to an unacceptably indeterminate negotiation with the United Kingdom. What Argentina needed from the mediator was sovereignty guaranteed—not immediately, but without fail.

Such a guarantee, tacit or explicit, was not to be had from this mediator. It would have contradicted the mediator's own longer run values and interests. Thus the last U.S. proposal could not take the Argentine approach and on April 30, Haig could still only say of the British reply that the United States had reasons to hope that Britain would consider it the basis for a settlement, but Argentina was unable to accept it. Haig assured Pym in a message that: "We will, of course, continue to support you in the OAS and in the U.N. and will be prepared to veto in the Security Council, or vote against [in] the General Assembly, any resolutions which, in our judgment, depart from Security Council Resolution 502."[78]

PLAYERS: THE CHEMISTRY OF THE MEDIATOR AS NEGOTIATOR

The interaction of the Argentine and U.S. governments[79] was complex and highly personal. Its more interesting aspects lead to as many questions as answers. Whether derived by analysis or directly stated by the participants, they are highly personal and subjective. They are nonetheless valuable as raw data needing further confirmation, assessment, and tying together for their *relative value in explaining the course of mediation*.

Argentine policymakers had taken their case to the OAS on April 26 in order, among other things, to get a more favorable reaction from the United States. They had the impression that they were provided with Haig's proposal 72 hours after the British that is, they were presented with an Anglo-U.S. document rather than a proposal originating from the United States as mediator. Costa Mendez wanted to discuss it with the United States but was overtaken by the April 30 U.S. statement and the U.S. decision to back Britain.[80] If they felt rushed and pressured by the series of U.S. statements on the 27th and the 30th, they also felt betrayed by the logistics and materiel intentions of the United States.

In later April and early May, the Argentine decision-making process was refined by Argentina's experience with Haig and by the sinking of their cruiser, the *Belgrano*. That the Argentine leaders were engaging in a rational, sophisticated decision-making process is evidenced by their handling of the Russians. The Junta did not see Perez de Cuellar's early May plea that there be no unnecessary violence as aimed at them. The U.K. had never accepted a Peruvian call for a cease-fire. Argentina considered its vessels to have been wrongfully attacked, believing the *Naral* a fishing boat and the *Sobral* to have been on a rescue mission when attacked. The Argentine Government was coming to be of the view that the British were not behaving like the British in the graduated application of political military power.

Diplomatic historians will need to sort out the interplay of personalities. All the characters acquired colorful semi-public attributes. General Lami Doso was hesitant. Admiral Anaya was correspondingly firm. Costa Mendez's experience was, in a sense, invalidated in that his nationalism was of the crudest type, and he equated it with toughness. Ros was often said to be weak in his decision making and implementation. Personality was certainly a fractionating force in the Argentine decision-making structure.

The Argentines felt that Haig was transmitting a feeling of their weakness both to the British, where he served as reporter, and to the Argentines, with whom Haig sought to use that feeling as a method of influence. Haig was courteous to the extent of encouraging the Argentines' sense of grandeur. He was distant, yet frank enough that Costa Mendez is said to have told him at one point that Argentina would understand if the United States were to side with Great Britain. The Argentines believed that Haig twice said that he would try to stop the British at Ascension. They are sure, in turn, that they never asked any of the mediators to halt British military actions as a precondition to beginning talks.

The Argentine Foreign Minister found Haig in need of education on the basics of the "Malvinas" problem. The Argentines felt that they had to educate Haig for an initial two days about the South Atlantic. (No U.S. contacts of the Secretary seem to have had to mention even the most detailed agendas to him twice.) Costa Mendez felt Haig to be rigid: operating from a script, and a NATO script at that. Haig did not seem to him to be functioning creatively, but negatively. Haig felt that Costa Mendez was more firm about guaranteed Argentine sovereignty than were the military leaders. "The British won't fight. In this judgment, I believe, [Galtieri] had the agreement and not the tutelage of Nicanor Costa Mendez, the Foreign Minister, who was reportedly the main opponent of my advice. On a number of occasions after Galtieri had showed some movement in the negotiations, Costa Mendez met with me privately and countermanded what his president had said, hardening the Argentine position and making resolution impossible."[81] It may well be, however, that one's Foreign Minister is simply the person that the Junta or any other government sends to make retractions and other conveyances of bad news. Galtieri would certainly not like to be in the position of retracting what either the rest of the Junta or the wider groupings of the Military Senior Officers rejected. This and other confusions may well have stemmed from the U.S. failure to perceive what was a perfectly clear, indeed formal, decision-making system on the Argentine side: Serious decisions required the approval of 8 Flag/General-Rank Officers of all three services. This may be awkward, imprecise, time-consuming, and inconvenient in a negotiation/mediation, but it was nonetheless the law of the land in Argentina. In this and other matters it would have been highly valuable for the U.S. mediators to have had the full and constant participation of the resident U.S. Ambassador, who knew his host government well.

Inhabitants of the United States and Great Britain are prone to use the word "machismo" in discussing the psychology, operating style, and bargaining tactics of the Argentine Military Government. This does not mesh well with, for example, Galtieri's courtliness, or Anaya's tears at the loss of sailors. Machismo is a particularly Latin concept and not entirely native to Argentine society, which is far more pan-European than Hispanic. Broadly influenced by Central and Southern Europe, and indeed to this day not entirely linguistically dominated by Spanish, Argentines are a unique civilization. Argentines, like U.S. citizens, are not easily subject to broad cultural generalizations.

The Junta's behavior with the negotiator certainly involved bravado, a nearly universal gambit in negotiating. One puts the best face possible on one's situation and outlook. Their collective behavior was indecisive and self-contradictory, neither classic attributes of the Hispanic *caballero* or the military officer. At times it lacked precision, a most un-Argentine trait. The Falklands crisis produced in the Argentine Government not exaggeration but instead dilution of national traits.

Indeed, serious international crises have a way of bringing into play the full range of human emotion and intellect. A form of machismo was also diagnosed in the Thatcher government and the Prime Minister herself. While Haig would perceive it, the Argentines would be repelled by it, and the press would concentrate on what Haig called the "icy scorn and iron will of Mrs. Thatcher." That aspect of her character and behavior are likely not in her view inconsistent to the concern expressed almost nightly to her Permanent Representative in New York at the impending loss of young lives should diplomacy fail.[82] Resolve is criticized by no society—public backing for Costa Mendez in Buenos Aires was expressed by dubbing him the "Iron Foreign Minister." If there was anything approaching bloodlust in the Falklands crisis, it was in parts of the British press and public reaction to the invasion, not at 10 Downing Street. The determination evinced there had no sense of adventure and heightened experience to it; it was pure political challenge and response.

Some members of the Argentine "team" thought they detected a bias in the mediator, with Anaya representing the extreme view that he was simply the agent of British imperialism in the South Atlantic. They saw collusion in his "permitting" the U.K. to declare the TEZ. (It was a *fait accompli,* announced before Haig touched down in London.) They found further cause for suspicion in the U.S. refueling of British units at Ascension. (The United States was so obligated by the terms of its use of the British island of Ascension.) They viewed Haig's behavior in London as acting as though he had returned home, seeming relaxed and happy. They also thought they detected an increase in his pro-British attitude between his two trips. The press story of April 14 concerning U.S. intelligence, especially the purported moving of spy satellites, fueled these doubts about the mediator.

The dominant opinion in the Argentine Government, however, was that, ideal or not, the U.S. Secretary of State was Argentina's only serious option for a negotiated settlement with the British once the Task Force got under way. Many conceded initially that Haig was growing in his command of the issue as the mediation progressed, but that sense was lost in Round Two as culture dominated the process.

Anaya and Galtieri consistently felt that Haig changed in his mood with each return to his hotel. He would leave their talks pleased about progress and then return from his hotel shaken and in low spirits. Their assumption was that he was talking by phone with Washington or London and encountering British intransigence.

The Argentines consistently note that Haig never said what Great Britain wanted, except on his last day in Buenos Aires. The Argentine perspective on the mechanics of drafting is that all during April there was no British proposal to discuss. The Argentines submitted four or five drafts of which two or three were given to the U.S. team. The Argentines began to feel that that this was a one-sided exercise in negotiation in which it fell to them to suggest the solutions, which were then rejected by London or the mediator.

On April 18, Haig said that he could not take the Argentine draft to the United Kingdom; it simply would not wash. By his last day in Buenos Aires, he recognized as a "miracle" the result of his request for a "gray" draft, that is, a colorless, low-key, nonpolemical text. However, that text fell flat with the British War Cabinet. Apparently perceptions about settlement had not come any closer during the whole Haig shuttle.

U.S. General Walters had separate missions from those of Secretary Haig. Were his talks and his signals parallel to others from other representatives of the United States? Does a special relationship sometimes prove too special for practical use in a crisis?

Haig did not understand why the Argentines could not budge. Was it that the survival of the government depended on their bluffing to the very end; was this an all-or-nothing strategy as regarded their own population and that of the U.K.?

Galtieri seemed swayed alternately by Anaya's patriotism and Lami Doso's realism. The Army, senior Argentine military service by size, was led in the Falklands invasion by the enthusiasm and expertise (specialization) of the Navy. The reluctant Air Force, however, acquitted itself best. Could the Air Force have made peace? Was the senior peacemaker, Costa Mendez, making smoke, or was he just unable to deliver the Junta?

The Argentine negotiating team consisted of Foreign Minister Costa Mendez and Armed Services Representatives Brigadier Jose Miret, Admiral Benito Moya, and General Norberto Iglesias. The three military officers had to work via an interpreter. The Foreign Minister could and sometimes did communicate directly in good English, in which he is precise and cultivated. He was a Falklands expert, a lawyer, and a student of Anglo-Saxon culture—his own best translator and direct negotiator in English when alone.

This was one scenario: One evening, toward the end of Buenos Aires Round Two, things were looking very good, and Haig received a call to come to the Foreign Ministry to sign an agreement. A call came an hour early and he was asked to come see the Foreign Minister as there was a hitch. The Junta had told the negotiating team to start all over. Smaller but parallel reversals characterized Argentine negotiating and decision making throughout. Why did a military government work in fits and starts?

The U.S. role in the tripartite administration plan was a definite irritant to the Argentine sensitivities toward North America. Why take a mediator you don't want as guarantor? Argentines speak of biased mediation in the Falklands crisis and even betrayal but does anyone really want a neutral mediator?

At one point, the United States suggested an administrating presence of Canada and Peru, an exceptionally clever combination. Why was it not taken up?

Operation Rosario was a plan for combining Beagle and Falklands "recovery" operations. The less ambitious, one-front war was at least tried first. Perhaps the U.K. reaction reinforced the "mainstream" values in territorial disputes sooner than observers will ever know—by heading off the other half of Rosario. The mediators never seemed to link the several unredeemed Argentine dreams. Could they have formed a "package deal"?

The plan as of the 4th of April was still only to leave a token garrison of Argentine marines. Who decided for and when occupation is unclear but it was linked to the April 3 reaction and the beginning of Argentine diplomacy in the OAS.

The idea of force in Latin thinking is a completely neutral one and, indeed, it is positive when force is used in support of a legitimate aim, such as to right injustice, especially invasion (for example, the legend of El Cid). Violation of legal and moral norms, especially the invasion of a peaceful people (for example St. George and the maiden menaced by the dragon), drove the British equally strongly. Falklands then became the stuff of powerful political/social belief systems and heroic mythology: El Cid versus St. George.

The Argentines mistook the deference of Haig and Enders toward their colleagues and a foreign Chief of State as a sense of inferiority, possibly a social one. The urgency of the question may have been exaggerated, and certainly seemed this way to the Argentines. "With the British fleet steaming down the South Atlantic at a steady eighteen knots and the Argentinians daily reinforcing their garrison in the Falklands, the opportunity for negotiations would last only a few days."[83] Such an attitude assumed not only that the British were coming all the way but that they intended from the start to prosecute their views militarily. Argentine thinking in the first round in Buenos Aires certainly did not fully accept either point. The timing of the mediator appeared to the Argentine side to be merely one more form of U.S. pressure in favor of the British enemy.

Related to timing was the feeling that this was the only possible mediation and mediator: another view the Argentines did not share.

It was my opinion, tested in a series of freewheeling staff discussions, that the United States alone had enough influence with both sides to provide an outside chance of success. The United Nations, with its vociferous, anticolonialist coalition of Third World and Marxist members would probably not be able to act quickly enough to be effective, and the debate was certain to digress to issues that would exacerbate a situation that could only be resolved by quiet diplomacy. The OAS was unsatisfactory for similar reasons.[84]

Argentina not only could but was already considering both the U.N. and the OAS as alternatives for securing its positions. It was precisely the nature of their membership and their way of conducting business that appealed to the Junta. If the U.S. could not secure for them what Argentina wanted, Argentina would turn to other mediators. In no sense did Argentina see Haig's mediation as a critical opportunity to be grasped as the sole alternative.

War, of course, was a solid alternative in the view of the Junta. Not desirable, but seeming daily more likely and perhaps ultimately necessary, the resort to force was not to their mind the catastrophe it seemed to the mediator.

The mediator was also more interested in abstract justice and propriety (i.e., in formalities) than was the Junta. His attitude showed clearly in his public statements concerning Resolution 502, which the Argentines took to be biased, power-based politics. There was indeed a sense of chastening that the Argentines found not only improperly judgmental but in their view factually, legally, and historically incorrect. Secretary Haig has written that he felt that "a sincere, high-level effort by the United States could do much to strip away the confusing ambiguities of the situation and help to establish who was right and who was wrong."[85] Beyond a judgmental preference for the United Kingdom, Secretary Haig held and may have betrayed the view that the United Kingdom was calling the shots. This was certainly not the way the situation appeared in the initial weeks to the Junta, yet the new mediator saw himself essentially to be negotiating with the Argentines what was acceptable to the British: "It was decided that I would go first to London, in order to know what was possible, before traveling to Argentina and talking to its unpredictable leaders."[86]

PROCESS

Less personal were the two systems' readings of each other, a more mild, self-conscious, and analytic process. The Argentines read Haig's consultation process with the British as a successful upgrading by the U.K. of the special relationship; the case of the British tail wagging the U.S. dog. Unconsciously grouping the Anglo-Saxons, and misreading a partnership that comes as close to sovereign equality as any in the modern world, the Argentines clung to their hope that the United States would wish to restrain the U.K. and be able to do so both militarily and politically. With the Suez analogy in mind, they ignored the modern special relationship of the Trident era and the force, in the mainstream politico-legal culture, of the principle of non–resort to force (especially against the interests of major states).

Galtieri's reaction to Haig's approach was critical. Two elements of the U.S. approach in particular hardened Argentine attitudes. The first was the insistence on Argentine withdrawal as the key element of what the Argentines saw as the larger and ongoing problem. Founded on U.N. Resolution 502, this U.S. core element was nonetheless seen by the Argentines as the enforcement of British interests and not equity.

The second major irritant was the increasingly clear fact that not only did Argentina have to get out, but that if it didn't, the United States would help the United Kingdom. While the emphasis was clearly on punitive action by the U.K. and the cost to Argentina, which the United States wished to avoid, the Argentine perception was more on the fact that the United States would help the U.K. if Argentina did not get out.

These two perceptions led to hardened Argentine positions, including the insistence on the 31 December deadline for the transfer of Argentine sovereignty, and poisoned both the U.S. and Peruvian peace initiatives. They also led to led to fallback thinking, such as: "Even if we lose, we can still obtain the original objective of getting the United Kingdom to bargain seriously."

Foreign Minister Costa Mendez felt that the greatest stumbling block in the Haig proposals was British insistence on consulting the population of the Islanders. He read return to British administration without a fixed date for ending the negotiations as status quo ante, in that the population would clearly not choose Argentine sovereignty. He harbored equally grave doubts about the U.S.-U.K. majority vote in interim administration. Argentina was again playing all-or-nothing poker: full sovereignty, no need to trust the U.S. mediator (not surprising from an Argentine perspective, in light of the years of negotiations.

Finally, Argentina failed to adjust the plan, militarily or diplomatically. It was preparing for siege warfare in both these fields. Amphibious warfare doctrine attributes a strength to dug-in defenders ashore of such disproportion that overwhelming superiority (six to one) in attacking amphibious troops is needed for a successful attack. Thus, the uncoordinated Argentine planning concerning holding the Falklands focused not on the brevity of the 13-month conscription period (only recently begun for the bulk of the troops on the Falkland Islands) nor on the lack of combat experience for the few hundred career officers and non-coms whose services had not fought a war since the Chaco in 1876, but on the simple preparation of trenches and lightly fortified positions for what they considered an overwhelming number of defenders.

DIPLOMACY AND ARMS, DELAY AND ACTION

Sir Nicholas Henderson has pointed out that when the Task Force was dispatched few of those responsible for the decision had any idea how the Argentines were going to be ejected by force from the islands. Admiral Sir John Fieldhouse put it in stark relief: The Task Force was the most difficult British military mission since World War II. The Task Force was clearly dispatched as a political as well as a potential military instrument of policy. How the Argentine Junta and public read it as a signal is open to considerable debate. Ambassador Henderson has pointed out that the government of Argentina misread publicly expressed doubts about the dispatch of the Task Force as indicating an ultimate British lack of determination.

INHIBITORS: FRIENDS, GAMBITS, AND TIMING

If the elements of a possible settlement were clear to the parties and to potential mediators, the factors that would inhibit mediation were more specific and unpredictable. Nonetheless, they too run like common threads through the three major mediations.

British diplomacy was creative on the tactical level. It was hampered, however, by policy and political considerations, principally the unyielding requirement that the Kelpers approve any solution that could be negotiated. In addition, National Honor demanded that British administration, dislodged by force, be reimposed by negotiation if possible, or by force if necessary (and possible). As in the years of bilateral negotiations, Britain found itself with little to bargain with. Its concessions could not be on what its National Honor determined were questions of principle: self-determination and non–resort to force in settling territorial disputes.

Argentine diplomacy had the advantage and constraint of being single minded: The goal of sovereignty had for 150 years been embedded in the national consciousness. The Argentine position was widely known and, better still, known to be firmly held. No Argentine diplomat needed to wonder about overarching goals, or his backing in pursuit of them, yet this also limited the creativity of Argentine diplomacy. Argentine diplomacy in the pre-invasion years had been a relentless but creative pursuit of one goal through such diverse means as naval gunfire, the establishment of weather stations, and the agreement to supply oil and education to the Islanders. In the crisis stage it became cautious and inflexible, a prisoner to its own consistency. The need to posture as the underdog alternated with absolute assertiveness about *force majeur*. First abandoned in favor of force, diplomacy was then called on to prevent counterforce—an inconsistent and self-defeating use of this instrument.

As important as the internal restraints and contradictions in British and Argentine diplomacy were their views of the mediation process, of the role and value of other parties, and of the graduated use of force as a policy instrument. Most of these elements in their diplomacy worked against peaceful settlement, especially in the Argentine case.

TIMING: WHEN TO NEGOTIATE, WHEN TO MEDIATE

Tactical military developments and prospects seemed to determine to an unreasonable degree the negotiating postures of the parties to the Falklands dispute, yet larger strategic developments were ignored by one side as they gave firmness to the other. The mutual failure to interpret the other party's reactions to a fluid military scenario was a serious hindrance to the mediations. The mediator too may have had an overdeveloped sense of the relative urgency of the crisis.

The declaration of the 200-mile exclusion zone around the Falklands should have pointed out to Argentine authorities how limited were their options. Resupply by air is inefficient and expensive. It limited the defenders of the Islands to a low volume of military material and, as the Antarctic winter approached, even more important shortages of food, fuel, and supplies. The superannuated Argentine fleet, while it might use the ship and air-launched Exocets and the air arm to inflict deadly harm on the British, would certainly not itself survive such attacks. The sinking of the *Belgrano* made this all too clear to the Argentine Navy, which played no further major role in the Falklands conflict. (The Navy took the Islands and then left attack to the Air Force and defense of the islands to the Army and Marines.)

The equipment and supplies already sea-lifted to the islands would have to suffice. The Argentines had indeed established a strong defensive position since the British naval blockade was not put into serious effect until long after its April 12 official declaration. The initial landing force of 4,500 Argentine Marines was reinforced by sea and air to around 13,000 ground troops. Their inventory included major artillery and armor. An effective air-defense system was installed, and the overall effort was well enough done that with the establishment of the British beachhead on May 21, the Argentines had numerical superiority in ground forces in the Falkland Islands as well as a more telling advantage in tactical air.

What compelled Argentina to pursue the military rather than diplomatic course at this juncture? Certainly, the air bridge was an encouragement. C–130 transports were able to continue supply and personnel changes through early May to the main airport at Stanley. Thereafter, however, the British air attacks at Stanley and Goose Green which began on May 1 made the runways ever less useful, and the trend must have been clear. The de facto withdrawal of the Argentine surface Navy reflects the realistic assessment that the U.K. Royal Navy was superior in numbers of combatants and the level of their electronic sophistication. This was clearly balanced, however, by the ability of the Argentine Air Force in mass attacks to inflict serious damage on British vessels with conventional bombs.

The illusion of the magic high-technology weapon—the Exocet maritime cruise—was also telling: The buoying effect of the attack on HMS *Sheffield* cannot be underestimated. (A critical question thus becomes how sure Argentina was of resupply of the Exocet missile. Starting with a very limited stock, reloads were critical to whether Argentina could count any further on their newly discovered "super weapon.")

The Argentine air inventory of over 50 A–4Bs and over 50 Mirage IIIs, a few Canberra bombers, and Super Etendards became the core of the Argentine defense of the Falklands and must have been thought to be sufficient to overcome both Britain's naval and ground-force combat efficiency. Argentine air forces were able to operate out of Stanley during April but, thereafter, only out of Rio Grande and Rio Gallegos, thereby cutting both their range/payload and their operating time.

By mid-May, the air bridge would be partially closed,[87] British air superiority firmly established, and the full use of marginal landing surfaces such as the road between the airfield and Port Stanley denied to the Argentines.

FAILURE: THE UNITED STATES AND ARGENTINA PART WAYS

On April 30, President Reagan announced full U.S. support for the United Kingdom, framing Argentina's recapture of the Islands as "armed aggression," ordering partial economic and arms sanctions against Argentina, and offering material support to the United Kingdom in any armed conflict.

Foreign Minister Costa Mendez felt Secretary Haig's statement of April 30 to be gratuitous violence—the mediator making a statement in addition to that of the President. The statement stemmed from Haig's moral and political judgments that Argentina was causing war and that the chance for peace was past because his mission had failed:

War was now inevitable. The Argentinian government had simply been incapable of responding; now it would fall like a house of cards, with unforeseeable consequences. On April 30, I announced the breakdown of negotiations to the press and stated that the United States would support Britain. We suspended military exports to Argentina and withheld certification of Argentinian elegibility for military sales, suspended Export-Import Bank credits and guarantees and Commodity Credit Corporation loans, and adopted a policy of responding favorably to British requests for military material.[88]

There would be two more mediation attempts before the occurrence of hostilities in the Falklands themselves. Even if time had run out for talking with no fighting, the two need not always be incompatible.

Former Argentine Ambassador to the U.K. Ortiz de Rosas feels that the U.K. request that the United States "take sides" was fatal to peace and to U.K. interests. He argues that the U.K. knew that U.S. military support would be available if needed, and ought to have recognized that U.S. good offices (read neutrality) should be maintained and the United States kept in reserve as an ongoing interlocuter. His assessment is that the U.K. operated out of short-term interests and convenience in this move, and brought itself to the verge of disaster as well as doing great and unnecessary harm to U.S. interests, especially in Central America. His view is that neither U.S. nor EC (European Community) help was "volunteered," and should not have been given.

The military government also found it politically impossible to "declare victory" and call itself home in glory from the recuperated islands. If "handback"—simply giving the Falklands back, having made Argentina's point with the invasion—was ever a serious option, it evaporated in the Plaza de Mayo in the heat of the national reaction to recuperation although General Galtieri had doubts right from Resolution 502's passage that "handback" would have resolved the problem elegantly. In this assessment, the military was now, at the end of April, without the withdrawal options and without real control over its situation. Foreign Minister Costa Mendez also maintains that the idea throughout was to get negotiations.

In the next two days, the first British bombings of the Falklands took place, Argentina tried to launch both naval and air sorties against a British-lead element now within range, and the cruiser *General Belgrano* was sunk with the loss of over 300 of her crew. The next Anglo-U.S. meeting included Ministers of Defense. U.K. Foreign Minister Pym flew on to New York to discuss with the Secretary General of the U.N. his offer to mediate the dispute, clearly turning the page on the U.S. mediation. Argentines do not understand why the United States did not simply step back; why it chose a side. On May 3, *Noticias Argentines* reported that Argentine Ambassador to the United States Esteban Tacaks had delivered a note charging that the United States had failed on Friday April 30 to "clarify several points of President Reagan's last minute peace proposal" and thus had "accelerated the clash with Britain" just as "Argentina was most flexible and with a vocation for negotiation." Argentina saw the "finality" of the U.S. plan as a gambit and countered with one of its own: "clarifications."

The American mediation spanned the last three weeks of April, 1982. Between April 8 and 20, the Haig shuttle logged over 35,000 miles and 70 air hours. It was undertaken with the publicly stated goal of averting conflict. One of the major methods for this was to impress on Argentina the British political will and military capability to recover the islands. This has been called biased mediation, yet the U.S. positions on sovereignty and the invasion were separate, clear, and unchanged throughout. The United States was and remains neutral on the Anglo-Argentine dispute on Falklands sovereignty. President Reagan had urged General Galtieri not to intervene. He then urged him to show flexibility and restraint, that is to withdraw his troops. If he did not at first characterize U.S. options or obligations, much less make threats, the U.S. position was clearly that Argentina should not undertake, and once it had done so, should undo, its military aggression. The mediation of Reagan's Foreign Minister was equally clearly premised on opposition to that invasion as a precedent for the resolution of disputes. His effort took UNSC Resolution 502 as a starting point, and the Argentine military withdrawal called for in Resolution 502 as a primary goal. There were U.S. interests, systemic and national, behind the U.S. mediation. They were not incompatible with constructive intent, and they did not preclude mediation.

V

THE PERUVIAN ATTEMPT

The men in the icy water were many of them wounded, some in the last stages of exhaustion, horror-haunted and burnt. There was no rescue for the struggling bodies in the water. Quarter of an hour later, when the *Carnarvon* passed over the spot, neither survivors nor wreckage were to be seen.

> —Account of the Battle of the Falklands, December 8, 1914, in which German losses alone were 2,260 men.

Submarine warfare. At least two British nuclear-power submarines, the *Superb* and the *Splendid,* are on station off the Falklands, an overwhelming match for Argentina's four diesel subs. The British submarines could easily intimidate the Argentine fleet in deep waters. Torpedoing a ship would not win the battle of the Falklands, but it might persuade the Argentines to negotiate more seriously.

> —Newsweek Magazine, April 26, 1982

For many a fathom gleams and moves and moans
The tide that sweeps above . . . .
Nor where they sleep shall moon or sunlight shine,
Nor man look down for ever . . . .
And over them, while death and life shall be,
The light and sound and darkness of the sea.

> —Algernon Charles Swinburne, "Tristram of Lyonnese"

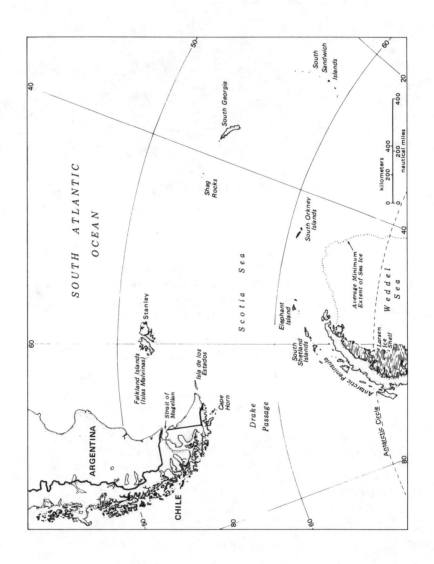

PERU, ROUNDS ONE AND TWO

Peruvian President Fernando Belaunde Terry's May initiative was a peace plan based on UNSC Resolution 502. It was attempted in two rounds on May 2 and May 5.

The final bare-bones text suggested by Peru to Argentina and the United Kingdom called for cease-fire, withdrawal, non-reintroduction of forces, interim administration by a contact group, consultation with the Islanders on a definitive settlement, acknowledgment of the conflicting claims of the two parties, and consideration of both the *aspirations* and the *interests* of the Kelpers (which Argentina considered its formula at this point), with the contact group seeking to bring the British and Argentines to a definitive agreement before April 30, 1983.

The Peruvian proposal was designed to simplify the negotiating and political processes. It was skeletal in nature and limited to the Falkland Islands themselves, leaving aside the question of the Dependencies (the British had reoccupied South Georgia on April 25). The cease-fire and mutual withdrawal of forces were, of course, "packaged." A contact group of Peru, the United States, Brazil, and the Federal Republic of Germany (FRG) was to have been established as an arbitrating and supervisory body as well as to administrator of the Islands *ad interim*. This was a new element over Haig's second proposal. The balance of the group (and that it should be perceived as impartial by Argentina) was most important; in the skeletal framework, all the implementing detail for the military cease-fire and withdrawal as well as administration of the Islands in consultation with the Kelpers was left to the discretion and joint decision of the contact group. Even more importantly, the contact group would work with the parties in negotiating the basic dispute. The Argentines were offered the firm time frame that they desired but there was no statement about the necessary eventual recognition of Argentine sovereignty.

Peaceful settlement was still possible in May, but peace itself was past. By May 1, 1982, there was no longer any political or legal doubt that Argentina and Britain were at war. South Georgia had been recovered by the British on April 25. A Total Exclusion Zone around the Falkland Islands had been declared on April 30. Nonetheless, the conflict was still limited. East Falkland was bombed and shelled on May 1, but British forces were not yet militarily engaged in large-scale hostilities. While the fleet had been known to be near, the use of Vulcan bombers as well as Harrier fighters came as a shock—an unanticipated British capability with more political impact than military effectiveness against Stanley Airport. Galtieri was three hours late for his last national television appearance. There was apparently a firming up of the collective nature of the leadership as the enemy became real in the Falklands, but the Argentine government below the Junta there was dissent against all-out war with Britain. Even following the occupation of the Islands by Argentina, the dispatch of the British Task Force, the failure of the U.S. mediation, and Britain's attack of Saturday, May 1, on the Falklands themselves, the Peruvian initiative seemed to offer a last chance for peace. That chance was twice lost in a tightly knit string of events, spread over five time zones (see chronology at end of chapter), with different players holding different key pieces of knowledge.

On the evening of Saturday, May 1, Peruvian President Fernando Belaunde Terry initiated the venture by passing his plan to U.S. Ambassador Frank Ortiz in Lima at about 6:00 P.M. and calling President Reagan via Peru's Washington Ambassador at 10:00.[1] Reagan was in Tennessee and Belaunde reached the U.S. Secretary of State late on Saturday, May 1. Belaunde and Haig decided on one last try via a simplified plan. There would be no details (in sharp contrast to the U.S. draft of April, which reached 20 pages), simply open-ended possibilities for each side to pursue to advantage in a bare-bones draft. The original Belaunde four-point plan as put to Ambassador Ortiz and Secretary Haig was designed to avoid further deterioration in the military situation, which had heated up that Saturday. It called simply for a truce, mutual withdrawal, negotiations based on U.N. and OAS resolutions on the Falklands, and U.N. interim administration with U.N. peacekeeping forces. After a discussion of the points, Haig took the proposal under advisement, and four hours later, at about midnight in Washington or 11:00 P.M. in Lima, Haig called Belaunde with some proposed modifications; these resulted in their agreement on a seven-point plan: cessation of hostilities; mutual withdrawal; interim administration by a third party; recognition of conflicting claims; inclusion of the points of view and interests of the inhabitants; a mediating group of Brazil, Peru, West Germany, and the United States; and definitive agreement by April 30,1983. Even the seven-point plan was an outline compared to the detail of the U.S. mediation. The concomitant risk of imprecision was felt to be better than the war that was looming.

The plan as of Saturday night (Draft Two) was worked out *ad hoc* by phone by the two intermediaries without consulting the parties. Haig and Belaunde had worked out what each believed to be the essential points from the perspective of the country with which each shared a common language and culture. In their second talk, lasting three-quarters of an hour, Haig defined the minimum points Britain would have to have and Belaunde Terry critiqued these from an Argentine perspective. They agreed on a seven-point plan which would be put to the two sides. Belaunde was to call Galtieri. Haig would see Pym the next morning. The plan was to have a concrete package *approved by Argentina* which Haig could in turn present to Pym the following morning. (The Peruvians, however, believed Pym had made the counterproposal between the drafting of the four-point plan and the agreed seven-point proposal.)

Belaunde outlined to Galtieri the seven Draft Two points phrased in language which the mediators believed Britain could accept. They were of course without value without Argentine agreement. The seven points as clarified and further simplified to Galtieri were:

—Cease-fire;
—Withdrawal;

—Temporary interim administration by third parties;

—Recognition of conflicting viewpoints on sovereignty;

—Recognition of the need to take into account the "viewpoints and interests" of the Kelpers;

—A supervisory group to commence operation Monday morning in Washington consisting of the mediators plus Brazil and West Germany (not yet consulted by the co-mediators); and

—A deadline of April 30, 1983, for a definitive solution.

Belaunde described the plan to Galtieri as "dictated" by Haig and modified and made concise by himself. Galtieri objected from the first to the makeup of the administering group but gave no negative reaction that night. The United States was not to have any further role in Argentina's fate concerning the Falklands. Belaunde asked for an answer by 10:00 A.M. Sunday morning Washington time, (12:00 noon in Buenos Aires) when Haig was to meet Pym. Brazil and West Germany had not been consulted.

Galtieri promised an answer not necessarily by 10:00 A.M. but certainly by the next day. He said, however, that Argentina was not going to change; not going to exchange sovereignty over the Falklands for anything.

When Belaunde phoned for an answer at 10:00 A.M. in Argentina he instead got Foreign Minister Costa Mendez and several hours of negotiation. Costa Mendez had been on the phone since 8:00 that morning and was clearly engaged in negotiating by "query." This is the first of several points at which Argentina has been said to have accepted the Peruvian plan in principle. This "acceptance" seemed promising to the Peruvians; however, they read too much into it.

Optimism was increased considerably when Galtieri phoned Belaunde in the early morning. The high command, he said, was almost unanimous in approving the terms, though there were a number of small points to be negotiated. Throughout that morning, Belaunde negotiated these points in calls to Washington and Buenos Aires. . . . He accepted the Peruvian plan and would put it to his Junta that afternoon.[2]

The call was placed 12 hours before the torpedoing of the *Belgrano*. Neither then nor at any time did Argentina agree to the plan firmly. It was still considering its trade-offs and other options when military events intervened. It is perhaps more accurate to say that at mid-morning Sunday, Argentina accepted the *negotiation process* in principle, not the terms of the seven-point plan which inter alia called for Argentine withdrawal and factoring in the wishes of the Islanders. Costa Mendez sought clarification that there would be no remnants of British administration, by which he meant participation of the Kelpers in their own government. Argentina would not tolerate any constructive ambiguity on that point. The Peruvians' and Argentines' points five and six were modified to have the "interests and opinions" of the Islanders taken into account, and the mediation group left open to agreement between the two parties by mutual consent. This would not do for the Argentine Foreign Minister.

The principal Argentine objections to the 2 May proposal were: (1) the presence of the United States among the four guarantors—they had not given up on Haig as co-mediator (indeed, the Argentines believed that Haig turned to Peru in order to keep the U.K. from using Haig himself as their instrument) but only as guarantor; and (2) continuing British insistence on having both the interests and wishes of the Islanders reflected in the settlement. At this stage, the draft included "the wishes" of the Islanders, which the Argentines objected to. Costa Mendez offered "aspirations." Costa Mendez proposed to Peru that they propose to Haig the substitution of the "views of the islanders, concerning their interests" early on the morning of May 2. "Points of view and wishes" became "needs and aspirations." The point never was agreed on, for on it hinged the whole Falklands issue. None of the mediators had or would arrange the basis for deciding the Islands' future. Agreeing on all but a few words or indeed one word points out how far apart the parties had been, were, and were to remain. "Interests" versus "wishes" amounted to a question of who would inhabit the Falklands.

Also during the morning of May 2, Argentina conceded the U.S. participation in the interim government. Later however, it retracted it, excluding the United States.

At 2:15 P.M. Buenos Aires time, Belaunde checked with Galtieri to confirm that his Foreign Minister was empowered to pose and agree to language. Galtieri confirmed that Costa Mendez was so empowered.

Galtieri then told Belaunde that the plan was acceptable in principle even without the specific language excluding any remnant of British administration.[3] Costa Mendez assured Belaunde that the military committee would approve the proposal that evening before 8:00 P.M. local time. This was transmitted to Haig at least three and a half hours before the sinking of the *Belgrano*. Costa Mendez dates Argentine acceptance in principle from noon Buenos Aires time. It is difficult to envision the agreement as agreed on with the number and basic nature of the points being raised by Argentina. Costa Mendez, Iglesias, Moya, Miret, and Ros had had the plan for 12 hours at that point. There had been between four and ten phone calls of clarification and negotiation to Lima. Ratification by the military committee of Galtieri's acceptance in principle was promised by 8:00 P.M. Early in the afternoon, Galtieri confirmed to the Peruvians what his Foreign Minister had verbally "initialled": that Argentina would that evening formally accept the proposed terms. The Argentine approval, which had been asked for by 10:00 A.M. Washington time, would possibly be available at 7:00 P.M. Washington time.

There was, however, a problem. Britain was only assumed to be engaged in the process.[4] The peace proposal was accepted in principle but not in detail. The gap between the "wishes" or "aspirations" of the Islanders left unsolved the problem of self-determination. Argentina could not place its future in the Islands in the hands of the Kelpers, who it knew very well had no desire to hold Argentine passports.

There was also an overreading in Lima and Buenos Aires of the silence coming out of Washington. Haig was clear that this meant no agreement, but Arias Stella was so sure that silence meant acceptance that he began making signing arrangements. Belaunde Terry began making press arrangements. However, as Arias Stella has said, Peru had negotiated mainly with Haig, whom it always took to be speaking for Britain. The Argentines believed that Pym was about to commit for a second and final time to their ideas.

Secretary Haig recalls that Belaunde Terry "represented these to both sides" and "gained acceptance in principle from both parties."[5] Haig must be referring to the second round of Peruvian negotiations. Belaunde had not contacted Britain in Round One, and probably did not in Round Two. He could not at this stage have gained acceptance in principle from the U.K. as he had not contacted the British. This leaves unclear exactly who first received the proposals for the United Kingdom and when. Costa Mendez recalls that at 11:00 A.M. in Buenos Aires Belaunde Terry called and said the U.K. had agreed to consider his plan. Who gave such U.K. agreement in principle? Haig had not yet seen Pym, though he believes he might have phoned him the evening before. Pym thinks not. Had the Peruvians had U.K. approval from the British Ambassador in Lima? He learned of the plan at 6:20 P.M. on his car radio in Lima, that is 8:20 P.M. in Buenos Aires. Thus in the morning he had not yet been to the Palace and had not talked to London on the situation in the South Atlantic.

Furthermore, the British did not undertake to "agree in principle" to the Peruvian initiative while Pym was with Haig. They discussed terms, presented de novo to Pym by Secretary Haig in the late morning of Sunday, May 2. It was more likely Haig than Belaunde who obtained British agreement in principle, if anyone did. It is equally unclear who accepted in principle for the United Kingdom. Pym and British Ambassador to Peru Charles William Wallace were the only officials contacted; Pym was the only one contacted at this point. There was certainly a negotiation, tacit or explicit, but it constituted a three-way demarche on Britain. As of Sunday noon, one cannot say that there was British agreement to anything, even in principle.

The process itself was not smooth or close to conclusion on Sunday afternoon. The co-mediators noted resistance on each side to one another. Haig mentioned resistance by the U.K. to Belaunde. Belaunde Terry said to Haig that he encountered a certain obstinance on the Argentine side. (The thesis ran that a Latin intermediary could not be the instrument of U.K. manipulation.)

Galtieri had told Belaunde that he, as Argentine President, must still ratify the Peruvian plan with his Senate, by which he meant the Argentine Officer Corps. Belaunde pressed for an answer and was promised that the 7:00 P.M. meeting would consider the proposal favorably and that he would have firm Argentine agreement by 8:00 P.M. Buenos Aires time (6:00 P.M. in Lima).

Belaunde scheduled an 8:00 P.M. Lima press conference to announce peace in the South Atlantic.

The timing and meaning of Belaunde's conversation with Galtieri is key to an understanding of the Peruvian initiative. At 2:15 P.M. on Sunday, May 2, in Buenos Aires it was 1:15 P.M. in Washington and 12:15 P.M. in Lima. (See the chronology at the end of the chapter.) Belaunde had taken the initiative to confirm Costa Mendez's statement that an agreement was possible. Costa Mendez had so informed his staff at 2:00 P.M. Buenos Aires time. Galtieri would not, however, commit. It is likely an overstatement to say that Argentina had agreed in principle. The drafting of the last few key words was everything in this negotiation. There was nothing from a British source to indicate any corresponding enthusiasm at the other end of the chain. One gets the feeling that Galtieri was engaged in a holding action. True, one member of the Junta was out of Buenos Aires, but the two sides' military forces were trying to change the picture totally. The Argentine Air Force and Naval Air arm were seeking the British fleet to make a decisive first attack. At the same time, a parallel peace effort was being explored by the United Nations.

U.N. Secretary General Perez de Cuellar's proposal to mediate the dispute was known to the Junta on May 2. Argentine U.N. Ambassador Ros had seen the Secretary General around 6:00 P.M. in New York. It was accepted on the 5th of May. The formal proposal was received after midnight but before Moya and Iglesias left for Peru, and was one of the reasons they gave Belaunde for deferring his effort. The expectation of a U.N. proposal had not only aborted a planned major Argentine effort in the U.N. Security Council, but perhaps been a factor in the delay in accepting the Peruvian plan.

As an alternative for the Argentines, U.N. handling of the crisis may also have *unintentionally* undercut the Peruvian effort. By that evening, the U.N. alternative was already being discussed with the British Foreign Secretary by Perez de Cuellar in New York. Enrique Ros and Perez de Cuellar learned only then of the Peruvian plan. Pym had already discussed it with Haig. In Costa Mendez's opinion, Perez de Cuellar was never happy with the Peruvian effort and, in any case, Pym and the U.K. Ambassador were scheduled to have a working dinner with the Secretary General to discuss his initial proposal on May 2. This implies that the U.K. was focused on the U.N. mediation. Ironically, Argentina was focusing at that moment on the Peruvian plan and believed Britain to be similarly engaged, but began to consider the tactical advantages of the U.N. where their case had so much paper on its side. Regardless, the two competing plans were about to be dealt a blow by the other approach to conflict management—the graduated use of force.

TORPEDOED: ARGENTINE PERCEPTIONS

At 3:00 P.M. Washington time, at early dusk in the South Atlantic, the British nuclear hunter-killer submarine H.M.S. *Conqueror* put two venerable World

War II–vintage Mark 8 torpedoes into the port bow and side of the Argentine cruiser ARA *General Belgrano,* sending her to the bottom within the hour.[6] Symbol of her nation's navy, the 10,650-ton *Belgrano* had upgraded electronics and the significant firepower of another era. Equally as important, she bore a name carried by Argentine warships for over a century. Like the carrier *Veinticinco de Mayo,* there was an ARA *General Belgrano* at the siege of Montevideo in the 1840s. These names are symbols of Argentine nationalism. The *Belgrano's* loss meant even more to Argentina than one of her two capital ships; it was the loss of a major national symbol.

As the Argentine Junta met to decide on the Belaunde Terry plan on the evening of the 2nd, it seemed that the *Belgrano* had been lost with most if not all of her complement of over 1,000 enlisted men and officers.[7] The meeting had been called to "ratify" the Foreign Minister's recommendation that the Junta accept the Peruvian plan, which was based on his belief that peace had been obtained with a combination of honor and a certain open-endedness which would allow further dogged pursuit of Argentine interests. "Ratification" may assume too much precision and agreement as of the start of the meeting: The Navy Chief's reaction to the first reports is said to have been "Over one word?"— that is, Argentina could not accept inclusion of the term "wishes" of the Islanders; Britain could not accept "interests." Many lives and valuable time in the search for a peaceful solution had been lost over just such single words in the month since Argentina opened hostilities. In tears, Admiral Anaya said that he would resign as Chief of the Navy when the hostilities were concluded as he could not continue in office with the blood of so many sailors on his hands. He said, however, that he would neither veto nor second-guess a decision by the Junta to accept the Peruvian peace plan and avert more widespread hostilities.[8]

Anaya thus provided the rest of the group with leeway to either accept the Peruvian terms, continue exchanges through the Peruvian intermediaries, or pursue other channels such as the United Nations. He did not make (nor did he provide for others) any excuse of nonbelligerent intent for the cruiser and her escort of two destroyers. He himself knew full well what her orders had been and that any run for the cover of the coast had been ordered before the Peruvian plan and was not done as a peace gesture. The British Task Force could not be found, the Navy was vulnerable and the fleet was withdrawing in favor of air attacks.

He also understood that the naval war was on in the South Atlantic. British Defense Minister John Nott had warned on the Wednesday before the Sunday on which the TEZ (Total Exclusion Zone) came into force that, "We will shoot first. We will sink them, *certainly within* the 200-mile limit" (emphasis added).[9] At least two nuclear subs were known to be on station enforcing that zone. Argentina would make much in public of the *Belgrano's* being outside the zone. A lack of clarity about the center (middle or shores of the islands) and radius (statute or nautical miles) did not cloud the fact that it was the *minimum* area in which combat would be joined, or that the two countries were at war. The wider area was the South Atlantic: On April 23, the U.K. had announced that any Argentine ships threatening the Task Force would be attacked. Indeed, the April 23 warning was more strict than a caution not to attack: The 200-mile Maritime Exclusion Zone was held to be without prejudice to the right to self-defense and "any approach on the part of Argentine warships . . . which could amount to a threat *to interfere with the mission of British forces* in the South Atlantic will encounter the appropriate response" (emphasis added).[10] (Unknown to the Argentines was that subs were on a tighter leash than this.)

Argentina had also declared the war at sea: Her statement in reaction to the TEZ was that Argentine forces would sink any British vessel that sailed either within 200 miles around the Falklands or a within a 200-mile belt off the Argentine coast. Thus they declared a *mare clostrum* and a free-fire zone tantamount to declared war from the 47th to almost the 60th parallels, and from the Argentine coast well toward Africa, and thus they tacitly defined the outer limit of the declared war at sea as the U.K. had defined the minimum contested area. The lead element of the British Task Force was within the Argentine declared war zone. Soon 10,000 British soldiers and sailors would be within it and vulnerable.

There was indeed already a state of war between Great Britain and Argentina. Even ignoring the invasion as an act of war, as Argentina did, they had fought in the South Georgia Islands on April 25, and had lost the Argentine submarine *Santa Fe*. Costa Mendez had said on that day that the two parties were technically at war. (The Argentine public learned only later of the opening rounds of the South Atlantic war.) On May 1, Britain had bombed and shelled the Falklands. Sadly for the officers and men of the *Belgrano*, the Junta had begun to believe its own statements that it had not committed an act of war in landing in the Falklands, and continued to so protest.

It also seemed to believe itself immune from the clear, declared British intent to use force. Admiral Juan Jose, Lombardo turned *Belgrano* away from the islands and the zone on which she had been closing when an expected British landing did not materialize. The point of wave-off was clearly based on an assumption (perhaps unconscious and certainly unthinking) that she could hunt and hurt the Royal Navy with impunity outside the zone; that the TEZ was a barrel in which Argentina could shoot British fish. This ignored the specific warning not to endanger the task force or even its mission. An Etendard/Exocet attack on the British Task Force had just aborted when aeriel refueling could not be completed. The Argentine forces, sea and air, were in sum at war. Their orders were to find and destroy the British Task Force. Its forward elements found and destroyed the *Belgrano* first.

Whether or not the Junta believed it, the Argentine public and a good deal of world opinion thought the *Belgrano* was an isolated, unjustifiable act of war in a state of armed peace. Former Foreign Minister Costa Mendez firmly believes that Prime Minister Thatcher ordered the *Belgrano* sunk precisely in order to torpedo the Belaunde negotiation.[11] The former Foreign Minister is sure the plan had been accepted by Argentina on the basis of the text of May 2. In the view of the Argentine military and the Argentine public, and hence in the political calculus of the Junta as a whole, the sinking of the *Belgrano* made compromise at that moment unacceptable for Argentine National Honor. Within hours of the sinking of the *Belgrano,* Galtieri informed Belaunde that the deal was off. It still has not been established that it was ever on.

BRITISH PERCEPTIONS

The British Government is adamant that the *Belgrano* was sunk for purely military reasons, since London knew nothing of the Peruvian proposals, and the Government also believes the statements by Admiral Lombardo on *Belgrano's* orders and how he would have acted confirm its contention.

The British view of the state of negotiations on May 1 and 2 was very much conditioned by the military situation. Pym had returned to Washington stating that he was there to visit an ally rather than the mediator of the previous week. South Georgia had been retaken on April 25. Port Stanley had been bombed and other attacks had been made on the Falkland Islands themselves.

After midday May 2, the British War Cabinet met at "Chequers," the country residence of the Prime Minister, and decided to approve the sinking of the Argentine cruiser *Belgrano* by the nuclear submarine *Conqueror*. At 8:00 P.M. London time (3:00 P.M. EST), the order was carried out.

Pym had met with Haig for two hours on Sunday morning in Washington. His signals to the British were mixed: While conveying President Reagan's conviction that U.K. forces were doing the work of the free world, he also pleaded that large-scale hostilities were unnecessary. He outlined the Peruvian initiative in general form. Haig noted that the ideas were similar to his own of the previous month, but thought they would be more acceptable to Buenos Aires having been posed by another South American government. He tried not to convey his personal skepticism.

Henderson's view is that the Haig-Belaunde terms could not possibly be described as proposals. Pym was not moved. He replied that while he was, of course, ready to consider new ideas, the seven-point Peruvian plan was not all that different from the Haig proposals he had rejected. Pym said that he would need to discuss any new ideas with the Cabinet on his return to London.

Haig agreed that both more time and more work were needed. They met again for lunch at the British Embassy and then were in touch via Henderson in the afternoon before Pym's departure for New York. The Belgrano was hit at 3:00 P.M.. If Haig's call was to relay Argentine acceptance in principle of what had been discussed in the morning and over lunch, the close timing was a tragedy for the *Belgrano*.

Henderson's account is that only at this point (in the late afternoon) was it possible to make a report to London. The telegram was dispatched at 5:15 P.M. EST; that is,10:15 P.M. in London, or 2 hours and 15 minutes after the captain of the *Conqueror* carried out his instructions of that morning to torpedo the *Belgrano*. The British view was that

Nothing had happened in Washington to suggest that any new peace initiative was afoot, or that anything more significant was likely than the numerous proposals that had been made in previous weeks, to which the Argentines had always responded negatively.[12]

The British Foreign Secretary's perspective was that discussions were going on *between Washington, Lima, and Buenos Aires* about the possibility of some new ideas for peace being put forward with Peruvian blessing.

"GRADUATED" FORCE/POLITICAL SHOCK

In determining whether there was a viable negotiation in progress, one must look at British strategic thinking and receptivity to a peace initiative over the weekend of May 1–2. Britain clearly was involved in a carefully thought-out process of using graduated force to apply political pressure. It does not appear, however, that after the bombings and shellings of Saturday, May 1, that the Cabinet or the Foreign Minister were particularly atuned to the Argentine reactions. To reap the political benefit, one must be able to interpret it. Secretary Pym gave every indication of this while he was in the United States functioning more in his former role as Secretary of State for Defense. He spoke upon his arrival Saturday evening of concentrating the minds of the Argentine government. Before departure for home on May 3 (even after the *Belgrano* incident), Pym said in New York that Britain wished to maintain diplomatic, military and political pressure on Argentina in order to force Argentina to bargain seriously. He was clearly thinking in terms of not only the initial actions but further, *continuous* military pressure. The continuity was meant to produce not marginal but rather major change in the Argentine position.

This explains in large measure Pym's apparent "insensitivity" to the *Belgrano* incident and the consistent nature of his statements concerning the use of force in pursuit of a diplomatic settlement before and after the sinking. The British were quite clear and consistent about meaning to use force all along. They said it before the Task Force was dispatched, while the Task Force was en route to Ascension, and after the Task Force arrived in the Falklands area. The warnings were consistent both unilaterally and via Haig during his mediation. The *Belgrano* sinking would not have struck Pym as an escalation since before his departure from London on Saturday, May 1, he had been fully briefed on the planning for the attacks on the Falklands. The use of strategic bombers to attack the Islands from Ascension, as well as the first engagements of the enemy by naval gunfire and strafing and bombardment by the Task Force's Harriers constituted a fulfillment of the threat that force would be used should Argentina not choose to abandon the Islands via a diplomatic settlement. Whatever his knowledge of Argentine actions, intentions, or capability on the military side during Saturday and Sunday, Pym knew before he saw Haig that Argentina's time for diplomacy without being subject to the sanction of force had run out. More than a full day before the sinking of the *Belgrano,* Britain had moved past that point in the trade-off between the use of force and the use of diplomacy. It was not the British intention to move beyond that point in the fully measurable way that had been possible in South Georgia with a limited number of Argentine defenders employing unsophisticated weapons.

In taking on Argentina at sea, on land, and in the air in the area of the Falklands themselves, Britain was choosing to use all the military assets which it could bring to bear against any Argentine targets that would seem to have a demonstration effect *or that should present themselves in defense of the Islands.* In what it viewed as self-defense, Britain had chosen to wage fairly unrestricted warfare. This decision making was already completed and indeed was well into implementation when Pym left for Washington. Decisions and actions known to him already had the two parties engaged in active hostilities. There was from the British viewpoint no question of ''escalation'' or ''disproportionate reaction'' in decisions such as the *Belgrano.* In this sense, Britain was very definitely not atuned to peace overtures along lines already rejected. The United Kingdom saw the situation as already escalated and due to escalate further as the Argentines no doubt would react to their attacks on the Falklands proper. Britain was thus not in a receptive frame of mind for the Peruvian initiative. Any successful appeal to the United Kingdom at that stage in the trade-off between force and diplomacy would have needed to offer much more.

In failing to perceive the point events had reached, the mediators and the other party continued to advance elements that might have been adequate at a former stage but were not now sufficiently appealing to compensate the hurts and risks of the United Kingdom. Just as critically, Argentina and Peru relied on Secretary Haig's judgment as to what would suffice to secure a cease-fire from Great Britain. Haig's judgments about the trade-offs were colored by his experience of the previous month, when British priorities and possibilities had been considerably different. Thus, three out of four links in the chain of communication were operating on a different vision than what the United Kingdom could accept, and when the trade-offs were set before a U.K. representative for the first time, he found them out of date and unacceptable; they looked more like the trade-offs of the previous month's bargaining, before Britain had had to pay the price of recapturing South Georgia and run the risk of entering Falklands waters with the exposure to submarine, surface, and air attack which this implied in disproportionately risky terms for the British Task Force. Thus, to the British Foreign Secretary there was no negotiation progress, no new terms offered, no sign in this initiative of what he was looking for: Argentine concessions in response to the large-scale British use of force beginning Saturday morning. Indeed, the Peruvian initiative would have seemed to a British observer to have taken no account of the punishment Britain felt it had dealt Argentina on Saturday; to be, in a sense, an effort to ignore increasing applicability of British power. Any favorable consideration of that initiative would be tacit acceptance of an apparent Argentine statement that the arrival of the British Task Force in the area could not be translated into diplomatic advantage.

However, while internally consistent, the British missed one point in their view that carrots alone or carrots with the threat of the stick had failed and that it was time for a light use of the stick in order to produce political change. Argentine perceptions of the initial British attacks were not that these were limited or being gradually intensified. To the garrison on the Falklands, which had expected the British onslaught for some time and feared the worst, the initial military actions generated complete panic, at least in some quarters. More than one rumor and more than one signal to headquarters spoke of full-scale British invasion having been repelled. Weeks later, Argentine military analysts were still speaking of the repulse of full-scale British amphibious operations and the *Belgrano* at one point was indeed closing on the Islands in order to assist in defending against what was seen as an invasion. The shock wave from this overreaction to what the British saw as chastisement was not only military but also political. If the military effects were few, with casualties probably under 100 and little damage to the key runway, the Argentines were shaken in two senses. First, their own capabilities were revealed as less than they had thought. The submarines failed to torpedo any British ships. The planes from their only carrier could not be launched. The new air-to-ship cruise missile could not be brought to bear for lack of a well developed air-to-air refueling capability. This created a second shock effect as military reassessment led to political reassess-ment. After May 1, no one could delude themselves that the British had not come to fight. Senior officers and possibly the Junta itself suffered their *first* doubts as to whether Argentina could hold, much less win, in the Falklands. The Government faced in bleak perspective for the first time the prospects of losing not only the war but also its own power. However, the doubts were stayed by the illusion that Argentina had repulsed a British landing. Thus the sinking of the Belgrano had all the more politico-military impact. What was seen by the British as a one-step escalation came in several senses as a massive blow to the Government and the military structure of Argentina.

There is some doubt as to whether massive pressure or military "sticks" can produce political change. There is certainly a point past which any political system goes into the equivalent of shock. While the political half-life of the Junta was no concern of Pym's ("I'm afraid I don't mind what happens to the Argentine government. . . . Whether they fall or change two or three times"), it was very much his concern whether that government could continue to take effective decisions and give force to them.[13] It was, principally, vital that they be able to make key concessions and exercise military restraint in order to manage the crisis they had created. Pym hinted in his departure press conference at open-mindedness about the eventual political status of the islands but was quite clear that the right of people to choose their government for themselves would deter-mine British positions.

After Washington, Pym met with the Secretary General to discuss his ideas for a solution to the Falklands crisis. Here, too, the emphasis was not on compromise but rather concession. He discouraged U.N. involvement, be it the good offices of the Secretary General or the further convening of the Security Council.

From May 1–3, Pym expressed quite clearly his own and his government's determination. (Though this was no warhawk. Leaks of Pym's comments and arguments throughout the crisis revealed a statesman very much concerned with humanitarian issues, regular warnings of intent to use force, and remaining open to peace.) He clearly saw force in both tactical and strategic terms. He said, after the *Belgrano* incident and after becoming aware of the Peruvian peace plan and its likely fate following the sinking, "When we succeed, and we intend to succeed—if possible by negotiation, if not by force—the world will be a safer place." However, in early May a "little" force was to be used to produce results but did not because it was not so perceived—Argentina viewed the sinking of the *Belgrano* as a major escalation.

THE THREAT: FORCE FOR ITS OWN SAKE

Differences in Argentine and British judgments about the threat each represented to the other were radically different by the weekend on May 1–2 when the British fleet arrived off the Falklands. Each Government in general perceived the other as hostile and on the attack. One crucial distinction, however, is that the British fleet was primarily "softening up" or making initial attacks against the Islands themselves in support of the politico-military goal of producing negotiated change, but while units of the Argentine Navy such as its Marines and probably a submarine were engaged in the defense of the Islands, the nature and role of the Argentine Navy over that weekend were different: Its contribution to Argentine interests was to be the destruction of the British "armada." That mission led to a change in British planning and operations: The day after the first softening up attacks on the Islands, the British Navy sank a major unit of the Argentine Navy.

From the British perspective in early May, Argentine air and naval forces were real and immediate threats. On May 1, the two sides attacked each other directly for the first time in the Falklands area. The Argentine effort was by the Air Force from shore bases. Some of the planes were shot down, but the Task Force Commander had come face to face with the vulnerability of his units. There were still Argentine naval, submarine, and naval air power to be dealt with: The *Veinticinco de Mayo* group (the carrier, and the destroyers *Hercules* and *Santisima Trinidad,* spotted by a Harrier and tailed by the nuclear submarine [SSN] H.M.S. *Splendid*) was north of the islands. The *Belgrano* group (the cruiser and the Exocet-armed destroyers *Bouchard* and *Piedra Buena*) was cruising back and forth on patrol in the south between Isla de los Estados (Staten Island) off South America and the Burdwood Bank south of the Falklands. Her patrol took her in both directions in a screening pattern. At either end she had shallow water for protection from submarines. The modern diesel submarine *ARA San Luis* had been at sea since mid-April with "free fire zone" orders.[14] The orders to all parts of the Argentine fleet were to find and engage the enemy. There was no restraint order; no rules of engagement to avoid a clash. This was not armed peace while negotiation was pursued. The British Task Force east of the Islands felt vulnerable from both directions:

> Early on the morning on 2 May, all the indications were that *25 de Mayo*, the Argentine carrier, and a group of escorts had slipped past my forward SSN barrier to the north, while the cruiser *General Belgrano* and her escorts were attempting to complete the pincer movement from the south, still outside the Total Exclusion Zone. But *Belgrano* still had *Conqueror* on the trail. My fear was that the *Belgrano* would lose the SSN as she ran over the shallow water of the Burdwood Bank, and that my forward SSN barrier would be evaded down there too. I therefore sought, for the first and only time throughout the campaign, a major change to the Rules of Engagement to enable *Conqueror* to attack *Belgrano* outside the Exclusion Zone.[15]

Argentine military events ran during May 1 and 2 with their own logic, independent of the political process; even independent of the Argentine military, as senior officers let the Junta know that they were not prepared for full-scale war with Great Britain and would not countenance it. The pace of military events was also independent of the Peruvian peace process. (This was not by accident or oversight, lack of receptivity or overconcentration on the tactical, as in the British case but as a matter of high policy.) The S2 patrol aircraft of the *Veinticinco de Mayo*, for example, located the British Task Force northeast of the Falklands and at about 300 miles distance at 11:30 P.M. Buenos Aires time. They were ordered to close on, engage, and destroy the Task Force, which was accompanying what appeared to be one of the carriers. They steamed at approximately 20 knots all night and were able to close the distance to 180 miles separating the two Task Forces, normally good range for the Skyhawks of the aircraft carrier. Two factors conspired against this air attack of pre-dawn on May 2: The carrier had generator or engine problems, and it could not make flank speed. At the same time, the wind in the South Atlantic was absolutely still (quite a rare event). Thus, neither the natural wind nor the carrier's speed were sufficient to launch the Skyhawks with full bomb loads and full range.

Then the two fleets lost each other. The attack had to be broken off on May 2. Admiral Lombardo ordered his northern groups to seek safe home waters until the attack could be reassembled. The military operations in question covered the period from before Galtieri was called by Belaunde Terry until after his purportedly affirmative answer (rather more an agreement in principle from which a debate of no less than ten phone calls ensued with Belaunde and positions were traded back and forth between Lima and Washington). The pattern of Argentine search for advantage in both the diplomatic and military areas in parallel would continue on May 2 as its Air Force was ordered to try to carry out the mission at which the Navy had failed. While the Argentines argued about fine points (for example, whether the United States would be in the group of guarantor countries or not), the first Super Etendard mission was launched to try to destroy the carrier with Exocets.

There are two elements to the judgment of a military threat: intentions and capability. In a naval engagement, capability must include both steaming times from present position and the ''reach'' of weapons systems. Present intentions (even if known or estimated) must take second place to capability—the maximum harm that could be inflicted.

British and Argentine perceptions about the *Belgrano* Task Group diverged by the hour. The *Belgrano* was on a patrol line that took her back and forth below the Islands. Whether she was going toward or away from the South American coast at any particular point did not affect her mission: She was to find and destroy enemy warships. The Argentine Navy may have thought of her as being a separate unit with distinct purposes. Such internal assumptions are lost on an enemy commander. From the point of view of the British Task Force, its task group was another combat element of the Argentine navy with considerable reach and fire power. Added to misperceptions about staying out of the minimal TEZ, this may have lulled the Task Group into a sense that they were not in the war that had begun at dawn the day before, if not on South Georgia the previous week.

H.M.S. *Conqueror* probably picked up the first signs of the *Belgrano* task group, or more likely their oiler, after 4:00 P.M. on Friday, April 30. On Saturday she approached the task group using her passive sonar. She closed at periscope depth on Saturday afternoon and from 4,000 yards observed them refueling at sea. (Had the Royal Navy wished to produce carnage it could have most efficiently done so then: a flaming chaos of three combat vessels, their full stocks of fuel and ammunition engulfed in the flaming fuel of their fully loaded tanker. Two thousand or more casualties might have resulted.) *Conqueror* tracked the group overnight Saturday from 10,000 yards. No changes in the rules of engagement were requested. To understand the request of May 2 and its approval one must factor in Argentine naval orders of later that night (full-scale attack on the British fleet) and the unknown positions (therefore unassessable threat) of the task groups in the north.

What specific threat did the Southern Argentine surface units represent? The British view was that the *Belgrano* task force was itself a threat: that she and/ or the two escorting destroyers, at least, were equipped with Exocet missiles and were on patrol in search of British surface units.[16] Whatever *Belgrano's* position or course at the time of the attack,[17] she was likely known from intercepted messages to be searching for the British Task Force, if not herself executing the Argentine Navy order to the main task force to seek and destroy Royal Navy surface units.[18]

Belgrano and her group were a mobile asset, and became an immediate threat and a priority target when the other Argentine units were ''lost.'' An older ship, she was a survivor as the U.S.S. *Phoenix* of the attack on Pearl Harbor. Her

1939 generation of light cruisers had watertight compartments and up to 4-inch waterline armor. Perhaps the last fully armored ship afloat, she also had the heavy firepower of another era: five triple-gun turrets of 6-inch guns, and eight 5-inch guns, and two quadruple Sea Cat surface-to-air missile (SAM) launchers. Well able to defend herself or destroy a ship 13 miles away with gunfire, her reach was in effect doubled by the 26-mile range of the Exocets of her escorts. *Belgrano* also had the length that conveys speed in ship hulls. She was not using it on the return leg toward Latin America when she was torpedoed, but it could have been used to close distance overnight to defend the Islands, engage the Task Force, or attack individual units southeast of the Falklands. She also blocked any southward movement and foreclosed operations in her direction as she could call in land-based air strikes by Argentine planes against any targets she might spot or engage. In this sense, she was a focus for the real source of Argentine strength in operations off her coast: the considerable reach of maritime and land-based air forces. She herself kept carefully within the range of the Super Etendard-Exocet fighter bombers, the innermost of three rings of Argentine air capability.

The British Task Force on May 2 was within the reach of the Mirage and Sky Hawk jets. With the whole Argentine Navy deployed as Task Force 79 in search of the British fleet, it was no mean feat to be able to say where the enemy was not. The Argentines were having difficulty locating the British units and to be able to foreclose any area was a considerable asset. In this sense, *Belgrano* and her group could confirm the presence or absence of British units south of the Falklands, confining the search area to the east and northeast. Thus, when the *Belgrano* task force was not serving as one end of a closing pincer, it was an anvil for a hammer from the north.

When contact was lost with the *Veinticinco de Mayo,* the Task Force had to assume she was closing on them and that *Belgrano* could do the same. At that point; *Belgrano*'s route on a direct heading for the British Task Force would take her across the Burdwood Bank, putting *Conqueror* in depths in which one cannot "run deep," and she would within 200 miles close on the forward radar picket position where Sheffield was to be hit 36 hours later.[19]

If the carrier group and other northern task groups were closing on the British forces, they had been lost and therefore there was no way to affect their intentions. Any move to stop full naval engagement would have to be against the *Belgrano* group. Thus, the only way to blunt the Argentine attack in the early hours of May 2 seemed to be to strike at the only Argentine target: the flag ship of Task Group 79.3.[20] The change was agreed to by 1:00 P.M., received aboard *Conqueror* by 6:00 P.M., and the attack carried out at 8:00 P.M. London time.

Indeed, whether the *Belgrano* herself or the whole fleet was attacking or retreating did not change the strategic reality for the British Task Force Commander: The Argentine fleet was an active, even aggressive, enemy overnight on May 1–2. Whether on the offensive or awaiting better conditions for one, its mission was clearly not politico-military pressure but the destruction of British power as projected into the South Atlantic. (The British Task Force could be argued to have maintained both roles until it landed troops.) Argentina was operating offensively in familiar home waters, close to its bases and sources of supply. Returns toward the continent were tactical moves of advantage, not political or strategic withdrawals. Argentina was still occupying and supplying the Falklands by sea. The British Task Force lacked early warning, reconnaissance, and air defense capabilities. The Task Force was therefore, in its own estimation, highly vulnerable.

The Peruvian effort was not known to the British War Cabinet then at Chequers. Two alternative scenarios involving the threat suggest that military factors would have led to the sinking *even had* the British known. Had the Pym proto-plan been weighed against the security of the British Task Force, especially following the three weeks viewed as Argentine diplomatic evasion, the likely conclusion would have been to proceed with action against Argentine forces. Such action might have been taken *additionally* or *solely* in the judgment that further direct and heavy military pressure was more likely to secure than prevent diplomatic progress.[21] That assumes, however, that the other party has seen the process as one of increasing real pressure, and that it is ready and able to make concessions in proportion to both the costs of bringing that power to bear and the costs of *not* using it.

THE DEAL?

The Peruvian peace plan was both of necessity and by design left in outline form during Round One. Dealing only with the elements of the problem and not the details for implementation, the plan had the possibility of being worked out quickly.

Designed for ease of negotiation by each mediator with his assigned party, it was a tool for the convenience of the co-mediators. The shorthand nature of the procedure, however, had different implications from the perspectives of the two parties.

Argentina's problems with the settlement proposed were both with individual pieces of drafting language (political implications) and with some elements of the structure of the enforcement group, particularly membership (to exclude the United States).

When the plan was presented to him, the British Foreign Secretary was faced with several additional considerations. Beyond his possible substantive and procedural disagreements with the proposals, as an outline the Peruvian plan would offer none of the detail and hence assurance that was inherent in British goals. Any arrangement that did not *guarantee* self-determination for the Kelpers conveyed no benefit or advantage to the United Kingdom.

The trade-off between force and diplomacy was a shifting balance. It had shifted considerably by May 1 as the U.K. had already borne the costs of moving a major fleet to the South Atlantic and retaking South Georgia by force. The Task Force had then been moved to the Falkland Islands, and on the previous day had not only bombed and shelled the Argentines from the sea but had conducted a bombing directly from Ascension with mid-air refueling. Britain had borne all the costs of the failure to agree over the previous month of diplomatic effort at the U.N. and through the Haig shuttle. The price to Argentina referred to constantly by Haig for failure to agree had not been paid. The use of force had been one-sided by Argentina at the beginning of April. At the beginning of May, counterforce was used. Any diplomatic effort had to take account of that set of British perceptions. The least likely form for doing that was an outline settlement in which only the implementation period would disclose the exact meaning of the terms arrived at. After May 1, only *clear* guarantees would correspond to the fully developed ability of the U.K. to apply power.

On Sunday, May 2, there was midday discussion amounting to negotiation of a package solution to the Falklands crisis. Secretary Haig (as well as his special assistent Woody Goldberg and his press spokesman Dean Fisher) recalls that the U.K. had accepted the Peruvian draft to within a few words of final agreement.[22] When someone said after the sinking, that he thought there had been an agreement, Fisher replied that there had. The impression that a deal was struck, indeed that an active negotiation of meaningful content was in process, seems to have been shared certainly by Argentina and its co-mediator Peru, and probably by the U.S. co-mediator. The British perception of the situation was quite different.

Haig's recollection seems at first glance quite different from Pym's:

We had progressed rather well on the telephone. We were down to words, single words and specifically in two paragraphs of the six points, and of course these words were critical to know whether or not they would be acceptable to the British government. . . . Basically, we arrived at some articulations that appeared that they might be [acceptable]."[23]

This implies the British were negotiating, but Haig means he had derived these formulae with Peru and Argentina by phone. The terms up to Sunday at 10:00 A.M. quite literally "appeared" that they might be acceptable—Britain had not seen them as they evolved.

Pym's recollection of the same Sunday morning meeting was that:

There was no text discussed between us on Sunday, no actual words. We discussed ideas and headings . . . but there was no actual piece of paper with a text being offered—there was nothing like that.[24]

Both Haig's specifics and Pym's lack of a text are accurate: This was an outline. The discussions were with others. The details were not spelled out. This was a deliberately sketchy outline; what the British call "heads of agreement." However, in the heads-of-agreement working method one works backward to details of implementation. In this crisis, the *details* were the substance; the fine points were the points for which men were going to die.

Former Foreign Secretary Francis Pym has made it clear that he did not see
Britain as engaged in a negotiation. He states that he did not fly to Washington
on the evening of May 1 for last-minute peace talks but rather to review with
the U.S. Secretary the new situation resulting from Argentina's rejection of the
U.S. draft. On May 2 he met for two hours with Haig late in the morning.[25]
During that meeting he states that Haig first informed him that

> The Americans and Peruvians were discussing a new possible basis for progress towards
> a diplomatic solution. . . . He outlined the elements to me briefly. I made it clear to him
> that while I was very ready to consider any new proposal, what he had outlined was in
> essence not very different from his own scheme which had just been totally rejected by
> Argentina.[26]

In effect, Pym turned down the feeler from the U.S. about the Peruvian proposal.
There would thus seem to have been no basis even by mid-afternoon, Sunday,
May 2, for anyone telling Buenos Aires that Britain was interested or was
considering it in principle. He expressed doubts about Argentine final acceptance
"if and when the details had been worked out"[27] and said that on the other side,
Britain would need time: "I would, of course, need to discuss any new proposal
with my colleagues in London on my return."[28] However, Pym did discuss
language with Haig and did agree to take the idea home. The discussion of
desiderata left Haig and the U.S. with further hope and means to pursue a process
in which they were now deeply immersed along with Lima and Buenos Aires.
The problem was that neither Pym, much less London, realized they were involved in that process. Like the Junta, Pym was dragging his feet. The impetus
came from the mediators, not the parties. The British government has said that
Haig had no contact with it over that weekend.[29]

Pym did not behave in Washington like an ally aware of specific orders to
sink a ship. He may well have been aware of the change in the orders of the
rules of engagement late on Sunday afternoon after leaving his lunch with Haig.
He is widely assumed even by British officials to have received news of the
change by phone and to therefore have had or to have missed a chance to tell
of the Peruvian plan. Embassies more often work by secure encrypted radio
cablegrams, and they tend to be one-way conversations.

By whatever means Pym learnt of the change, there is little difference between
his Saturday night and Sunday night statements on military pressure on Argentina.
Whenever he learned of the potential attack on the *Belgrano* (such an order for
the 25 de Mayo never could be implemented), it would seem to have been after
his session with Haig. With Haig he conveyed no sense that a ship was about
to be sunk in the middle of what Haig certainly saw as a negotiation. Neither
he nor Haig seems to have had any idea that time was about to become critical:
"Mr. Haig fully agreed that more time and more detailed work were needed."[30]
The two saw each other again for lunch, at which the Peruvian peace plan was
not the subject at hand, and exchanged messages (Pym originally said they spoke

on the telephone) before Pym flew to New York in the afternoon for evening talks with the U.N. Secretary General. Pym states that Haig was in agreement that further clarification and work on the plan would be needed. Timing was simply not critical in Pym's view:

I would hardly have left for New York if I had thought that anything remotely approaching an agreement—let alone peace—was at hand in Washington. Lengthy and detailed peace efforts had just failed because of the Argentine attitude. What Mr. Haig had outlined to me was at best a promising basis for further work. If the Peruvians had prepared the treaty ready for signature on the evening of May 2, they certainly gave us no indication of this neither in Lima nor in London. Nor did Mr. Haig say or suggest any such thing to me.[31]

What stage had the drafting of "the deal" reached by midday Sunday in Washington? The shape of the deal changed Saturday night and all day Sunday in parallel with but *behind* British military decision making. On Sunday morning, May 2, the War Cabinet was sitting down for its afternoon session as Pym was arriving for his Monday morning meeting with Haig. Haig's recollection was that by this stage:

We had progressed rather well on the telephone. We were down to words, single words and specifically in two paragraphs of the six points, and of course these words were critical to know whether or not they would be acceptable to the British government.[32]

The dialogue, however, is rather more a three-way U.S.- Peruvian-Argentine discussion. These three parties thought by late afternoon that the shape of the deal had narrowed to a single word. A fourth player, critically, was not in the game: The deal, however concrete, did not include the views and—what was to become critical within hours—the actions of Great Britain. The British Foreign Minister was a party, but thought that he had in effect declined or taken under advisement for his return to London for what was offered in the rough outline of the Peruvian plan. He proceeded to New York to discuss a U.N. effort. The British Government was not even yet aware of the outline format presented to its Foreign Minister.

The attitudes of the three participants in the British dinner for the U.N. Secretary General that evening are instructive. British Ambassador Sir Anthony Parsons recalls that the expectation was that the U.N. Secretary General Javier Perez de Cuellar was about to take over the peace effort in the wake of Haig's announced failure. The British Government viewed the agenda as a working dinner to discuss a negotiating initiative that the British knew the Secretary General was about to launch. Sir Anthony Parsons in testimony before the Foreign Affairs Committee of the House of Commons on Wednesday, April 11, 1984, said that he had received the impression from Pym that the Peruvian plan was in a heads-of-agreement (outline) form with no details. The U.N. Secretary

General, himself a Peruvian citizen and long-term Peruvian diplomat, knew little or nothing of the Peruvian initiative. Indeed he crossed wires with it.

Scattered news reports were brought to the participants during the evening. The three were focused on Perez de Cuellar's initiative. Nothing as strong as even British agreement in principle was indicated, and even in their private talks before the Secretary General's arrival, the British diplomats did not discuss the Peruvian initiative in any way other than in passing. It was not thought to be novel, did not seem to advance any new ideas beyond those of Secretary Haig's, and held promise little since most of its elements had been previously rejected by Argentina. These are not innate failings but rather due to following the Haig shuttle effort. Options which were of themselves viable were poisoned by previous rejection or acceptance followed by rejection by the other side. At heart, however, it was just too late. Argentina should have made its concessions 8,000 nautical miles sooner if peace were its plan.

Most tellingly for the British, Perez de Cuellar seemed neither to have much knowledge of nor interest in the Peruvian initiative. While it was hours too late for the bluejackets of the *Belgrano*, the Peruvian effort might have been merged with the U.N.'s interest. Neither the U.N. nor the British seemed to find it promising, and instead pursued in earnest a possible U.N. initiative. "Throughout that whole evening I have absolutely no recollection of that thought [holding off on the U.N. initiative in favor of the Peruvian proposals were they in such an advanced form and of such a nature as to stand a strong chance of producing results] being voiced by anybody round the table."[33]

THE LONDON CONNECTION

The Team B thesis poses several challenges to the Prime Minister's contention that the first indications of the possible Peruvian peace proposals reached London from Washington at 11:15 P.M. London time, and from Lima at 2:00 A.M. London time, May 3.

As regards Washington, Sir Terence Lewin is cited as believing that there was telephone contact between the FCO and Pym in Washington by secure lines, and Cecil Parkinson is cited as contending that there was regular contact between Chequers and Washington during the War Cabinet meeting on Sunday, May 2.

Team B contends that throughout that Sunday, Mrs. Thatcher was kept in the closest touch with the discussions in Lima on the Peruvian proposals, but does not say by whom. Cecil Parkinson is cited as having told the media that the War Cabinet during their meeting on Sunday was fully aware of the diplomatic initiatives in Washington of which he said the prime example was President Belaunde. His specific example would seem to indicate that what Parkinson meant were diplomatic initiatives in general and perhaps the ongoing interest of Belaunde. Since the crisis began on April 2, the Peruvian President had generated several proposals, including a cease-fire; none had been successful.

THE PHONE CALL

Having spent the morning with Haig (two hours at the U.S. State Department) as well as lunch (approximately one hour at the British Residence), Pym, as he was leaving Washington, was called by Secretary Haig. Pym originally recalled that he had spoken to Haig, but has since said that he authorized Henderson to speak to Haig. In any case, Haig's message seems to have been passed thus: The Peruvian plan should be given serious consideration. Pym's reply was passed along as: serious peace initiatives would be considered (but this did not appear to be such an initiative), and he would raise the plan upon return to London with the Cabinet.

A separate but more interesting question is: What was the full content of that message? Was Haig passing along further developments and details that should have piqued the interest of the British Foreign Secretary? Haig's call to Pym was made at approximately 2:30 P.M. Washington time. Thus, Haig would not have had significant additional information since Belaunde's call concerning the withdrawal of Peru and the United States as mediators.

In the Team B scenario, Pym declined to take the call in order not to have to confront his ally later with what he had learned from London: that the *Conqueror*'s Rules of Engagement had been amended and possibly that the *Belgrano* would be sunk. His urgency to get to New York is said to be inexplicable in the light of the availability of a shuttle flight between Washington and New York. Thus, it is concluded that between lunch and Haig's call, the U.K. Foreign Secretary had been told by London of the change in the rules of engagement. It is surmised that if there was a call that the Foreign Secretary either knew why or should have asked and did not want to let Haig in on this.

It is equally possible that Pym had known all day of a general change in the rules of engagement. Given the clear and indeed stated British attempt to convince the Argentines to take negotiating concessions through a display of force on Saturday, May 1, it is highly likely that the Foreign Secretary did not see an expansion of the area in which Argentine ships could be sunk as a radical change. From his defense briefings at Northwood before his departure he knew that the two navies were looking for each other with serious intent. He then learned that the *Belgrano* was now a permitted target, but perhaps that is all he was told.

There would be good reason not to tell the Foreign Secretary when abroad of any operational details such as the location of the *General Belgrano: Operational* orders are very closely held. Even where political advantage would be gained by early notification and diplomatic and press preparation for major military events, operational security does not permit. The British Submarine Service is a highly compartmentalized and almost separate part of the Royal Navy. The Silent Service is even more concerned with operational secrecy than other sections of the Senior Service. Were Pym aware of the change but not actual targeting (and certainly not of any intercepts of an Argentine fleet withdrawal order), he would have felt that he had already conveyed a two-part message: (1) in his arrival press conference to the effect that Britain meant to turn the military screw on Argentina, was entirely earnest about its stated principles, and would have them implemented, either at the negotiating table if possible or in the field by force if necessary; and, (2) that the Peruvian proposals were too vague and substantively inadequate, although he would put them to the Cabinet on his return to London (in several days), and hence that force was in order until and unless concrete concessions were made.

CLOSING THE LOOP: RISKS OF MULTILATERAL MEDIATION

Haig was making a last try at favorable immediate British consideration, and called Henderson with a message for Pym as the latter was leaving Washington for New York to emphasize the importance of the Peruvian ideas. Pym instructed Henderson to emphasize Britain's openness to new ideas of substance, but to emphasize that the Peruvian proposals seemed vague, indeterminate, and were not a solid basis for peace. Henderson reported to London that he had completed this demarche to Haig on the British approach by 6:00 P.M. Washington time, or 11:00 P.M. London time.

The diplomatic loop, from Pym's point of view, was closed. The Peruvian plan had not been accepted because of its vagueness, its similarity to previously rejected suggestions, and what was seen by the British Government as the vague state of its preparation. It could be pursued the next day in London.

That was not at all the impression of the other mediator and party. In Argentina it was felt that an active negotiation was underway and Argentina was about to accept the general terms. In Lima, the co-mediator believed that he had put together peace in the South Atlantic. Only in Washington was it possible to judge the lack of immediate and enthusiastic British response. This was conveyed to Lima. It probably did not seem profitable to the Peruvians to convey it to Buenos Aires, but that, along with the Peruvian non-reaction to Argentina's gambits, encouraged the Junta to ''string out'' the decisions.

It is indeed debatable whether the British Foreign Secretary believed himself engaged in a negotiation of any kind judging by his reticence not just about the degree of generality but the actual substance of the Peruvian plan. A key indicator of whether Britain felt engaged in a negotiation would be British knowledge of and reaction to the Argentine ''acceptance,'' subject only to approval by the Military Committee (the expanded executive meetings of the Junta) scheduled for that evening at 7:00 P.M. in Buenos Aires. The last Peruvian relay of Argentine positions and reactions to Washington was around 1:00 P.M. Washington time. A key question remains whether and when Haig learned of the ''ratification'' procedure and whether and when Haig told Pym the Argentines were on board? If Pym (and only Pym for the U.K.) knew of acceptance in principle, his reaction judging by his actions was that the Junta would not accept and no further exploration via Peru would be profitable. That judgment was a sound allocation of his efforts if and only if he did not know of a scheduled "ratification." Were the conveyance of that "acceptance in principle" of a fixed and final set of terms the message Haig was passing by telephone to Henderson for Pym, it was certainly to be judged a significant development. Whether it was a key development depended on British views on the terms.

There seems to have been no general, much less firm or specific, communication to Great Britain of an Argentine intention to ratify the Peruvian effort within hours. Otherwise, it seems unlikely Haig would have let Pym leave town. Still less was it clear to the "Anglo-Saxons" that Argentina thought it had said yes, subject only to Cabinet-level ratification. At whichever stage, this was a critical failure of communication if (but only if) Argentina was to be bound by the Peruvian framework. The four Foreign Ministers were in touch, but there seems to have been failures to pass the full message—if there was a full and meaningful message—along the chain between: (1) Argentina and Peru; (2) Peru and the United States; (3) the United States and the U.K. in Washington; and (4) the U.K. Minister/Ambassador and London/Chequers.

The lack of direct contact between London and Washington on even the fact that more than bombings were in the offing was tragic. The U.K. never did tell the United States about the *Belgrano:* By around 8:00 P.M. Washington time, Haig informed Henderson of the attack. Haig did not express a definite idea about the effect this would have on the Argentine Junta, but both knew what it implied for the Peruvian initiative. Pym, meeting in New York with U.N. Secretary General Javier Perez de Cuellar, found out from the press at midnight.

An alternative circuit which did not connect, if indeed there was a message of Argentine "preliminary acceptance," was via the British Ambassador in Lima. Peru chose, apparently, to ignore this direct channel to London, either by accident or design, by focusing on Haig's definitions of British minima and his replies based on his talks with or speaking for the British Foreign Secretary. The Peruvian-U.S. failure to distinguish between times when the Secretary was interpreting British needs, when he was conveying the reactions of Pym, and when (if ever) he was conveying definitive positions of Her Majesty's Government based on decisions by the Prime Minister and/or the War Cabinet is a part of the tragedy of the Peruvian intervention.

The British Embassy in Lima might have been actively used by the Peruvians as a confirmation channel to sort out the distinction between the three kinds of "bargaining."

The British Ambassador to Peru, Mr. C. W. Wallace, met with Peruvian Foreign Minister Arias Stella at London's initiative on Saturday, May 1 to brief the Peruvian on the situation in the South Atlantic.[34] Arias Stella asked if there were any way in which Peru could help, but did not give the British Ambassador any indication that Peru was considering a peace initiative. Belaunde called his Washington Ambassador later that evening and the peace process began. Haig and Belaunde put their initial contact in the evening.[35] Thus there was nothing for Wallace to be aware of on Saturday. He was briefing the Peruvians. On

Sunday, the fact that they were briefing *him* may have been precisely the problem. He and his post were excluded from a high-level, personalist loop. (He would not know until later that his Foreign Secretary was also partially cut out and his Prime Minister not even informed.)

The question is not, as defined by Team B, why Wallace sent no cables on the Peruvian initiative following the point—set by the Peruvians as noon Saturday—from which Wallace was kept informed. There was no Peruvian initiative at noon Saturday Lima time. There was a debate beginning Sunday morning Lima time between Peru and Argentina over the terms which had been worked out by Belaunde and Haig late Saturday night. What, then, was Wallace told on Sunday which would or should have been reported? If informed at Sunday noon, it was that Haig and Pym had worked it out. Nothing to report. It is highly improbable that he was told with any frankness of the Peruvian debate with Buenos Aires. Belaunde as co-mediator nonetheless saw himself as the person able to communicate with—and in that sense the agent of and guarantor for—Argentine interests. This left Peru with no incentive to be at all frank with the British Ambassador, even a British Ambassador who was a friend. He more likely found out on the way to his 6:00 P.M. briefing at the Foreign Ministry—too late.

At most, Wallace was likely told midday Sunday that a peace process was under way. One cannot assume (as in the Team B thesis) that this information was flashed to London. To understand why the British Embassy in Lima might not have done so even had they known, one has to look at the role, if any, of Ambassador Wallace and his staff in the Belaunde-Haig mediation between Galtieri and Costa Mendez in Buenos Aires and Foreign Secretary Pym in Washington.

The British Embassy in Lima was certainly underutilized by Pym and by Belaunde. London ordered Ambassador Wallace to brief the government of Peru. Assuming his orders were part of a round-robin briefing for all Latin Posts (else why Peru and why on a weekend?), Britain was probably "stage-setting" for reaction to the first bombings of the Falklands. Whatever Wallace would be told, was too low-key, too vague, and too guarded: The mediator had access to Pym via Haig, and did not "need" Wallace. The "information" passed him was probably procedural and possibly appeared to cut him out of the circuit, as in this hypothetical phrasing: "Your foreign minister has agreed through Haig that . . ." This "marginalization" of one circuit in the process denied the effort a backup channel which might have led to peace instead of chaos. It may come to be a classic case in diplomatic folklore of the damage done by marginalizing your resident ambassador.

At 6:00 P.M., Sunday, Lima time (midnight in London and four hours after the *Belgrano* sinking), President Belaunde authorized Foreign Minister Arias Stella to inform Ambassador Wallace. Wallace got his first "briefing" enroute—from his car radio and Belaunde's premature press talk. Arias Stella, still unaware of the torpedo attack, told Wallace, four and half hours after the sinking of the

Belgrano: (1) that on Saturday (*sic*) he had called Costa Mendez on behalf of Belaunde to urge that Argentina accept the U.S.-Peruvian plan, and that Belaunde and Haig had discussed the plan and evolved the seven-point formula; (2) that the plan had the approval of Argentine Foreign Minister Costa Mendez; (3) that Argentine President Galtieri had told Peruvian President Belaunde that he was inclined toward accepting the plan, but that Galtieri needed to consult with "his Senate" *and convince them;* and finally, (4) that the Junta was, at that moment, meeting, and that their reply was expected shortly.[36]

THE COST OF HIGH-LEVEL PERSONALIST DIPLOMACY

If indeed the British Ambassadors in Lima and Washington had known in time of the Peruvian proposals, it may not have been possible politically for either to have reported or evaluated them directly, as they knew that their Foreign Minister was personally engaged with the U.S. Secretary of State in negotiating them. In this sense, either embassy would have been constrained from doing its own reporting or analysis, which might have alerted London. The "marginalization" of those on the scene and equipped with the first-hand experience and knowledge of the situation is one of the costs of direct, admittedly efficient, high-level diplomacy. A combination of these two syndromes may have denied the British government precisely the needed cross-checking and pooling of expertise and information from its resident diplomats abroad.

Had Ambassador Wallace in Lima indeed had detailed, frank information from the Peruvian Foreign Ministry as to what was going on, its form was likely to have been by way of the passive brief; information as to what his foreign minister had already agreed on. This is hardly the stuff of a good telegram. It would convey second-hand information hours late, in probable duplication of reporting by the Foreign Minister himself, and with risk of inadvertant harm to the peace process, even internally. It was not until after Wallace was told of original, local developments in Lima that concerned his country and the host country directly; that is, local developments involving local characters that may have been news, such as Peruvian reactions to the knowledge that the *Belgrano* had been sunk, that Wallace sent his first reporting cable, received at 2.00 A.M. London time or 8:00 P.M. Lima time, a lapse of only an hour and a half after Wallace was briefed by the Peruvians on the scope and supposedly imminent outcome of the Peruvian first round. At that point, the "marginalized" Ambassador had something to say, and said it.

On Monday, May 3, the Peruvian Foreign Minister told the British Ambassador that on Sunday evening, May 2, the Argentine Junta had rejected the Peruvian proposal because of the torpedoing of the *Belgrano,* but had "not entirely closed the door."[37] This was probably too low-key a version of the wider Argentine reaction. Haig told Henderson in their Monday meeting that Belaunde had complained bitterly that the torpedoing had wrecked any chance of peace. Haig introduced the Buenos Aires rumor that U.S. intelligence and special weapons had allowed the sinking of the *Belgrano*.[38] He cautioned also about a general world reaction to the British use of force: that Britain had severely escalated the conflict. That is the most valid and telling critique of the torpedoing of the *Belgrano*. It is not a criticism, only a cost in a calculated balance of benefits and costs that nation-states including Argentina must make between diplomacy and force.

"GRADUATED" USE OF POLITICAL-MILITARY PRESSURE

Haig was then informed by the British Ambassador of the renewed Argentine attempts to locate and sink British ships. This Argentine withdrawal or non-ratification was what the U.K. would have expected, with or without the *Belgrano* incident. Britain was confirmed in its view that three weeks of relative military restraint had produced no Argentine flexibility; that it was time for force in support of diplomacy. The corollary is that one must be prepared to sense when force has been sufficient to produce progress in negotiations. Great Britain should have been looking for diplomatic "give" in response to its Saturday morning bombing of Stanley; it should have been sensitized to feelers and should have caught the Peruvian initiative if only by chance. The back-up for an earlier report by Pym would have been information from Peru relayed by the British Embassy in Lima.

Britain should have waited for some reaction to the bombings before pursuing a second round of force that weekend had its goal been only to exert graduated military pressure on Argentina. Argentine forces indeed seemed to expect a lull after the last air attacks at dusk.

There were several additional realities to be factored into a decision like that concerning the *Belgrano* beyond turning the political screw: Power projected by sea needs itself to be protected as it becomes increasingly exposed; such bringing to bear of power may not be viewed as leverage but only as bluster; the finely tuned steps may be shock waves to the enemy who misses the cues.

One can schematicize the British tacit bargaining position about force and diplomacy as a scale proceeding along an arrow aimed from the British Isles to the Falklands.[39] There is evidence in the timing of British diplomatic and military moves that British leaders at least tacitly saw their trade-offs as depending on the point reached along that scale. While public positions and negotiating tactics reflected it less clearly (and indeed may blur the situation for political reasons), the Argentines at a minimum set store by several significant points along that scale: the British departure from Ascension; the retaking of South Georgia; the escalation reflected in the May 1 bombings; and most prominently the May 2 sinking of the cruiser *General Belgrano*.

While the locations of the Task Force, which at times was deployed in of different stages, were a classified matter, rough positions from press reports and estimated steaming times can be used to fix the approximate *perceived* progress

of the Task Force toward the Falklands. These can be usefully correlated with
diplomatic events and attitudes. Overall, Britain felt (and therefore was) more
committed to the use of force the further south it had to go without securing its
minima by negotiation. Those minimum goals were therefore less, and not more,
"negotiable" as the British Task Force approached the Falklands. The countervailing Argentine accounting took little account of force, discounting it first
absolutely and, after Ascension, still in insufficient proportion to proximity.

One contributing factor to the failure of the two Peruvian peace efforts was
this differing Argentine perception of the interrelationship between force (the
"progress" of the Task Force) and diplomacy. From Buenos Aires, the question
was a defensive one—only invasions of the islands proper counted, and Argentina
was dug in and felt itself prepared. This siege view of the military part of the
strategic/settlement equation made the Junta see other incremental actions (South
Georgia, the Vulcan raid, the naval air bombardment of Stanley) as *shows* of
force rather than the true exercise of force—bluster rather than escalatory warning. Thus the *Belgrano* was the first real shock—more immediate and convincing
than the loss of the submarine *Santa Fe* and the troops in the South Georgias.

It was such a hammer blow, especially in light of what the public yet knew,
that it confused Argentine decision making rather than coming as the fourth turn
of the military screw. The effect in Buenos Aires was not a gradual increase in
pressure but a radical escalation.

While they had perhaps seen the "arrow" as really beginning at Ascension
(as it entered the South Atlantic worldview), the Argentines saw its tip as aimed
at the beaches of East Falkland. They imagined that the fleet was solely *diplomatic,* then mainly *amphibious,* in purpose. The sinking in daylight of the pride
of their fleet would make them realize they were at war . . . limited but general
war.

The political decision making structure at the top of the military was already
divided. The direct bombing as well as shelling from the task force on Saturday
had reinforced tendencies in the Argentine services, especially in the predominant
army, to avoid full-scale war, particularly after the "easy" British retaking of
South Georgia.

However, the effect of the *Belgrano* sinking was in its timing: It overloaded
the decision-making capacity of the Junta, which was already split and therefore
ambivalent. Coming when it did, literally during the decision meeting on the
Peruvian plan, it stifled and may even have reversed for a period the political
movement among the senior officers to avoid open warfare with Great Britain.
The suddenness and concreteness of the new reality harmed the tenuous peace
process which they were considering at that moment, but was only the beginning
of a realistic assessment of military realities in Argentine decision making.

This is not to say that a clear chance for peace was lost. That is a separate
conclusion dependent on other requirements: principally that the Military Committee would have accepted the Peruvian plan fully and finally (surrendering its

military gains without major military engagement; healing the deep divisions
between hard-liners and those who preferred compromise; and putting Argentina's future in the Malvinas firmly in the hands of third parties). It would also
have been necessary for such acceptance to have made a critical political difference in United Kingdom decision making, allowing the Thatcher government
to meet Argentina halfway in order to avoid full-scale war. That second requirement in turn assumes that at least self-determination for the Islanders, if not the
reimposition of British or at least Islander administration, could have been obtained. (It seems highly *unlikely* that the British government could have dispensed
with both major elements.) The increased British military pressure of early May
could achieve the *perception* of military advantage, but it could not create the
diplomatic channel by which that perception could be turned into concessions
and settlement.

Argentina failed to appreciate the dual nature of the tip in the balance after
Ascension: Not only was the show of force less diplomatically profitable with
time, but a force deployed in distant, hostile waters takes on a dynamic of its
own: To remain deployed and applicable, it must defend itself as well as its
diplomatic effect. Argentina's crucial failure of perception about the Total Exclusion Zone and the stand-off order was to ignore the fleet as a naval force that
had to command the sea. It had to do so not only to land troops against a
weakened enemy if so decided (using the TEZ) but to survive (via unrestricted
naval warfare in whatever its area of operations, as declared on April 23). If
such warfare is not planned, it is nonetheless a necessity for an expeditionary
force. It was inevitable that it dominate events in the South Atlantic absent a
formal cease-fire and given (known) Argentine attempts to engage the force.
Any peace process, known or not, had to take second place to the loss of a ship,
even at the eleventh hour.

Even had both British embassies known and reported the Peruvian peace
initiative, and known of and pointed out the inherent conflict with the widening
of the TEZ, there was a basic problem that no amount of unfortunate coincidence
or irony can explain: Argentina was simply not ready to offer terms proportionate
to the British diplomatic (credibility–National Honor) and military (risk–National
Interest) investment in bringing its fleet all the way to the Falkland Islands,
which they reached with effective fire power from the carriers on Saturday,
May 1.

Like the Polar Star, that arrow was not visible in the Southern World. Argentina
did not see the British politico-military effort which had brought the Task Force
to the shores of the Falklands as a straight thrust but as a difficult project hemmed
in by politico-legal norms—norms made in the North, which Argentina, as
representative of the South, could use but need not observe. It saw force and
diplomacy as opposed, not complementary. Thus, from an Argentine perspective,
there were at least three moments in which military events were matched, national
honor satisfied, and Britain should have agreed to a ceasefire in place: (1) after

retaking South Georgia, when each side held an island group; (2) after each side had lost a ship in the *Belgrano* and the *Sheffield*; and (3) after the San Carlos landing, when each had troops ashore.

At each of these junctures, Argentina saw Britain as wanting and needing more and more to avoid further force and fall back on diplomatic compromise, especially in observance of norms concerning avoiding the use of force—a norm it had not felt constrained by in opening the conflict.

The British perspective was the opposite: Each price paid made any negotiated terms except full Argentine withdrawal less acceptable. Each demonstration of force not heeded, as on May 1, made further force not only increasingly necessary but more justified.

Thus the two parties approached Saturday May 1 and the opening Falklands hostilities, and then the escalation of Sunday May 2, ever further apart in their perception of relative bargaining strength and what constituted rational behavior on the part of the opposition.

The positive indications about the terms as they stood on Sunday, May 2, come from the U.S. and Peruvian intermediaries, and were said to be obvious and acceptable to the Argentine government, though not so obvious that they agreed on language; it was to ratify the agreement without the United States or the wishes of the Kelpers that the Junta was to meet. They were not apparently advantageous or appealing, nor one would indeed say even interesting, to the chief foreign policy official of the United Kingdom. This reflected a price Argentina did not wish to recognize or pay: Argentine negotiating behavior during the Haig round and the first Peruvian round was on the assumption that the British fleet could in political terms be ignored without cost; that is, Britain would pay no price in sending the fleet first to Ascension, then to South Georgia, and then to the Falklands; and Argentina could ignore the specific threat to use force if British terms were not accommodated diplomatically, and the very clear statement of these potential costs by the U.S. mediator over a full month of diplomacy preceding in parallel with the application of force.

Such an Argentine calculus would have to be based purely on National Interest in terms of which it was conceivable that a British force could be dispatched to the South Atlantic much as if on maneuvers and returned without being employed. This ignores National Honor and the problem of credibility in the future deployment and employment of force in support of stated interests. It also ignores the increasing exposure of the fleet to exhaustion of supplies, severe weather, and the geometric increase in the applicability of Argentine power as the fleet neared the islands and thus came within air and sea reach of Argentine forces.

It is difficult to calculate the overall result of the *Belgrano* sinking for the Falklands crisis. If there was a tactical loss to the peace process in the evening meeting of the Junta, it is probable that strategically the conditions were not up to British requirements for a settlement; that is, they provided few benefits and major costs since Britain had already made the investment in political and military terms of bringing power to bear and exposing it to major risk off the Islands.

In the overall campaign, the military effect of this politico-military decision was clearly summed up by the Rattenbach Commission which investigated the conduct of the war by Argentina: The Naval Commander did not conduct isolated attacks with surface vessels as a way of preventing the British from making unrestricted use of their naval superiority. Such an attack was not even made on the occasion for which it was definitely scheduled in the overall "schematic plan" for the naval defense of the Islands: the British landings at San Carlos Water in the week following May 21.[40] Argentine Vice Admiral Lombardo had recognized that only under very favorable conditions could the Argentine navy use its surface units, especially given the threat from British nuclear submarines. A strategy of running these risks was adopted; a strict stipulation that only worthwhile targets would be worth the risk of the Argentine Navy. The arrival of the British fleet in the area, unoriented as yet and without firm control of the seas or any control of the air, was such a moment. Argentina decided to take the risk. The next such moment was the British landing three weeks later. Argentina did not this time put its fleet to sea. The difference between the situations was the sinking of the *General Belgrano*. Further, and more importantly, "The knowledge that its surface forces were not even being used in a restricted manner to combat the enemy, given the risks inherent in the battle, affected the nation's morale."[41] It was the sinking of the *Belgrano* that brought home to the nation, despite the seamanlike handling of the disaster by her partially draftee crew, that the Argentine Navy was not ready for war with Great Britain. In that sense, from the time of the sinking of the *Belgrano,* Argentine forces on the Falkland Islands were surrounded and largely cut off, and military means should have given way to diplomaticization in an assessment of Argentine National Interest. The Argentine perceptions prevailing when the *Belgrano* was sunk led instead to an assessment founded in National Honor: After such an unexpected and stunning blow, concessions were "impossible."

PERU, ROUND TWO

The sinking of the *Belgrano* did not in any direct diplomatic sense doom peace efforts. A second Peruvian try took place within days. (The U.N. was already trying at midnight on May 2. Peru would try again on May 21.) On May 3 the text was reworked and put to paper. The conditions were more violent but, ironically, perhaps more conducive to peace.[42] The second round failed on its own.

By May 4 there was a new Peruvian text:

PERU-U.S. PROPOSAL, MAY 5, 1982

Draft Interim Agreement on the Falkland/Malvinas Islands

1. An immediate cease-fire, concurrent with items 2–6.
2. Mutual withdrawal and non-reintroduction of forces, according to a schedule to be established by the Contact Group.

3. The immediate introduction of a Contact Group composed of Brazil, Peru, the Federal
   Republic of Germany, and the United States into the Falkland Islands, on a temporary
   basis pending agreement on a definitive settlement. The Contact Group will assume
   responsibility for:

   a. Verification of the withdrawal;

   b. Ensuring that no actions are taken in the Islands, by the local administration,
      which would contravene this interim agreement; and

   c. Ensuring that all other provisions of the agreement are respected.

4. Britain and Argentina acknowledge the existence of differing and conflicting views
   regarding the status of the Falkland Islands.

5. The two Governments acknowledge that the aspirations and interests of the Islanders
   will be included in the definitive settlement of the status of the Islands.

6. The Contact Group will have responsibility for ensuring that the two Governments
   reach a definitive agreement prior to April 30, 1983.

"Aspirations and interests" (a Costa Mendez contribution) of the Islanders
bridged one former sticking point. The Dependencies were not covered. Cease-
fire was inseparable from the withdrawal. The quadrilateral contact group was
to oversee both these military provisions and interim administration in consultation with the Kelpers. Its discretion would determine law, the role of the
Governor and councils, and all ties with Britain. Interim administration was
essentially open-ended, a risk for each side, but the geographic balance of the
four countries in the Contact Group was the guarantee of reasonableness (were
either party willing to settle for reasonableness or compromise). A realistic
one-year period was left for negotiations—which took pressure off the U.K. but
gave Argentina its fixed period. The negotiation terms and process were again
completely in the hands of the four countries.

   To accept the Peruvian proposal would have been a leap of faith for either
party. The new draft went to Buenos Aires by hand. The first-round Belaunde
terms had been considerably better for Argentina. In the Argentine Foreign
Minister's view this was because Haig realized that he had not given Argentina
enough in his suggested solutions of April. The Argentines believe that the
Belaunde second-round (May 5) terms and the British stipulations on them were
harsher because Britain thought the *Belgrano* sinking gave England the upper
hand.

   The further try made on May 5, after Argentina's attack on the *Sheffield*,
suffered from a change of outlook on both sides stemming from the sinkings:
The spirit of compromise was lost. Argentina was already in the process of
internal agreement to the good offices of the U.N. Secretary General, and likely
felt it could maximize its gains in the politically hospitable forum of the United
Nations. The U.K. had already paid the cost in logistics and lives to project
counterforce into the South Atlantic.

POLITICAL PRESSURE

On May 5, Great Britain initially indicated it could seriously consider the proposal[43] and responded favorably to the second round,[44] but, crucially, the U.K. upped the ante again: Their redraft of the May 2 agreement reply added the element of reimposition of British sovereignty. Britain pursued pressure, military and then diplomatic, on these two key days of early May, and twice lost chances for a negotiated peace without military cost.

The British government expressed itself as still willing to negotiate the possibility of *diluted* British sovereignty as in the first Peruvian proposal. (The first Peruvian plan was, in their view, rejected by Argentina, not by the United Kingdom.) Whether or not the Thatcher government could have shepherded the Peruvian plan through the Parliament is an interesting but academic question. It made the political commitment to the United States and Peru to negotiate on the basis of the Peruvian proposal, demonstrating considerable political courage.[45] Its need for ratification, as Galtieri had felt compelled to take Peru Round One to his military "senate," might have run a severe risk of rejection, but if British concurrence in the terms were indeed also subject to other factors, such as ultimate approval by Parliament, this condition applied to any agreement, formal or informal, done at a distance or over the negotiating table. Peru had worked through the United States to secure some of the British concessions and had produced what the United States could not: the basis for an enduring peace.

The possible Peruvian attempt to mediate the Falklands crisis had the personal participation of the President of Peru. It was perhaps the most nearly successful of many less noted attempts by the friends of Argentina and Great Britain—individuals, The Vatican, other nations—to avoid conflict over what seemed, to most observers, a negotiable issue, susceptible of compromise and nonviolent solution.

The effort was criticized as not being an original and fresh one (that is, it emanated from earlier efforts by the United States); as not being "serious," as it did not involve a convening of the parties; as biased, involving a Latin American with strong sympathies for Argentina in the Falklands crisis; but principally, it seems, for being an *ad hoc* and straightforward effort. However, its very simplicity and the ease of conveying its points were what made it almost work—twice.

The first Peruvian efforts may also have come closer than any others to avoiding major bloodshed in the Falklands because its compromises were realistic, and vouchsafed as such to Argentina by a Latin government. These compromises were very probably in the *process* of being accepted, and ways of explaining them sought, in Buenos Aires when Great Britain (not yet aware of the effort) moved upscale in its mix of persuasion and pressure.

In the first Peruvian round, the Argentines expressed themselves as more flexible. They might have so proven. In reaction to the sinking of the *Belgrano*, however Argentina returned to its maximum objective: guaranteed sovereignty via "negotiations." In response to the gutting of HMS *Sheffield*, Britain sought its minimum: reimposition of British administration. In the second Peruvian round, Argentina was less flexible (seeking cease-fire now without withdrawal) while Britain was more flexible. Forced to continue the conflict, the U.K. would increase the price and return to its maximum: full British sovereignty. That was also stated by Argentine Defense Minister Amadeo Frugoli to be his country's goal; without guarantee of sovereignty Argentina could not start negotiations.

The timing of the two parties remained out of synch; their willingness to compromise came at different times. It is, however, less than informative to state as did the British White Paper of May 20 that (as the Foreign and Commonwealth Secretary had told Parliament on 7 May) Britain had been willing to accept the final version of the Peruvian proposals, but Argentina had rejected it. British diplomacy had worked to amend the Peruvian plan through the United States. Presumably, the direction of such charges was toward points the U.K. could accept and, thus amended, it is not surprising that the "final version" was rejected by Argentina.

At 5:00 P.M. London time on May 7, the Peru Round Two cease-fire would have gone into effect. The British Foreign Secretary expressed regret on May 6 that Argentina had declined the Round Two offer. The Prime Minister noted to Parliament that discussions were under way both at the U.N. and with Peru, claiming that a constructive response had been made to Peru via the United States. Argentina was focused on the U.N. in New York. The U.K. would accept the U.N. mediation on May 7. Argentina wanted only one negotiation at a time but would turn again to Peru on May 21/22 after the U.N. effort collapsed.

The Peruvian efforts demonstrated the advantages and costs of multiple intermediaries. More multinational than international, the pairing of the United States to reassure and convince the U.K. with Peru to reassure Argentina was inspired. As a mediation team, however, it was rejected as a part of the supervisory group, but would clearly have remained the ultimate guarantors.

The effectiveness of the potential guarantor roles, however, was never tested, due to the complexity and imprecision of the six-way communications required: from the party to one of two co-intermediaries, to the other mediator, to the opposite party, and back. In the complexities of that communication, one could not control the delicate process of graduated and coordinated use of political persuasion and military might with the required precision, nor be sure that fine points on the diplomatic side, or even the more blunt messages of acts of force, were well and quickly communicated all the way to the other party, with shades of meaning intact. Who, for example, told Peru that Britain had accepted in principle Sunday morning? To whom in the U.S. government was the message clearly transmitted that Argentine agreement was all but a formality away and would be confirmed within hours? When did Peru tell the United States? When did the United States tell the U.K.? The cost of the lack of clarity was two failed mediations in one week and a further slide toward war.

Foreign Minister Costa Mendez feels there was an equally real if informal second of Peruvian peacemaking. The reply by the United Kingdom, he recollects, was not transmitted officially but rather phoned to Costa Mendez by Peruvian Foreign Minister Arias Stella.[46] Arias Stella said that he had no instructions to transmit the British reaction but thought it would be constructive. By now, however, the similarities of Belaunde I and II to Haig II were dominating the Junta's discussions, Exocet[47] reload seemed in the offing, and as Thatcher began to prefer Peru to the U.N., Argentina leaned the opposite way. Costa Mendez informed Arias Stella that Argentina had already accepted the mediation of U.N. Secretary General Perez de Cuellar. The second Peruvian round also ended in tragic and unnecessary failure.

Chrono-map: The Use of Force and the Round One Peruvian Mediation

This chart is an attempt at precision in two dimensions—diplomatic time and space. There are many conflicting versions of the events and their relative timing in five cities and the South Atlantic during the weekend the *Belgrano* was sunk. Many accounts do not give times or the recollections of the participants are inexact. Many facts surrounding that weekend are classified diplomatically or militarily, or are simply closely held by the players. Some events will, with disclosure or declassification, have to be reordered. The dimensions to watch on this "chrono-map" are *what* was known *when* and most importantly *where* as the actual events unfolded. This analytical tool is designed to pierce to the extent possible the ignorance and confusion inherent in fast-moving politico-military events—the diplomatic equivalent of the confusion recognized by military analysts since the Greeks as "the fog of war." Time zones given for the Spring of 1982 are British Summer Time for London and the Home Counties including Royal Navy Headquarters at Northwood, Greenwich Mean Time (GMT) or Universal Standard Time, Buenos Aires/South Atlantic, Washington and New York, and Lima, Peru. The spatial dimension of this chronology is that an entry under a time zone shows where an event took place or was known to have taken place. The GMT column contains no events and is not a spatial dimension but rather a simple timeline flowing through the chart to help track events in relative chronological order. A blank indicates that the precise time of an event is not in the public domain. An entry in parentheses highlights that the event was unknown in that place or was hypothetical—a scheduled event which never took place. Hours are given in the 24-hour time, and hours beyond 2400 are given cumulatively into the next day for comparison, that is, an event at 1:30 A.M. after midnight on a given day is given artificially as 2515 hours.

```
April 2    Argentina takes control of the Falkland Islands
April 3    U.N. Security Council calls for Argentine withdrawal and
           negotiations
           Argentine Marines take South Georgia
April 5    Britain sends naval Task Force to retake the Falklands
April 7    U.K. Defense Minister John Nott announces an April 12 imposition of a 200
           n.m. Maritime Exclusion Zone around the Falklands
April 12   Britain imposes the MEZ around the Falklands
           Nott tells the Commons Argentina used force first and Britain will not
           hesitate to do so
April 15   Argentine fleet puts to sea
April 17   British Task Force reaches Ascension Island
April 19   British hunter-killer sub HMS Conqueror reaches South Georgia
April 23   British warning to Argentine navy to stay away from the Falklands
           Also warning for all Argentine ships and planes to avoid UK Task Force
           (from 23 April Rules of Engagement are that all surface ships may defend
           themselves by firing first should they sight an Argentine warship.
           Submarines being less vulnerable to over-the-horizon missilry were held to
           more strict Rules of Engagement.
April 24   The U.N. and publics are told of the warning to Argentina that any approach
           which could threaten to interfere with the Task Force would encounter the
           appropriate response (no geographic restriction -- aimed first at Argentine
           scouting planes off Ascension Island)
April 25   Britain retakes South Georgia by force
           Sinks Argentine submarine and takes 190 Argentine prisoners of war
           Task Force heads for the Falkland Islands
           Argentine Foreign Minister observes that technically UK & Arg. are at war
           OAS convenes as organ of the Interamerican Treaty of Reciprocal Assistance
           (Rio Treaty)
April 26   Argentine heavy cruiser ARA General Belgrano leaves Ushuaia for sea
           Proceeds to Staten Island off Tierra del Fuego
April 27   Viscount Trenchard assures the Lords that nuclear weapons will not be used
           in Falklands
April 28   Britain declares 200 mile Total Exclusion Zone to be effective 30 April
           HMS Conqueror departs South Georgia for Falkland Islands
April 29   Argentina declares its own exclusion zone around the Falkland Islands
           Helicopter brings Belgrano sealed orders; patrol 250 mile line
           back and forth South of Falklands (110 degrees ESE; 290 WNW)
```

Friday, April 30, 1982	UK	GMT	ATL/BA	DC	LIMA
	+1	0	-3	-4	-5
British War Cabinet includes the Argentine carrier					
Veinticinco de Mayo (25 May) for attack in	1000	0900	(0600)		
Rules of Engagement for subs incl. HMS Splendid					
U.S. Secretary of State Alexander Haig abandons					
his mediation		1530		1130	
U.S. announces measures of support for U.K.					
(Peruvian President Fernando Belaunde Terry sends					
telegraphic offer of support to Argentina)					P.M.
HMS Conqueror on station some 200 n.m. South					
of the Falklands in Belgrano's picket area			___		
Conqueror picks up sonar signals of Argentine ships					
Conqueror goes to periscope depth			___		
seeks Belgrano Task Group 79.4		1900	1600		
Conqueror is told that 25 de Mayo is within scope					
of the Rules of Engagement			___		

Saturday, May 1, 1982	UK	GMT	BA/ATL	DC	LIMA
	+1	0	-3	-4	-5
Vulcan bomber departs Ascension Island,					
opening this stage of armed conflict	0101	0001			
Refueled by 14 Victor tankers in flight					
Vulcan drops 21 thousand-pound bombs in area					
of the Stanley Airfield, East Falkland Island	0823	0723	0423		
Pym is briefed on war before departing UK	___			1000?	
He raises issue of a further warning to					
Argentina of intention to employ force					
British Task Force closes on islands at dawn					
UK carriers Hermes and Invincible launch aircraft		0700	0400		
Carrier-based Harriers begin all-day bombing		0740	0440		
Lombardo believes troop landing imminent					
Abortive torpedo attack by Argentine sub					
San Luis on British Task Force			___		
(British depth charge counterattack)			___		
To the South, HMS Conqueror catches Arg. Task					
Force 79.3 refueling and vulnerable		1400	1100		
Course was then also "westward unawares"					
24 hrs after sonar find of her fleet oiler					
Peruvian President Fernando Belaunde Terry says he					
proposes plan to Argentine Junta head Gen. Leopoldo					
Galtieri & urges acceptance "that same Sat. morning"			___		___
Vulcan bomber returns to Ascension Island		1500			
Costa Mendez arrives B.A. from New York		1530	1230		
Lombardo has Belgrano on a pincer movement,					
East and then North toward UK Task Force			P.M.		
(but not part of May 1 attack order in North)					
Second phase of diplomatic negotiation for					
ceasefire and negotiation (US-Peru effort)				"midday"	___
Arg. Mirages bomb British ships shelling Falklands		1625	1325		
Argentine Seahawks attack HMS Glamorgan					
20 Arg. senior officers declare for avoiding war			p.m.		
British Ambassador Wallace briefs Peruvians		1700			1200
Peru claims informed UK Embassy Lima from 12:30		1730			1230
Peruvian Foreign Minister Javier Arias Stella					
says his Pres. contacts U.S. State Department	(1830)	1730		1330	1230

Belgrano antisurface Task Group forms up					____
Northern Argentine Task Groups 79.1 & 79.2					
are ordered to engage the enemy	(1955)	1855	1555		
(Attack order would make no sense for Belgrano,					
nor would cancellation order then apply to her)					
Argentine Super Etendard aircraft damage HMS Arrow					
& HMS Glamorgan off Port Stanley		1940	1640		
Nautical Dusk in the South Atlantic		2130	1830		
(The Guardian says Belgrano is ordered to port)		2200	1900		
British Task Force withdraws East out of air range	2300	2200	1900		
concluding all-day softening-up "demonstration"					
Meeting of the Malvinas Working Group on diplomacy					
& protest note to Haig on his May 30 speech		1915			
Net differing Argentine perceptions of the day:					
UK "attack" "failed" therefore less respect for UK;					
Others: 56 Arg. casualties. There will be war.					
25 de Mayo (w/o 1 engine) fails to launch Skyhawks		1930			
Galtieri tells Peru's Belaunde: No Argentine decision					
as yet between UN and 3rd Party Mediation					
Peruvian President Fernando Belaunde Terry calls					
American Ambassador in Lima Frank Ortiz	2300				1800
TF 79 Commander Allara aboard 25 de Mayo overflown		2000?			
by a Harrier but unable to launch Skyhawk defense					
Anaya orders Task Force 79 to cancel attack	2307	2007			
(the attack perceived as "pincer" by UK TF)					
Conqueror observes Belgrano from 10,000 yards	2309	2009			
Galtieri told of Generals' meetings: sense of the		2030			
flag officers groups was to avoid full scale war					
Argentines say carrier heads to port		2030			
Pym arrives Washington, speaking of use of force	2400	(2100)	2000		
(Belaunde under misapprehension he & Haig meet)					
Argentine S-2 carrier aircraft finds UK TF at					
300 miles from the Veinticinco de Mayo	0230	2330			
Peruvian FM Javier Arias Stella calls Costa Mendez	0230	2330			2130
Belaunde call his Washington Embassy ("night" = N)	0245			2245	2145
Tells Amb. Fernando Schwalb that Haig and Pym					
must find solution or there could be a disaster					
Adm. Lombardo perceives UK had no intention of					
landing; orders naval forces to safety	2700	2400			
Adm. Allara orders N. & S. Task Groups to ports		0019			
Arg. Navy has lost UK TF, esp. wary of carriers					
(but had located UK TF less than 1 hr before;					
probably therefore queried recall)					
Secretary Haig returns Belaunde's call (N-hour + .5)	0315			2315	2215
(but one Peruvian account puts 4 hours between Belaunde calls)					
Belaunde and Haig fix their format (N + .5 + .75)	0400			2400	2300
Cancellation of Northern Argentine attack reconfirmed	0419	0119			
Belaunde calls Galtieri "immediately", at earliest=	0430	0130			2330
(transmits the 7-Points orally)					
Galtieri calls day a "bloodbath"					
Buenos Aires Malvinas Working Group analyzes Plan	0500	0200			
The two fleets lose each other North of Falklands:					
Last Argentine fix is that UK carrier is 330 mi.					
from 25 de Mayo at 2330;					
UK carrier Harrier spots 25 de Mayo after dark					
but British submarine loses her overnight	____	0300			____

	UK +1	GMT 0	BA/ATL -3	DC -4	LIMA -5
The Task Forces search for each other before dawn			OVERNIGHT		
Belaunde calls Galtieri with new Haig proposals(?)			0130		
Belgrano actually receives order to make for coast			0200		
U.K. Task Force Commander Adm. John Woodward is unable to find 25 de Mayo carrier task group and must assume it has evaded his forward picket line of nuclear submarines and is closing on Task Force					
Belgrano swings to the homeward leg of picket line South of the Falklands on usual course (B-11)		0800	0500		
Morning Twilight, sun 12 degrees below horizon =		1000	0700		
Conqueror reports Belgrano in her sights					
Adm. Lewin asks change in Rules of Engagement	1100	1000	(0700)		
Belgrano sets course of 290 for Ushuaia at 100mi. from Staten Is.(more direct than 270 picket line)		1000	0700=B-9		
Planned Argentine carrier "dawn" naval air attack but no wind to launch carrier planes,					
(nautical twilight at 58 degrees south latitude)		1025	0725		
(Arg. sources say only attempt was 1900 May 1)					
Veinticinco de Mayo aborts Skyhawk launch		1057	0757		
(at 180 mi. from UK Task Force and closing)					
(UK TF out of range of land-based Arg. aircraft)					
British War Cabinet reconsiders Rules of Engagement	1200	1100		0700	
Malvinas Working Group assembles			0800		
Belaunde sends 7-point plan to Galtieri by telex			0840		
War Cabinet agrees change in Rules (B-7)	1300	1200			
(only discussion of Belgrano)					
First Peruvian call to get Arg. reaction to plan	1300	1000	(0900)	0800	
Belaunde Calls Galtieri, who says talk to Costa Mendez					
(3 interrupted Belaunde - Costa Mendez calls in all)					
Arg. wants Canada vice US in interim administration & the Islanders' "viewpoints regarding interests" vice wishes					
Peru insists on Arg. answer for Haig-Pym meeting					
They agree on Islanders'' "aspirations"					
Northwood signals Conqueror that attacks are permitted on all Argentine vessels on high seas	1330	1230	(0930)		
(Haig said to have called Belaunde before recall of Argentine Task Force?)		1315?		0915?	0815?
Adm. Lombardo orders Northern Task Groups to safety		1030			
Argentina rejects U.S. as participant in the Plan		1100			0900
Pym meets with Haig for 2 hrs. at State Department				1000	
Argentine "acceptance in principle" (‡1) of process, but with debate and queries on substance of plan	1400	1100		1000	0900
Conqueror tells Northwood Belgrano's positions as of 0900 & 1500 BST. (Conqueror sending, not receiving. Unaware of orders changing ROE.)	1500	1400	(1100)		
Peruvian PM Ulloa calls Haig to ask 24/48 hr truce				1100?	1000?
Haig tells Belaunde to put wishes back into Plan (if after Pym meeting, this is no workable plan)					
US Amb in Lima calls Belaunde on 2 text changes: "views concerning interests US role in interim administration					
Peru tells Arg. of UK agreement in principle (by what British authority unspecified)					
Argentine acceptance in principle ‡2 (at B-4 per Costa Mendez)	1500	1200	1100	1000	

Peruvian negotiators say UK is informed	___	___		___	___
(Haig says UK informed overnight)					
Belaunde calls Costa Mendez & Galtieri		1500	1200		1000
Some Arg. objections are met					
Differences are down to a single word					
One UK wording change unacceptable to Arg.					
So Arg. proposes "Third Formula"					
Belaunde says Third Formula" might work					
Arg. judges it has approved (#3) Peru Text					
Galtieri tells Belaunde acceptable peace plan					
and will be put to the Junta for "ratification"					
Belaunde communicates "success" to Haig, and					
Belaunde calls press conference for ratification hour		1510	1210?	1110?	1010
Peruvian PM Ulloa urges ceasefire on Haig		1500	(1200)	1100?	1000?
Peruvian PM Ulloa calls Costa Mendez					
Costa Mendez believes Arg. agreed (#4) at B-3.5	( )	1530	1230	1130	1030
Parliamentarians say Belgrano course change is					
communicated to Royal Navy headquarters Northwood	1640	1540	(1240)		
Arg. Foreign Minister drafts press statement					
on disagreement being reduced to one word		1600	1300		
(aspirations vs. wishes or viewpoints)					
Conqueror reports she has received & understood new ROE	1708?	1608	1308		
Intensive Argentina calls to Belaunde in Lima		1615	1315?		1115?
U.S. sure Argentina rejects its participation				1220	1120
Haig tells Peruvians that Brits object to Peru		1630	1330	1230	1130
but he will make proposal his own					
First Exocet mission aborts due to non-refueling					
Costa Mendez tells press "We have an agreement"(#3)	(1800)	1700	1400	1300	1200
(1800 BST in London, B-2)					
Pym is informed of change in Rules of Engagement	___			___	
(presumably at British Embassy in Washington)					
Conqueror receives order (5 hours after issue)	1800	1700	1400		
Haig tells Belaunde he is going to lunch with Pym					
(indicates no British reaction during morning)		1700		1300	1200
Galtieri says Costa Mendez is empowered on language		1715	1415		
Pym and Haig lunch at British Embassy				1300	
(thus Haig is not at State Department when Galtieri					
gives his most firm version of "agreement"					
Last Peruvian Call for Argentine reactions		1730	1430	1330	1230
Military Comm. must ratify agreement (#4) B-1.5		1730	1430		1230
Belaunde says he talks to the press and makes					
Peruvian press announcement of "success" at B-1.5=	(1830)	1730	(1430)	(1330)	1230
Arg. Malvinas Working Group approves proposal					
Adm. Moya, Galtieri approves Plan (#5),					
will show to the Military Committee, and	(1830)	1730	1430	(1330)	1230
and will be approved by 2000 Peru time, that is..	2600	2500	2200	2100	2000
(Peruvians state this still not an approval)					
Belaunde says Haig tells him no conclusions reached					
(presumably with Pym) on Arg. reply which had					
arrived after 1000 Washington time, Haig going to		1800		1400	1300
lunch with Pym. Belaunde concludes this is stall					
to give Pym time to check with London.					
Peruvians begin preparations for a signing		1800			1300
Pym and Haig part after lunch at British Embassy					
Conqueror goes to Action Stations	(1700)	1800	1500		( )

	UK	GMT	BA/ATL	DC	LIMA
Peru informs Argentina no UK approval.	( )	1815	1515	( )	1315

(Each assuming London knows. Therefore no viable
peace effort if both knew Peru Plan not accepted
by Pym & assumed London also knew.)

	UK	GMT	BA/ATL	DC	LIMA
HMS Conqueror launches three Mk-8 torpedos			1559		
UK War Cabinet formal afternoon meeting ends	2000	1900	1600	1500	1400

No afternoon discussion of Belgrano
Seven hours since Belgrano included in Rules at ...   (1300)

(It is now 20 hours since Argentines state Belgrano   2000 1900 1600
and rest of TF 79 ordered to port (May 1 2307 GMT).
In 20 hours at 10 knots, Belgrano would have been
200 nautical miles West of the center mark of her
long picket line where she was sunk, that is,
back past Staten Island, through the Beagle Channel,
and safely at dock in her home port of Ushuaia.)

(If Belgrano had headed for the continent at 0100   2000 1900 1600
BA/ATL Time that morning, she would now be 14 hours
steaming time from her picket line or inside Staten
Island in shallows and safe from submarines.)

	UK	GMT	BA/ATL	DC	LIMA
TORPEDOS STRIKE ARA GENERAL BELGRANO [B-HOUR]	(2000)	1900	1600	(1500)	(1400)

Course: 280 degrees toward Argentina;
Position: 55.27 S, 61.25 W, 35-70 NM outside the TEZ;
200NM SW of UK Task Force; 45NM off Burwood Bank)
ARA Hipolito Bouchard, on far side of Belgrano, takes
the third torpedo but suffers only light damage

	UK	GMT	BA/ATL	DC	LIMA
Belgrano Capt. Hector Elias Bonzo last off his ship			1640		
Haig tries to reach Pym to emphasize importance		2000		1600	

Leaves message at British Embassy

	UK	GMT	BA/ATL	DC	LIMA
Belgrano sinks		2001	1701		

Bouchard homes on Conqueror with SQS 30 & SQA 10 sonar
Bouchard depth charges Conqueror which dives to 500 feet

	UK	GMT	BA/ATL	DC	LIMA
Pym proceeds to contacts with United Nations in N.Y.		2100		1700?	
Conqueror to periscope depth to report her kill		2100	1800		
Amb. Henderson returns Haig's call to Pym		(___)2100		1700	

Assures him Foreign Secretary will overlook no
peace proposal; that Peru effort as far as it goes
is a basis on which one could work
(Pym plans to discuss Peru & UN plans on return)

	UK	GMT	BA/ATL	DC	LIMA
UK Embassy Washington makes Pym's report to London	2215	2115		1715?	
Belaunde meets w/press to "preannounce" agreement		2130	1830		1630
Argentine Naval HQ Buenos Aires learns of Belgrano		2145	1845		
UK Ambassador is called to Peruvian Foreign Ministry		2200			1700
Costa Mendez walks Junta through the Plan at MOD		2400	1900		
Junta is informed of Belgrano, drops Plan		2420	1920		

Argentina sees Peruvian mediation suspended, not off
Decides to send envoys to Belaunde
Junta also has UN text before it since that morning

	UK	GMT	BA/ATL	DC	LIMA
Belaunde calls Galtieri to ask for promised 1700 reply				____	X-10
Haig tells Belaunde of torpedoing of Belgrano				____	X

Belaunde drops contact with Argentina				___	X
Argentina's Amb. Ros meets with UN Secretary General		2200	___	1800	
London aware of Peruvian Proposals (B+3)	2315	2215	1915	1815	1715
(telegram from Washington Embassy)					
UK Rules expanded to include sinking all warships	___		___		
Pym arrives Amb. Parsons' Residence in New York		2230		1830	
British Embassy Washington reports to London	1830	2230		1830	
(Pym does not himself communicate with London)					
British Ambassador in Lima learns of Plan on car					
radio enroute Foreign Ministry for briefing		2320			1820
British Ambassador in Lima fully briefed at ...		2330			1830
Military Committee "ratification" expected at ...		2500	2200	2000	
UK Embassy Lima report on Plan reaches London	2603	2503			2003
UN Secretary General learns of the Plan from press			(2100)	2000	(1900)
Pym dines with Parsons and SecGen Perez de Cuellar				2000	
Haig tells UK Ambassador Henderson of Belgrano				2000	
Nautical Dusk in the South Atlantic		2430	2130		
Reuters carries the Belaunde announcement	2530	2430	2130	2030	1930
Arg. officials believed confirmation promised for...			2200	2000	
Belaunde formal press conference had been set for..)		2500	2200	2000	
London receives Lima Embassy report (0203 ON 5/3)	2603	2503		2003	
Reuters reports UK Gov't unaware of Peruvian Plan	2609	2509			2009
Reuters carries the last Belaunde running summary		2523			
Reuters carries UK announcement of sinking		2558			2058
Costa Mendez cables the UN: no negotiation under way					
will consider UN Good Offices		2630	2330	2230	
Pym-Perez New York dinner ends		2800		2400	
Argentines believe Belaunde calls Haig		2800	2500	2400	2300
Galtieri tells Belaunde of Junta's reaction		2800	2500		2300

May 4   Arg. Super Etendards successfully refuel and cripple HMS Sheffield with Exocet missile; Conqueror signals Northwood that she is returning to area where she sank Belgrano; ordered not to interfere with any ships rescuing Belgrano survivors.

May 7   UK extends the TEZ to 12 mi. from Arg. coast to keep Arg. fleet in port and make clear that the war does not extend to the Argentine mainland

May 8   Argentine boat Narwal is sunk 66 n.m. South of Stanley

May 10   (Per Argentines, Gen. Vernon Walters assures them that no U.S. satellite data was involved in the sinking of the Belgrano)

May 16   The EEC extends sanctions for only one week.

May 20   United Nations mediation breaks down

May 21   Britain lands troops in the Falklands

VI

INTERNATIONAL GOOD OFFICES: THE U.N. MEDIATION IN NEW YORK

A quiet professional use of the facilities here, where everyone's represented by professional diplomats, may in some cases be far more effective than rushing about in all directions.
— United Nations Undersecretary General Brian Urquhart

U.N. good offices mediation as proposed on May 2 by Secretary General Javier Perez de Cuellar ran effectively from May 8 to 18, 1982. It was the most visible yet the most closely held of the Falklands mediations. During intensive exchanges in New York under the Secretary General's auspices, agreement was almost reached.

On May 6, Perez de Cuellar announced that the parties had accepted U.N. mediation of their dispute. The next day, Peru and the United States formally abandoned their effort. Britain turned the screw, moving the TEZ to within 12 miles of the Argentine coast. The siege scenario was becoming mutual. After talks from May 8–14, the U.K. conveyed a final offer on May 17. In the late evening of May 18 at U.N. Headquarters in New York, Argentina failed to grasp a historic opportunity to diplomatically consolidate what it had gained but could not keep militarily. The United Nations secured from Great Britain concessions on the full return of British sovereignty, but Argentina declined.

UNITED NATIONS MEDIATION—THE NEAR MISS

The United Nations Secretary General, had maintained a close contact with Argentina and the United Kingdom from the opening ''intelligence indicators'' phase of the Falklands crisis. The Secretariat was alerted to the bilateral talks and their sad ending. It was, far more than the Security Council, conscious of the South Georgia crisis. Fact finding and contingency planning in a low-key way on the part of the Political Secretariat were already underway when the full crisis broke on April 2. The U.N. had prepared itself to be able to offer assistance in finding a peaceful settlement of the dispute, in support of the Security Council.

As a former Under Secretary General, Perez de Cuellar was well aware of the shortcomings of the United Nations as a peacemaking body. As he would state in his first annual report as Secretary General, the failures of collective action to render the U.N. more capable of carrying out its primary function are many. During the Falklands crisis, the Security Council would endeavor to narrow the differences between the parties, but competing claims, rather than being resolved, seem more often to lead to what the Secretary General has called the use, misuse or non-use of the United Nations as an instrument for peace. Often able to help nation-states avoid war or reestablish peace, the United Nations has nonetheless never achieved a consistent record in this, its primary purpose. The Secretary General bluntly recommended that the U.N. also improve its capability to anticipate and prevent political dispute and war.

The Secretary General's personal intervention was more productive and more nearly successful. He dealt with the Falklands in its widest implications, even to making sure that the fervor of the Latin American cause did not spread to Venezuela and its analogous claim to the Essequibo region of Guyana. If the "legislative" side of the house was divided and ineffective in deterrence, the "executive" showed more promise as a mediator. Both parties, as in any dispute, appealed to the U.N. Charter and other international norms. The Secretary General's exercise of good offices in support of Article 1 could be undertaken, in the light of Article 40 of the Charter, without prejudice to the positions of the two parties. Forced originally to defend his "passive" role while he allowed the U.S. Secretary of State a try, Perez de Cuellar wanted the Security Council to instruct him to provide good offices.

Argentine Permanent Representative Eduardo Roca took up his duties in New York earlier than expected, in March 1982. He called, almost upon arrival, on the U.S. Ambassador who was chairman of the Security Council for March. He told her on March 31, as British intelligence confirmed that the Argentine fleet was bound not for South Georgia but for the Falklands, that Argentina was considering the option of asking the Council to take up the South Georgia incident. Costa Mendez informed the British Ambassador in Buenos Aires that diplomatic channels were finished as a means of settling the Falklands dispute. Argentine forces had been issued their "jump-off order." The U.K. press disclosed previous deployment of a submarine. Nonetheless Argentina wanted a Security Council meeting on its citizens on South Georgia as the focus it preferred for events it was about to precipitate. This position was circulated in a letter to the Council the following day.

At noon on April 1, the U.K. Permanent Representative received firm warning of the Argentine invasion. Great Britain called for a Security Council meeting. Informal consultations were convened in a matter of hours in the private room that allows the Council to operate in a rapid, discreet, non-polemical way. The Argentine letter of April 1 brought to the attention of Security Council what it called the situation of grave tension between Argentina and the United Kingdom resulting from differences over the entry of Argentine employees of a private company into South Georgia. The U.K. stated that an Argentine invasion was planned for the next day. It was agreed that at a public session the Council would make a statement through its President, calling on each side to exercise restraint and avoid the use of force.

The Secretary General also made an appeal, but Argentina moved militarily before the Council met again, and then took South Georgia while the Council was still discussing the Falklands action. Argentina blithely ignored the calls of the collective security mechanism, which had "functioned" perfectly, but had not worked.

However, as British Ambassador Sir Anthony Parsons has pointed out, for once in the history of the United Nations, the debate was absolutely crucial. The discussion in the Security Council would form the principal material on which the nonaligned governments would formulate their positions on an issue familiar only to specialists on U.N. Decolonization matters. Passing Resolution 502 depended on securing three of the four nonaligned votes in order to be sure of the necessary nine votes for passage. In fact, the votes of Guyana, Togo, Zaire, Uganda, and Jordan were favorable, and with the United States, U.K., France, Ireland, and Japan, gave ten "yes" votes against Panama's "no" and abstentions by Spain, Poland, China, and the USSR. Resolution 502 set the framework, if not the terms, for the Secretary General's good offices. The finding of the Council that there had been a breach of the peace was critical in that it put the Council's proceedings on the crisis under Chapter 7 of the Charter rather than Chapter 6, and left the U.K. its veto. Without that definition, Argentina might have preferred more emphasis on the Council and less on mediation. Without the underpinning of Resolution 502, Britain might have wanted to have nothing to do with the U.N., and would have had far less international backing. The mediation efforts might have aborted or wandered without 502. Resolution 502 also gave a clear line of march to U.N. peacemaking: military cease-fire and withdrawal, then diplomatic solution.

While the Haig shuttle pursued a U.S.-mediated solution through the month of April, Perez de Cuellar had his Under Secretary General, Raffuddin Ahmed, set up a Task Force to do contingency planning for U.N. good offices and other potential contributions. The working group produced a list of possibly helpful U.N. roles and activities. This was not a motion to supercede Haig, serve as interim administrator, or guarantee the agreement. The Secretary General offered only what might be termed technical assistance for a political problem: U.N. observers and administrators, and U.N. auspices for either military withdrawal, interim administration, or both. The list was given to the parties and to the United States as the current mediator on April 19, which was probably not helpful timing for Haig. The two potential mediators crossed each others' bows several times, as did Peru. Haig held out little hope for a U.N. effort.

One final attempt was made to resume negotiations. Javier Perez de Cuellar, secretary general of the United Nations, responding, as he told Mrs. Kirkpatrick, to appeals from the king of Spain, the president of Colombia, and other dignitaries, attempted to bring the parties together. It did not seem to me that there was much prospect for success in this initiative, and I informed the secretary general that the United States would oppose any settlement that appeared to reward aggression or derogate from the rule of law, but encouraged him to try.[1]

This ignored what Ambassador Kirkpatrick pointed out as making the Falklands the perfect U.N. subject matter: A new question that had not yet been framed in bloc or ideological terms. This was accurate in East-West if not North-South terms. The Secretary General had the confidence of both parties—Argentina by long experience, the U.K. by its recent role in his election. The U.N. had set Haig's yard-stick in Resolution 502 and was fully conscious of the precedents for international order. Perez de Cuellar had waited long enough letting the U.S. effort play out. With no briefings or help from Haig's experience, he turned to a Falklands crisis already gone critical. If the timing of the U.N. effort was late, with blood spilt and National Honor fully engaged, it had the compensating advantage that both parties now knew in real terms the price of failing to find a negotiated settlement.

As the Haig mission appeared stalemated, there were calls for Security Council action in April. Perez de Cuellar knew that this would not help Haig, and did not encourage a meeting. He also likely knew that it would not help the credibility of the Council to attempt to enforce its mandatory calls in Resolution 502 for Argentine withdrawal and peaceful settlement. Neither was looking likely, and even (politically unobtainable) Chapter 7 sanctions would not produce compliance. The Security Council had done what it could.

PERSONAL GOOD OFFICES

Perez de Cuellar was with the Argentine Foreign Minister when the United States announced its failure. The U.N.'s time had come, and he began to plan in earnest. After the British recapture of South Georgia, and without information about the Peruvian efforts, Perez de Cuellar consulted with the British and the Argentines, and then on May 2 gave both parties his "set of ideas" concerning the shape a negotiated settlement to the Falklands crisis might take. He was operating as the U.N. "executive branch," providing good offices through systematic contact between the parties which now were clearly at war. How far the situation had degenerated became clear with the arrival of the news during his dinner with the British Foreign Secretary that the Argentine Navy had lost its cruiser. Perez de Cuellar went ahead without the formal Security Council mandate he had earlier planned on before committing the prestige of his office to a settlement effort—the Council would have to catch up.

As in the other mediations, his "set of ideas" included military disengagement and withdrawal; negotiations for peaceful settlement of the sovereignty dispute; the lifting of sanctions and exclusion zones; and interim arrangements for administration. Specifically, the U.N. would supervise mutual military withdrawal of forces, there would follow an interim administration by the United Nations, and, in parallel, there would be longer-term negotiations under the Secretary General's auspices to settle the territorial/sovereignty dispute. (The sovereignty negotiations would be direct talks. The parties were not to see each other across the table until the military disengagement phase was agreed on and executed.)

On May 5, the Secretary General got his Security Council backing and formally undertook a good offices mission, announced the next day as agreeable to the parties.[2] He insisted on a distinction between mediator and provider of good offices, between discussion of procedure (cease-fire/administration) and substance (sovereignty), and between U.N. "ideas" and proposals: "All along I have been presenting ideas to the parties. It is not United Nations 'proposals,' but we were constantly presenting ideas to the parties. . . . I have never exposed the parties to proposals. I provide them with ideas, that is all."[3] Call it what you will, Perez de Cuellar's practiced, expert, and effective intervention began to narrow the differences between the parties. Some took the distinction to mean he would not personally be involved: Reuters reported on May 6 that

Mr. Perez de Cuellar has ruled out for the time being a mediator's role for himself. Rafuuddin Ahmed of Pakistan, the Under Secretary General leading his so-called Falklands/Malvinas task force, has been mentioned as the official most likely to be asked to undertake diplomatic consultations with the parties.

There was no doubt whose effort it was, but its modest nomenclature continued as late as May 10 when the Secretary General was asked outside headquarters, whether he would call himself a mediator. The Secretary General responded that he was simply a man of good faith.

By noon on May 6, each of the parties had accepted Perez de Cuellar's intervention and thus tacitly agreed to the "set of ideas" as an agenda. Argentina's agreement the night before was "in principle"; Great Britain's was somewhat more detailed and substantive. In exercise of his good offices, the Secretary General made specific proposals for interim arrangements that might serve as the basis for a settlement. The set of ideas specified:

1. Immediate cessation of all hostilities;
2. Withdrawal of Argentine troops;
3. Withdrawal of the British fleet;

4. Beginning of negotiations under U.N. auspices;

5. Suspension of economic sanctions against Argentina; and

6. "Transitory measures" by the United Nations.

Transitory measures meant a U.N. Administrator to govern the South Atlantic islands. He would remain, for a period of time to be agreed upon, while both parties negotiated at the United Nations. He would have advisors from each side. This would allow both governments to have a presence on the Islands and a first-hand view of their administration.

METHOD

Perez de Cuellar began a series of separate meetings with each side on May 8. Working with position papers solicited by each government, as well as his "ideas," he looked for the common ground. Initially this was a scarce commodity. The respective positions seemed not just contradictory but confrontational. From the center, the Secretary General "buffered" the raw positions of each party, exploring forms of presentation and substance that might be more acceptable. British U.N. Permanent Representative Sir Anthony Parsons and Argentina's Deputy Foreign Minister Enrique Ros would come in alternately. The Secretary General would hold over 30 such sessions in which he would sound out the parties without precision as to what their opponent was seeking or would settle for. There might be two meetings with each side per day, but they were kept to about an hour per meeting. This kept the sessions focused. It was enough time to give the parties the chance to fully develop the instructed position of their Government. It was recognized that the time between sessions was as useful as time "at the table"—a chance for creative drafting and consultation with their respective capitals. Mechanics were not a problem. Most U.N. missions need first-rate encoded communications. London was on a different time zone, but achieved a three-to four-hour turnaround time on answers. Buenos Aires took longer to react firmly but was only one hour off New York time, and so had overnight for its policy process. The Secretary General was able to speak, when he felt it valuable, with both Foreign Ministers and the heads of government. He not only "received," but at times helped formulate, national responses. He then controlled their presentation to the other side. He introduced his own ideas to guide both toward what might prove common ground. Perez stated that his mediation was not a matter of proposals. Rather, he and the parties worked around the same ideas and then the parties took them back to their governments for their reactions. He drew a procedural distinction between his "exercise" and direct talks that might come later.

Indeed, as if determined to prove that U.N. norms and documents were not to be part of the solution, the parties had only days before appealed to the same sources in support of *opposing* positions:

—In a letter to the Security Council dated 30 April (S/15016 and Correction 1), the U.K. asserted that the Security Council had not been effective in restoring international peace and security because of Argentina's refusal to comply with the provisions of Resolution 502. The United Kingdom would therefore exercise its inherent right of self-defense, for which the U.K. said no mandate from the Council was required by the terms of the Charter.

—The Argentine letter of April 30 (S/15018) reiterated the Argentine intention to comply with Resolution 502 but said that the punitive actions by the U.K. had compelled Argentina to exercise its right to self-defense.

The Secretary General's effort was the first to be carried out during full-scale hostilities. In the 24 hours before it began, two attempts to sink a British carrier were mounted and the *General Belgrano* was sunk. Diplomacy would be used as much in support of the use of armed force over the next month's mediation as to avoid violence. The parties would maintain an escalating use of force throughout the Perez de Cuellar mediation.

The Secretary General was also clearly starting from scratch in his mediation. He had no briefing from Haig or his party on the points of congruence which they had reached, much less any of the drafts. It may have been just as well not to bring preconceptions to the table, but a full background might also have saved time on the probing process.

Given the opposing appeals to U.N. norms, the start of full-scale hostilities, and the lack of negotiating history, the New York talks got off to a slow start. It was not a sterile exercise but, like all exploratory phases, the first days turned up as many differences as areas of possible agreement.

The outlook and actions of the parties did not help the process. As of the start of talks, the British Cabinet was confirmed enough in its strategy of negotiation and pressure to dispatch the invasion force from Ascension (with an expected D-day between May 18 and May 22).[4] Naval and air hostilities increased in intensity. Britain declared a further "zone": All Argentine ships would be considered hostile if found beyond their 12-mile limit. A lull in the fighting after the *Belgrano/Sheffield* sinkings ended on May 9 with British naval bombardment and helicopter attacks on Argentine vessels and positions at Stanley and Darwin. Harriers attacked and captured an Argentine oceangoing trawler. On May 11, a British warship hit an Argentine supply ship in Falkland Sound. The Special Air Service (SAS) advance party for the Pebble Island raid was put ashore on West Falkland. The next day, two Argentine A–4 Skyhawk fighter-bombers were shot down, and on May 14, the 22nd SAS Regiment conducted a raid on the Argentine airfield on Pebble Island off the north coast of East Falkland.

PROGRESS AND PROMISE

However, real diplomacy continued in parallel to the use of force: In response to the deaths at sea and the loss of the Peruvian opportunity, the U.K. gave on pure self-determination but on May 6 insisted on Argentine surrender of the guarantee of sovereignty. Britain's concession on direct self-determination lay on the table for three days. The press reported the Prime Minister as having said she would give the talks four more days. The Junta pondered until May 11, then said it would drop guaranteed sovereignty as the precondition for starting negotiations. The Secretary General was emphasizing step-by-step, procedural handling of the problem, as he explained outside U.N. headquarters on May 11: "The whole problem is on the sovereignty of the islands. It is the underlying issue. Of course, it is the real issue. But at this stage we are trying to work on the basis of a procedural mechanism."[5] That day, through his "procedural mechanism" of indirect communication and narrowing of the gaps between positions, Perez de Cuellar achieved a major breakthrough. The pace picked up with sessions with the Argentines (Ros) at 10:45 A.M. and 5:00 P.M., and with the British (Parsons) at 3:00 P.M.. It was a major step forward. Talks might be possible.

The two sides edged closer. The British in turn threw in U.N. administration rather than the return of British administration. Britain, however, still sought symbolic and de facto return of British institutions in the form of an elected Island Council as part of the interim administration. Argentina saw even Kelper as well as British institutions as inconsistent with its sovereignty and therefore not possible under U.N. administration. How, or indeed whether, that administration would end came to define the differences between the parties: Argentina wanted it to expire with the calendar year 1982, implying that negotiations would result in sovereignty for Argentina by then, with the penalty being chaos in Stanley and New York if it did not. Britain could not enter a fixed-term negotiation that Argentina had only to wait out, any more than it could enter one with a pre-conceded outcome. On May 12, the Secretary General said the talks were at a very delicate stage but that progress was being made. Pym characterized the situation as promising, but Perez de Cuellar was cautious; a few more days of work would be needed; the exercise might be completed by the end of week.

By May 13/14, the outlines of a settlement were emerging: U.N. supervision of withdrawal, U.N. administration, and U.N. auspices for negotiations to conclude within the year. The prominence of the United Nations in the solution was not imposed by the mediator; instead, it was the best avenue of peaceful settlement to be explored. The parties had tried several sets of bilateral and multilateral arrangements over two mediations without success. Perhaps in internationalization of the territory and institutions lay the tradeoffs in National Honor and National Interest that would permit compromise. After six very intensive consecutive days of the indirect talks, a solution was taking shape. Also taking shape, however, was an impending war—the British Task Force reached a reported 25,000 men in 100 ships.

The U.N. package of phased mutual withdrawal under U.N. observers, completed by a fixed date; the dropping of sanctions and zones; and sovereignty negotiations to begin immediately, was intact. The problem was what transpired next under the U.N. process. There would be interim U.N. administration under the U.N. flag, but what could the two parties do in the Islands under the "without prejudice to claims" formula? This was not specified in writing—it was in the U.N. view a minimal governance question which could be handled like a peace-keeping force. The parties were allowed liason offices with flags, and that was likely all the U.N. wanted them to do: serve as liasons. What kind of sovereignty talks would occur? Good faith negotiations were to be held under the Secretary General to try to conclude the question in calendar year 1982. Talks could be put together later, but what if there were no agreement? Both interim adminis-tration and sovereignty negotiations posed major problems. Argentina still ex-pected to be free to bring people into the Islands as a price for surrendering military control. Argentina wanted, and the U.K. resisted, a fixed ending date as opposed to a target date for the sovereignty negotiations. Less vital but not agreed to was the distance to which the U.K. would withdraw its forces when they left the Falkland Islands.

Argentina did not accept that withdrawal, for example, to South Georgia was equivalent to Argentina's withdrawal from the Falklands to the mainland. Finally, Britain resisted Argentine insistence that the U.N. settlement cover all contested territory in the South Atlantic rather than just the Falkland Islands. The Secretary General had proposed solutions (which were undisclosed) for the distance of withdrawal for the Royal Navy and the more difficult question of Argentine immigration and its management. The U.N. proposals were deliberately open-ended in nature, especially on sovereignty. The distance for withdrawal was not to be defined within the specific proposal but left to U.N. experts—the field of peacekeeping is certainly the U.N.'s province more than anyone's. Precision as to number of miles would have denied the Argentines their demand that ships return to home ports or normal bases. The line between creative ambiguity and insufficient precision to satisfy either party is debatable. Certainly sovereignty had to be left open. Other issues might have been resolved in favor of one party or the other in an attempt to give the most benefit for the least offense.

By Friday, May 14, the parties and the mediator sensed a lull at best, a stalling of the talks if nothing could be worked out. They had come far, yet despite the mutual concessions each seemed to assume that more would be forthcoming. The U.K. was looking for an Argentine concession to match British willingness to consider U.N. interim administration and thus grant abandonment of the reinstallation of its administration. The British team thought a role for the (Falk-land) Islands Council was a fair compromise. It would fulfill the minimal duty to guarantee the Kelpers the self-determination or at least local-level self-rule that England had once provided even ethnically foreign peoples under the pro-tection of the Crown, for at least the interim administration period.

Perez de Cuellar said before beginning the eighth day of talks that the next few days were to be critical. He had artfully avoided press questions trying to characterize the timing of the progress of the talks. He had emphasized that he had no schedule, much less a deadline. Now he was supplying a time judgment unsolicited. Putting pressure on the parties, he indicated that the next days would be decisive; he did not contemplate endless negotiations. He expressed the hope that he would have a final answer from the parties that day or the next. First there was the press of time, and then the possibility of deadline or failure. Apparently the Argentine view on guaranteed sovereignty was equivocal, or so it seemed to the British who were seeking clarification that Argentina would enter the sovereignty talks without the premise of ensured future sovereignty, which they feared could lead again to Argentine frustration and the possibility of renewed hostilities. Certainly Britain still sought a role for the Council.

British Ambassador Parsons took the emerging deal to London to personally explore its advantages and disadvantages with his government. He received orders to return to London on consultation over the weekend of May 15/16. The parties were not impossibly far apart on the military aspects, including cease-fire and withdrawal. Britain would insist that there be a strict timetable. Time was growing short, meterologically and logistically, in the South Atlantic. There was agreement on a package of: Withdrawal of forces under U.N. supervision, and a provisional administration of the islands by the United Nations, with observers from the two parties, and communications similar to those existing before 2 April. These steps would be undertaken as provisional measures under Chapter 7 of the Charter, meaning that they did not affect sovereignty claims. There was considerable divergence over local input to U.N. governance, with Argentina seeking U.N. appointment of an equal number of British and Argentine "residents" on the islands as the administrator's advisors instead of the Island Council and one Argentine representative. Each side could agree to the lifting of prohibited zones and sanctions. Parsons felt that the resumption and duration of sovereignty negotiations could be agreed. The principal stumbling block seemed to be reinstitution of the Islanders' democratic institutions (the Council) during U.N. interim administration.[6] It looked workable, and would have to be approved in Cabinet were it to move into details and initialling by delegations in New York. Parsons took it to the Cabinet.

At first the package didn't sell in London, but it was judged a start. Major points were still unspecified, and might increase the political costs: How would local government make its input to the U.N. administration, if indeed real input could be guaranteed? How could the Blue Helmets of the U.N. peace keeping force keep the Argentine military from "resolving" any disagreements? In the week since the landing force had been dispatched from Ascension, the Cabinet had accustomed itself to the possible costs of a military solution. These costs were, however, growing daily. This appeared to the Cabinet to be the basis of Argentina's bargaining strategy, not only in New York but for any resulting negotiating period. Parliamentary pressure was mounting. As the Prime Minister and the Foreign Minister briefed the Commons on British minimum conditions in the negotiations, there were cries of "sellout." The landing was now an option: The troops aboard *Canberra* entered the war zone, with *QEII* en route. The risk to the Task Force was growing daily—two more Skyhawks and a chopper were shot down during attacks.

The War Cabinet met with Parsons and Henderson on May 16. Parsons detailed the progress of the negotiations and the many pitfalls of the compromise that had been hammered out. His professionalism and personal presence got the document a fair hearing and kept the possibility of avoiding larger-scale hostilities alive. They decided that an offer of the text with amendments would be made, but it itself would be unamendable and *final*. They made some of the more vague points of the draft agreement only as specific as they had to be to win U.K. approval. Some points indeed may still not have passed Parliament.

If Argentina did not gain sovereignty firmly, Britain certainly agreed in its proposal to the effective end of British administration. It was judged to be the price of avoiding war, and worth it. It was worth it only, however, if accepted right away to clearly end the need for hostilities while logistics and weather still made an effective British response possible.[7] The U.K. concessions made in the Peruvian effort were not to be put on the table again because Argentina was not giving any weight to the increasing "applicability" of British arms. Landings were scheduled for May 21–22. The Cabinet decided to force the Argentine diplomatic hand; to see whether Argentina, after three mediations and extended delay since the call for withdrawal of Resolution 502, was prepared to leave the Falkland Islands without war.

The British withdrawal proposal was thorough. It provided for the withdrawal of all armed forces following a complete cease-fire and an end to hostilities; the elimination of all exclusion zones; and the lifting of all blockades and economic measures by the parties and third countries. The two parties would jointly submit a draft U.N. resolution establishing the agreed terms and a U.N. administrator acceptable to the U.K. and Argentina to manage the government of the islands.

The administrator would govern in consultation with representative organizations established on the Islands, the Island Council, and one representative of the small Argentine population normally residing on the Islands. In addition to his mandate of supervising withdrawal of all armed forces on the Islands, the administrator was to draw up an effective plan to prevent armed forces from returning.

This administrator would govern by consulting the "Representative Organizations Established on the Islands," the Island Council and "one representative of the Argentine population normally residing on the islands," and would also be in charge of supervising the "withdrawal of all armed forces from the islands" and of drawing up "an effective plan to prevent them from returning."[8]

Under the British proposal there would be three observers from each of the parties on the islands. Bilateral negotiations would be resumed as would regular air (i.e., Argentine Air Force) and communication links. There would be relative *status quo ante bellum* normalcy under U.N. administration.

Britain insisted on an ex post facto clause that nullified much of the Argentine strategy of gradualized peaceful absorption:

During administration of the islands by the United Nations. . . . The two countries' claims of sovereignty over the archipelagos would not be affected by any development [such as

Argentine immigration and settlement] that might take place after the agreement was signed. None of the points of this provisional agreement will affect the rights, claims and position of each of the two countries in the final peaceful agreement over the islands.[9]

Further, no act or activity while the provisional agreement is in force would be grounds on which to base support or deny a claim of sovereignty.

The ongoing negotiations would be under the aegis of the U.N. Secretary-General and aimed at finishing a framework for a peaceful solution to the dispute by the end of December 1982. If this implied a U.K. willingness to make concessions, it was nonetheless an important point of principle in the U.K. position that "the negotiations should be started without . . . affecting the right claims and positions of the parties and without a preconceived position regarding their results," and that the parties would then *seek* to end by December 31.

Parsons took the amended deal back to New York on May 17. In a side-letter he brought the latest major amendment: The agreement was not to apply to the Dependencies. It was described to Perez de Cuellar in the morning as a final offer. Argentine Vice-Minister Ros was informed of its contents in the afternoon and was asked to respond clearly within 48 hours. For the first time, Perez de Cuellar seemed pessimistic about his mediation effort: "I am more than ever convinced that time is not on the side of peace." London was equally pessimistic.

ARGENTINA DECLINES

Argentina balked, making a counterproposal on May 19 that also provided for the withdrawal of forces and provisional administration of the islands by the United Nations. It provided for dual flags and equal representation on an advisory council.

Argentina committed a historic mistake in declining a package of these rough dimensions made four days before the British landing in the Falklands. The U.K. was willing at this point, before having had to expend human life on the conflict of National Interests and National Honor, to compromise. As the reality of a British counterattack in the South Atlantic had became more clear to the Argentine Government, the real desire for a negotiated settlement appeared. Even Galtieri rejected the option of continued popularity and election to the Presidency. By mid-May, the pressures from within his government for settlement were growing. They were overridden, however, by those who wanted total victory. Admiral Anaya was insistent, as were the Peronists, on staring down the British. Brazil had just provided the long-range patrol aircraft needed to find the Task Force. The ship-to-ship Exocets had not yet been brought to bear. Argentina commanded the skies and could thereby hold the ground she had rewon. The Junta chose full-scale war.

The decision does not appear to have been a reasoned one. It was not staffed out to the crisis staff for analysis or options. It is clear that Argentine decision making by this juncture in the crisis was confused, awkward, and imprecise.

The image that many held of an autocratic government, with the presumed attendent advantages of centralized power enhancing the clarity and speed of decision making was sadly far from the reality. The process the U.K. chose for forcing closure or rupture was misread as simple pressure, and therefore subject to counterpressure. Assured by friends that it was committing political and military suicide, Argentina pushed back. Concentrating on procedure and drafting over substance, it found the "final" character and the drafting of the British version of their common paper unacceptable. The tactic of final offer/fair offer was read as a bluff. A counteroffer was made.

Argentina felt that it had conceded the following in the Perez de Cuellar negotiations:

—Not prejudging the sovereignty issue;

—Leaving the Island Councils (local government) in place;

—A lower number of Argentine members of the governing body;

—The omission of the U.N. resolution numbers; that is, only vague and passing reference to what Argentina felt it had gained politically over the years at the U.N.;

—Allowing the U.K. to withdraw only to an equal distance; namely; to remain in South Georgia and not pull all the way back to Ascension Island; and

—Retreat from guaranteed sovereignty by year's end, to an understanding that the negotiation process, in time, yield restoration of Argentine rule, to dropping guaranteed sovereignty as a condition for opening the talks on long-term settlement. From its opening position that sovereignty was not negotiable, Argentina had come around to agreeing to negotiate for sovereignty over the Falklands.

Argentina felt that its proposals in the Perez de Cuellar mediation met, at least in part, *all* U.K. doubts. Argentina had worked from May 7 to 13 with Perez de Cuellar and provided him promptly with the separate positions that he asked each side to give him. The Argentine team thought that mutual concessions had led the two sides very near to peace by mid-month.

Foreign Minister Costa Mendez himself had felt that by May 14, the New York negotiations had reached the point where positions were converging and a real understanding might be reached. Argentina had accepted that there need be no specific mention of sovereignty and that there would be language referring to entering talks with the mutual recognition that each party had its own position. With these concessions, the Argentines understood that the Secretary General would be able to resolve the remaining differences through British concessions. At this juncture, however, Ambassador Parsons departed for London and returned with what Argentina saw as an ultimatum. While Argentina did not meet the British-imposed reply deadline, which it viewed as arbitrary, it did not, in its view, reject the British paper. Indeed, the Junta was discussing the paper when it was told that Perez de Cuellar was ending his efforts.

That weekend, however, saw the first major land battle: the British attack on Pebble Island. The Junta had believed that the U.K. accepted the Perez de Cuellar mediation because of the loss of the *Sheffield;* in other words; Britain had been planning to pursue a military solution but had backed off from that option in favor of negotiation. (It appears that these courses were, rather, consistently parallel throughout the crisis in British Cabinet thinking.) The Argentines realized then that a major British counterattack was imminent unless terms were agreed on. The menace of Ascension and the real application of power on South Georgia were now at hand off West Falkland. Perhaps, they now reasoned, the British were looking to gain time by their consultations with their U.N. Ambassador and his recall to London. They believed that the weather and the disposition of the fleet and its long supply line argued for almost immediate British invasion, but perhaps it could not yet be imminent as the landings scare of May 1 had shown. Perhaps Parsons would return without power to agree.

He returned instead with a concrete but unilaterally final plan. Perez de Cuellar received Parsons around noon and passed his paper to Minister Ros in the afternoon. The Argentines could only see as an ultimatum the British redraft of Monday, May 17. They were told that it would be made public on May 20. In their view, Perez de Cuellar (who was thus seen as Argentina's protector) had his back against the wall at this point. Argentina had made its last concessions. They judged that the U.K. was not negotiating in good faith. They decided that Argentina had to put down a marker. If necessary, Argentina would go directly to the Security Council. They conveyed to Perez de Cuellar their position that Argentina felt itself to have been flexible but must now be firm.

Perez de Cuellar told Parsons late on the 18th that he had the Argentine reply and would send it over the next day. Between the 17th and 18th of May, Perez de Cuellar, facing the impending failure of his mediation, had called Prime Minister Thatcher. When, late on the 18th, Argentina turned in its position, Perez de Cuellar told the Government of Argentina that he was ending his mediation. Already convinced of the self-fulfilling prophecy of collapse, and with their eye again on a next forum for a favorable hearing with the impending demise of the mediation, Argentina had formulated its position in a very tough form in order to serve as the opening position in some further hoped-for mediation. The parallels to Argentina's successive rejections of mediators who ruled against their definition of their interests is striking. Very much conscious of the fact that Perez de Cuellar's common paper looked more like the U.K. draft than their own, Argentina again thought in terms of a new arena in hope of finding political advantage to shore up an increasingly bleak military posture. Parsons asked for and got the essence of the reply immediately: It was no time for nuance. The British gambit on response precluded shades of meaning and further strategic delay. Without seeing the full text, which was delivered on the morning of the 19th, the British Ambassador knew diplomacy was exhausted. The U.N. Secretary General seemed more cautionary than hopeful in a midnight statement:

The Argentine government has conveyed to me this evening its reactions to the British position which was communicated yesterday. I relayed these reactions to the British government. There will certainly be further exchanges tomorrow. For the moment, all I can say is that we must continue without respite our efforts to achieve a durable peace through negotiation and accommodation. This is clearly in the common interest of both parties.[10]

The Secretary General's assessment ("Solo peudo decir.") is perhaps better rendered "I can *only* say" that efforts must continue. They did so the next morning (May 19) but the effort never recovered its momentum. Gambit (final offer to force cloture) had been met by gambit (unsolicitated amendment). Entering U.N. Headquarters at 9:35 A.M., the Secretary General characterized the negotiations as "alive" and said that Argentine ideas were in the hands of the British, but noted, "We are living the last hours."[11] Parsons met with Perez de Cuellar for an hour-and-a-half discussion of the Argentine reply. He told the Secretary General that Argentina's reply was unacceptable. *Canberra,* with 2,000 troops embarked, had reached the war zone—one of the last pieces in the Task Force puzzle. The war was already joined in South Georgia. Only Argentine withdrawal could now stop full-scale hostilities.

COUNTERPROPOSAL AND COLLAPSE

The Argentine counterproposal was in line with the British proposal on withdrawal of forces, U.N. supervision of that process, and reopening of communications and transport. They were also parallel on the critical issue of provisional administration by the United Nations with observers and advisors from each of the parties.

The remaining fundamental disagreements were Argentine insistence on:

—Thirty days' time to be allowed for withdrawal;

—Inclusion of the Falklands Dependencies, already again in British hands;

—The number of advisors being equal and substituting for the Island Council, which would have caused the most difficulty on administrative arrangements;

—Rejecting the opening of Article 1 of the British proposal, which was that none of the points of this provisional agreement should affect the rights, claims, and position of each of the two countries in the final peaceful agreement over the Islands;

—An exclusively U.N. administration with no role for the Islanders, thus denying Britain the appearance of the continuity of local if not British administration;

—Free access during the interim government period, with the implied invasion of Argentine settlers;

—Rejection of self-determination in any form, even after a further period of persuasion and demonstration of the benefits of Argentina, as mother country or metropole;

—Retaining the advantage of military proximity to the Islands while insisting that Great Britain should withdraw to the other end of its 8,000-mile line of march (Britain's offer of a two week, two-stage mutual withdrawal to 150 miles would have left Argentina with a considerable air cover and logistics advantage, able to negotiate *ad nauseum* while British units faced the Antarctic winter at sea or on equally bleak South Georgia) and;

—An end of the year deadline on negotiations, after which the General Assembly would decide sovereignty.

At that stage, it is likely that Argentina could have secured three quarters of its interests in the Falklands in the following approximate form: U.N. Administration, with both the British and Argentine flags flying along with that of the United Nations. There would have been no return to traditional British administrative or military presence in the Islands. The inevitability of full Argentine sovereignty would have been established. It would have been most difficult for the United Kingdom to reestablish any sense of political or diplomatic momentum for a return to the status quo. Indeed it can be argued that Britain had no desire, except insofar as the Kelpers were not convinced by the idea of an Argentine role, to return to the prewar insecurity of administering contested territory—if the population were persuaded, Britain could be persuaded.

Foreign Minister Costa Mendez found the U.K. proposal tougher than previous British positions. However, in his view, Argentina did not reject that proposal but rather modified a text said not to be subject to negotiation. The proposed Argentine amendments:

—Rejected mention of Article 73;

—Objected to the reimposition in toto of British administration;

—Called for some fixed limit on negotiations; and

—Noted the British resistance to any mention of relevant U.N. resolutions.

The British offer of May 17 proposed withdrawal of the armed forces of both parties and administration of the Falkland Islands by the United Nations, all without any precedent or effect on the sovereignty question. The Argentine counterproposal of May 19 matched the proposal for withdrawal of the forces (though still to normal—that is, unequally distant—bases) and U.N. provisional administration, but called for Argentine and British flags to be hoisted alongside the blue U.N. flag. Argentina wanted the Dependencies covered, and felt it needed 30 days for a dignified withdrawal. It emphasized the parties as *observers* of U.N. administration, denying the U.K. even partial restoration of governance. Less symbolically, it called for the U.N. administrator to have equal numbers of Argentine and British advisors drawn from residents of the Islands.

The period of U.N. administration would likely have led to *eventual* full Argentine sovereignty. Argentina would not have had to expend more lives and could indeed have kept victory—military and diplomatic—almost bloodless. The risk of military defeat would most probably have been averted, since it would be very difficult for the U.K., no matter what the course of the negotiations, to reassemble not only the Task Force but the national consensus needed to retake the Islands by force.

Argentine "national will," on the other hand, needed neither elaborate construction of political consensus (which could have been fairly easily maintained in any case) nor the complicated logistics of conducting operations at a range of 8,000 miles.

Thus an imaginative diplomatic solution at this point would not only have consolidated Argentina's territorial and diplomatic gains but indeed her military gains in the sense of politically blocking reintroduction of British forces and maintaining the edge on reinvasion of being close at hand. Far more than the miscalculations resulting in the decision to invade, the decision not to accept U.N. administration on May 18 was at the root of Argentina's tragedy in the Falklands. If not her last chance, it was certainly her best.

Argentina's refusal of the compromises that evolved in the United Nations setting proved to be the final and fatal failure in a series of failures of political imagination. In their de facto rejection of the final British offer on May 19, the Argentines exhausted the British patience with diplomacy proceeding in parallel with armed conflict.

Independent Television News reported, without identifying its source, that orders had already been issued to the Task Force Commander. Great Britain released and interpreted its final offer as it in effect told the Argentines it would invade should they decline it. The "gloss" is as important as the terms: the British news report stated that the agreement provided for complete *Argentine* withdrawal within two weeks. It termed this withdrawal an act terminating aggression and upholding international law. British withdrawal is not mentioned, and seems contingent on Argentine withdrawal, although under the British proposal withdrawal would occur simultaneously. Also, U.N. interim administration would maintain the democratic structure, and the future of the Islands would not be prejudged, thus safeguarding the British position on sovereignty. With these interpretations, the British provisions seem to clearly favor the U.K.; they certainly seem less conciliatory. The Argentine negotiators knew British politolegal reasoning well after 17 years, and were clearly able to discern these underlying interpretations. In light of the gloss the U.K. would put on the agreement, one can understand why the Argentines may have been hesitant to accept these terms as open-ended.

Perez de Cuellar judged that his good offices had ended with the rejection of the British final offer tactic. What gave force to the tactic was the gambit of public revelation of the text on a fixed date (May 20). In so doing, Britain set an end to the process as Perez de Cuellar cared to conduct it—privately. That gambit is certainly the end of negotiating confidentiality; of "open treaties secretly arrived at." In this sense, Perez de Cuellar did not end his own negotiation; rather, the parties did. With disclosure of texts and the end of the confidential process, Perez de Cuellar had no more reason to resist the confrontational formal Security Council meetings which he had held off for the whole of his three-week process on the grounds that the *Stürm und Drang* was inimical to effective mediation.

Perez de Cuellar made one last effort late on May 19, calling the two Heads of Government to let them know that he was sending each side reformulations of the interim administration and diplomatic negotiation of the draft agreement. In a statement (SG/SM/3283) of the evening of May 19, he said:

I must state that we are at a very dangerous point in the efforts for an agreement between Argentina and the United Kingdom. The time left for negotiations must now be measured in hours. In my judgement, substantial progress has been made over the past two weeks. This will be lost if the present opportunity for negotiations disappears.

I have suggested certain ideas which I believe might be of assistance in overcoming the remaining points of difference. This afternoon, I have spoken to both President Galtieri and Prime Minister Thatcher to express my views and my very great concern. The cost of failure in terms of human life and suffering is too high to permit us to give up our efforts.

At this decisive moment, a last urgent effort is needed to reach the accommodation necessary for a reasonable settlement. I am persuaded that this can be done without prejudice to the rights, claims or positions of either party. We must continue to work for peace without jeopardy to principle.

Britain informed the Secretary General on May 20 that while the Secretary General's formulations (put to the Heads of Government) were not entirely in line with British views, they would not react negatively or comment in detail before seeing the Argentine reaction. That Argentine reaction was not available within the Secretary General's deadline for response to his final aide-mémoire.

U.S. Permanent Representative Ambassador Jeane Kirkpatrick made a last effort to save Perez de Cuellar's mediation. Argentina had already decided to concur in the abandonment of the effort before Kirkpatrick saw Argentine representatives in New York, and she reached Costa Mendez two hours after the British landings at San Carlos Bay.

Convinced that the U.K. would remain absolutely intransigent, Argentina again confronted the fact that she could not or did not wish to make any political concessions to avoid combat.[12]

The U.N. Secretary General was unfortunately incorrect on the morning of May 20 when he described the negotiations as in intensive care but still alive. Late on May 20,1982, he had to inform the President of the U.N. Security Council that his efforts did not offer the present prospect of success. The following day, he so informed the Security Council:

The Secretary General informed the Council that the time for reaching agreements through negotiations . . . was extremely short and although, in his view, substantial progress had been achieved in the preceding two weeks, the necessary accommodations which were still needed to end the conflict had not been forthcoming. He added that . . . the efforts in which he had been engaged . . . did not currently offer the prospect of bringing about an end to the crisis nor preventing the intensification of the conflict.[12]

On May 21, the British forces established a beachhead at San Carlos Bay on East Falkland Island, and the British campaign to regain the Falkland Islands militarily was under way. U.N. Security Council President Ling Qing of China ordered urgent closed consultations to consider the collapse of the Falklands peace process and the new fighting in the South Atlantic. The Council decided during a 90-minute private meeting to convene an emergency public session at 2:30 P.M. An Argentine Government Spokesman said Foreign Minister Nichanor Costa Mendez would go to New York to ask the Security Council to call a cease-fire. International diplomatic mediation and negotiation had failed their most crucial test: the ability to prevent the conflict of National Interest and National Honor from leading to deaths which do not solve the problems which lay at the core.

As the Security Council reconvened on May 21 at the request of Ireland and Panama, it seemed clear that the Secretary General did not hold out much hope of the U.N. resolving the Falklands crisis before a major confrontation and violence occurred. The Secretary General reviewed his conduct of the negotiations between the parties. He noted that agreement in principal had been reached on the majority of points, but that four remaining differences were key: details of interim administration; the outside limit of time for the sovereignty negotiations, and hence the duration of interim administration; details of mutual withdrawal; and the geographic area covered by the interim agreement.

Argentina told the Council that it was willing to negotiate on the basis of Resolution 502. Great Britain emphasized that it was negotiating the Argentine withdrawal that had already been demanded by the Council. Britain had moved so far as to have offered mutual withdrawal and abandoned reimplementation of the British sovereignty which prevailed before the Argentine breach of the peace. In order to regain any democratic institutions for the Kelpers, Britain had agreed to accept the proportional inclusion of Argentines in such bodies. The inclusion of the Dependencies was, however, a separate question and not in play here, nor was withdrawal to unequally distant home ports.

The Commonwealth then took Britain's side and Latin America that of Argentina. Argentine Delegate Eduardo Roca was no more optimistic. The Argentine military felt itself prepared now for a full-scale British assault on the Falkland Islands. While Argentine Foreign Minister Costa Mendez insisted that Argentina had not given up on the U.N. talks, this was more than likely a position communicated to the media before the Secretary General's pessimistic assessment of his own efforts and his frank statement that his peace effort had failed.

On May 26 in Resolution 505, the U.N. Security Council requested the Secretary General to undertake a renewed mission of good offices on the basis of Resolution 502 and the approach outlined in the Secretary General's statement to the Council. He was requested to seek agreement between the parties for the terms of a cease-fire.

By unanimous vote, Resolution 505 reaffirmed Resolution 502. The resolution [S/RES/502 (1982)] expressed ''appreciation'' to the Secretary General ''for his efforts to implement 502''; requested him, on the basis of the present resolution, to undertake a renewed mission; urged both parties ''to cooperate fully'' with him; and requested the Secretary General ''to enter into contact immediately with the parties with a view to negotiating mutually acceptable terms for a ceasefire, including, if necessary, arrangements for the dispatch of U.N. observers to monitor compliance with the terms of the ceasefire.''

The Secretary General was less than eager for the renewed ''mandate.'' *Before* the Council session he noted: ''Everything is now in the hands of the Security Council. I understand that today they will approve a resolution. . . . It seems that they are giving me a very difficult mission. . . . What can I do in seven days?''

On Thursday, May 27, the Secretary General met with the parties at 4:00 and 5:30 P.M. Exhausted and desperately trying to maintain the evenhandedness that had brought him close to avoiding full-scale war in the South Atlantic, he allowed himself an ''editorial.'' He was reminded by the press that both Resolution 502 and the British called for Argentine forces to withdraw and asked if he was in effect saying that Argentina was what was stopping the peace process. Perez de Cuellar replied quietly that the questions sounded like they came from a member of the U.S. or British delegation. The Secretary General had put the final round of questions to the parties on Wednesday, May 26, and demanded their answers by the close of business on the 27th.

On May 28, the second battalion of the Parachute Regiment took Goose Green and Darwin in extended fighting. The 1,400-man Argentine garrison surrendered the next morning. The first Kelpers had been liberated and the British campaign took on political as well as military momentum.

After a week of further intensive exchanges, the Secretary General on June 2 informed the Council that the positions of the two parties were not compatible with a cease-fire. On June 4, the Council almost watered down its position in Resolution 502 with a draft resolution calling for a military cease-fire. British troops had been within sight and range of the surrounded Argentines at Stanley since June 2. The nine countries in favor were China, Ireland, Japan, Panama, Poland, Spain, Uganda, the USSR, and Zaire. Japan's vote was perhaps the least predictable, politically the most interesting, and thus in a sense the ninth ''yes'' vote necessitating the U.K./United States veto. It would have been in good political company in the abstain column. France, Jordan, Guyana, and Togo abstained. The United States and U.K. vetoed the draft, although the U.S. Permanent Representative asked that the record show that abstention orders arrived only minutes too late (from the U.S. Secretary of State in Paris via the State Department) for the vote. The U.S. Delegation in the Security Council Chamber had maintained an open phone line to the Department, even after the vote was taken.

Britain clearly viewed the idea of a ceasefire as overtaken by events.

Parsons noted that:

My Spanish colleague took the lead with Panama on behalf of Argentina and . . . they pressed to the vote an apparently innocuous cease-fire resolution which, in our judgement, would have precisely the effect which we refused to contemplate. The vote was deliberately timed to coincide with the ministerial meeting of the Non-aligned Movement Coordinating Bureau which was taking place in Havana.[14]

The United States had indicated through the press that Secretary of State Haig was ready, if asked, to resume his shuttle diplomacy.[15] A well-publicized, high-level meeting was convened by U.S. Vice-President George Bush to discuss the collapse of the U.N. peace effort and thereby indicate U.S. concern and interest. The U.S. press was questioning the first U.S. mediation effort at this point, pushing the idea that the United States should have insisted on a further mediation rather than declaring its support for Great Britain. It was also saying that the United States had made its arrangements to supply the British with ammunition and spare parts before the British made any such request.

The Secretary General had almost put the United Nations back on the map in terms of peace and security affairs. That he came so close is testimony to his professionalism and patience. He himself said that from the beginning of his efforts the fact that the parties were negotiating did not stop them from fighting: "That is in a way the rule of the game."[16] Now, however, fighting while negotiating was no longer on either party's agenda. They turned to war to solve the Falklands crisis of spring 1982.

It is important to note that the Secretary General's mandate from the Security Council to seek a solution to the Falklands crisis is still in force. While not conducting active negotiations, he has nonetheless remained in touch with both the Argentine and British Governments, who are fully aware that U.N. good offices are available if desired.[17]

Falkland Islands

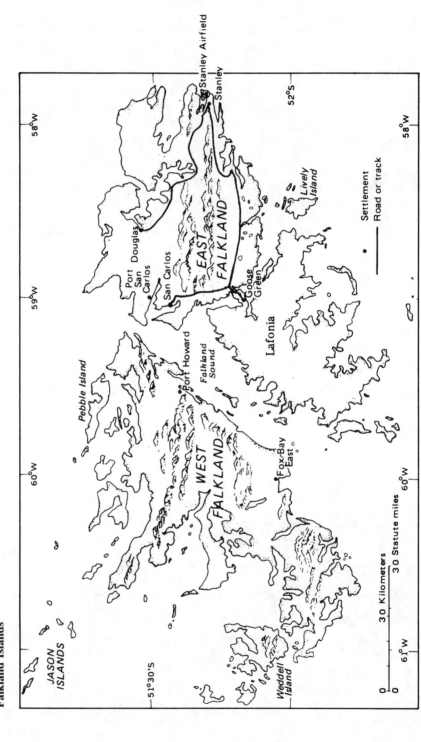

VII

STATECRAFT AND FORCE

The opportune presence of a ship of war may avert a disaster which can only be remedied later at . . . considerable sacrifice.
—British Foreign Office Report, 1907

There were no contingency plans on the shelf, we had to improvise.
—Chief of the British Defense Staff, 1982

There cannot be good laws where there are not good arms. . . . The chief cause of the loss of states is the contempt of this art.
—Nicolò Machiavelli

To find security without fighting is [the] acme of skill.
—Sun-Tzu

Generals should mess with the common soldiers. The Spartan system was a good one.
—Napoleon

The overall diplomatic and military scenario that comprised the Falklands crisis of spring 1982 is varied and complex, a mass of detailed, nuanced proceedings and acts spread from pole to pole on three continents. The negotiations can be best understood as a diplomatic process by laying out their elements or components as they developed through the many proposals for solution of the crisis. The "solution" to the Falklands crisis was in the end the military campaign of May 21 and the month following. Statecraft failed: It neither produced a "win" nor a negotiated compromise. War produced a "win" but did not solve the dispute. The politics leading up to crisis and war have as many instructive politico-military points as the war itself.

Diplomacy and the use of force interacted throughout the crisis. With the expenditure of billions of dollars and thousands of casualties, the Falklands War may have been the costliest conflict per square foot of contested territory or per capita of population in history. The implications of the Falklands crisis for crisis management are highly specific and disturbing in their implications for world order. Equally disturbing are the mislearned "lessons" about politico-military affairs and international relations which many governments drew and some may act upon. There are a few novel instructive points. There are more, equally valuable, reminders about the use, effects, and causes of interstate violence over territory. Understanding the cause does not lead to the cure. However, understanding may at least lead decision-makers to a sparing and effective use of violence and the nation-state system to better shape incentives to keep a just peace.

NEGOTIATIONS: AN OVERVIEW OF THE ELEMENTS

The proposals and counterproposals advanced by the two parties and the mediators during the Falklands crisis bear examination as a whole if we are to try to understand why the conflict was not solved by diplomacy. The principal proposals were:

—Statements on Negotiations from January–March 1982 (especially the Argentine bout de papier of January 27 on "The Argentine Position")[1]

—Elements Britain was Prepared to discuss

—The Argentine Proposal of April 19,1982[2]

—The US Proposals of April 27,1982[3]

—The Argentine Response to the 4/27 US Proposal, in a Letter from Argentine Foreign Minister Costa Mendez to Secretary Haig dated April 29[4]

—The Peru–US Proposal of May 5,1982[5]

—The May 2 Perez de Cuellar Initiative[6]

—The British Interim Draft Agreement (British Counterproposal of May 17)[7]

—Argentine Response of May 19[8]

—British Government White Paper of May 21,1982[9]

—Argentine Diplomatic Note to the US Department of State, May 26,1982[10]

—U.S. and British Reactions to the Final Argentine Position.[11]

The elements which were in play throughout these negotiations were in constant flux. Some factors were more emphasized than others at various times. Throughout the diplomacy of Spring 1982, however, there were key issues which had to be addressed:

—Military Provisions: Ceasefire, Withdrawal and Non-reintroduction of Forces into the Islands
—References to Resolution 502
—Geographic Scope of the Negotiations
—Normalization of the Situation in the Islands and of Relations between the Parties
—Interim Administration of the Islands
—Followup negotiations on the Sovereignty of the islands.

The flow of each of these subjects through many documents and talks gives one a sense of the dialogue on each critical area. It points out strongly how slim some gaps between the sides were, and how others seemed at heart unbridgeable. (Key phrases are in quotes only to highlight their precise content but are *not* footnoted since their origin is cited by document, above, and most of the documents are one or a few pages.) While the turn of a phrase or timing of a small concession on language may at times be only a tactic within a wider strategy, the language in which a crisis was negotiated tells one the subjects formally thought to be in play and the formally acknowledged to be legitimate.

Military Provisions: Ceasefire/Withdrawal/Non-reintroduction

All plans and proposals in the Falklands crisis of Spring 1982 called for military disengagement of some kind. A cease-fire was an obvious precondition. Roughly mutual or parallel withdrawal of forces was a common element throughout, and the time frames were relatively short because neither side had impossible logistics requirements. Most had an explicit or implied commitment not to reintroduce forces into the area. Verification was provided for by a third party in most cases. This element was reinforced in the respective negotiations by the call of UNSC Resolution 502 at the opening of the crisis in its operative paragraphs 1 and 2 for a cessation of hostilities to take effect immediately and the withdrawal of Argentine forces from the Falkland Islands.

When initially approached by a mediator, the British Government's sense in early April of military provisions in any diplomatic agreement was that these should consist solely in possible arrangements for supervising the withdrawal of Argentine forces in line with UNSC Resolution 502. In this sense, military provisions were the only British diplomatic goal at the opening of the crisis: peaceful Argentine withdrawal so as to obviate the use of force. This was the pure trade-off that the dispatch of the Task Force envisioned. Argentina of course saw any military withdrawal as contingent on a cancellation of all initial British military preparations and a firm and permanent recognition of Argentine sovereignty.

The U.N. Security Council enjoined against the use of force in a statement of April 1 by the President of the Council. In Resolution 502, the military provisions called for an immediate cessation of hostilities and the immediate withdrawal of all Argentine forces from the Islands as well as calling on the parties to seek a diplomatic solution. The essence of a diplomatic solution on April 3 when Resolution 502 was passed would have been of only Argentine withdrawal, since no British forces were operating as units in the area at that time.

As the Haig negotiations took shape, the agenda expanded, and by the 19th of April, Argentine officials were engaged in drafting a proposal with Secretary Haig, which included a very precise formula from the United States. Beginning on the day after signature, both sides would cease introducing forces into circles of 150 nautical miles from the three island groups. Within 24 hours, they would begin withdrawal, with Argentina withdrawing half its forces within a week and the rest within 15 days; and the United Kingdom withdrawing within a week to at least 2,000 nautical miles and within 15 days to their bases or usual areas of operations. The United Kingdom found the disproportionality of the distances for withdrawal unacceptable, but by April 21 the U.K. had clearly accepted that a wider package than just military withdrawal was going to be needed. On April 21, U.K. Foreign Secretary Pym told the Commons that negotiations and interim administration would have to be part of the package. He was still phrasing the military element, however, as "arrangements for Argentine withdrawal."

In the U.S. proposal of April 27, the United States called for a cessation of the United Kingdom's "zone of exclusion." Argentina was to suspend operations in the same area, also within 24 hours. Each side was to withdraw half its forces within seven days, with the Royal Navy to stand-off seven days steaming time at 12 knots. Argentine forces were to be at such a distance or in such a state of readiness that they "could not be reinserted with their equipment and armament in less than seven days." After 15 days, all Argentine forces were to be removed from the three zones around the island groups. British forces were to withdraw to "their usual operating areas or normal duties," which relieved them of the requirement to return to bases at which they might not have been at the opening of hostilities. Both sides were to cooperate with the United States, which undertook to verify compliance with the military measures of paragraph 2 of the U.S. plan of April 27. Cease-fire was integrally linked with withdrawal. The U.S. formula for reinsertion time was an ingenious attempt to overcome the problem of geographic distance and achieve military balance. The non-reintroduction was much more specific, and was a commitment integral with cease-fire and withdrawal, thereby protecting the parties from military arguments against the diplomatic process. The strong U.S. role as verifier and guarantor was the underpinning for the Haig military proposals.

In the Argentine response to the U.S. proposal, Costa Mendez in his April 29 letter to Haig sent a tacit message that Argentina was in military control of the Falkland Islands and saw no reason in the Haig proposals to surrender that advantage. The power in occupation of the Islands could speak of "difficulties that it is essential to overcome," as it still could so define the question. Costa Mendez spoke of a provisional regime for administration of the Islands "as an essential step in the process of separating the two military forces.'' While stating that it was willing to consider withdrawal in line with Resolution 502, the Argentine emphasis was on separating forces and avoiding direct clashes rather than military withdrawal and non-reintroduction. Recognition of Argentine sovereignty and power in interim administration of the Islands had to be resolved in Argentina's favor before ''solution of the remaining problems.'' The remaining problem in this Argentine order of priorities would be military withdrawal, which was considered by both the United Kingdom and the mediator to be the initial and prerequisite order of business.

In his statement of April 30, Secretary Haig noted that large-scale military action was likely in the South Atlantic and that his effort to restore peace through implementation of Resolution 502 had as one basis the call of Resolution 502 for ''an end to hostilities, the withdrawal of Argentine forces from the islands; and a diplomatic settlement of the fundamental dispute.'' He noted that his proposals had involved ''a cessation of hostilities, withdrawal of both Argentine and British forces, termination of sanctions.'' Adding a new element to the politico-military equation, he noted that President Reagan had ordered the suspension of all military exports to Argentina, cut its eligibility for military sales, and decided to respond favorably to British requests for war materiel.

The Peruvian proposal's military provisions called for immediate cease-fire ''concurrent with'' mutual withdrawal and non-reintroduction of forces. The schedule was open-ended and was to be set by a Contact Group which was to ensure that the provisions were respected. There was, however, no provision for enforcement or a guarantor role: the Contact Group was to ''verify'' the military provisions. (The language was stronger, for example, on the Group's role in ''Ensuring that no actions are taken in the Falkland Islands by the local administration which would contravene this interim agreement'' in the interim administration provisions). Britain recognized that the revised Peruvian proposals would provide for complete and supervised withdrawal of Argentine forces matched by a corresponding withdrawal of British forces, with immediate cease-fire to *follow* the Argentine agreement to withdraw. The Contact Group would, in the British view, supervise withdrawal. Exclusion zones would be suspended. Thus the Peruvian proposals still required Argentine withdrawal, which Argentina was not prepared to carry out in exchange for the interim administration and sovereignty provisions.

The Secretary General's initiative as put forward in his points of May 2 to the parties included provisions for military withdrawal by both sides; that is, Argentina from the Falkland Islands and British forces from the area around the Falkland Islands. Britain was already in possession of South Georgia, and the U.N. effort applied only to the Falkland Islands themselves. The military blockades or zones in effect by each side were to be rescinded. Hostilities were to cease. In the U.N. negotiations, the British position on May 6 was acceptance of the general terms of the Secretary General's points, but Britain made it clear that Resolution 502 (i.e., Argentine military withdrawal from the Falkland Islands) had to be implemented without delay and that any cease-fire must be clearly linked to the beginning of Argentine withdrawal within a fixed number of days.

The Secretary General was clear at all times that his initiative was based on an implementation of Resolution 502. The resolution had nothing to say, however, about British forces, and therefore nothing about the order, precedence, mutuality, or equality of withdrawal by two militarily engaged sides. The Secretary General was quite clear in his statement to the Security Council of 21 May that he believed the implementation of Resolution 502 was absolutely necessary for peace in the South Atlantic, and he made no further indications that the need for Argentine withdrawal was ever in doubt in the U.N. negotiation. In the British draft proposal of May 17, a cease-fire would take effect 24 hours after signature. Argentina would then begin withdrawal from the Islands, completing 50 percent drawdown to at least 150 nautical miles within 7 days and drawdown of all forces within 14 days. Great Britain would begin withdrawal at the same time to at least 150 nautical miles away (half within 7 days, half within 14 days). As withdrawal began, 24 hours after signature, the respective exclusion zones would be lifted and each side would undertake not to reintroduce any armed forces in a zone 150 miles around the Falklands after the completion of withdrawal. The United Nations Administrator was charged with verification of all armed forces in the Islands and devising an effective method of ensuring that they were not reintroduced.

These elements of the British final offer on military conditions were not acceptable to Argentina. In the Argentine response of May 19, Argentina counterproposed the completion of withdrawal within 30 days (i.e., deep into Antarctic winter to about 1 July, at which the time the logistics operations of the British Task Force should have become impossible) and full return to normal bases and areas of operations, thus setting British forces 6,000 to 8,000 miles from the Falklands with the sole exception of the patrol ship *Endurance*. Earlier content to secure advantage solely in distanced withdrawal, Argentina now wished under the military provisions to reassert the advantages of her operating capability in Antarctic winter and retain—past Britain's ability to affect the situation—her occupation of the Islands. While one cannot judge intentions, this clearly left the capability to default on the military provisions with little expectation of effective British response from frozen-in South Georgia. The British capability under the British proposal of withdrawing to a distance of only 150 miles would have allowed Britain the possibility of establishing a major base at South Georgia and beginning to develop the operational capability to maintain naval forces in the area on a fairly large scale. A relative disadvantage would have been the ability of Argentine air forces to cover the Falklands area from half the distance from which British forces in South Georgia would have had to operate. Each side found the other's military provisions unbalanced and unacceptable.

In its White Paper of May 21, Britain noted that in its proposal at the U.N.

it had been willing under Article 2(3) of the draft agreement to withdraw to a distance of 150 nautical miles in exchange for Argentine withdrawal within 14 days. It had also been willing to comply with international verification under Article 6(4) of the draft. Britain was willing to have aerial surveillance from third parties to confirm all military withdrawals.

In its note to the U.S. Department of State of May 26, Argentina noted that during the U.N. negotiations it had proposed withdrawal of forces of both countries on a gradual and simultaneous basis, to be completed within 30 days. The phrasing, however, was constrictive on British forces in that it stated that within a maximum period of 30 days, "All armed forces shall be in their normal bases and areas of operations." By requiring that at the end of 30 days British forces be in their normal bases and areas of operations, the Argentine drafting would have compelled most British units to set sail almost immediately. Thus, at the end of 30 days, the British fleet would have been at least a month from being able to return to the area in an operational mode. Argentine provisions in the U.N. negotiations for supervision and confirmation were quite specific. Under Article 3, Section 1 they called for supervision of withdrawal by "specialized personnel of the United Nations whose composition shall be agreed with the parties."

U.K. insistence on cease-fire with immediate withdrawal of all Argentine forces was in line with its legal position that under Article 51 of the Charter it was acting in self-defense and was also acting consistently with Resolution 502. It viewed the distances of withdrawal of the two sides as totally unbalanced. Great Britain accepted the principle of U.N. verification of military disengagement and withdrawal, but remained insistent, however, that the only acceptable kind of cease-fire was one unequivocally linked with the immediate beginning of Argentine withdrawal. Thus, moves in the United Nations for cease-fire resolutions were unacceptable to one party. The Secretary General told the Security Council on June 2 that the two parties had provided statements on what they would view as acceptable conditions for cease-fire. They concluded that there was no possibility of a mutually acceptable cease-fire. Britain reiterated in the Council that any cease-fire not linked to Argentine withdrawal was inconsistent with Resolution 502 and the Council's call under that resolution for Argentine withdrawal. Any cease-fire would have left Argentina in possession of the disputed territory. The Council voted on a draft resolution calling for both sides to cease firing on June 4. The resolution also called for the simultaneous implementation of Resolutions 502 and 505. While the resolution received nine favorable votes, enough for passage and extentions, it was vetoed by Britain and the United States and thus not adopted.

While the military provision of the several proposed agreements on the Falklands crisis would seem to have been semiautomatic and somewhat a preface to other more "diplomatic" provisions, they provided a *contretemps* of their own, and were in a sense the price Argentina was being asked to pay in the negotiations. The other elements never outweighed the military price in the judgment of

Argentina, and the settlement was thus not possible. In the varying proposals, one sees reflected the relative military advantages each side sought to preserve, with Argentina consistently pursuing withdrawal to home bases and a longer withdrawal period, and Britain seeking, once it had regained South Georgia, to reserve the right to use it as a base from which to ensure compliance with any possible agreement.

References to Resolution 502

While Britain drafted and secured the passage of U.N. Security Council Resolution 502, it was accepted (via different interpretations) as the basic international, legal, and political document through the spring of 1982, and appeared in the earliest proposals and drafts in the several forms.

In the initial round of Secretary Haig's shuttle, both the British and the United States appealed to Resolution 502 regularly, emphasizing the call for Argentine withdrawal. The Argentine proposals of April 19 had both parties agreeing on the steps to be undertaken "on the basis of United Nations Security Council Resolution 502." The U.S. proposal revealed on April 27 contained the same language in its preamble to the memorandum of agreement. The Peruvian proposals drew on the fundamental elements of 502, and the U.N. Secretary General made clear in his statement to the Security Council on May 21 that the implementation of 502 was imperative and was the basis of his mediation effort. As they moved toward war, both Argentina and Britain appealed to 502, Britain citing it as the formalization of the fact that a breach of the peace had taken place and thereby using it as the basis of its claim to be acting under the Charter in self-defense. Argentina made appeal to the call for an immediate cessation of hostilities, ignoring the call in 502 for the immediate withdrawal of all Argentine forces.

In the British interim draft agreement of May 17, the U.K. called for both governments "responding to Security Council Resolution 502 (1982) adopted on 3 April 1982 under Article 40 of the Charter of the United Nations." There was reference, however, in the preambular language also to "obligations with regard to non–self-governing territories set out in Article 73 of the Charter of the United Nations, the text of which is annexed hereto." Britain saw itself as acting under an inherent right of self-defense under Article 51 of the Charter and fully justified in the use of force (without any negotiation required). In the British view, HMG made major efforts to achieve peaceful settlement under Resolution 502 rather than relying purely on Article 51 self-defense. British references to 502, however, were often in terms of ending Argentina's "unlawful aggression," which was not, of course, the language of the resolution. Britain sought and received in 502 only an acknowledgement that Argentina's actions had been a breach of the peace. U.S. policymakers saw Resolution 502 as a form of diplomatic pressure; the clear condemnation in both the U.S. and British views that the Security Council resolution was mandatory (or binding), but Argentina refused to comply with it.

To both the mediator and the British, what they called Argentine procrastination or intransigence dated from the passage of 502 and their time horizon was thus longer than that of Argentina, which took 502 as simply an expression of universal norms which did not apply in this specific case of historic injustice. In that sense, Argentina's time frame for judging its firmness or determination was really to start from the time when force could be brought to bear against it; that is, the arrival of the British Task Force, rather than from April 3 at the beginning of the crisis. When to the Argentines the clock was just beginning to tick on implementation of Resolution 502, the clock had practically run out in British eyes.

The essence of 502 was reaffirmed by the Council in its unanimous passage of Resolution 505 on May 26. In addition to the steps of 502, the U.N. Secretary General was asked to undertake a renewed mission of good offices. The parties were called on to the end the hostilities in and around the Islands.

Scope

The geographic scope of the drafts, documents, proposals, and discussions which made up the diplomacy of the Falklands crisis varies considerably. In their *bout de papier* of January 27, the Argentine Foreign Ministry transmitted to the British Embassy in Buenos Aires on January 27, 1982, the full-scope demand that would be the essence of the Argentine position throughout: Argentine sovereignty over the Falklands, South Georgia, and South Sandwich Islands. The three Island groups were represented in both Argentine and U.S. drafts during the Haig shuttle by zones of 150 nautical miles around three sets of coordinates. The Dependencies were thus included. By the time of the Peruvian initiative, Great Britain had already retaken South Georgia and it was clear that neither South Georgia nor South Sandwich were in play, although the Argentine station at Teniente Esquivel in the South Sandwich chain was as yet unchallenged as it was militarily and politically marginal. When Britain presented its final offer in the United Nations mediation, a side letter to the Secretary General accompanied the text making clear the British position that the Falkland Islands dependencies were not covered by the draft interim agreement. This had been the British position throughout the U.N. negotiations.

Britain held that South Georgia and the South Sandwich Islands are geographically distant from the Falklands, have no settled population, and have a British title not derived from or related to the sovereignty of the Falkland Islands. Hence, the Dependencies were attached to the Falklands only for administrative convenience and were not a related political question. Argentina's May 26 reply called for the inclusion of all the island groups in Article I.1.: "The geographical scope of the area within which the withdrawal of troops is to be carried out shall comprise the Malvinas, South Georgia, and South Sandwich Islands." The

British reaction to this was that this full-scope proposal would have had the import that British forces would have to withdraw from South Georgia, which they had already retaken. It was totally unacceptable to the United Kingdom that South Georgia and the South Sandwich Islands be included in the U.N. solution. With such scope, it was not even necessary for Argentina to secure return to normal bases and areas of operation as the British would have had at a minimum to withdraw to Ascension Island.

Normalization

Most of the proposals and drafts in the Falklands crisis called for rapid normalization of the situation prevailing between the two parties. Nuances of scope and timing, however, were significant. Argentine thinking during the Haig shuttle called for action as of the date of agreement to end economic and financial measures, including restrictions on travel, transport, communications, and transfer of funds between the two countries, as well as the EEC and third-country sanctions. Until definitive arrangements were made permanent, those subjects as well as others related specifically to the Falklands (residents, property ownership, communications, and trade) would be available on an equal basis to each party. The U.S. proposal similarly called for the ending of economic and financial measures.

The language relating to the Islands was even stronger: transportation, travel, and trade were to be promoted and facilitated without prejudice. Similarly, the U.N. Secretary General's initiative called for the rescinding by each side of blockades, exclusion zones, and economic sanctions. The British proposal called in Article 5 for each party to lift economic measures as from signature (time "T"). Argentina wanted not only the lifting of zones and sanctions but freedom for its citizens to seek residence, property, and work in the Islands as part of normalization. The British saw this as outside the scope of normalization, and viewed normalization as of far more benefit to Argentina than to Britain as there were few effective sanctions to the economic side against the U.K. Britain was willing under Article 7 to agree to the reestablishment of communications, travel, transport, postage, and so on, as before the invasion. The U.K. viewed this as normalcy rather than the additional openness to Argentine residents and ownership that Argentina had always sought but never obtained as in so many other matters. Thus Britain was seeking the status quo ante and enhanced position as compensation for its military withdrawal. The May 19 Argentine note of reply in the U.N. round stated in Article II:

With effect from the signature of this agreement, each party shall cease to apply the economic measures which it has adopted against the other and the United Kingdom shall call for the same action by those countries or groups of countries which, at its request, adopted similar measures.

Argentina went on, however, to call for "freedom of movement and equality of access with respect to residence, work and property" as well as "freedom of communication . . . [to] include the maintenance of freedom of transit where the state airline, . . . merchant ships and scientific vessels, . . . communications, Argentine television transmissions and state petroleum (YPF) and gas services shall continue to operate freely." The British saw such expanded access as changing in very short order the operation and character of the Islands.

Interim Administration

Of the proposals and views on interim administration that involved third-party control, oversight or supervision of local government, not all provided for open Argentine access during the period of interim administration. The role of the third party varied greatly. At the beginning of the crisis, interim administration was not envisioned as a diplomatic solution. A diplomatic solution was seen as involving simple Argentine withdrawal or military expulsion of Argentine troops. In either case there was no clear conception of an interim or transition period. In initial discussions with Secretary Haig, two kinds of multinational or international supervision arose: supervision of military withdrawal and supervision of interim or transition arrangements. Britain's thought in interim administration arrangements was to secure freedom for the Falkland Islanders to participate in their own governance through elected representatives and to express their wishes about the Island's future.

In the Argentine discussions with Haig, Argentine views as reflected in their April 19 draft were that interim administration should take the following form:

A Special Interim Authority (SIA) would approve decisions, laws, and regulations of the local administration. To the traditional local administration (the Executive and Legislative Councils) would be added two Argentine representatives on each council appointed by the Argentine government, and one on each council *elected* by resident Argentines with an open-ended formula: "The Argentine population whose residence is equal to that of others who have the right to representation will elect representatives, there being at least one representative in each council." There would also be Argentine representatives in the local police, and the police, while under local administration, would be subject to supervision of the Special Interim Authority. The national flag of each member of the SIA would fly at its headquarters.

Among other freedoms, freedom of movement, property, and employment, as well as cultural links with the countries of origin were to be guaranteed. Freedom of movement, employment, and property were particularly important to Argentina's view of how the interim period should affect events. The period of interim administration in the Argentine April 19 draft would end on December 31,1982, and, starting January 1, 1983, and until full Argentine sovereignty, "The head of government and administration shall be exercised by an official designated by the Argentine government." Thus, interim administration as of

1983 would be entirely Argentine, and the only British role would be as a member of the ongoing sovereignty negotiations. The United States would also still be a member of the Special Interim Authority. Having taken over the roles of Head of Government and administration of the Islands at the beginning of 1983, Argentina would be in a position to pass to the other two members of the SIA only those questions on which there was no disagreement, and would in effect take over the Falkland Islands as of the end of 1982. In this case, the functions of the third party were not so much to assist Argentina and the U.K. in implementation as to simply serve as comfort to the United Kingdom. The Argentine advantages (the time pressure of only eight and a half months before Argentina took over government and administration, and the considerable expansion of the Argentine role in local administration even during the interim period) were not counterbalanced. It is not at all clear from the text that a majority vote within the SIA (for example the United States and the U.K. against Argentina) would be conclusive. In the local government, as Argentine population expanded, that country would eventually obtain the majority on the two councils. Thus, while the April 19 proposals submitted to Secretary Haig before he left Buenos Aires might have been seen as workable bases for more negotiations, they clearly contained elements highly prejudicial to British positions and interests concerning local interim administration.

The U.S. proposal retained the SIA with roughly the same role: the task of verifying the execution of obligations in the agreement became that of verifying compliance. Each party was limited to ten staff members for its SIA contingent. Expansion of Argentine representation on the councils was retained. The minimum of one elected and two appointed Argentines on each council was retained, but the suffrage requirement was made more specific: "Representatives in each Council of the Argentine population whose period of residence on the islands is equal to that required of others entitled to representation, in proportion to their population." Two appointed representatives would serve in the senior Executive Council. The civil service would still be under the direction of the first nonreplaced official below the rank of the Governor. Most significantly, there was no firm end to the interim administration. This arrangement was to stabilize rather than bring to a head or make critical the situation during any interim period.

In the April 29 Argentine response, Costa Mendez said that since provisions in the Haig proposal for "recognition for sovereignty are imprecise, for us it is necessary—if we do not wish to return to the frustrating situation that prevailed before April 2—to establish mechanisms that give us broader powers in administration of the islands." He called for a provisional regime for administration of the Islands which would overcome the "unfavorable changes" made by the United States in the drafting of mid-April. Costa Mendez noted that

The number of Argentine representatives involved in the administration of the islands has been decreased, and the opportunity of expanding my country's control in the event that negotiations on the basic issue go on endlessly without a solution has been barred.

Thus we are faced with the real possibility of establishing a predominantly British administration with no fixed expiration date.

Missing from the U.S. proposals were the Argentine appointment of the Head of Government and administration should the target date of negotiations not be met.

The Peruvian text of May 5 called for a Contact Group of Brazil, Peru, the FRG, and the United States to ensure that the local administration of the Islands took no action contravening the interim agreement. Thus the Contract Group would assume administration of the Falklands in consultation with elected representatives of the Islanders. The Contact Group would assume many key decision-making functions including deciding which would be the applicable law, what the links to Britain would be within government, and the extent of the powers of the governor. The period of interim administration in the Peruvian proposal was defined at least tacitly by the responsibility of the Contact Group for "ensuring that the two Governments reach a definitive agreement prior to April 30, 1983." There was no penalty for not making the deadline and no turnover to Argentine administration once it passed. Following Argentine administration (interim or permanent), Argentina would clearly have to put its faith in the composition of the Contact Group to guarantee its interests during the interim administration period.

The U.N. proposals included transitional arrangements with a different character: They were to meet interim requirements. This implied, even more strongly than previous arrangements or reservations that the period of interim administration was not to change the situation. This prohibition would certainly be consistent with the spirit of Resolution 502. The length of interim administration was implied by a requirement for negotiations to seek a diplomatic solution for their differences by an agreed date.

In the British interim draft agreement of the U.N. process, a United Nations administrator approved by each side would be appointed by the Secretary General and would administer the government of the Falkland Islands. He would do so in consultation with the Island Councils with the addition of an Argentine representative from the preexisting Argentine population. On each of the two Councils, U.N. administration would under the British plan be "in conformity with the laws and practices traditionally obtaining in the Islands." Argentina would be allowed up to three observers in the interim administration period. Interim administration under the British proposal would last until a definitive agreement about the future of the Islands was implemented. Britain put heavy emphasis on the fact that the system of Legislative and Executive Councils had been developed in compliance with Article 73 of the U.N. Charter and thus had a preexisting U.N. legitimacy.

In the Argentine May 19 response, administration of the Islands was to be an exclusive U.N. responsibility with equal numbers of British and Argentine advisors. In the interim period, Argentina was to be free to sponsor immigration of its nationals to the Falkland Islands, and they were to have open access to residence, work, and ownership of property. Of course, none of this was in keeping with the traditions, law, and practices referred to in the British draft. Argentina also rejected the provision of the British draft that interim administration should last until definitive settlement. The two Councils that represented democratic institutions and freedoms to Britain represented the continuance of colonialism to Argentina. Britain saw the allowance for 1 representative from the Argentine population as already a concession and disproportionate to the 30 resident Argentines in a population of 1,800 Britons. The Argentine note to the State Department of May 26 proposed that there be only non-Argentine and non-British officers of the Falklands government in all areas, including executive, legislative, judicial, and security. While local law and legislation would be maintained, U.N. interim administration would use advisors in equal numbers from Britain and Argentina and the two flags would fly during interim administration together with that of the U.N.

The U.K. saw an agreement to U.N. administration as a substantial concession. They viewed the falling back from maintenance of administrative links to Britain to purely local self-rule under U.N. supervision as something Argentina should match with further flexibility. Particular details were left open-ended and subject to joint decision. Argentina, however, rejected even a local role, and required that interim administration should be exclusively in the hands of the United Nations, advised by equal numbers of Argentine and British citizens. In the British view, this would leave the Kelpers with a U.N. administration subject neither to local law and practice nor to local political bodies. Purely U.N. administration of course left no role for the United States as guarantor of either evenhandedness or of British interests. Thus, the parties were no closer at the end of the negotiations on the subject of interim administration than when they had begun.

Sovereignty Negotiations

While each of the peace plans included longer term face-to-face negotiations with the aim of resolving the underlying sovereignty dispute, the approaches to these negotiations were varied. All included a deadline or an ideal "target" date with varying degrees of enforcement or penalty. All included a third-party role, but again it varied greatly.

At the end of January 1982, the Argentine Foreign Ministry *bout de papier* to the British Embassy in Buenos Aires recapitulated the Argentine position on sovereignty and called for *conclusive* negotiations to effect Argentine control of the Falklands. The proposed negotiations were seen by the Argentines as the last negotiations. They were to resolve the sovereignty question in Argentina's favor peacefully, definitively and rapidly. Talks were to go into permanent session as a negotiating commission, meeting in the two capitals alternately. The time frame proposed was one year.

The novel element in the Argentine proposal was that the Commission and its work were to be open to denunciation by either side at any time during the year. The Junta had already decided to reclaim the Falklands one way or the other within the year, and the 27 January proposal "denunciation" element would provide them with the open-ended excuse to denounce and break off the talks, thereby indicating the exhaustion of peaceful means, at any point at which it suited their military convenience. Ironically, they never had to invoke the clause; they used the talks at which their *bout de papier* was discussed and deliberately *not* rejected as a means to break off discussions and proceed to war.

The British reply of February 8 confirmed that negotiations on sovereignty could be discussed in the New York talks. The aim of the talks would be an early and peaceful solution acceptable to both sides and to the Islanders. Britain did not of course accept the time table or the guaranteed result of the sovereignty negotiations called for in the Argentine proposal; it reserved the British position on sovereignty and therefore, in its call for a peaceful solution implied compromise by Argentina.

In the February 26–27 New York talks, the delegation headed by Under Secretary Richard Luce of the British Foreign Office sought to work out a compromise accommodating the Argentine proposal for institutionalized talks without conceding either the deadline or the guaranteed outcome. Across the table, Argentine Under Secretary of the Foreign Affairs Ministry Enrique Ros expected a substantive reaction to the Argentine proposal at the opening of the meeting. Britain, however, was *not* prepared to simply accept or reject the proposal as the Junta had hoped—either (1) setting sovereignty negotiations on track for Argentine title or (2) providing the final diplomatic "straw" to justify military action. Ros could not implement his instructions. The British delegation presented a working paper on how the U.K. would see the Commission functioning: not on greased skids toward full and immediate Argentine sovereignty but as a substantive and standing negotiation of differences on the sovereignty issue. Ros made a fallback proposal to the Argentine opening demand of a make-or-break British reply: a firm reply within a month coupled with a first meeting of the Standing Commission on April 1. Following extended discussions, Ros worked out a compromise: Each side would take an agreed-on version of the Argentine proposal back to their capitals for calm and confidential consideration. The text, an informal working paper on the purposes of the Commission, was in a standard diplomatic practice agreed on preliminarily at the discretion of negotiators, or "initialled" as opposed to signed. Initialled documents are confidential between the parties, and this was explicitly agreed on so as to keep the "political temperature" low.

It would thus appear that Ros was not informed that in the Junta's judgment, the fully viable option of military action was a preferable alternative to an ongoing diplomatic discussion; that the political temperature was not supposed to stay low. The inner circle of Argentine decision-makers wanted a decisive outcome from New York talks as regards sovereignty negotiations, implying a real round of negotiations of differences. That was an unforseen and therefore enraging event to the Junta. The confidentiality of the February 26–27 talks was violated, and the initialled agreement rejected by the Junta even before Ros could return to Buenos Aires.

The Argentine Foreign Ministry made a statement on 1 March belying the word cordial, disclosing the confidential talks and drafts in detail and threatening that were Argentina's vision of sovereignty negotiations not adopted, Argentina would "choose freely the procedure which best accords with her interests."[12]

The British Government nonetheless continued to consider the process begun in New York in March as called for in the negotiations. A draft reply to Argentina was passed to the Falkland Island Councillors. It was positive in tone, with reservations designed to keep it a real negotiation. A public affairs statement was readied about the British reply, explaining the negotiating arrangements following their announcement. Before the message could be cleared with the Islanders, the Argentine scrap-metal on South Georgia party raised the Argentine flag on March 19 and began a different process. The British responded with *Endurance,* which the Argentine Foreign Minister on March 28 called a dispro-portionate, provocative response. The Argentine statement linked South Georgia and the dispatch of *Endurance* to the negotiations discussions then underway. Argentina declined Lord Peter Carrington's proposal that he send a personal emissary, and on April 1 stated that the negotiations and indeed diplomatic channels between the two countries were closed.

Both the United States, in President Reagan's call, and the United Nations, in Resolution 502, urged negotiations on the parties. Resolution 502 called on the parties "to seek a diplomatic solution to their differences."

Britain was initially prepared to enter into negotiations for a long-term settle-ment of the dispute, but only if these were really negotiations. Implied was the idea that Argentina had to be prepared to make concessions as well. At a min-imum, the Islanders had to have a voice in their own government and their future political system.

Argentina in its April 19 draft called for negotiations to achieve a definitive arrangement for Argentine sovereignty. Negotiations would begin within 15 days and end by the New Year. Argentina would take over executive powers as of January 1, 1983, until full Argentine sovereignty were implemented. Negotiations would remove the Falklands from the list of non–self-governing territories and would define their definitive and final status. Both the rights of the inhabitants and territorial integrity were to be considered. The Charter, Resolutions 1514 and 2065, and the GA resolutions on the Falklands were also to be considered. Under the Argentine April 19 document, the United States would "help" in the negotiations.

The United States proposal of April 27 referred only to principles of the Charter and "relevant" UNGA resolutions. Rather than "help," the (tripartite) Authority was to consult with the Executive Council and make specific proposals and recommendations to the two Governments on a broad range of subjects, including the wishes ("based on the results of a sounding") and interests of the Islanders. Wishes and interests were to be a factor only for islands with a settled population, and the sounding was to be agreed on "without prejudice to their respective positions on the legal weight to be accorded such opinion." Were no agreement to be reached by the end of the year, the United States was to make specific proposals for a settlement and conduct direct negotiations. The parties were to respond within one month to formal proposals or recommendations submitted by the United States.

Britain recognized that, as Pym told the Commons on April 21, any satisfactory negotiations had to deal with a framework for negotiations on a long-term solution to the dispute. Britain said it was willing to consider negotiations proposed under the Haig initiative but, in its view, Argentina had rejected them by demanding guaranteed sovereignty or a controlling role in interim governments.

The objective of Decolonization was open-ended as to means, and subject to mutual agreement. In the negotiations, the legal positions of each side were protected by (1) the references to competing principles and (2) the specific reservation that the wishes of the population expressed in a plebiscite or poll would be without prejudice to the respective positions.

The Argentine reply to the Haig proposals (in Costa Mendez's letter to Haig of April 29) said that either the negotiations had to clearly result in Argentine sovereignty being recognized in the end, or Argentina needed a stronger hand in temporary administration so as to guarantee the recognition of sovereignty, which was Argentina's "unrenounceable goal." Costa Mendez recognized that sovereignty negotiations were necessary given the "logical impossibility of formalizing their final fate at this time," but the key word was "formalizing." It was on this point that the Argentine reply really constituted a rejection of the Haig proposal as they regarded sovereignty negotiations. The negotiations were to be, in Costa Mendez's view, about "recognition of sovereignty." He found "provisions relating to the recognition of our sovereignty" imprecise, and therefore proposed the recognition/administration trade-off: "If it were clear that Argentina's sovereignty would be recognized in the end, then we could be more flexible regarding the matter of temporary administration." He stated that the "new element of a virtual referendum to determine the 'wishes' of the inhabitants is in open opposition" to U.N. Resolution 2065 and the Argentine position. Costa Mendez made no comment on the fact that the U.S. proposals applied the question of the wishes of the Islanders only to inhabited islands.

In his statement of April 30, Secretary Haig referred to the call of Resolution 502 for "a diplomatic settlement of the fundamental dispute." He noted that the U.S. proposal included a framework for negotiations on final settlement, which would take into account the interests of both sides and the wishes of the inhabitants. Haig characterized Argentina's position as requiring "assurance now of eventual sovereignty or an immediate de facto role in governing the Islands which would lead to sovereignty," and even in announcing the U.S. decisions in support of Britain, said: "In the end, there will have to be a negotiated outcome acceptable to the interested parties. Otherwise, we will all face unending hostility and insecurity in the South Atlantic."[13]

The Peru-U.S. proposal dated May 5 was open-ended on the structure and conduct of sovereignty negotiations. The negotiations were clearly intended to constitute the status of the Islands. Parties acknowledged differing and conflicting views on this but agreed to acknowledge that the "aspirations and interests" of the Kelpers were to be "included" in an unspecified way in the definitive settlement. The Contact Group was to be responsible for ensuring that a definitive settlement was reached by the end of April 1983. The role of the Contact Group in doing so was unspecified.

The Perez de Cuellar mediation included negotiations by the two sides aimed at a diplomatic solution to the sovereignty question. The Secretary General's aide-mémoire of May 2 called for the negotiations to conclude by an agreed date. Several potential roles for the United Nations in the ongoing sovereignty negotiations were discussed in May 1982. Argentina preferred eventual decision by the U.N. General Assembly; Great Britain and probably the Secretary General and his staff more likely envisioned the Secretary General providing good offices for an ongoing bilateral negotiation between the two parties. During the Secretary General's negotiations, it seemed for a while that the Junta had approved a formula that would not prejudge the outcome of future sovereignty negotiations. Almost immediately, however, contradictory statements were made in Buenos Aires and it became clear that there was no such agreement. The Secretary General was quite clear in his support of the elements of Resolution 502, including settlement by peaceful means.

In the British final offer in the U.N. mediation, the Interim Draft Agreement counteroffer of May 17, the United Kingdom proposed that no provision in the interim agreement, including those on negotiations, should prejudice the rights, claims, or positions of either party. It also made the negotiations on sovereignty definitive by stating that no acts or activities under the interim agreement would constitute a basis for "asserting, supporting or denying a claim to territorial sovereignty . . . or [to] create any rights." The negotiations were to be real negotiations. Under Article 8 of the May 17 proposal, they were to take place under the auspices of Perez de Cuellar, and the parties would aim to complete them by the end of the year. Balancing the previous positions of the two parties, no outcome was excluded and no outcome was predetermined.

In its response of May 9, Argentina agreed that the negotiations concerning the Islands' future should be begun without prejudice to the positions, rights, or previous claims of the parties. Argentina did not accept, however, the concept that the outcome should not be prejudged, nor could Argentina fully accept the provision of the British draft that called for the interim arrangements to last until a definitive settlement could be implemented. Argentina could not accept that the negotiations be open-ended either in outcome or the timing of the end of the talks.

The British White Paper in reply to the Argentine response noted that Great

Britain could not accept *inter alia* the call of the Argentine response for "long term negotiations which led in only one direction." In the White Paper of May 21, the U.K. said that it had no doubts about its claim but had been willing to negotiate sovereignty at some points without prejudice under successive British Governments. It stated that since the Argentine invasion, Britain had again been willing to consider negotiations as long as they were not prejudged in their outcome, and to set a target date of the end of 1982.

In the Argentine diplomatic note of May 26 to the U.S. Department of State, Argentina proposed negotiations without prejudice; recognition of divergent positions (but on all three Island groups); and respect for and safeguarding of the "customs, traditions and way of life of the inhabitants" as well as their "social and cultural links with their countries of origins." Negotiations under the auspices of the U.N. Secretary General were proposed, and the December 31 deadline was kept as a target date. A single option to extend the deadline until June 30, 1983, was added, as was reference to specific U.N. resolutions (in order to comply with the Charter of the United Nations, Resolutions 1514, 2065, and relevant resolutions). The site was specifically given as New York. The Secretary General, in the Argentine May 19 proposal,

may be assisted in the negotiations by a Contact Group composed of representatives of four states members of the United Nations. To that end, each party shall nominate two States and shall have the right to a single veto of one of the States nominated by the other.

If agreement were reached by the end of the first renewal period, the Secretary General was to draw up a report framing the question for a General Assembly decision. Argentina thus rejected the British idea of the interim arrangement staying in place until a definitive solution was reached by negotiation. The Argentine redraft emphasized Decolonization and territorial integrity as the basis for sovereignty negotiations.

Resolution 505 of May 26 called on the Secretary General to renew his talks, which had included eventual sovereignty negotiations. The Security Council also reaffirmed and called for implementation of Resolution 502. The emphasis, however, was now on military cease-fire, not sovereignty negotiations.

The elements which ran through the Falklands negotiating proposals had come full circle. Military matters dominated when the crisis opened, and again loomed large as the crisis moved beyond diplomatic remedy. The other elements seemed vital at stages, but at heart interim administration and the other ingredients of a solution hung on the larger questions of sovereignty and its expression in military force. This review of the flow of the elements through the various mediations tells us that there were moments on each subject when the parties were very close to each other's positions. The challenge remaining unmet is to build on those near-conjunctures and—the critical element—to so array the several elements so that they can be agreed upon at the same time. The pattern in the Spring of 1982 was to narrow differences in one area just as another gap widened.

ENDGAME

Speed, daring (strategic and personal) and flexibility were the most striking elements of the British repossesion of the Falkland Islands in May 1982. The Argentine defense was determined but overly reliant on air forces, static, focused on the capital and not on quick reaction forces deployed to the site of a landing. The major actions of the South Atlantic war have been extensively and thoroughly analyzed for their lessons for Western defense. There were also however, in- structive politico-military points for nations which would protect territory at a distance, and those that would seize it. Those who would mediate territorial disputes would also do well to watch weaknesses in these areas as barometers of crisis in the making, especially since some of the lessons for the West have been taken to heart by the South.

Keeping up the Pace: The Campaign in Brief

Following Argentine recuperation of the Falklands on April 2 and (their first) occupation of South Georgia, Britain launched a Task Force on April 5, which was led by *Hermes, Invincible,* and *Fearless.* A month of diplomatic activity followed, in which the principal politico-military measures were the exclusion zone announced on April 7 and the sailing of the *Canberra* with a large additional increment of troops, indicating a major landing and occupation, on April 9.

Actual hostilities between large units began on April 25 as British forces retook South Georgia from Captain Alfredo Astiz and his Argentine Marines. The Argentine submarine *Sante Fe* was damaged by British helicopters and beached. The first Argentine prisoners were taken.

On April 30, the *day before* the ''impossible'' bombing of the Falklands from Ascension, the United States publicly sided with the United Kingdom. The Vulcan raid as well as attacks by carrier Harriers and naval gunfire opened the naval and air war in the Falklands on May 1. The combination of diplomatic and military ''punch'' jolted the Junta, which had believed against all external advice that neither could come to pass. The following day, the cruiser *Belgrano* was sunk, and on May 4 the first British ship was severely wounded as H.M.S. *Sheffield* was hit by an Exocet (she was afloat for another six days before scuttled); the first Exocet did not explode and the other Exocet launched with it likely dropped into the sea; hardly the ''superweapon'' performance in which much of the arms-buying world believes.

By gaining naval control over Falkland Sound, British forces split the two Argentine garrisons and restricted the supply lines of each one. The destruction of a tanker in the sound on May 10 signalled the end of Argentine supply by sea. The two Argentine garrisons were cut off from each other by sea, but Argentine forces did not read the signal that a back door to amphibious landings had also been opened.

That same day, Argentina declared that all British vessels in the Falklands area would be regarded as hostile. The (rather tardy) declaration of this free-fire zone characterized the measure as necessary in self-defense in the face of British aggression.

In the second week in May, press reports had the United States discussing the loan of KC135 aerial tankers for mid-air refueling, portable long-range radar for use ashore, and other elements of an extended list of materiel. Again, the signal that the U.K. was coming ashore did not seem to register. Key elite units were kept in Argentina.

Little noticed also, but of great significance for the Argentines was the May 15 British special Air Service/Special Boat Service commando raid on Pebble Island which eliminated a tactical airfield and several Pucara aircraft. The war had come ashore in the Falklands. Its first stage was characterized by slow steaming and steady diplomacy, then by persistent hard blows in each field.

On May 21, war came to East Falkland as the British 3 Commando Brigade landed. At San Carlos settlement, the 2 Para and 40 Commando went ashore. Forty-five Commando landed at Ajax Bay and 3 Para and 42 Commando at Port San Carlos. The British had a beachhead.

The Argentine reaction to the landings was neither flexible nor in force. It was fought from static positions set up to defend against a landing such as the Argentines themselves had made at the island's capital. The British force was not interested in political symbolism. While outpost troops and island-based air units responded directly to the English landings, Argentine ground forces did not bring the war to them. Counting on the traditional 3:1 advantage of a dug-in defense against attacking infantry, Argentine Army strategy was to turn to the Air Forces to wear down the British invasion.

The Argentine diplomatic response was equally lacking in subtlety: The power that was *de facto* claiming that possession was nine-tenths of the law now pushed for a U.N. ceasefire. The Junta could no longer discount Haig's warning that the British were coming as biased mediation and dispatched Costa Mendez to New York.

On the first day ashore, the British began consolidation of the beachhead with patrols out onto the Island. The Argentine response was air attacks on the ships, principally in Falkland Sound; between May 21 and May 26, 11 British ships were hit.

The British break-out from the bridgehead began on May 27 as 45 Commando moved toward Douglas via Port San Carlos. Three Para moved out for Teal Inlet and Estancia. In the first telling action of the campaign, 2 Para moved on Darwin and Goose Green via the Camilla Creek House. On May 28 they moved to Camilla Creek House which they reached at dark on the isthmus from Burntside

House. There was intense fighting outside Goose Green in the predawn of May 29. Attempting to personally make the critical breakthrough, the Commander of 2 Para was killed.

By the next day, May 29, over 1,000 Argentine troops and airmen surrendered at Goose Green. A week after the British landing, Argentina lost not only those prisoners and an airfield but the sense of invulnerability that had pervaded their planning.

From May 30 on, the campaign can be considered as a closing noose on a surrounded Argentine garrison centered on Port Stanley. That day, 42 Commando took Mount Kent, and on June 2, 5 Brigade landed at San Carlos. Other British units pressed forward:

—The Ghurka Rifles to the Sussex Mountains;

—2 Scots Guards to the Verde Mountains;

—1 Welsh Guards to Bonner's Bay; and

—2 Para to Fitzroy and Bluff Cove.

By June 3, the units at Bluff Cove included 2 Para and a battery of Royal Artillery, as well as 3 and 4 Troops of B Squadron of the Blues and Royals. Forty-two Commando finished its move to Mount Kent. In the rear, the Ghurka Rifles were taking over Goose Green and the Argentine prisoner detail, freeing 2 Para to move to the front again. (Long the nightmare of Argentine draftees, and the object of much racist propaganda, the Ghurka Rifles had few engagements with Argentine troops, but the myths spread in the Argentine trenches bred more fear than ferocity.) On June 5, 42 Commando reached Mount Challenger, being relieved on Mount Kent the next day by 45 Commando.

On June 8, Argentina made its first major counterattack since Falkland Sound. Again, the task fell to Argentine airmen. The U.K.'s amphibious warfare ships *Sir Galahad* and *Sir Tristam* were caught at anchor at Bluff Cove and gutted by an Argentine air attack. British casualties were 53 dead and 46 injured. The Welsh Guards had just arrived at Port Pleasant on *Sir Galahad*, together with a Rapier battery which was not yet operational.

On June 11 and 12, 3 Commando Brigade, including 2 Para and 1 Welsh Guards, attacked Mount Longdon, Two Sisters, and Mount Harriet along three axes:

—3 Para against Mount Longdon with 2 Para in reserve;

—45 Commando against Two Sisters from Mount Kent; and

—42 Commando against Mount Harriet.

By dawn on June 12, the three positions were taken. The noose was closed, and the Falklands campaign was all but over.

The next critical action was an attack by 2 Scots Guards on Tumbledown, aided by diversionary attacks by the Blues and Royals. The Ghurkas saw action in this June 13–14 campaign, attacking Mount William. (The Argentine defense here was tenacious and broke only on the morning of the 14th.) The Welsh Guards attacked Sapper Hill. Argentine resistance was crumbling in the draftee and nonelite units. White flags began to be seen over Stanley on June 14, and on June 15 a formal surrender was signed covering both East and West Falklands. The same day, 40 Commando moved without resistance to West Falkland to accept the surrender of Argentine units there.

Quality Over Quantity

The British Task Force attempted to have a qualitative as well as quantitative edge on Argentine forces and weaponry in the South Atlantic conflict. Where both were not possible, British doctrine emphasized quality where a trade-off was needed. This seems to pay off far from home where only limited amounts of equipment can be sent. Each side had four submarines in the Falklands battle area, but the Argentine subs were diesel-powered and the British subs were nuclear-propelled. The two British aircraft carriers *Hermes* and *Invincible* were "pocket" carriers with VTOL aircraft but together were more than a match by class for the *25 de Mayo* and the cruiser *General Belgrano,* the capital ships of the Argentine navy. Argentina fielded 3 corvettes as well as 8 destroyers, 2 type–42, 2 Fletcher class, 1 Gearing class, and 3 Summer class. The United Kingdom matched these with 4 type–42 destroyers, 6 type–21 frigates, 2 County class destroyers, and 2 type–12 frigates.

Argentine aircraft by mission pitted 74 Skyhawk and 9 Canberra bombers with 43 Mirage fighters against a total of 32 Sea Harriers and 3 Nimrod AEW aircraft.

The British qualitative/quantitative disadvantage in aircraft was partially made up for by the unique characteristics of the Harrier aircraft, and the *qualitative* superiority of 32 Sea King helicopters (with radar and missilery) over 14 light- and 25 heavy-armed helicopters on the Argentine side.

Furthermore, of course, instead of having an extended coast-line and several major naval bases, 300 to 400 miles away, Britain had to rely on a vulnerable, slow-moving Task Force of Royal Fleet auxiliaries: tankers, fleet replenishment ships, a stores support ship, 5 landing and logistic ships, 2 troop and hospital ships, 2 roll-on/roll-off cargo vessels, and a scattering of smaller utility craft.

In the modern missilry category, Argentina possessed Sea Cat point-defense SAM, Sidewinder or other AAM, Sea Dart SAM, the Gabriel antiship missile and both surface and antiship Exocet, which were all but the last two antiship missiles also in the British inventory. In addition, some British vessels or aircraft had Sea Skua, Sea Wolf and Sea Slug, but in this field where quality is so costly not all British vessels were "state of the art," and the price in ships and lives was heavy.

Combat Effectiveness

Quality of leadership is essential, and one of its leading elements is the willingness to share hardship and risk with the combat soldier. Distasteful as that may be to some civilians, combat deaths are a unifying and inspiring factor in the collective identity and cohesion of military units. Casualties among officers have an even more exemplary value than those from the enlisted ranks. To the extent that the enlisted ranks are drawn from the population at large and the officer corps is also expanded from nonprofessionals in war-time, broader social values than even unit cohesion are appealed to. Thirty-three percent of the German aristocracy was killed in action during World War II.[14] The aristocracy was less than 4 percent of the Officer Corps, yet took 7 percent of the casualties.

The combat readiness and combat efficiency of Argentine forces was clearly not up to that of British forces. Good organization, however, and the time to entrench and prepare active defenses ought to have been able to overcome this problem. This is where leadership both before and during combat made the crucial difference.

The performance of Argentine submarines cost the Argentine cause dearly. The captain of the A.R.A. *Salta* is sure that he fired torpedos at H.M.S. *Hermes* on May 5. Royal Navy experts feel that this may have been a completely aborted firing; that the only sonar "tracks" on May 5 seemed to be the screws of *Broadsword* in her screening role for H.M.S. *Invincible,* the other carrier. Since sonar records are kept and would normally show the propellers of an attacking torpedo, it would appear that *Salta's* torpedos, if launched, never got far from the submarine itself.

The cost to flexibility and operational options of bad intelligence was clear. Brilliant Argentine flying could not compensate for the waste of Argentina expending her penultimate Exocet on the Atlantic conveyor rather than the carrier *Invincible,* which had been her target. It may be that the loss of the Atlantic conveyor was tactically more crucial to the ground forces. For Argentina to then, however, expend her final Exocet on the already crippled merchantman was a lost opportunity of tremendous proportions. It might have been saved for one of the carriers. Good offensive equipment well employed is largely lost unless it is properly directed and coordinated according to a good assessment of targets and priority among them.

Bombing as a tactic had very mixed results in the Falklands War. The Argentine Air Force, unable to maintain altitude in face of the antiaircraft defenses arrayed against them, courageously flew low-level bombing missions with telling effects against the Task Force. This is clearly a capability to be developed by an irredentist nation. (The limitation on the pilots' skill was that their weapons were often not properly armed or fused, and therefore had a lower rate of detonations and kills for the tonnage dropped.) The instructive point for the Navies was clear: Close-in ("point") air defense is just as important as the sophisticated longer-range protection of forces meant to project power by sea.

British bombing of the Argentine forces was less effective. The first bombings by refueled planes from Ascension were telling psychologically on Argentine forces at first, but eventually began to produce the counterproductive results seen in World War II by uniting those bombed in a feeling of camaraderie against an unseen and apparently unfeeling enemy.

Cratering of airfields might have been the most effective use of bombing by the attacking British forces, but the Argentines seemed to be able to both fake and repair damage to the field, which operated right through British recapture of the Islands.

British troops displayed a remarkable combat efficiency, more than countering the fact that they may have numbered half the number of Argentine troops on the Islands. The British Task Force included units counted among the best assault infantry in the world: the second and third battalions of the Parachute Regiment; the Special Air and Special Boat Services; and 40, 42, and 45 Commandos, Royal Marines.

Battle Management—Restraint

Restraint and moderation consist not only in initial strategic decisions such as avoiding main-force combat and attacks on the Argentine mainland, both of which confer tremendous advantages in limiting the conflict, but also in tactical flexibility and good political judgment in handling political affairs in the field.

Accounts of the conduct of the campaign are notable in the regular calls for surrender, pauses for talks under white flags, actions designed to save life rather than taking it with cold efficiency. First-hand accounts and interviews indicate a constant preoccupation with the contradiction that this dangerous, well dug-in defender was often an unwilling draftee and might, on a small unit basis, be talked out of giving up his life for these islands.

If there is a key line in the instrument of surrender signed by Argentine General Mario Menendez and British Major General Jeremy Moore, it is the initialled cross-out in the second line of the document before the word "surrender." It very likely read "unconditionally." The surrender was a full one. The word "unconditionally" would only have served to humble the Argentine Field Commander further. No aspects of a conditional or limited surrender, even the ceremonial provision for officers to retain swords, are contained in the document's stipulations.

From the conception of the campaign through surrender, restraint paid diplomatic as well as military dividends. The longer-run dividend is that there are some 10,000 Argentine veterans who have met the enemy and found him fierce and unforgiving only in combat.

Flexibility

The ability to adjust to changing circumstances is clearly vital. The loss to the U.K. of four Chinook helicopters, six Wessex helicopters, shelter for 4,000 men, and the steel "instant airfield" (aboard the *Atlantic Conveyor* when she was lost) called for a new plan for advancing across the Island. Without the capability of the four Chinooks to carry forward waves of 160 troops in a flight, the whole character of the advance was changed to the "hike" that took place across East Falkland.

A key point in the battle for Goose Green was the ability of the British 2 Para to instantly replace its Commander when he was killed. Colonel Herbert Jones had established a duplicate command unit to remain in the rear until needed. His planning paid off for his unit when he was killed. Any lack of momentum in addition to the pinned-down position before the final ridge (which led Colonel Jones to attempt a push through a vital route through the center) would have made the situation far worse, and might have indeed resulted in a counterattack from the considerable Argentine forces at Goose Green. A rout of the attack on Goose Green could have been critical. Major Chris Keeble was able to immediately move forward, assess the situation, and redirect the attack, setting the stage for the psychologically stunning capture of 1,500 Argentines at Goose Green by a force less than one-third their number.

While the military value of such flexibility is in maintaining offensive momentum, the politico-military value was also considerable. Any halt in a campaign produces the political temptation (at home or among third parties) for ceasefire. This had the potential to leave a negotiation or mediation not only still unresolved, but perhaps even unresolvable between parties with each others' blood now on their hands.

Command and Control

The integrated command of ship and shore units was crucial to the success of the British Task Force and landing operations. Conversely, while Argentina did a credible job militarily in its initial takeover, it was in a situation of unopposed landings. Thus, a power that had little if any capability for amphibious landings beyond its crack marine units could handle a *lightly guarded* disputed territory. The country with what were supposed to be first-rate NATO-level capabilities was forced to improvise: While the British landing counted a lot on the Royal Marines, the British army had not for years conducted amphibious operations. The northern flank reinforcement mission for Great Britain is handled by the Marines. The British Army is stationed well inland along the Rhine, and does not on a regular basis practice coastal invasion with the Royal Navy, making all the more creditable the skill with which staffs were merged, the operation mounted, and a successful landing conducted.

There was little political interference in British operational needs. The risks and decisions made at the principle turning points in the operation were those of the military commanders. Within the broad guidelines of a War Cabinet with a rich personal acquaintance with war, the politicians in London left command to the military. Major policy questions were mainly (and rapidly) decided in favor of the recommendations of the commanders in the field. In sharp contrast to Argentina's conduct of the war, political interference in tactical matters, whether from the government or distant military overlords, was recognized as most likely to produce disaster—diplomatic, military or both. Only the broad rules of engagement up to the decision to go ashore were controlled by the War Cabinet and these were adjusted regularly as the Task Force Commander requested, based on his perceptions of his needs. Overall, British decision making was a decentralized as Argentina's was centralized.

The command and control implications of both joint forces operations and decentralization would thus seem parallel for both the power seeking to retain control of territory and that country seeking to wrest control: beyond the diplomatic stage, in which force is exercised mainly to intimidate or deter, war is too complex and fast-changing to be left to multiple central service commands, or to civilians. Within broad guidelines, the local commander must in the end make the tradeoffs between political restraint and prosecution of a military solution. This is so not only as regards preserving the means to fight if so ordered (force preservation), but because the other side—where they meet—will signal its true intentions on the scene, not at the negotiating table. The reiteration of the will to peaceful settlement can be camouflage or can simply change in the calculus of the parties. That both sides have forces on the scene of a crisis means they may have to use them. In the final analysis, only the commander's judgment can keep those forces disengaged but ready, threatening but not attacking. Only he can determine the actions as opposed to the stated intentions of the opposing side. Thus he must be kept informed of the wide diplomatic and political context, and also given the freedom to defend his force not only from attack but even from being put in *a position of disadvantage in event of hostilities*, which is itself a temptation to the other party to opt for force. Should armed conflict come, by design in opposing capital cities, or by error on the scene of confrontation, his orders must be to secure superiority as fast as possible.

Deterrence

Holders of territory in dispute must clearly retain the means to defend it. Clearly is the key word. Ironically, when Francis Pym was Defense Minister from 1979 to 1982, he had questioned the decision to trade conventional naval units for an augmented seagoing nuclear deterrent. The Argentine perception of diminished British naval and amphibious capabilities was a major factor in the Argentine decision to invade.

A credible level of defensive forces must also be matched by their deployment within striking distance of disputed territory. British decisions to bring *Endurance* home and not to rebuild the Marine barracks at Stanley were "overread" in Buenos Aires. If distances must be great, then the investment must be made in aircraft and holding-time at site to overcome them.

Whether by deployment or by rapid deployability, the overarching consideration for the power of a state seeking to retain control of distant disputed territory is that sufficient resources need to be applicable *within a reasonable time frame* in order to make any political difference.

In the initial stages of a crisis, it would appear that any unit is better than nothing. One of the most flexible and useful units is the nuclear (attack or even cruise or ballistic missile) submarine, whose presence can be announced to (or absence hidden from) the possible opponent as political judgment and the changing situation dictate. The multipurpose patrol craft, especially a hydrofoil, is a good in-place investment. Any platform from a truck to a helicopter makes a good base for smart, modern missilry.

Finally, such a credible deterrent must be *known* to the potential opposition, and should be multifaceted and flexible. Cross-training among services and specialized forces is indicated. One's ability to handle the recherché task or the specialized mission should be advertised, along with general skills and training for difficult jobs. Cold-weather sea and amphibious operations, as well as refueling at sea, were key skills of the Royal Navy and Marines, but Argentine attachés let Argentina forget the analogy of NATO's northern flank to the Falklands.

POLITICAL "LESSONS" LEARNED AND MISLEARNED

Good News/Bad News

Public affairs and press policies for the two sides were markedly different. Argentina gave "good," often misleading, news to buoy morale. Britain delayed news, good or bad, until fully confirmed (and often without effect on ongoing operations). Only under the first approach is truth the first casualty of war. The other casualty is credibility in controlling the interaction of National Honor with negotiations: One might do better to admit losses but translate them into directed anger in the streets and across the negotiating table. As a tool for mass motivation, propaganda is losing its effectiveness except to hearten the uninformed and the uninvolved. Elite opinion has access to international journalism and broadcasting. Creating a split between the two is counterproductive in crisis. Better to say little or nothing and say it late but regularly, and then interpret the event and state or imply effect and action.

Easy In, Easy Out

One disturbing point about modern crises (including that surrounding the Falklands) which is conveyed by high-technology and military operations is that the use of force is now more precise and thus by implication more limited in its locations for retaliation for the reconquest of territory. The illusion is conveyed by the possession of modern equipment that renders armed forces both highly maneuverable and "compact" in terms of effective force and firepower which can be applied by small units. Whether a small invasion fleet of amphibious troops, mobile air cavalry, or paratroopers, the small, highly disciplined force that seizes disputed territory with an overwhelming strength resulting in a low planned level of casualties seems in political decision making to convey the illusion of having used less (or more acceptable) force. The high-tech, high-mobility forces also encourage thinking of the "Plan B" fallback kind: Even if we lose, we can extract our forces and thereby, in some sense, undo the political damage. It is highly likely that the damage to the National Honor of the nation-state will be as great even with such a failed and withdrawn "raid" mentality. Certainly the ability of the offended party to make negotiating concessions is greatly reduced in terms of National Honor.

The "easy in, easy out" approach is the more dangerous in that it lowers the threshhold of resort to force. It encourages total surprise and thus could tend to warp negotiating processes by making negotiations appear a second-best option should they slow, as in the case of the February 1982 New York talks. One party thus goes into the talks with an absolutist approach in which it must win either by negotiation or by force. However, such determination must be in large part veiled and thus loses any negotiating leverage, which it might have given had the massing of forces, mobilization, and more open preparations of con-ventional large-unit conquest been involved.

Superweapons

One non-lesson for the future is that a regional power can take on a more militarily powerful opponent because modern weaponry will, *within its region,* allow military superiority. The air/maritime cruise missile is cited as one of the superweapons that will bring about military equality.

This ignores several factors in military balances other than sheer firepower: depth of commitment, domestic political support, and the industrial depth and flexibility of the opponent.

It also ignores the fact that the world arms bazaar is open to all comers and the opponent is as likely to be able to acquire (if he is not already in possession of) the same or better "superweapon." He may indeed be a manufacturer of it and may have exported a less than first-class "export model." He may also be equipped with or able to obtain very effective specialized countermeasures.

The Near Thing

A non-lesson widely learned from the Falklands crisis was that Argentina came very close to winning. This may be true in several senses: If the priming and arming devices of Argentine bombs had been as sophisticated as her pilots were brave, conventional bombs would have done even more damage than they did to the Royal Navy in the amphibious landing stage in Falklands Sound. If the preparation time had been longer for the Exocet as fitted on the Super

Etendard, the use of these weapons might have been even more efficient. Other major possibilities for a different direction for the military outcome are few in number and begin (with such options as a successful submarine attack on the British carriers or a flexible-response land defense by the Argentine army) to enter the realm of speculation rather than the probability of differing outcome.

The idea that Argentina almost won is true tactically. The question, however, is a strategic one: Would even an initial Argentine repulsion of British forces have settled the military question?

A second-order defense, such as nuclear-submarine blockade of the Islands, would have been politically difficult in that shipping could not for long be torpedoed without changing the world political climate and, in any case, resupply by air was realistic and might have become more possible as Argentine air superiority was fully asserted and a forward capability moved to the Islands.

Britain would have had to reattack. Assuming the loss of one carrier and up to half her surface ships, could she have done so? The answer is probably yes: The new carrier *Illustrious* was being rapidly readied for sea and indeed was commissioned in June. Her sea trials and fitting-out would have had to be done enroute to the Falklands, but she could have been brought to bear in time to protect the troop ships in a delayed landing from South Georgia.

All military actions, especially expeditionary operations at great distance, are "near things." The Falklands, however, could have been handled in a second round by the United Kingdom, and the Falklands was a special case in another sense: Neither offensive air power nor the ability to land troops by air (rapid deployment) were available to Britain in this case. "Nearby" facilities were not available either. There are few other places on the globe where both conditions apply so thoroughly because of politics and geography.

NATO: The Out-of-Area World

The Falklands crisis had some interesting consequences and implications for the North Atlantic Treaty Organization. While the crisis was entirely beyond the treaty area and there was no attempt to invoke the Alliance, Britain did have to go through NATO procedures to withdraw forces and earmarked units from the area and thus from NATO's common shield. The principle effect was on the Northern Flank where there was a short-run loss, and, perhaps, a long-run gain. There were certainly precedents for national withdrawal in national emergency, including withdrawals of U.S. forces. While the Northern Flank lost some contingency protection, it gained very real experience by British combined-forces operations in an environment that was the mirror image of the Norwegian coast. Winter operations in bad weather, under very difficult supply conditions, were more than well "simulated" by the Falklands operations.

There was also a significant benefit in long-run terms for NATO's Northern Flank Mission in that the British units, which would support Norway in crisis, bringing with them the Royal Dutch Marines, gained not only competence but also confidence in this deployment. Making the Northern Flank a very costly penetration for the Red Army would require precisely the imagination and initiative that characterized U.K. military actions in the Falklands campaign. There may also be significant long-run benefits in slowing the trend toward scrapping and reducing the Royal Navy's complement of amphibious-landing ships.

British Minister of Defense David Hazeltine has pointed out several ongoing realities for the U.K. of the Falklands:

—Britain, as the third naval power in the world, is changing its emphasis in naval affairs from surface to submarine vessels and from a concentration on platforms to weapons systems;

—NATO's Northern Flank strategy is dependent upon the U.K.-Netherlands amphibious force, supported by U.S. and Canadian Marines;

—The Falklands experience has led to further measures to increase the United Kingdom's "out of area" capabilities; and

—Men proved to be far more important than machines.[15]

NATO and the EEC

The crisis saw the EEC's global role in political matters overshadow NATO's limited scope. While NATO as an alliance took no formal action against Argentina or even in military support of Britain, one should note that the economic sanctions imposed by the Common Market were also joined in by Norway. In terms of their 1982 memberships, such a self-definition by the EEC "Ten" began to look more like the (then) NATO "Fifteen."

The Common Market as a forum neatly excluded the New World allies: the United States and Canada. Ireland was the first EEC country to balk on sanctions.

Spain was not a member of NATO or the Common Market. The accession of Spain to the North Atlantic Treaty on May 30, 1982, however, aptly encapsulates the problem of out-of-area activities for NATO: Internal to the alliance there is, of course, a specific restriction on NATO activities south of the Tropic of Cancer. Non-European territories of member states are excluded from the general call to consult when any member is threatened and to consider an armed attack on one as an attack on all. NATO protects the North Atlantic area. The Out of Area restriction foresaw quite realistically the problems with colonies. Mother country of Latin civilizations, Spain was vocally pro-Argentine in the South Atlantic crisis, and any attempt to use NATO in support of the United Kingdom might well have peeled her off from her new political association. If not, it would certainly have reinforced any tendency for the new socialist government to immediately cancel membership.

The sanctions against Argentina were at heart political. They preceded and lasted until after the armed conflict. The EEC was the chosen organ of European political consultation and cooperation, and was deemed a more appropriate in-

Table 7.1

NATO Members	Common Market Members (1982)	European Free Trade Association
		Austria
Belgium	Belgium	
Britain	Britain	
Canada		
Denmark	Denmark	
		Finland
France	France	
Greece	Greece	
Iceland		Iceland
	Ireland	
Italy	Italy	
Luxembourg	Luxembourg	
Netherlands	Netherlands	
Norway		Norway
Portugal		Portugal
		Spain
		Sweden
		Switzerland
United States		
Turkey		
West Germany	West Germany	

strument than NATO for this "out of area" activity. It will not be lost on the South that this body which chose to speak for the West has since grown to near co-identity with NATO's membership and to an even more powerful economic bloc.

"They Write the Rules"

One of the saddest lessons "learned" by the Third World was that Western powers emphasize law and precedure to their own advantage: "They write the rules." The West drafted the rules in the nineteenth century. They are then felt to hold all the legal cards, making force not only necessary but even legitimate. Just territorial demands unmet by negotiation must be sought through arms.

The international law of territory, sovereignty, and conquest has evolved in the twentieth century into a set of international norms that constitute the only real protection against force that most nation-states enjoy. Neither their own military nor the self-interest of their allies can provide national security. Their security and hence their very sovereignty lies in large measure in an international politico-legal system that makes change of sovereignty difficult. The smaller the state, the more its existence is inextricably bound up in the West's definition of the rules.

Restraint Unrewarded

Too much of the world read British actions over the years in the Falklands were disputed as weakness—either military weakness stemming from distance and reduction of forces, or political weakness: paralysis and decline brought on by the "colonial" (and therefore to their mind illegitimate) nature of Kelper society and Falklands sovereignty.

This is part of a wider syndrome of Western restraint in the use of force which is perceived in the more ideological quarters of the Third World states as a relative weakening of world-class military powers. In parallel, the reach of the mainstream politico-legal culture is felt to be shortening with a decline in will or assertiveness. As the assertiveness of the radical political culture has risen, restraint has been misinterpreted.

Channels

The first political action of the Falklands crisis was a break in diplomatic relations, with Argentina telling the British that the diplomatic channel was closed on the subject at hand, and Britain recalling its ambassador. The nation-state needs to rethink the idea of recalling diplomatic representation in crisis. It should search, perhaps, for an institution of functional internment in which diplomats would be protected and supervised but left in place to maintain the channels of communication that become all the more valuable when two nation-states are at risk of going to war. The response of the British Government of Lord North (Prime Minister from 1770 to 1781) to the Falklands crisis of 1770 is instructive. In June of 1770, the Governor of Buenos Aires confronted the British garrison in the Falklands with an overwhelmingly large task force, parallel in its dispro-portion to the Argentine invasion fleet facing 27 Royal Marines in 1983, and successfully asserted control over the Islands. In both eras Britain had extended comittments elsewhere, and certainly had higher priorities elsewhere.

The need to demonstrate that force could not legitimate the transfer of territory was strongly felt in England, and Britain had its settlement established in 1763 at considerable risk. The British Government sought to contain the crisis. While preparing to make its power applicable through a major fleet, it left diplomatic relations open with Spain and offered the Spanish Government a way out:[16] the

Spanish Government was given a chance to disavow the act of its Governor in Buenos Aires through long negotiations and secret agreements. Even with France eagerly standing at Spain's side, Lord North's government managed to quell the internal pressure for war, though he could not save his Foreign Secretary, who was branded an appeaser. The situation evolved. France lost its heart for war. Britain was allowed to reestablish its settlement and in all probability had made a secret agreement to abandon it after a decent interval. In any event, the British settlement was abandoned 2 years later and, for 50 years, Spain and its successor, Argentina, used the Islands (mainly as a penal colony) with no challenge from Britain. We should in no way view the 1770s as simpler times with different rules. Diplomatic similarities are quite valid across that time gap. In the 1770 crisis, the Islands were not fought over because they were not valuable. In the ensuing half-century, they were not seen as valuable because they had not been fought over.

THE SUEZ SYNDROME

One of the lessons the Third World should *not* learn from the Falklands crisis of spring 1982 is that Great Britain had to go it alone. First, the support from its allies, friends, and Commonwealth partners was immediate. The scale and deviation were considerable, both logistically from the United States and economically from the European Community. There were hesitations and slippages of timing, and there were questions of means rather than of ends. The larger coordination of the West, in political terms, is all the more impressive in that this was not a NATO Alliance question; indeed, it was the type of situation specifically excluded in the negotiating history of the Western alliance and geographically quite deliberately delimited by drawing the Alliance's southern area of concern at the Tropic of Cancer and excluding New and Old World possessions of Alliance members as a subject of common concern or the object of mutual defense commitments.

No analogies to Suez 1957—major splits in the ability or willingness of the First World to defend the major interests of its members—should be drawn. The situation is quite the opposite: The invasion by Argentina united the West in a way that the territorial question had always divided it. The United States, Canada, and Common Market members always held differing views from that of the U.K. on the question of sovereignty of the Falkland Islands. The United States, for example, is traditionally neutral on the territorial question as it is on all New World territorial disputes.

The way in which Argentina chose to assert its claim determined where the West came down on the until then somewhat marginal question of the Falklands: The question became the principle of the rule of law. While they differed greatly about the territorial merits of the sovereignty dispute, there was little or no difference about the proper response to the settlement of territorial dispute by force. In tandem with the fate of the Kelpers and the question of self-determination, peaceful settlement of disputes and non–resort to force would seem to be the "bottom line" for the West and the North. It is on these questions that the dialogue with the South needs to be developed as regards territory.

A REDEFINITION OF THE VALUE OF TERRITORY

Such a dialogue might begin with a redefinition of the worth of territory in the last quarter of the twentieth century. In an increasingly postindustrial era, the North and the South should reconsider whether conquest conveys resources and other goods that traditionally went with territory. There is a good case to be made that in highly interdependent, complex, skill-oriented, manufacturing and electronics industries it is impossible to make conquered people work. While extraction of basic raw materials might be possible under forced-labor conditions, the potential for sabotage and inefficiency ("passive resistance") as well as for urban terrorism should make any country considering the subjugation of a population think twice.

Even raw materials extracted from conquered territory require transport over long distances, and are again very vulnerable to passive and active resistance.

In the agricultural two-thirds of the world, efficiencies are so low that it is literally only the land one would be capturing, and there are few breadbaskets in the Third World. Thus, conquest would imply working the land oneself, but modern agriculture is so dependent on a complex interaction of factors such as seed type, rainfall, timing of moisture, and the complexities of soil chemistry that it would be a good deal of time indeed before an agressor would be able to arrive at the correct factor mix to make agriculture pay.

If not for economic reasons, why invade? In military terms, a specific piece of soil also has less value per se in the last quarter of the twentieth century. Strategic islands and peninsulas, for example (once the jumping off point for the projection of naval power) are less and less relevant as nuclear submarines and surface units are able to go months and years without bunkering, to distill their own fresh water, and to be serviced for supplies, munitions, oil, and lubricants by seagoing tenders. Large carriers to some extent replace airfields. The cruise missile makes any and every piece of rock or coastline a potential base, with a portable or "turn-key" technology that can project power ground-to-sea and ground-to-air. A specific or key place is less vital. Many can be replaced as a "fire platform" by ships. All of this is not to say that forward bases and especially airfields and deep-water, protected anchorages are not valuable, only that they are less frequently the only ways to accomplish a given mission. The accuracy of nuclear and conventional smart munitions now argues against fixed facilities. There are also increasing costs to fixed bases as both political sensitiveness and local resistance might make their high technologies vulnerable. The nation-state might want to consider keeping more of its resources safely in its heartland. It could also be that the speed of modern war, even land war, would dictate something other than a forward defense in contested territory.

THE RULES: POWER AND LAW

Power in the modern world is diffuse. It is spread among and between all kinds of political systems in differing ways. It has many forms, and they rise and decline in relative importance. Economic wealth may not be combined with political stability; gifts for organization may be unevenly distributed with military power; all the various attributes of national strength can even be present but be badly combined or organized, resulting in a state with less ability than one might have estimated to effect its will. The basic politico-legal rules of the nation-state game are still defined by codified and customary (Western) international law, and are seen as embodied in the Charter of the United Nations. Normative international law suffers from political inhibitions to sanctions or even censure. In the name of sovereignty, even key, reasonably "powerful" Third World countries will not, for example, condemn the action of a progressive superpower such as downing a civilian airliner.

There seems to be less inhibition in condemning the behavior of states not deemed "progressive." The general Third World approach is to condemn Western and Northern Hemisphere power and action, to profess awe and distaste in the face of it, and yet in the end game to feel, given post-war Western behavior, that that power will not be applied, much less applied ruthlessly.

Powerful states have less difficulty in working within international law to enforce their interests, since the basic rules of the game favor the established nation-state and particularly those large nation-states that have codified, accretive international law. This is the cumulative effect of centuries of working out the inconsistencies between the norms and the nation-states' longer-run basic interests. In this sense, the more powerful players in the game have less problem working out geopolitics and international law.

If the international politico-legal "rules" have no international army backing them up (no enforcement), it is still nation-states and collections of nation-states that enforce the widely if not universally agreed-on rules in self-defense or even preemptive attack. Whether acting politically or militarily through the United Nations and regional organizations, or acting individually, nation-states are still the basis of the system.

As a nation-state it could be said that Argentina was the focus of no political or military sanctions following its actions in the South Atlantic in the spring of 1982; that there are no penalties in the modern world for solving problems by force. This is true in a technical sense only.

The heaviest price Argentina paid was in political support for its claim to sovereignty. During the crisis in which it tried to firm up that claim, it lost a good deal of support because of the way in which it had chosen to enforce it. While this is less true since the Falklands crisis, there is no doubt that strength of support for the case, if not the Argentine case itself, was gravely wounded by Argentine military action on April 2, 1982.

Economic sanctions imposed from abroad by other governments were a clear cost during the crisis. Harder to measure but possibly greater in their effect on a nation opting for force would be any lingering doubts in the world trading community in years to come. The use of force still conveys not moral but economic judgments about security for capital and even for engaging and becoming dependent on major trade flows.

Argentina has, despite its military surrender (which was characterized as a cease-fire), maintained a state of belligerence with the U.K., increasing de facto leverage without de jure penalty. The lesson that it was able to do so was lost on few. Argentina lost, it lost overwhelmingly. Nonetheless, it was able to salvage some of the domestic component of National Honor. It was also able to use the state of belligerence to maintain normative pressure on its neighbors to isolate the Islands.

By that isolation, Argentina was able to impose a blockade as regards South America, which it could never have obtained before its military breach of the peace. This further helped the Argentine cause diplomatically as it forced up British costs and prevented resumption of trade and other British and Kelper links with South America. Perversely, in the future that state of isolation may freeze a situation in which time is not on Argentina's side. The "penalty" should this prove to be the case will be real rather than normative.

TIMING AND NATIONAL HONOR

Whether and how firmly to fight over territory is a calculus that can change rapidly and will vary with differing perceptions. A matrix of *relative* interests in a mutually beneficial solution as opposed to a zero-sum outcome can be laid out in rough form for the Falklands crisis as follows.

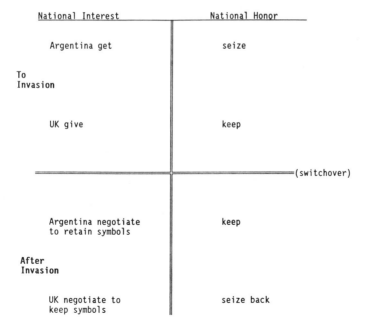

National Interest and National Honor are separated here into their most
extreme (nearly artificial) forms for emphasis. Before the switch-over point
on April 2, the National Interests of the two sides were in congruence in the
sense that the U.K. had several significant and outstanding reasons to make
concessions, and Argentina felt itself under heavy pressure to continue to
push for concessions. This implied further, if increasingly nasty, negotiations
and public exchanges. Allowing for the sway of the components of National
Honor, however, the most extreme formulations of national positions were
that Argentina should grab and the U.K. should hold at extreme cost. In
these formulations, the distance between the two sides grows as the components of National Honor are folded in.

After the switch-over point, each side, again on the grounds of National
Interest, had significant reasons to make concessions provided (some) of its vital
interests were met. Each had reasons to trade, and a solution again became highly
plausible. Folding in the components of National Honor, however, it became
"vital" that Argentina, now in possession of what it views as its territory, hold
it at very high cost and ironically, it became all but inevitable that Great Britain
should take the Islands back with loss of life on both sides.

How could a negotiator keep the crisis confined to such quadrants as to have
recurring chances at a likely congruence of willingness to negotiate in earnest?
The search moves like a "Z" through this pattern. How can you keep things
principally on the left-hand side of the graph so that before a "switch-over"
point to mutual "desire" for conflict, one side has significant reasons to make
concessions in a match, as it were, with the other side's desires to gain concessions, or at least to keep both parties in a trade mode where they may find a
mutually agreeable middle solution via mutual concessions and mutual gains?

The idea of mediation may at certain stages be politically undigestible. It is
probable that when a crisis is too new or when the sanctions for failure to agree,
such as war, are too distant or not credible enough, no mediation can evoke
compromise and produce a solution. It requires not only a threat hanging over
the mediation but a stalemate or deadlock that is painful for both parties.[17]

It is vital in this case to view each party's version, tacit and explicit, of when
the switch-over occurs. The British formal position was that this important
juncture came with the Argentine invasion. This position implies that Britain
could concede less easily once the act of forcible invasion had taken place when,
in fact, a cold assessment of its National Interest would be that the stakes (cost
of action) had increased without any corresponding increase in possible benefit
for British National Interests.[18]

Here the real meaning of National Honor becomes important: several basic
principles important to a middle power of world reach were violated: peaceful
settlement, non–resort to force, inviolability of frontiers, and the self-determination of peoples.[19]

Thus, the two dynamics were very different in national terms. In the Argentine
view, principle required the use of force. In the British view (of the world system

and stability), the use of force led to an important question of principle and thus to counterforce. Argentina's (and Britain's) increasing commitment led to loss of life. Loss of life led to an increased British commitment, in defense less of National Interests than National Honor. Here the scaled distinction between a middle power of global reach and a major regional power becomes vital. Here one sees, in operational terms, the importance of the insularity of Argentine politics and the regional, southern-hemispheric nature of its geopolitical outlook.

"NONE FOR FIVE": "PLAN B"

The combination of the two internally consistent, internally rational calculuses that led the Argentine military to attempt the recuperation of the Falkland Islands does not bode well for world peace. The temptation of the superweapon and the pattern of defense drawdown and the slighting of conventional forces (especially irregular warfare, mountain and arctic warfare, and other troops trained for special environments), add external impetus to the internal logic. The necessity of planning in a vacuum in order to preserve operational security, as well as the operational difficulties of cancelling or amending planned actions, further reinforce these tendencies. The closed loop of radical nonaligned political thought on Decolonization, the radicalization of U.N. activity and resolutions, and the increasing ineffectiveness of the U.N. Security Council in avoiding or applying sanctions to breaches of the peace further exacerbate the trend. A major contributing factor is the general relegitimization of resort to force by the nation-state or by a people, as self-defined. The festering of a sense of grievance in territorial questions not only is an increasingly frequent cause of or pretext for war, but a factor that makes preventive, mediatory, or even post-dispute resolution of differences between nation-states measurably more difficult. For all these reasons, we can unfortunately expect "more and better" territorial brushfire war for at least the remainder of the twentieth century. Not only are the Falklands crisis and possibly conflict not at an end—they may indeed be a prototype of Third World decision making about territorial causes.

VIII

THE ROAD TO THE FUTURE

In War: Resolution.
In Victory: Magnanimity.
In Peace: Good Will.

—Winston Churchill

Without power of administration, sovereignty will come to nothing.
—Chinese academician rejecting a transitional role
for Britain in Hong Kong

There is no durable treaty which is not founded on reciprocal advantage, and indeed a treaty which does not satisfy this condition is no treaty at all, and is apt to contain the seeds of its own dissolution. Thus the great secret of negotiation is to bring out prominently the common advantage to both parties of any proposal, and so to link these advantages that they may appear equally balanced to both parties. For this purpose when negotiations are on foot between two sovereigns, one the greater and the other the less, the more powerful of these two should make the first advance.
—de Callières, *On the Manner of Negotiating with Princes*

Developments since the Falklands War of spring 1982 have not been promising. That war did not solve the dispute. It may not even remain quiescent—there is no peace treaty. Argentines are undiminished in their claim to sovereignty—all parties and several democratic governments insist on this tenet of their foreign policy. Indeed, at times the Falklands seem to constitute Argentine foreign policy.

Rearmed and moving year by year away from the memory of defeat, Argentina under a future government will reconsider at some point the military option. The declared resource zones of the Islands and of Argentina overlap at one point and are patrolled. The potential for armed confrontation is maintained by each side. The future promises further Nonaligned rhetoric and confrontational use of the United Nations, if not indeed a return to hostilities, whether accidental or planned.

There are alternatives. The same menu of theoretical politico-legal status options remains, but the best way to reach one of them may now be to set the whole question aside in favor of a focus on real politics and governance. It may be that the limits on third-party mediation, and indeed on bilateral formal negotiation have already been reached in the Falklands dispute and it is time to return to the preferred operating mode of the nation state: unilateral action in its own interest.

The clear and overriding first interest of each party is normalization of not just bilateral relations but the situation in the South Atlantic, that is, agreement to disagree politically on the politico-legal question of sovereignty. This would leave Argentina free to continue what it has always done in politico-legal terms— legislate for its 23d province. It could construct a regime binding and well enough resourced to appeal to the Kelpers, and obviate the political perceptions on their part that are the less-appreciated heart of the Falklands question. The second part of the accord (tacit for now, explicit later) would be agreement for Argentina and England to jointly preserve, develop, and exploit the living and mineral resources of the South Atlantic world. With perpetual resource sharing as one way to defuse questions of economic interest and indeed create an expanding "pie" to be divided, this might open the way to creative diplomacy on territory and a modern redefinition of sovereignty.

ARGENTINA CREATES AND REACTS TO "FORTRESS FALKLANDS"

In the years following the Falklands crisis, Argentines developed a new rationale for change in the Falklands: The presence of British military forces, it is now argued, made this a security problem. It is specifically an Argentine security problem, and in those terms is deemed unacceptable. The world, and especially the United States, is asked to recognize the British garrison as a new and dangerous fact in South Atlantic security affairs, a political-military problem without regard to the events of 1982. Its context should include Brazilian-U.S. cooperation on ship building and Chilean-U.S. amphibious maneuvers. The Falklands is, in a word, no longer simply a case of colonialism but now an example of imperialism.

The Falklands garrison argumentation was placed at the end of a long list of problems foreshadowing doom for Argentina. Violations of human rights, terrorism, narcotics, and unemployment already weighed down the republic, but were widely admitted to be internal matters. "Fortress Falklands" was added to the list of externally caused problems, along with debt and denial of nuclear technology. Oblivious to suggestions that framing the Falklands as a frontier problem rather than a colonial problem might set a better framework for negotiations, Argentines tried to transmogrify the results of the invasion into another justification of the invasion.

FALKLANDS DIPLOMACY BECOMES FALKLANDS FOREIGN POLICY

By the first anniversary of the April invasion, recovery of the Falkland Islands had become the predominant concern of Argentine foreign policy at the expense of its traditional neutrality, export promotion, and arms-length dealings with other nation-states. The Government's attitude was expressed by its declaring April 2 an annual national holiday of celebration and reaffirmation of Argentina's military bid for sovereignty. A foreign policy notably centered on National Interest had shifted heavily to one focused on a single issue and based principally in National Honor, and promises to become more so over time.

Only domestic politics proved consistent: Everyone was using the war of one year before to support and defend his domestic political views. Those who did not support the military argued that the Falklands campaign had proved it bankrupt as a governing institution. Those who supported the military argued that it had made the only significant effort to assert Argentina's legitimate demands and indeed that such an effort would have to be tried again, and that the military therefore needed resources and power if not the actual reins of government.

In foreign policy, the defeat was blamed on the United States. The conclusion flowing from that logic was that Argentina must side with antiimperialist powers or that Argentina must make itself a significant part of the nonaligned movement.

Argentine twentieth-century neutralism was nothing like nonalignment in the 1980s, but now Argentina had an entirely different sense of priorities—in many ways opposite to the maximization of National Interests. National Honor would now become the driving force. Argentine foreign policy was directed almost entirely to recovering the Malvinas.

There was nothing direct about the attempt, however. Just as the Decolonization mythology lay in part at the root of the military attempt to recover the Islands, so the effort to regain them was centered on the nonaligned movement and particularly on the hard core of radical nonaligned states. The special relationship with Cuba, developed during the war, blossomed in the following year. Cuba used its full authority as the informal whip of the nonaligned movement to rally the NAM behind the Argentine cause.

As one diplomat observed, however, Argentina is not going to recover the Falkland Islands by negotiating with Mozambique. In the group repetition of radical shibboleths lies the kind of diplomatic sterility and destabilization that characterized Guatemala's claim to Belize, Venezuela's claim to the Essequibo, Ecuador's campaign for a connection to the Amazon, and Bolivia's struggle for a sovereign outlet to the sea. Valid or not, territorial claims are not implemented by nonaligned communiqueés.

ARGENTINA REARMS

One year after the Argentine surrender, Argentina was well enough rearmed to make another military attempt to recover the Falkland Islands. On March 28,1983, she had taken delivery at Bahia Blanca of the destroyer *Brown* which, symbolically, carried eight Exocet sea-to-sea missiles loaded at Brest on its way from West Germany where it was built.

Arms purchases of this quality and scale did not come easily to a blighted economy. Argentina was already suffering serious budget imbalances and a staggering foreign debt whose interest payments alone would swamp most nations' GNPs. Sanctions had cost Argentina $40 million in European trade each week and the damage was long-lasting. In the year following the Falklands War, the gross national product of Argentina dropped 5.7 percent, yet military spending was projected for the year 1983–84 at 16.5 percent of the national budget, compared with 9.5 percent for 1982–83. Unemployment climbed from 1.4 to 2 million persons, and the closed factories and general decline had reached such a stage that on the day the *Brown* entered port, more than 90 percent of Argentina's 12 million workers went out in a general strike.

West Germany, France, Israel, and Brazil were the principal arms suppliers of Argentina following the Falklands crisis. Argentina's orders were significant. The shopping list began with 16 more Super-Etendard fighter bombers and 25 Exocet missiles. While many items were shipments that had been interrupted by hostilities and equipment embargoed during the Common Market boycott, the orders began to take on the dimension of an arms upgrade and buildup. This had definite implications for Argentina's social programs in that the projected budget put military spending at twice the levels spent on education and almost ten times what was spent by the state on health care. An Argentine Central Bank estimate put military spending at more than $2.5 billion U.S. for 1983.

The spending extended even to using the surplus from wheat sales to the Soviet Union to purchase SAM–7 Soviet shoulder-held missiles via Bulgaria. Overcoming another traditional wariness, Argentina also turned to Brazil, which had answered its wartime needs by decommissioning and leasing two EMB–111 Bandereirante naval patrol turbo-props. That small but helpful gesture netted Brazil a $25-million dollar contract for arms for Argentina in the post-Falklands period.

Argentina has also ordered up to six conventionally powered but first-rate attack submarines, four built in Argentina, and two in the FRG. Whatever number are actually completed, the TR1700 models are reported to be capable of 70 days submersion, with high attack speeds and a low sonar profile; in a word, a submariner's dream. The six submarines are part of a wider Argentine effort to reduce its naval exposure, relying less heavily on major surface units and more on submarines in combination with marine infantry and land based naval aviation. Argentina's air inventory grows more and more impressive. This triad gives Argentina the ability it lacked in 1982 to take real advantage of its proximity to the Falklands and harness military technology in an augmented potential to defeat both British forces in and around the Falklands and any reinforcements that might be sent in response to a future attempt at recuperation of the Islands. Press reports regularly raise the medium term possibilities of nuclear weapons and the ballistic missilry to deliver them.

Such military planning, even if longer-range, highlights the technological and military resources at the command of the Argentine Republic. They are no doubt useful in support of either Argentine diplomacy; however, such instruments can, with the frustration of diplomacy, become means in and of themselves. They demonstrate that even without scenarios such as the development of nuclear weapons, it is more than likely that Argentina could in a medium-term future deploy sufficient military force to engage in a second Falklands War. The options available include submarine, air, and unconventional warfare scenarios, the most likely of which is a high-technology, missile-oriented, reduced British garrison overwhelmed by small numbers of Argentine beach-landing teams and hilo (high altitude/low opening) parachutists who crater the extended runway before British reserves can be flown in. In such a scenario, first-rate Argentine submarines would make a considerable difference in that the repetition of the British amphibious task force operation would be precluded after air reinforcement were denied. Unable to join the land battle either by air or sea, Britain might be reduced to Argentina's present position of only retaliatory or diplomatic options; an inability to effectively, efficiently, or humanely project force and turn it to effective control and exclusive use of territory. No matter what the technical or legal assumptions, or indeed who one assumes might win in such a scenario, the scenario itself is a nightmare for each party. Overall, the best traditions of the worldwide arms bazaar prevail, and Argentina has more than rearmed following her war—she has built hardware if not force levels to all-time highs.

PLAN B DISSOLVES

The Argentine decision to turn power back over to the civilians was in large part due to an implosion in the Army's political will as an institution. Defeat in the Falklands was the most proximate but not the only cause of that implosion. Indeed, it was not so much the military defeat as the contrast of that defeat with the image purveyed by the military's monopolistic information program that led to a sense of crisis.

There was no popular revolt in Argentina against the military because of the defeat. There was, however, deep and instantaneous division within the military itself. As officer turned against officer in the wake of defeat, the political divisions and the lack of self-esteem led to a failure of confidence or institutional will in the face of the need to form a new viable government following the departure of the Galtieri Junta.[1]

While the U.S. press may have seen demonstrations against the loss in the Falklands as revolts, this was principally a failure to understand that working-class demonstrations in Argentina have never forced anyone out of office. Demonstrations in Argentina are just that. As public opinion had not determined the invasion, it would not decide its political aftermath. The rallying around the Malvinas as a national cause, in fact, had gone much better than Galtieri could have predicted. The size and ferocity of the public reaction immediately following the crisis was beyond both his expectations and his control. They did not yet have the "rally-making" machinery in place for the crowds of the 2nd of April. That was a natural *porteño* (a porteno is a resident of Buenos Aires, where most Argentines live) response to something that had always been a national cause. The spontaneous reaction to victory, however, failed to gain the momentum needed for the impossible political task the Junta had taken on. If they aimed at a new Argentina with a restored sense of order and purpose, the enthusiasm of the 2nd of April could not effect such a deep transformation. Citizens did not retake the Islands or feel their loss deeply enough to risk life or career. The military was discredited before the war in most fields of public life, and the war simply added military failure to other mismanagement. Already on the way out in the medium term, the Argentine military moved its own orderly departure up to the near term.

Following the defeat in the Falklands, military morale was low. Reports were being leaked. Officers were criticized and even tried for their conduct. There was no military unity on which to plan, much less stage, a political comeback.

Civilian revulsion at the military had already been high, and was increased when the one thing that was acknowledged to be their exclusive field and an area of competence was instead shown to be another field of failure.

The military's only hesitation about leaving office was on accountability for their stewardship. Certainly the principal institutional problem facing the military as it considered return to civilian constitutional rule was the problem of missing persons from the antiterrorism campaign begun under a civilian government. The campaign is estimated to have cost the lives or liberty of between 5,000 and 30,000 Argentine citizens since 1976, with a range of 8,000 to 9,000 probable "disappearances." There were estimates that even toward the end of the Military Government, hundreds of persons remained imprisoned without charges, of whom many could have been in jail as long as eight years. Bodies were discovered in more than a dozen clandestine cemeteries. The governments of Britain, France, West Germany, Italy, Spain, and Sweden have officially requested information on their own citizens said to have disappeared in Argentina. Thus, the foremost of the military's conditions for elections was a moratorium on investigations into the disappearance of civilians. A moratorium on investigating the Malvinas campaign seemed secondary.

At the end of 1982, 100,000 people demonstrated in favor of an immediate return to democracy in the midst of a general strike. The military had less to bargain with each month. The Junta declared elections. It had to declare its own amnesty.

POLITICS RESUMED: THE MALVINAS LEITMOTIF

Argentina's solidified democracy will not meet one British expectation which has been widely shared in the world: There is no correllation between a democratic form of government and moderation on territorial issues. No one should confuse the Malvinas issue in Argentine politics with the military government. That government may have used force on a large scale, but force has been used by all manner of Argentine governments over the Republic's history when it comes to the number-one nationalist territorial issue.

Similarly, changes in governments between Radicals and *Justicialistas* will have little effect on irredentist policy toward the Falklands, unless it is to strengthen such policy. While the Radical party government has been moderate in its language about the islands, it has left no anniversary unobserved, no international forum unaware of Argentina's territorial goal. Likewise, the Peronist *Justicialista* party, indeed all Argentine parties, support that cause. Indeed, perhaps the most vociferous and effective supporters of recuperation will remain the Peronist unions, cadre and shock troops of the *Justicialista* movement, whose agenda has always been highly nationalistic and fervently irredentist about the Malvinas, Beagle Channel, and Andean Chile.

Nor has the redemocratization of Latin America now well under way changed the character of territorial disputes in the region. Both among themselves and collectively in opposition to non-Latin holders of territory in the Hemisphere, Latin America is quick to anger on territory and little given to solutions other than total and absolute inclusion in the claiming state. Reversion to military dictatorships is not the only risk facing a democratizing Latin America. While the continent is down to four military dictatorships, and most democracies are building bulwarks against the military in politics, populism may be the next menace to Republican Democracy. Should Latin America have to pass through irrational mass politics before achieving mature pluralist democracy, the politics of territory will be even more turbulent. Should populism fail where dictatorship and responsible democratic government are judged to have failed—achieving self-sustaining growth—then populism will turn more easily than have military governments to xenophobia and irredentism to hide, and hide from, its inability to govern.

BRITAIN: FORTRESS LONDON/FORTRESS FALKLANDS

Military victory in the South Atlantic helped the Conservative government in London to political victory in the elections of June 1983 and since. Further years of governance into the 1990s however, carry the continued responsibility for the Falkland Islands.

Following the war, a British garrison of more than 4,000 troops was stationed in the Falkland Islands. This is the major politico-military change that the Argentine invasion produced. A new set of Argentine accusations concerning imperialism and colonialism will not dislodge or discourage that presence, but added to such major commitments as Northern Ireland and the 55,000 troops of the British Army of the Rhine, even the third naval power in the world must consider itself highly extended.

The new look in British defense (subs over surface ships, weapons over weapons platforms) will not make the maintenance of the garrison any more practical, though the Mt Pleasant jetport makes its reinforcement feasible. NATO Alliance pressures remain for committment of large parts of that force to exercise with and be ready for the U.K./Netherlands amphibious force which, with U.S. and Canadian Marines, is earmarked for NATO's northern flank. If the Falklands experience led many militaries, including the British, to better prepare for out-of-area responsibilities, it did not provide them with the funding and capabilities to do so by expansion.

There are also political and commercial costs to Argentine hostility. Relations and trade with several Latin countries are strained. The Falklands and Dependencies are more than normally expensive to maintain on a "wartime" footing. Transport is indirect. Essentials must come greater distances. Thus, the United Kingdom has sought Argentine agreement to formally cease hostilities and to resume trade and diplomatic relations.

PARADISE RECOVERABLE: THE KELPERS, CULTURE, AND POLITICS

The attitudes of the Falkland Islanders are the little-appreciated heart of the Falklands question. In the years after the South Atlantic war of spring 1982, the Falkland Islands are a cautious but revitalized society. Few Falklanders any longer give serious thought to a role for Argentina in their political future. In the supreme irony of the Argentine recuperation and subsequent loss of the Islands, years of patient economic and social courtship of the Islanders were lost not so much to the experience of the sword and boot of Argentina but to the experience of watching the Argentines work with each other in the Falklands. If Kelpers are residually wary about their chosen (but many feel reluctant) motherland, they have full confidence in short-term British political and economic backing. Indeed, a sense of cautious economic and political optimism pervades Kelper society, which did not characterize it in the years before 1982.

The Falkland Islands landscape is characterized by gorse and heather moors. It is a bleak and forbidding land, but beautiful in its contrasts and colors, and reminiscent of Scotland or Maine in the northern hemisphere. A land of fens and glens, it yields a difficult living to sheep farmers. Theirs is the reality of outlying settlements called camps. The camps are settlements of individual family households. A few comprise towns. Most are collective sheep herding farms, many owned by the Falkland Islands Company (FIC), but the majority in private if sometimes absentee hands.

Falklands society has three major elements: The residents of the capital of Stanley and environs; the people of the camps or outlying settlements of the Islands; and the British military and construction teams. The three exist in a surprising harmony. Indeed, the populations rather complement each other. These three elements of Island culture coexist well precisely because they are British. Social science generalizations such as the negative impact of a military garrison that outnumbers the small local population are largely diluted by this cultural harmony. In the words of one Kelper, "I don't care how many troops there are here, as long as they're British."

The Government is that of a British Crown Colony. It is headed by a Civil Commissioner and includes, at least for the moment, a Military Commissioner as Commander of British Forces Falkland Islands. The traditional office of Chief Secretary has been vested in a Chief Executive who is in charge of administration of the government and economic development. The Financial Secretary is Chief Budget Officer of the Falkland Islands Government. Like all Crown Colonies, the Government is autonomous. The Falkland Islands Government includes both an Executive and a Legislative Council. In the case of the Falkland Islands, the traditional Consultative Council, which was usually appointed by Governors, is in part elected. Six of the nine members of the Legislative Council are chosen by the population. The Falkland Islands has its own currency and code of law.

Fortress Falklands is not a British policy but a political and logistical condition imposed by Argentina's denial of transport and communications via any point in South America. This may be fair enough—it is Argentina's only remaining card, along with the high costs it imposed on the United Kingdom for its support of the wishes of the Kelpers.

However, Fortress Falklands appears viable as long as it is a necessity. Indeed, the longer this economic isolation is imposed by Argentina, the more it risks denying Argentina the sovereignty it has always claimed and nearly had dropped into its lap. Great Britain has chosen to pay the price, to rehabilitate the infrastructure, to clear the minefields and unexploded munitions, to expand the economy, and eventually to increase the population. If Argentina maintains the isolation of the Islands, the Kelpers and the British taxpayer will have no alternative.

The medium-term effects may be not the wearing down of Kelper and British will that Argentina intends but a Berlin Airlift effect—an economic and then political determination to remain autonomous. Precisely because the interruptability of supplies and services on political grounds can be so expensive, any society strives for as much independence as is efficient, replacing imports with local manufactures so as to increase the scope of its autonomy and guarantee its own expansion via the new industries. Argentine "blockade" not only raises the threshold of that point of efficiency almost infinitely, but provides further political incentive to invest past a point where the Island economy has reason to find productive mutual advantage with the mainland.

Continuation of the situation as at present will also reinforce the antipathy of the political culture of the Falklanders for that of even democratic Argentina. Continued official hostility and isolation will reinforce the principal negative politico-social lesson that the Kelpers took from their brief military occupation by Argentina: The culture of the Falkland Islands is antithetical to that of Argentina as the Kelpers experienced it.

Culture is politics to the extent that it determines and incorporates our collective values. The Falkland Islanders define themselves as culturally and politically British. This means far more than which country provides defense and conducts foreign relations. It is less a question of the nation-state and its privileges than of the people of the Islands and their preferences. Their institutions and beliefs mirror those of the society they still, after generations, refer to as "home." As much as a taste for gardens, warm beer, and peat fires in the hearth, their civic but decentralized, individualistic, rights–oriented political tastes determine who and what the Falklanders are.

The primary source of the cultural lessons preserved in the collective memory of Island society about Argentine occupation was the way the Argentines dealt with each other on the Islands. No one enjoyed living under military government, with the attendant security measures and restrictions. Tension between the two cultures was high but well managed by both parties. Kelpers do not dwell on that, but rather on politico-differences. Between themselves and their occupiers and between their values and those they observed in the Argentine Military as a "society." No military can accurately reflect its civilian values and institutions, but the negative impressions are strong regardless. Kelpers noted the caste nature of the officer corps/enlisted ranks distinction, even down to field rations. They were bemused. In contrast, they were horrified by the reaction of an officer who was told his men had stolen peat for fires: The offenders were buried to their necks in the frozen muddy ground. No more complaints in that settlement were lodged above the noncommissioned officer level for fear of the punishment that would be meted out next. Similar lessons about Argentine society were drawn from the combat leadership of Argentine officers. The Kelpers concluded that this was not a culture by which they wished to be led.

The perceived incompatibility is more political (concerned with leadership and group goals, values and conduct) than social (concerned with "peers," behavior norms, and the conduct of competition). The Kelpers have known for generations the rough dimensions of Argentine life and customs. While Spanish is not widely understood (apparently a surprise to the occupiers), everyone knows some Argentines. Many Islanders have spent time in Argentina. Some have married Argentines. The two cultures (and especially the minority of rural Argentines) share some values common to frontier societies. (To the extent that Kelpers "reject" Argentine culture and society, it stems from a grudging lack of familiarity and of any desire to get below the surface aspects of culture, a universal condition of mankind.)

Island society, especially "in camp" beyond the capital, remembers the Argentine draftees with a compassion and understanding that they demonstrated at the time of their enforced acquaintance. There was tension born of mutual captivity, political differences, and the logistical burdens of war on a conquered population (e.g., requisitions of buildings and supplies). However, cold, wet, hungry troopers were fed in kitchens and told not to "make a habit of it." Infractions of the undoubtedly serious orders to treat the Kelpers well for political reasons were overlooked by Kelpers who knew they could trap individual Argentines in a draconian disciplinary response. Islanders comment regularly on the punctillious courtesy of Argentine officers and the concern of all Argentine personnel for women and children as defenses were prepared and hostilities loomed.

As in their disciplined and fortunate occupation (with no British combat deaths and only 3 Argentines killed), the invaders demonstrated a restraint and political sophistication throughout the occupation which did them credit. This was not enough, however, to overcome the cultural differences that the Islanders perceive or the natural hatred of an invader. Like the well-intentioned Argentine grants of orientation tours and scholarships at the best schools on the mainland, the overall experience of cross-cultural contact had the opposite effect of that intended.

There has always been a deep if not universal suspicion of Argentina as the claimant of sovereignty. Many rejected as completely self-serving and Machiavellian Argentina's claims and deeds in support of its proposition of the 1970s that it was the logical and natural partner for the Kelpers; that they might enjoy not only autonomy but preferred status in Argentine national life. They saw the air-and fuel-supply personnel among them as spies and a vanguard (indeed many were sources of information and even hard intelligence for the landings, and returned to administer the Islands). The invasion and occupation confirmed their worst fears about partnership with Argentina. Their resistance to economic and political compromise would lead them to emmigrate rather than hold an Argentine passport or work Argentine soil.

Indeed, many Kelpers who state that years ago they were beginning to despair of the *existence* much less the vitality of their society, now feel they have no choice but to develop their own way, with or without a better life due to infusions of infrastructure and capital from Britain. Once resigned if not enthusiastic about what they saw as the inevitability of eventual Argentine sovereignty, they are now equally resigned about a political future with no Argentine role at all and a parallel economic future that may not be as bright as is possible but will be freely chosen. Argentina has not only lost whatever political ground it had gained in the Falklands, it has convinced a generation of Kelpers that it is not to be let back into their world even for great economic gain in goods and services. Not only is there no longer any question for the majority of Kelpers of negotiating lease-back, conditional sovereignty or other political compromises, but even resumption of fuel and transportation via Argentina are no longer desired. The Argentines are not to be trusted, much less empowered.

It is the Kelpers' unification against any Argentine role in their political lives which is the most lasting effect of the occupation and the continuing isolation.[2] Those who have always mistrusted Argentina and those converted to that point of view will form the majority for generations. Whether Argentina has any role in their lives at all, or indeed any place in their collective consciousness at all, and therefore any chance to influence future generations, depends on Argentina.

The Falkland Islanders are well aware that intensive British political and economic support is not an automatic and permanent alternative future to that of Argentine support. They have always had a difficult time pressing for resources from a distant central Government with worldwide claims on its treasury. The Islands were significantly "underresourced" —with capital extracted and seldom reinvested in full; Kelpers indeed express the (perhaps fiscally inexact) sentiment that current costs do not measure up against 150 years of exports and taxes paid to England—which, they still, after 150 years, and in some cases 6 generations, simply call "home." If that is more of a political sentiment than an economic analysis, it is nonetheless true that the Islands were never the public-sector drain some African colonies were. The Falklands were largely self-supporting on balance. Expected to pay their own way, they were accustomed to a lower standard of living. Like their defense, their public-sector investment was prisoner to the desire for stability and the constant threat of major change. Great Britain hoped not to invest so much as to offend Argentina or alternatively relieve it of its responsibilities should it acquire sovereignty. To the costs of the war and repairing its damages must be added the costs of years of underspending on a colony whose productivity, and indeed whose very future political status, was in doubt.

However, that investment is being made. Its most striking example is the airport at Mount Pleasant, built to replace the field at Stanley. Capable of handling fully loaded wide-body and long-haul aircraft, the airport provides an air freight and passenger capability that the Falklands have never known. Its modern facilities, roads to the main towns, its own harbor and pier, and better weather prediction have radically improved transport and communications. With a deep-water jetty at Stanley and other infrastructure investments, there will be a real base for the lowering of public costs, diversification of the economy, and import substitution.

The extended airfield will allow the further reduction of the British Army garrison on the Falkland Islands. With the ability to reinforce rapidly by air, the U.K. can reduce ground forces to a contingency level—sufficient to hold the Islands and the airfield until reinforcements can arrive by air. Relying on sophisticated, all-weather radar which gives detailed, and now 360-degree early warning of approach by sea or air; Rapier antiaircraft batteries; and well-honed naval and aircraft response capabilities, British Forces Falkland Islands need not be a garrison several times the population they protect. Further reduced and concentrated, the troops will become less a factor in Island life than a well-managed community-relations program and sophistication on both sides had made them when they were at full strength after the British recapture of the Islands.

Beyond the repair and upgrading of infrastructure, the U.K. Government and the Island Government plan to revitalize and expand the economy of the Falklands. It is a gradualist approach, recognizing limits on rapid change such as the conservative nature of Kelper society; limited housing and therefore new manpower; and hence a reduced absorptive capacity for capital. This factors are, however, constraints, and not barriers. They mean that new or upgraded fields of productive activity will have to be introduced in a well-planned way, consistent with local conditions and resources, and thus self-generating and sustainable. In such necessities lies virtue. Too much economic-development work flounders on failure to plan for local conditions, to adapt to local values, and to enlist the longer-run enthusiasm and critical input of the population affected. The Kelpers themselves joke about the "Falklands factor" —the difficulties and inefficiency of doing even the most apparently straightforward task in their environment, so far from supplies, critical skills, and centers where the specifications and time-tables are written.

Betting against the difficulties of imposed and natural isolation is a population that not only salvages Land Rovers in farm machine shops but tears them down and lengthens the body to accommodate sheep dogs; that is practical, sacrificing, principled in its stoicism, accustomed to low levels of resources, economically maximizing, and oriented toward production rather than consumption.

The proven resource base of that population is marginal. Wool production dominates the economy of the Islands and faces major problems of overgrazing of not inherently rich pastures, increasing labor costs, and a declining world price for its product. Grasslands management, appropriate and available fertilizers, and new strains of hardy plants may help increase the number of sheep per acre to world levels. Experiments with putting more land in the hands of those who work it are underway, and alternative forms of tenancy are promising. The marketing of specialty wools as well as creative product differentiation (Colombian coffee; Falklands wool) offer hope and hard work.

Starting and sustaining new and supplementary industries such as fishing and shellfish will be no easier than turning around the long-term decline of the wool business but must be done.

There are, however, possible new forms of endeavor for the Islands that hold some promise. All new forms of investment involve large amounts of capital and risk. Some, if poorly implemented, will set back not only planning and investment but the very faith and hope of the Islanders, which must be the foundation of self-sustaining growth in the Falklands. Only a few such failures would make a reality of the Falklands Factor so strong that no external capital or entrepreneurship would overcome it.

However, the potential resources of the Southern World are immense. Already foreign fishing fleets extract massive amounts of protein from the Scotia Sea along the chain of the Falklands and Dependencies. The first and most obvious source of revenue for the Islands was the 200-mile exclusive resource zone so much in vogue around the world. This both taxes and allows the resource management of the fisheries of the area. The management and preservation at sustainable yields of the living marine resources is the more important benefit—it may well be that before the Kelpers can assess and attempt commercial fishing their seas will be depleted not only of the fish and squid that are feeding Poles and Russians but of the very krill that is the basis of the South Atlantic and Antarctic food chains. These miniature shrimp are quite literally the basis of life in the Southern World and are now being harvested themselves for human protein. Unless carefully managed, they and the rest of animal life in the South Atlantic may be reduced beyond the point of annual renewal.

The Falkland Islands need the resources zone for present investment and future resources. The U.K. is exercising great diplomatic restraint in managing and patrolling the zone. One palliative and confidence-building measure would be to share the zone with Argentina—allowing Argentine-registered civilian fishing craft to work the zone by simple registration, while "foreign" vessels continue to pay fees that could be put toward conservation and joint exploitation at renewable levels of the wider fishery. Should Argentina choose not to reciprocate, the fledgling Falklands fishing industry is not likely for decades to have the capability to take more than its own territorial waters produce anyway, nor even to fish up to the maintainable yield of its waters—a surplus that might as well be shared with Argentina.

Where does a viable Fortress Falklands leave Argentina and its historic claim to the Malvinas? Argentina will clearly not drop its claim, nor further moderate its political and practical insistence on that claim. Argentina rearmed following the war, but for the moment its methods are likely to be confined to politics and imposed economic costs; a strategy of diplomatic and physical isolation bordering on quarantine. No one should underestimate Argentine determination that these islands are their soil. A Peronist government or another generation will reassess options.

The United Nations and the Non-Aligned Movement will continue to provide the fora for Argentina's pursuit of its sovereignty claim. Only in the longer run will the effects be telling—if they prove to be increasingly successful. The tradeoffs in these processes are between strength of condemnation and numbers of favorable votes—the tougher and more one-sided or condemnatory the language, the harder it is to make the vote totals climb in one's favor year after year. Success when achieved is the moral equivalent of friction in a mechanical process—over time it is corrosive.

Corrosion by nonaligned declaration and U.N. resolution are not telling in international terms, as the very process of debate and voting emphasizes the debatable nature of an issue. Camps tend over time to stabilize on territorial issues and to maintain their positions largely out of the requirement of National

Honor for consistency. Absent new developments that are legally or politically telling, they dwindle toward rhetorical sterility. Without broad consensus, sanctions are out of the question.

Internally, political corrosion is reduced in its political effect should it emanate from institutions perceived to be inherently hostile. External victory may pressure the U.K. less than Argentina believes. It may indeed be perverse in its effect, solidifying domestic opinion to an otherwise unobtainable degree, especially if the emphasis remains on Decolonization in the name of territorial integrity. This invokes British National Honor in its disregard for the principled and deliberate nature of Britain's divestment of its empire by and in the name of self-determination. Discounting British motivations for tactical gain may result in strategic loss as first the British people and then others tire of the tactics of villification.

More telling will be any resonance that direct (rather than multilateral) Argentine positions find within British politics. In questions of National Honor as in the debate of National Interests, one party will often find potential sympathizers or even allies within the other system, especially in democracies. Debate is not subject to the disciplines of the policy process, while policy is influenced no matter how reluctantly by public and legislative debate. Subjects that are the object of public policy debate rapidly outdistance simple (primarily wartime) distinctions of a we/they nature such as treason or aid-and-comfort-to-the-enemy. The opponent must be admitted to be as valid if not as neutral a source of ideas as any.

In combination with costs that may not drop fast or far enough to suit many when measured against British National Interests or National Honor in the South Atlantic, Argentine equity arguments will find both principled and opposition-motivated sympathy in the British parliamentary system, public, and press. Appeals based in principle and Britain's self-image of reasonableness (a major component of National Honor in London) will, over time, fare well. The external and internal proponents of change (talks, if not at first talks about sovereignty) will reinforce each other, citing each other at home as a reason to be engaged in and continue the effort. Cumulative lists of means and ends will gain wider acceptance given the two symbiotic, ready-made audiences. It is a powerful tool of policy to be able to influence the opponent's debates on National Interest and even more so on National Honor.

This implies that Britain should do the same. Starting at home and extending to Argentina and multilateral fora, it should patiently explain the apparently overfine distinction of being willing to discuss everything except sovereignty; of having no fixed positions except self-determination for the Kelpers. If the ideological fight is uphill, it should not be a lonely one. The principle is less applied than accepted, and can be made less threatening to the majority of nations even if it it presents an implicit challenge to each.

Aware of these realities, Britain has never stopped insisting that it is ready, indeed eager, to resume relations and talks with Argentina. Even (perhaps especially) following military victory, Britain's self-image requires reasonableness.

What HMG insists is *not* on the table is sovereignty. That reflects the reality in a representative democracy that what the Kelpers as a constituency and their lobby—private and parliamentary—do not want, is not negotiable.

In one of the many political ironies of the Falklands crisis, the Kelpers were at one point granted full citizenship. In so doing, the U.K. opened itself to the criticism that it has lost its last political basis for the argument of a distinct population entitled to "self-determination." In this view, it is clearly inconceivable that a small group of English citizens can determine the interests of the whole of the British body politic.

To other societies, the picture of 1,800 people "dictating" the policy of 56 million more is a travesty of the nation-state. Long traditions of territorial arrangement and pre-Wilsonian handling of "subjects," as well as a morally casual tendency toward social engineering to which we are all subject, incline us toward resettlement of the geopolitically inconvenient.

To citizens of politically responsive governments, the reflection of the preferences of constituencies (even—indeed especially—minorities) is precisely what the state is all about. Self-determination will be a controlling element of National Honor in the Falklands for the British long after other major components such as the memory of military sacrifice in support of non–resort to force, the inviolability of frontiers, and peaceful settlement of disputes have begun to fade from the political foreground they now occupy.

MEDIATORS: PROPHETS WITHOUT HONOR

The particular nature of Kelper objections to Argentine governance renders mediation difficult. The past roles of the major mediators may now make a third-party role next to impossible; in broad terms, the U.N. may be unacceptable to Britain and the U.S. to Argentina. The road to a solution is thus first unilateral, and then bilateral.

To the extent that consistently held national positions are or have become contrary to basic National Interests, the active mediation process offers a player the option of change that is not perceived to be inconsistent or contradictory and therefore damaging of other stated interests or of the longer-run National Honor component of consistency.

To the extent that mediation is more than intermediary negotiation, it is potentially most useful when it breaks the deadlock of opposed, stated, formal national positions from which no apparent win/win solution can be obtained.

Thus, it is in unlinking National Interest from National Honor that mediation is truly a unique and valuable function in international crisis diplomacy.

To the extent that there are more than two major players, the synthesis of national or institutional interests becomes all the more complex. To the extent that complexity constitutes difficulty, the risks of failure increase proportionately with the value of success. This is the principle caveat for anyone considering the mediating role. As in brushfire war, there is no *real* "easy in, easy out" mediating role. Only a dynamic, active, power- or prestige-based mediating role is likely to synthesize these two very diametrical, or three or more opposed, sets of interests and firmly held long-term positions that have engaged National Honor.

Future U.N. Roles

While eliminated in the medium term as a mediator, the United Nations could still someday provide:

—Observers;

—Peacekeeping forces;

—Development advice and assistance; and

—Creative discussion of new forms of sovereignty for disputed and non–self-governing territories.

These contributions lie in a distant future. For the moment, the "world forum" is more likely to harm than to help. Political discussion of the Falklands crisis will continue at the United Nations. It will likely be increasingly polarized and polarizing. The annual Decolonization resolution will call, in effect, for Argentine sovereignty. To the extent that the C–24 and the Fourth Committee encourage a hard Argentine irredentist position and keep the U.K. defensive about what it had to retake in the face of U.N. impotence, other potentially useful roles for the U.N. Security Council and Security General will be delayed if not discredited.

The United States: Collateral Damage

The potential contributions of the United States as facilitator or guarantor will also not be politically applicable in the near future. Most Argentines will never completely understand the U.S. support for the U.K. position following Argentine rejection of compromise.

Argentina's poet laureate Jorge Luis Borges put the year's events in perspective when he pointed out that the military defeat was an unfortunate result of the mistake of initiating the war, but that the real harm to the country had been done by the government in not giving its people realistic assessments of prospects and developments. The United States was providing such realistic assessments to Argentina and will not be forgiven in our lifetimes.

It is a measure of the depth of the damage to the bilateral relationship that in a very real sense Argentina did not lose the Falklands War, nor did Great Britain win it. The winner was Cuba, and the loser was the United States: At least for the near term, their standing in the New World was reversed by the crisis. Their places in Third World and Argentine perspective were further unrealistically exaggerated. The United States is "burnt" as as a mediator for Argentina.

If their positions at the North and South Poles of the Americas has always been seen by Argentines more as contrapositions than symmetry with the U.S., the Argentines were reinforced in their view by the Falklands crisis. Perplexed, confused, and bitter, they find new grounds and new strength for their doubts about basic U.S. attitudes.

Argentina's tarnished image in the United States was not done any good either: To the past perceptions and misperceptions about the Argentine Republic were added the sins of the military government: military aggression, false grandeur, recklessness, and jingoistic self-indulgence and self-delusion. It is widely believed that narrow, short-term nationalist interests were chosen over world peace. Doubts about Argentina's nuclear and ballistic missile responsibility were fueled, and the question introduced as to whether Argentina was really ready or mature enough for membership in the small and dangerous circle of nuclear power and nuclear arms states.

The publics and media of Argentina and the United States have, over the decade since the Falklands, cast each other in a very harsh and unflattering light. However, traumatic testing of a relationship can be admitted and discussed realistically rather than in the usual sterile generalities about bilateral political relationships, especially between two nations who never were fast friends. Such analysis could perhaps, in the case of the Falklands, form the basis of a new, mature relationship, breaking an unfortunate half century of misperception, misunderstanding, and culturally bound diplomacy.

As we move toward the twenty-first century, democratic Argentina has in its hands the shape and direction of its relationship with the United States. It will find a receptive, open-minded country, not intent on determining either its domestic politics or overly concerned with its nominal foreign policy and "alignment." If we do not share a common perception of the security threats in the New World, neither are we in total disagreement about the source of those threats. If our forms of government and our approaches to politics are not identical and not susceptible to close alliance, we are nonetheless in a period in which our political ideas and values are converging rather than diverging. The temptation to engage in scapegoating on each side should by now be minimal and, if that temptation is resisted, a healthy, realistic, and constructive relationship ought to be possible since the United States and Argentina have more than enough substantive material for a constructive bilateral relationship:

—Maintenance of peace in the South Atlantic;

—Productive dialogue on hemispheric and global issues;

—Cooperation to prevent Soviet strategic inroads;

—Support for Argentine democracy, and tranquility at home;

—Support for self-sustaining growth in the Argentine economy;

—Increased cooperation to develop Argentina's capacity as a, major world food supplier;

—Cooperation in the Antarctic.

Building a solid bilateral relationship will have to suffice, for the United States cannot now help on the Falklands. The United States will in all likelihood maintain its 200-year-old tradition of neutrality as regards sovereignty disputes in the New World, neither associating itself with nor arguing against the new level of British presence in the Falkland Islands. The United States will not, however, give in to the temptation to be passive and reactive vis-à-vis the dispute as opposed to sovereignty. The Falklands crisis is not over, and will not be concluded until it is actually grappled and managed by both parties and possibly a mediator/guarantor. There was in the case of the Falklands a major U.S. attempt to react constructively to crisis. A realistic and revitalized U.S.-Argentine relationship may in future allow the United States to act as mediator/guarantor for a lasting Falklands settlement, but not under forseeable circumstances.

BEYOND MEDIATION

Each party to the Falklands crisis found itself sufficiently in conflict with the various mediators and their interests that they should revert for now to bilateral resolution of the Falklands conflict.

The two parties have rather burnt their bridges with each other also. They may therefore want to consider alternative forms of negotiation should they decide to proceed toward normalization.

One way to defuse the National Honor component would be to meet clandestinely. It may be that there are no secrets in the last quarter of the twentieth century, but they might aim at the pre-Wilsonian ideal of open convenants arrived at secretly.

More subtle still would be not to meet at all but to watch each other's actions and tacitly match or complement them, all without delegations or declarations. Tacit bargaining is perhaps the most subtle and difficult part of the art of negotiating, but it offers two sophisticated players the option of avoiding harsh words and unobtainable formalities and proceeding directly to real cooperation on real issues.

THE ILLOGIC OF POLITICO-LEGAL RESOLUTIONS OF TERRITORIAL DISPUTES

Several tries since the Falklands War at bilateral negotiation have failed to solve the territorial dispute over the Falkland Islands. The negotiators keep coming back to the fact that the holding power wishes to retain effective control in order to absolutely protect the rights of the Islanders, while the claiming power wants absolute sovereignty over the islands while stating its willingness to negotiate guarantees. The formula usually reduces itself to Argentina wishing to discuss all aspects of the problem and Britain stating openly that sovereignty is not at issue.

We face here the heart of the problem with territorial conflict: the essential indivisibility of control of land. The nation-state is not accustomed to external guarantee. While resources or even the freedoms of a population might in theory be guaranteed while territory were surrendered, examples are rare among equally sovereign and powerful states. Nor has division of territory satisfied many. The essence of sovereignty would seem to be complete control.

The parties have in theory multiple ways of assigning or dividing sovereignty:

British Administration

Whatever the military arrangements on the Islands, this status quo is likely to prevail for some time as it has (with some constitutional amendments) since 1833. It is the preference expressed by the roughly 1,900 Islanders who in the view of Her Majesty's Government are entitled to self-determination of their political future. Guards Regiments and the Royal Navy will likely deter any near-term Argentine attack or harassment, of which Argentina is again militarily capable but now perhaps politically less desirous. Annual UNGA resolutions will maintain normative pressure for negotiation, but the U.K. will likely reject such discussion of sovereignty as inconsistent with the expressed wishes of the population for which it was forced to fight a war in self-defense. The status quo enhances the British version of National Honor, proving with time that the mainstream politico-legal culture can assert and enforce its view of territorial and dispute-settlement questions; that nation-states must resolve these questions peacefully, and that where differences cannot (yet) be resolved, one must live with the nationalist/irredentist frustration. Short-run costs that can likely be borne by HMG include: U.N. and Latin American political objections; troop and naval misdeployments and expenses; and potential social disruption on the Islands.

Lease-back

Still the most viable of the compromise paper solutions, lease-back would put the Falklands under full but deferred titular Argentine sovereignty. Administration of the Islands with the (exclusive) use of the territory but not necessarily the sea or subsoil resources would remain without interruption with the United Kingdom. The Islanders would retain all aspects of their way of life but with a date certain fixed for full Argentine occupation and use. Should that date be far enough off (20 to 100 years) they would be able to prepare well to live culturally distinct lives within the Argentine body politic, as tens of thousands of Welsh and Anglo-Argentines do today.

Partition

Ignoring the realities of National Honor momentarily, one could picture scenarios in which the Falkland Islands would be split up between the two parties. The most obvious would be for the U.K. to cede West Falkland to Argentina in exchange for renunciation in perpetuity of Argentine claims on East Falkland and the Dependencies. The population would be resettled on East Falkland or might choose provisionally to test the decades of Argentine guarantees concerning their "life-style" in the majority culture. The permanence of such a solution would be compromised by several factors: Irredentists would see Argentina's concession as a tactical one until the full and inevitable national goal could be implemented by infiltration or invasion. The eastern margin of the Antarctic claim would be pushed out almost as far as with full occupation of the Islands, and the Argentine *mare nostrum* would be affected, but pressure for further gains would be maintained by compromised sea frontiers, exclusive resource zones, and National Honor. The focus would shift to the British "colony" on the "coast" of Argentina's recuperated eastern frontier.

Joint Use

Argentina would be offered the opportunity to utilize but not occupy the territory jointly with Great Britain. No permanent Argentine settlement or other non–resource-related privileges would convey. Joint projects would have the advantage of involving Argentines with British and Islanders on an individual and ongoing basis. The flow of resources and profits to the two sides would compensate them mutually for increasing investments in the area. This in turn would lower (and eventually obviate in development terms) the perceived risks of not solving the sovereignty question to their complete mutual satisfaction. If one could not solve the Falklands question in the medium term, one could at least help both the Islanders and the Argentines get on with their real-world tasks and, in doing so, jointly eliminate an incentive to focus on politics. Joint development would help define the extent of the resource bases in the areas not yet fully assessed. If there is oil, krill, or other wealth without limit, the perceived importance of sovereignty as opposed to access will diminish over time. If the resources are proven to be marginal, inaccessible, or unmarketable, the perceived importance of sovereignty may still suffer the same fate. The provision of equal capital for equal share at such great distance would seem at first glance inequitable for the U.K. Consider, however, the possibility that its subjects in the South Atlantic have at present a far less bright future than those of Argentina. In a twenty-first century strapped with overpopulation, starvation, and resource shortages, Argentina will remain self-sufficient in meat, grain, petroleum, *lebensraum,* and red wine.

Joint Occupation

Both Britain and Argentina administer the Islands, as proposed by the 1982 mediators, with or without a third-party administrator/guarantor. One immediate payback would be the possibility of joint resource exploitation. One disadvantage is that instability is built into the situation to an even greater degree than into standoff; Argentines would be on and around the Islands, with the temptation to misuse such persons (as the Argentine airport personnel and others present on the Falklands before the 1982 invasion prepared intelligence reports for the invasion and occupation). It would also be difficult to agree to a reasonable degree of Argentine presence, property ownership, and participation in Island affairs. The temptation to flood the Islands with citizens and make a de facto takeover by sheer weight of numbers would be immense.

Joint Sovereignty

The parties declare the Falklands to be their joint, commonly administered national soil; distinct in that the solution would be considered permanent rather than interim. Andorra and the New Hebrides have been so administered. The problem arises that for one party this would be a territory or possession while for the other it would be an integral part of national territory. Separate administration and favorable resource flows are more likely to be a price Argentina wants to pay only for full rather than shared sovereignty. For the Islanders, and therefore for the British Government, all the problems of level of Argentine presence (flooding) remain, yet renegotiation or control are no longer implied, much less guaranteed, by the political arrangement.

Trusteeship

Trusteeship is one of the proud chapters in the United Nations experience. Under trusteeship, a people are recognized as a political unit entitled to self-determination by plebiscite under U.N. supervision, including armed forces if necessary to ensure a real hearing. Thus the assumption is that a trust is a temporary status to allow for debate and voting on another status. There is a tradition but no requirement of moving on to independence. The status would be more formal and regulated than would be U.N. administration as proposed during the conflict. It would be governed by the U.N. Trusteeship Council unless set up otherwise—Argentina would probably want General Assembly direct supervision as in the case of Namibia, while Britain would no doubt prefer a Council of which it is a member and master. Beyond the tactical, however, neither side is likely to want its title questioned by the neutral and precedent-erasing status of trusteeship, and Argentina would not want a majority vote by the population as presently constituted.

Free Association

One widely recognized alternative to being a territory is to become a state but associate oneself freely with another state. While it is rendered in English as "Commonwealth," Puerto Rico is, in its Spanish-language terminology, a Free Associated State with the United States. As in the case of trusteeship, however,

Argentina would balk at the supposition of determination of status by the present population, but that is how the rules of the game stand. Britain, conversely, is unlikely to agree to any period of free immigration preceding the vote.

Neutralization

The Falkland Islands would be declared politically neutral territory, demilitarized in perpetuity, with a special nonterritorial status to be guaranteed by the two parties; a body non-politic that would confer residence rights and resource licenses. However, even were Argentina as a government to ignore politics, Argentine civilization would envelop the Falklands with the best of intentions and the most perverse of results for Kelper society. Territory, unfortunately, implies societal control. Even should Britain be able to live with neutralization, an eventual Kelper revolt against the "natural" flow (flood) of people, resources, and consequent influence, would likely result. The unhappy and probably bloody outcomes might include the obliteration of Kelper society or the Argentine residents.

Independence

While theoretically this is what self-determination and decolonization are all about, sovereign independence and accession to U.N. membership are the last thing Argentina wants for the Falkland Islands. Not only is this status theoretically final, but it obliterates previous colonial claims, be they Spanish or English, and devolves on a resident population the identity and legitimacy as a "people" entitled to self-determination and self-perpetuation whose denial is the core of the Argentine case.

Argentine Sovereignty

The clear and consistently—if not constantly—maintained national goal of the Argentine Republic for over a century and a half has been incorporation of the Falklands and their Dependencies into the Argentine nation-state. That goal will not be soon set aside by the people of Argentina, whatever their form of government. It will not, following the experience with armed violence by Argentina, be accepted by the Kelpers. In its pure form (with U.N.-supervised electoral decision to do so by the majority of the population), it would constitute *incorporation* of a non–self-governing territory (more usually into the administering power) and would satisfy international law. (So would incorporation into the United Kingdom of Great Britain and Northern Ireland, by choice of the population, Argentine and UNGA majority opinion notwithstanding. Obviously, neither scenario is likely to be implemented in this century.)

Unfortunately, this is also true of all the solutions on paper, from British sovereignty through Argentine sovereignty. These solutions run the full gamut of traditional methods of resolving territorial disputes—but they are solutions on paper only. They summarize a politico-legal package which by its very nature prevents addressing problems one by one, because the nation-state cannot address problems this way: it requires the certainty of sovereignty.

In this case the paper solutions are not working—nor do they hold promise for the medium term—basically because to succeed they require a perfect package. Long negotiations gain ground in several areas; the ascent up the mountain looks possible, then the whole agreement is swept away by a point of disagreement as by an avalanche. What is needed is an approach like the Dutch Route up Annapurna—a route of climb which is technically more difficult and less direct, but free of avalanches. Such a method might be to set aside the formal solutions on paper and simply act so as to avoid aggravating the conflict. Through long patient years of learning to live together and share the South Atlantic, a formal solution might one day be possible.

SOLUTIONS IN PRACTICAL POLITICS

If no diplomatic "paper" solution is feasible for the Falklands in the medium term, what then are the two governments to do about the responsibilities they feel?

Democratic politics at its best consists in legislating and governing in such a way as to produce the loyalty and support of the governed—maximizing their interests, both by economically bettering and politically enriching their lives. From blocks and wards up through nations and their coalitions, legitimacy and trust derive from effective performance of the political and economic responsibilities of governance.

In the case of the Falkland Islands in the 21st century, the maximizing of the interests of the Argentine and British peoples and of the inhabitants of the Islands lies in real actions of legislation and of governance. Real maximizing of the rights and resources of Islanders might yet be accomplished in the context of a politico-legal (paper) solution. This would have a longer run framework and clear outcome. However, if those rights and resources cannot be maximized in a such a framework, they should be sought in another way, not allowed to remain underfulfilled.

If they cannot be started jointly, they should be begun in parallel, but they should be launched lest the political aspirations and economic patrimony of all concerned be frustrated by short-range geopolitical and nationalist concerns which little touch the reality of those at the center of this ongoing conflict.

Political rather than diplomatic actions would seem to offer a concrete way to get back to the more firm and final "paper" solutions in the medium term. All the traditional, territorially focused solutions to sovereignty disputes would still be available to the parties. (Lease-back might remain the most promising if one found the future situation unacceptable or potentially unstable and could develop nothing truly joint in nature.) The problem with most of these solutions, however, is that they seem to involve an unacceptable level of compromise and concession, and to require a full and comprehensive agreement on all aspects before any can be implemented.

More promising in the interim might be a series of unilateral, purely national, internal actions, based upon incremental, self-implementing, and self-enforcing policies. While not constituting a final solution to the Falklands conflict, these steps would go a long way toward easing rather than exacerbating tensions, and make future agreements more rather than less likely.

These would begin with political steps by each side to demonstrate good faith, at its own pace and in its own terms. New political policies would then move into practical programs—first parallel and then joint—to preserve their common economic heritage in the South Atlantic. If this experience were positive for both parties, their potential to expand and develop the economic potential of the region would be limitless. Their political and social differences should over time narrow accordingly and politico-military peace come within their grasp.

ARGENTINE INTERESTS, ARGENTINE ACTIONS

A Very Special 23rd Province

It is no longer realistic, given her politico-military action of 1982 and previous offers aimed at securing Kelper confidence, for Argentina to pursue pure *incorporation* of the Falklands and the Kelpers into the Argentine nation like any other Province of the Republic. One realistic scenario for *tacit* Argentine presentation to Stanley and Whitehall would be *local self-government within the Argentine Republic* for the Falklands. Delay or transition are implied. So are guarantees, which would seem to infringe on sovereignty. The trick would be to make them unilateral, preemptive, internal, legal, and autonomous. The issue portfolio would even be transferred from the Foreign to the Interior Minister.

Sovereignty would not be infringed were Argentina to act as she has in the past to *unilaterally promulgate executive decrees and congressional legislation for the Malvinas*. Conditions would not need third-party guarantee or be at risk of annulment after transfer: Argentina would unilaterally and without conditions or expectation of immediate implementation or reciprocity *write into its own constitution political local self-government and cultural/linguistic autonomy* for an English-speaking community in the Malvinas.

The Islands are already a formal part of the Republic under Argentine national law, and matters such as development funds, social benefits, economic diversification, and limiting residence and commerce under regional planning would be a straightforward drafting exercise. The Argentine Federal Government also has it within its powers the ability to authorize consular representation and to set the conditions under which foreign nationals might enjoy dual citizenship at their option.

In such a process, Argentina could define for itself what it thought an equitable alternative to British sovereignty might be—openly, democratically, unilaterally, and without pressure or infringement of sovereignty of any kind. Such an internally derived solution ought to constitute a solid, dependable, incremental, and changing "fair offer," which would remain tacitly on the table until picked up as undeniably a maximizing solution for all parties.

Redefining Sovereignty

Argentina should, when it comes time to sit down at the negotiating table again concerning the Falklands, think in terms of new possibilities concerning its own relationship with the Falkland Islands. These possibilities should be construed, at least initially, in terms of relationships in *addition* to those with Great Britain; that is, Argentina should consider what it can do to supplement rather than supplant the desire of the United Kingdom to safeguard the self-determination and way of life of the Falkland Islanders.

This will not be an easy exercise in political science, in diplomacy, or in national politics. It would require redefining sovereignty; further, it would require modifying it in ways not yet explored. Easy absolutist sentiments are to be avoided as they are not going to gain any ground.

Modifications of the concept of sovereignty as the exclusive possession and use of territory might produce moderate gains or moderate risks on the part of Argentina. Certainly no such experimentation could either secure Argentina less control or less influence than Argentina possesses in the 1990s in the Falkland Islands. That control is now negative or nil. Argentina's principal bargaining point beyond her historic case for sovereignty are simply the strains on the budget of the United Kingdom, hardly an effective argument with the British Government.

A New Vision of National Interest and National Honor

It will be argued that negotiating limited or compromised sovereignty will do nothing for Argentine National Honor. This ignores the fact that the trade offs would be Argentine decisions. It fails to envision a wider National Interest—the South Atlantic as a resource zone (whose joint maximization is explored in the following pages). It defines national interests and honor purely in "onshore" terms. Argentine patriots will want to consider the proposition that in the next decade and century, it is entirely possible that a less absolutist approach to the territorial question of Falklands sovereignty would increase Argentina's standing abroad, amplifying and expanding international support for her traditional case, and providing a symbiotic complement to the return of democracy on the domestic scene. Indeed, even at home, limited concessions by the United Kingdom in response to limited goals on the part of Argentina would enhance the image of effectiveness of the National Government and provide a wholesome object lesson in what can be accomplished by the pen rather than by the sword. To the extent that Argentina's democracy should but cannot play "divide and conquer" in facing competing institutions and overwhelming national problems, relief on its number one foreign policy question, even if only a token of progress to be achieved in the future, might be most welcome. After several parties have legislated wisely under different Argentine democratic governments, and conserved and fostered national resources and a potential patrimony, National Honor will have been redefined as National Interest, and the vision of both concepts widened.

BRITISH INTERESTS, BRITISH ACTIONS

Such a gradualist approach to the preconditions for a solution of the Falklands dispute requires *parallel but not externally conditioned* concessions by the other side. Great Britain can only be expected to do what any party to an international negotiation, tacit or express, does: pursue its own National Interests. There are unilateral steps that the U.K. could take to both serve its interests as seen from London in the territorial status quo *and* contribute to the possibility of other solutions that Britain may in future judge to also be in its interests.

Confidence-building measures might include:

—Volunteered statements of position;

—U.N. observers;

—U.N. Decolonization visiting missions;

—OAS regional visits and observers;

—The inclusion of Argentina in a resources zone;

—Forces drawdown, including observation;

—Reductions in the protection zone and its applicability; and

—U.N. guarantor troops.

Volunteered Statements

Public declarations (such as the U.K. policy statement of December 11,1982 and statements at the U.N. since) which are positively phrased and emphasize what *is* open to political discussion, help the climate. Regular declarations of this nature cost the U.K. little but alleviate somewhat the pressure on the Government of Argentina to raise the issue regularly. A *reaction* by Argentina to reasonable British statements is far easier to formulate assertively but constructively.

U.N. Military Observers

To the extent that Argentina fears or *claims to fear* an offensive military presence in the South Atlantic, it would be most useful for the experienced U.N.

observer personnel from other hot-spots to certify that the Falklands is the site neither of increasing nor offensive military preparations. Nothing else would so thoroughly dispute recurrent Third World visions of a "NATO base" in the South Atlantic.

OAS Regional Visits and Observers

As an observer of the Organization of American States and a power with a long-standing interest in the hemisphere, Great Britain might find it in its interest to invite the OAS to send political and military observers to the Falkland Islands. Such missions could provide the assurances sought by Argentina concerning limits on offensive weapons and major bases, as well as providing the Islands with what will likely be for some time their only contact with the South American continent. To the extent that such missions also note formally or informally the British character and political preferences of the Kelpers, some major myths about the Falklands might be dispelled in favor of a real dialogue about the legitimate role and extent of the wishes of the Kelpers in a political solution.

Britain would not and could not expect from such visits OAS support of its position or even that of the inhabitants, but it is entirely possible that the OAS observers could be factual concerning what they observe in the area.

Despite its resolution and findings on the sovereignty question, the OAS should have no problem with visiting and observation missions under the aegis recognized by the United Nations: Britain is, according to the United Nations, the administering power in the Falkland Islands. This would seem to clear the way for a regional organization as recognized in the Charter, to accept current British administration as a de facto reality.

For Argentina, OAS visiting missions and perhaps military observers could provide both security assurances (that is, confirmation that the area is not being strengthened as an offensive British presence off the Argentine coast), as well as evidence to its public and press that the Falklands question remains open and potentially subject to debate and what Argentina would view as a just and lasting solution.

Both parties would give up little by the introduction of a mild OAS role, and might find a potential interlocutor that neither side has truly attempted to use in that role.

U.N. Decolonization Visiting Missions

Similarly, the United Nations could be invited through the Committee of 24 to visit the Islands under the aegis of and at the invitation of the administrating power in the order to review those socioeconomic and political questions that are normally the subject matter of U.N. oversight of dependent territories.

As an Administering Authority with a long-standing and highly creditable record in the Decolonization proceedings of the United Nations, Britain has an interest both in firming up her title as administering power and in establishing the continuing benevolence of her administration of the Falkland Islands.

Argentina, having based its claim in recent decades on the Decolonization argumentation, should have no problem with U.N. visits. British reporting on the Falkland Islands has remained in effect, and the U.N. Secretariat still prepares an annual socioeconomic and political report on the Falkland Islands.

The United Nations would benefit from a mild expansion of its continuing activity involving the Falklands as a possible prelude to a once-again expanded role in a political solution.

Force Reductions

As Britain drew down its force levels, both army and naval, in mid–1983, Argentine naval and air activity along its southern coast also declined. Whether coincidence or response, the lull was a very healthy indicator of what can be achieved by both sides in reducing the level of tension, whether or not the Argentine Government agreed to a formal cessation of hostilities. If it is difficult for Argentina to surrender this "bargaining chip," it may not be necessary to link the formal declaration (a matter of National Honor) with a de facto decline in the mutual levels of military preparedness (a question of National Interest).

Whether or not, however, Argentina sees its way clear to avoid saber rattling from its southern bases and probing the maritime exclusion zone, as well as possible encroachment by oil rigs, fishing craft, and other resource-related gestures, it is entirely and unilaterally in the interest of the United Kingdom to lower its force levels gradually, consistent with the security that is part and parcel of its foreign relations and defense responsibilities to the Falkland Islanders. Given improved defense infrastructure and high-technology defensive capabilities, such a lowering of the U.K. military profile in the Falklands is possible. (There might be public ceremonies as unreplaced units are withdrawn, to inform and reassure the Argentine public directly.) Not only would it lower the cost to the United Kingdom, but drawdowns also have value as confidence-building measures with Argentina, designed to both evoke and embarrass Argentina into similar stances.

Reductions in and Redefinition of Zones

Further reductions in zones,such as that of July 1982, would help the political climate. That reduction of the exclusion zone from 200 miles to a protection zone of 150 miles changed both the character and coverage of the zone. The definition of its center point between the two Islands kept the Argentines only some 80 miles from the coast of West Falkland. Further reductions might be made contiguous with join zones involving equal linear distance (from coasts) concessions by Argentina.

U.N. Guarantor Troops

Internally, London and the Kelpers themselves might want to consider the longer-term advantages of *having the United Nations secure the peace in the twenty-first century in the Falkland Islands.*[3] Lesser but not token numbers of U.N. forces could give force to the Security Council's resolutions and keep world attention focused on any potential Argentine threat to peace in the region. U.N. forces would as well relieve the U.K. of a considerable monetary and security burden, and Kelper society of some social stress. Like Argentina's undertaking, this would be a unilateral measure undertaken for national ends.

United Nations forces offer one of the few sound mechanisms for unlinking the political and military components in National Honor in territorial conflict. In the opening weeks following the Argentine invasion of the Falklands, a U.N. interim force might have avoided armed conflict. A token United Nations force in the Falklands might have and still might help provide the congruence between National Interest and National Honor that both the United Kingdom and Argentina require in order to reconsider their territorial conflict over the Falkland Islands.

The difference, the real long-run cost to peace of the Falklands War, is that following hostilities, the peace keeping force will be as much an object of negotiation as an aid to settlement; that is, it will have lost to some extent the advantage of avoiding rather than proceeding toward definitive settlement. Thus, they can no longer be thought of by either party as a way to simply delay full implementation of all its goals. Each party will have to realistically assess the implications of a U.N. presence for its long-run interests.

In that sense, however, a U.N. force is now promising in that, were it to be agreed to, it would be the first step in the solution rather than being subject to misuse as the first step in avoiding a solution.

If the Falklands War is over (and that is not at all clear), the territorial dispute is more sharply drawn than ever. The possibility of settlement by a mediator like the United States or the U.N. could be enhanced by a U.N. Interim Force Falklands (UNIFF).

For the United Kingdom, UNIFF would:

—End the necessity of maintaining the long supply line to a Falkland garrison into the foreseeable future;

—Allow the United Kingdom to fully resume its northern flank role in NATO;

—Pursue political compromise without fear that HMG would stand accused of not being militarily prepared or politically alert to further extreme Argentine reactions;

—Inhibit Argentina from pursuing any military solutions no matter how drawn-out the ongoing negotiations; and

—Avoid accusations of total intransigence and an unwillingness to consider the idea of changing the political status as evidenced by "military occupation," thus increasing their ability to defend self-determination at length.

Argentina, in turn, would derive the following benefits from a U.N. Interim Force:

—A visible if very indirect revivification of Argentina's claims so apparently unviable following her military seizure and military defeat in the Falklands;

—Concrete expression of the apparent nonaligned majority view that Argentina's case has merit and that the question of the sovereignty of the Falklands should be kept open and negotiated actively;

—A salutory limitation on Argentina's military and, indeed, political options, within which a newly democratic Argentine Government could explain patiently and realistically to the population that sovereignty would not be easily or quickly obtained but was neither impossible of attainment; and

—A significant salving of the military defeat of Argentine ground forces with the replacement of the physical remainder of British forces by a multinational unit.

Should the ongoing search for a lasting solution involve a third-party mediator, the mediator would find his situation considerably improved by:

—The longer political time frame allowed by a "temporary" U.N. force;

—The lower political temperature in each country (and in the Islands) allowing more open and creative debate on options;

—Increased normative pressure on each side in an atmosphere more free of military pressures;

—Less chance of military questions invoking National Honor;

—consequent restraint brought by a heightening of the role of the international community in the dispute; and

—A more solid juridical ground for possibly making some of the aspects of the dispute subject to binding arbitration.

If the National Honor tied up in the physical presence of armed forces could be put aside, the parties should stand a better chance of setting aside military considerations and harmonizing National Interests.

JOINT UNDERTAKINGS

Beyond (and even without) any such unilateral actions to normalize the political situation and move toward stability without prejudicing potentially negotiable issues, there are steps the parties could undertake jointly without harming their politico-legal cases, being called upon to make unilateral concessions, or acting in any but their own definitions of National Interest and National Honor. If not initially agreeable as joint efforts, the benefits (including net profits) could be assigned nominally or in escrow to the other party until it chose to participate and improve the joint results. Such a cluster of joint resource-oriented actions could include oil, living resources, and general exploration.

Joint Oil Exploration and Production

The normal situation on the Islands, which pertained before April 1982 and is now restored, makes development of any petroleum resources of the South Atlantic impractical. Transportation, operating distance, and political risk are the major hindrances to unilateral British exploration and exploration. The natural market is the Southern Cone of South America.

The costs could be halved, and the political risk and political factor in insurance cut to near zero by joint development with Argentina. Every step and every facility and crew would be 50/50. To the extent that the U.K. might bring more deep-water in-house capability to the operation, Argentina would have local resources at better factor costs, not to mention the best command of related petroleum geology. The oil experience would in itself be a confidence-building measure for each side. It might, whether petroleum turns out to be feasible or not, form the model for going after other mineral and marine resources of the area together. Possibly the biggest political payoff would be the finding that the reserves are insufficient to exploit—defusing the main resources argument for sovereignty on either side and calling into question some of the Antarctic resources arguments for the conflict.

If both sides would have reservations about the sovereignty implications and precedents of certain drilling areas, these could be agreed on in advance to be without political consequence. If either side were subjected to political objections about sharing finite resources, Argentina already has self-sufficiency but could use the hard currency, while viability of Kelper society (with immigration and environmental safeguards) would be secured, irrespective of its future political choices, or would at least know where its economic future did *not* lie.

Fisheries and Krill: A Living Resources Regime for the South Atlantic

A joint Anglo-Argentine resources regime for the South Atlantic would allow each party to exploit and preserve its fisheries better than at present. Undertaken without prejudice to territorial claims, it would be based on a 200-mile zone projected from *all land areas of either party*. Such a zone would encompass most of the South Atlantic down to the 60th parallel, which marks the northern edge of the Antarctic Treaty area. The zone might be negotiated for compatibility with the Treaty, and ways of merging the two areas for scientific purposes sought. The zones so shaded, without distinction as to whose territory the line was projected from, would be open to the commercial ships of either party up to a line 12 miles from any coast, which would be treated as territorial waters for purposes of customs, security, and other national priorities, and within which fishing would not take place. All exploration would be by registration without tax, with a central authority which would undertake to centralize and make joint analytical use of all data bearing on the living resources of the sea. This would allow the maximization of those resources at sustainable yields. Where limits needed to be imposed for conservation, the parties would take or license to the other equal shares of the available catch.

The political difficulties of declaring and enforcing the zone would be mitigated by its joint character. The parties each have sets of allies and friendly nations who would be less inclined than the international community at large to protest or violate the zone. The combined weight of British and Argentine prestige would be considerable. The political legitimacy of the regime as a confidence-building measure would also add to its acceptability.

Third parties could be licensed to fish the zone within conservative preservation limits and until parties wish to expand their own capabilities to exploit resources directly. Any such licensee would be of assistance in policing the expansive zone. Revenues could be scaled in from initially low levels for those nations already feeding their populations from the fisheries of the zone so as not to cause economic disruptions. They would have time to factor taxes and catch limits into their planning. Their present levels of catch could be guaranteed for the transition period unless markedly exploitive or demonstrably harmful to the resource base.

Conservation of marine life in the South Atlantic would be the central purpose of the zone. The miniature shrimp-like krill are the basis of life in the South Atlantic. They can be harvested for human consumption as well as animal feed and fertilizer purposes. In an increasingly hungry world they offer a potentially rich source of protein. Their principal fishery focuses on the islands of the Scotia Sea and principally on South Georgia. The basic and direct food of penguins, squid, fur seals, birds, and whales, krill themselves feed on plankton. They are thus the focal point of the food chain of marine life in the South Atlantic. As first sealing and then whaling declined in the area, the potential for using krill for other purposes has been more widely noted.

Krill are highly nutritious, consisting of approximately 65 percent protein by dry weight. Both the meat and the shell have utility, the latter being usable in glues and other industrial applications. There is interest in this potentially massive fishery on the part of Japan, Argentina, the United States, the U.K., the Federal Republic of Germany, Chile, Poland, and the USSR. Hundreds of thousands of tons might with good management be taken annually for everything from meat, paste, and food sticks to cattle foods to fertilizer. Like many marine proteins, there would be some problem in preparing the food in an acceptable form. However, in the face of declining traditional protein sources, the carefully managed krill harvest might someday be twice that of the current worldwide fish intake of mankind.

A 1982 convention undertook to manage krill stocks ecologically and to prevent any unnecessary depletion of this potentially renewable resource. It has been estimated that the reduction in the number of whales in the South Atlantic would allow for 150 million tons of surplus krill beyond past depletion levels. The potential with good management might be as high as an annual crop of six billion tons of krill or enough protein to feed the world.

The U.K.'s income and other benefits would be devoted primarily to the Kelpers and thus to what the Argentine Government could see as potential Argentine territory. The income from taxes would go first to research and conservation, and secondly to safety of life at sea, meteorology, and navigation. Again, the Kelpers and the Argentines would be the primary beneficiaries. From the Argentine perspective, there would not be "extraction" of resources from the area. From Britain's viewpoint, the welfare of the Kelpers would be considerably advanced in both the short and the long-run.

Science and Antarctica: A Joint Science Region, Emerging Planning, and Expeditions

The two parties could agree to initially share all the results of and eventually jointly undertake increased scientific and exploitative exploration of the South Atlantic and Antarctic. Both Britain and Argentina have considerable experience and expertise in the area, and joint expeditions would both reduce the cost to each and probably improve the results by cross-fertilization and specialization of roles in support of the expeditions.

In the longer run, such cooperation would make it easier both to share the exploitation of new, jointly discovered resources and perhaps even to approach on a common basis the upcoming major political decisions the world will face concerning the Antarctic region and its resources. Parallel interests and some political battles fought together could not but help the parties improve their bilateral exploratory process concerning the political future of the South Atlantic.

EPILOGUE

FALKLANDS: A CRISIS FOR NEGOTIATION AND MEDIATION

In the Falklands Crisis of Spring 1982, war was not in the end averted nor the underling dispute attenuated much less solved by negotiation and mediation of conflicting visions of National Honor and National Interest. Indeed the sovereignty dispute may not be solved in this century, and even under a continued democracy no one can guarantee the future limits on Argentina's sovereign options in pursuing its perceived interests.

Peace or even a ceasefire evaded and continues to evade efforts in all the classic third-party diplomatic methods of conflict resolution—national, multi-national and international—by some of the most experienced and influential players in the nation state game. The Falklands Crisis is not, however, an ongoing risk solely for the parties but for the system itself; not only a series of case studies in the weaknesses of the present international system but itself a series of precedents and potentially mislearned lessons which further destabilize that system, especially along North-South fault lines.

The reasons are a complex interaction of the contexts (universal to territorial violence in the last quarter of the twentieth century), the causes (specific to the Falklands), and the specific negotiations and parallel use of force that comprises crisis politico-military statecraft.

The overarching context is the nation-state system, with its emphasis on sovereign autonomy. Sovereignty in turn is focused on territory and thus puts it at the center of international affairs. While the value of territory in National Interest terms has declined, its importance to National Honor has, if anything, increased. This is particularly true for the radical nonaligned states, many of whom reject group norms which are useful to older and even bloc states; they discount the competing notion of a political ''people'' defined by itself in favor of historical or perceived territorial integrity. Increasingly well armed by a world arms bazaar with smart, high-technology weaponry, those states will act against major powers as well as, and indeed in preference to, more lightly armed neighbors. This is due to the delegitimization of the political holdings of First World states even where preferred by the population. The radicalization of the nonaligned has had a paralegal effect with the United Nations resolutions and paralysis of the collective security system, which favors the acquisition of territory, especially by ''progressive'' states, even against the wishes of populations. If each of these contexts is at first glance only permissive, the cumulative and collective effect over several decades has reached the dimensions of a political phenomenon that is motivating if not causal for territorial violence.

The parties to the Falklands crisis contested not only National Interests in possession and exclusive use of the territory in question, but centuries of what they perceived to be a zero-sum game for National Honor. Their actions and even their negotiating strategies tended to exacerbate rather than ameliorate the problem. They each invoked, and indeed created, domestic political opinion in support of their cause, and in turn became its prisoners at crucial junctures.

Negotiation failures in the three principal mediation tries call into sharp focus the underlying difficulties for third-party mediation which have given it such a sad track record in this century. In the first round, Argentina could not take force seriously; the mediator could not convince either party that there was urgency (and penalty to failure) to compromise; and the United Kingdom could not take seriously the mediator's allowance for the National Interest and National Honor of the other party. In the second round, the British could not control force with the precision that the paradigm of trading off force and diplomacy posits; the mediators were not truly communicating with each other or between the parties; and Argentina was seeking new mediations fora just as the focus of the crisis was becoming all but exclusively military—the continuation of political tacit bargaining is not the same as the continuation of real negotiation. In the third round, compromise was facilitated but could not be turned to agreement due to the timing and increasing incompatibility of simultaneous fighting and negotiating.

That dynamic is key to the relationship between force and diplomacy. That relationship can be (but cannot always be kept) complementary. In the South Atlantic autumn of 1982, the playing out of diplomacy was exhausted almost in direct proportion to the shift in the nature of projected force: Argentine forces built up their defense capacity in direct proportion to elapsed time in the opening weeks of the crisis, but then leveled off and, indeed, in their own perception began to decline as draftees suffered exposure and morale problems. They became a wasting asset; they had in a passive sense to be used or lost as an instrument of the state. Initially, British forces were a primarily diplomatic instrument, dispatched, so many including the Junta perceived, simply to pressure Argentina. Upon entering Argentine home waters and Argentine land-based airspace, the instrument of diplomatic pressure became, sooner than its wielders realized, a vulnerable and wasting asset unless turned to military purpose. So turned, it not only solved its own vulnerability (a push effect on decision makers), but also reestablished the politico-military credibility for which it had been publicly dispatched (a pull effect).

Both dynamics were underappreciated by mediators, those Argentines who saw the stated purpose of forcible repossession as a bluff and, at least as regards the speed of events, by the U.K. Government itself, which suffered (long past the point when many attributed pure political lust for military victory) for too long from the illusion that its options remained open.

The strength of the political history, the countervailing politico-legal norms established by the radicalization of the nonaligned U.N. majority, the world arms bazaar, and the trend toward national assertiveness through armed force in the name of unredeemed territory are little diminished by the war in the South Atlantic. The tendency for National Honor in several complex forms to predominate over National Interest was, if anything, reinforced by the crisis.

Only by working together on non-sovereignty questions and unilaterally but constructively on questions sovereign can the United Kingdom and Argentina avoid the sterile dialogue of the years before the Falklands War, seek the realistic limits of what National Interest and National Honor will allow to be negotiated, and reach a peace that both accept not as ideal but as just and therefore lasting.

APPENDICES

FALKLANDS CHRONOLOGY

1494

June   Pope Alexander VI arranges the Treaty of Tordesillas by which the Vatican attempts to solve the problems of Catholic Spain and Portugal in their maritime and colonial expeditions. The Pope's Line of Demarcation gave (for those recognizing his temporal authority) all lands discovered to the east of the meridian 100 leagues west of the Azores to Portugal, and all those to the west of that meridian to Spain.

1498   Columbus reaches Venezuela on his third voyage.

1499–1500   Brazil is discovered by Europe.

1502

April   Three ships out of Lisbon with the Florentine Amerigo Vespucci as geographer are driven in an Antarctic April storm in an area between 52 degrees and 53 degrees south along an unknown coast of about 20 leagues seen intermittently in dark and storm and abandoned as the expedition returned north for Portugal; possibly the first sighting of the Falkland Islands or the Jason Islands to the northwest.

1520   Pietro Appiano's World Map shows a cluster of islands in the middle of the South Atlantic. A map of two years later by Pedro Reinel shows the islands closer to the southern coast of South America and bases this on reports by Esteban Gomes returning (deserting) from a Magellan ship to Seville in 1521.

1592	British vessel *Desire* sights the Falkland Islands and John Davis is claimed to have discovered them. The Islands are again sighted by Hawkins in 1594 and by a Dutch vessel in 1600.
1690	A British party led by Captain John Strong lands on the Falklands and names the body of water between the two principal islands the Falklands Sound in honor of the Treasurer of the Royal Navy.
1713	
13 July	The Second Treaty of Utrecht. Argentina holds that Article 8 protected Spanish claim to areas in the New World against British claims or actions.
1764	Antoine Louis de Bougainville, sailing from St. Malo, France, established the Islands' first settlement at Port Louis on East Falkland. The Islands were designated Les Malouines (or las Islans Malvinas in Spanish America) and were taken in the name of King Louis XV.
1765–66	Britain's Commodore John Byron takes possession of the Islands in the name of George III and establishes a settlement at Port Egmont on Saunders Island.
1966–67	The Spanish Government purchases the French settlement and France's claim to the Falklands for 24,000 pounds. A Spanish Governor of the Falklands is appointed, under the jurisdiction of the province of Buenos Aires. Spain garrisons a settlement at Port Louis, renaming it Soledad.
1770	A Spanish force of 1,400 men expels the British garrison from Port Egmont.
1771	The British expel 1,400 Spaniards from Port Egmont and Spain and Britain almost go to war which is averted by negotiations. The British renegotiate their return but Spain reserves its prior right to sovereignty.
1774	British settlers withdraw from Port Egmont leaving a plaque claiming sovereignty for King George III. Spanish governors, under the authority of the viceroyalty of La Plata in Buenos Aires, govern the Falkland Islands without effective legal or military challenge from 1774 to 1811.
1806	British troops land on the South American mainland and march on Buenos Aires. They surrender two months after taking the town on August 12, 1806. The Spanish viceroy surrenders military and civil power to the leader of volunteer troops who defeated the British and a legislative council (''cabildo'').
1807	British troops again try and fail to take Buenos Aires.
1810	In opposition to the Bonapartist Spanish throne, the governing junta of the provinces of the Rio de la Plata takes over

	the viceroyalty in the name of the deposed Ferdinand VII. The commandant of the Falklands requests payment for his services from the governing junta.
1811	The Spanish/Buenos Aires garrison is removed because it is too expensive, and a plaque similar to that of the British is left behind as a symbol of sovereignty. Spanish forces withdraw from the Falklands.
1816	The Republic of Buenos Aires (Argentina) declares its formal independence from Spain.
1820s	Argentina garrisons the unpopulated Malvinas on the basis of a disputed version of a secret eighteenth-century Hispano-British negotiation.
1823	The Government of Buenos Aires designates a Governor of the Falkland Islands. U.S. President James Monroe first enunciates the Monroe Doctrine to the U.S. Congress.
1825	United Kingdom recognizes Argentine independence.
1829	Louis Vernet, under the authority of the Buenos Aires Government, revives the settlement of Puerto de la Soledad. Buenos Aires declares it the capital of a military commandancy of the Falkland Islands. Great Britain protests the establishment as inconsistent with British sovereignty.
1831	The United States requests that the Argentine Minister of Foreign Affairs punish or extradite Luis Vernet for the seizure of two U.S. schooners and a cargo in the Falklands during 1831.
	First U.S. armed action against a Latin power—a U.S. Navy warship routs fishermen and whalers from the Falkland Islands. On December 30, the U.S.S. *Lexington* enters the harbor at Puerto Soledad and destroys the settlement.
1832	Puerto Soledad settlement is reestablished by Argentina.
1833	British landing party of HMS *Clio* expels 25 Argentine soldiers and reestablishes British settlement on January 2, 1833.
	British forces evict the Argentine settlement from Puerto Soledad. The United States is said to assist Britain's takeover of the Islands in the first contravention of the Monroe Doctrine (1823).
1839	U.S. Supreme Court case on the schooner seizures evokes Executive Branch position that the Falklands are not Argentine territory.
1843	Formal civil government is established by Great Britain for the Falkland Islands and Dependencies.
1852	The Falklands come under the control of the Royal Falklands Company.

1884   Argentina formally reaffirms its sovereignty over the Falk-
                              lands based on proximity to the Argentine mainland.

1904   Argentines construct a whaling station at Grytviken on South
                              Georgia. A meteorological station is operated by the Argen-
                              tines from 1905 to 1943. The U.K. grants lease for 500
                              acres to the Argentine Fishing Company in 1906.

1908   South Georgia, the South Orkneys, the South Shetlands, the
                              Sandwich Islands, and Graham Land become part of the
                              Falklands Dependencies.

1913   Negotiations are opened on ceding the South Orkneys to Ar-
                              gentina. The talks deadlock. In 1925, Argentina unilaterally
                              establishes a wireless station on Lourie Island and applies for
                              an international call sign. In 1927 and 1928, negotiations
                              again fail to go beyond the preliminary stage.

1947   Argentina declares at the Rio Treaty Conference that it does
                              not recognize European colonies or possessions. Regarding
                              colonies or possessions of European territories within the se-
                              curity zone established by the Rio Treaty, Argentina reserved
                              its position of sovereignty over the Falkland Islands, South
                              Georgia, South Sandwich, and the Argentine Antarctic sector
                              (presumably the entire British claim). The United States held
                              that the Rio Treaty does not effect questions of sovereignty.
                              (The radio station continues to operate and other effective
                              exercises of sovereignty or civil government continue at
                              Gritviken.)

                              Argentina lands mountain troops from two cruisers on De-
                              ception Island in the Antarctic. British base across the harbor
                              from Argentines calls for military assistance, but Argentine
                              ships depart before Royal Navy arrives.

1947–48   Argentine cruisers and six destroyers conduct maneuvers off
                              the Falklands. British naval task force is sent in reaction and
                              Argentine maneuvers cease.

1948   Special department founded in Argentine Foreign Ministry to
                              press claim. Navy makes shows of force and presence Ant-
                              arctic. From 1948 Argentina demonstrates the political will
                              and military capability to recover the Falklands. HMS *Ni-
                              geria* is sent to the scene by the British.

                              Britain yields to force and international opinion and with-
                              draws from Palestine.

1950   The United Kingdom repossesses the Argentine meteorologi-
                              cal station at Gritviken in South Georgia and returns all
                              property to the Argentine Fishing Company.

                              Argentine Senate and Chamber of Deputies declare Falklands
                              to be Argentine territory.

1952	British expedition to Deception Island to rebuild meterological station which burned in 1948 is evicted by Argentine troops.
1953	Attempted naval occupation of Deception Island by Argentines. HMS *Snipe* sent by British to expel intruders.
1955	Argentina rejects jurisdiction of International Court of Justice or of any other tribunal.
1956	The Argentine Navy summers on Southern Thule on the South Sandwich Islands. The next year, the Argentines attempt to investigate a source of bootleg alcohol at Gritviken. As they had in 1947, the British authorities refuse to let the officer land without a passport.
1957	Argentina establishes the national territory of Tierra del Fuego, Antarctica, and the South Atlantic Islands, including the Falklands Dependencies.
1960s	Argentina reasserts its claim at the U.N. HMG's internal options include developing the Islands jointly under a leaseback. However, a gradual shift in British policy begins under pressure from the Falklands lobby to take account of the wishes rather than just the interests of the Kelpers. The British diplomatic counterthrust is based on self-determination, which meshes nicely with emerging Decolonization doctrine and practice at the U.N.
1960	The U.N. General Assembly passes Resolution 1514 on the granting of independence to colonial peoples. Self-determination, nationality, and independence (territorial integrity) are asserted as paramount principles in international relations.
1961	The Antarctic is demilitarized.
1962	The Special Committee on Decolonization includes the Falkland Islands in the List of Non–Self-Governing Territories. The United Kingdom is the administering authority.

Great Britain separates the British Antarctic territory from the Falklands Dependencies. |
| *1963* | Britain withdraws from Kenya. |
| *1964* | Argentina asserts its claim to the Falkland Islands in the Decolonization context before the United Nations, resulting the next year in a General Assembly resolution inviting Argentina and the U.K. to proceed to immediate negotiations. Reference is made to the declaration on the granting of independence and to the *interests* of the Islanders. Similar resolutions continued be passed, but negotiations did not lead to a settlement. |

1965 16 December	Resolution 2065 urging Britain and Argentina to negotiate a peaceful solution to their long-standing dispute on sovereignty over the Falkland Islands approved by the United Nations General Assembly.
1966	The U.K. and Argentina open 16 years of bilateral negotiations concerning the Falkland Islands.
	G.A. Resolution 2065 urges the parties to seek peaceful resolution of the Falklands dispute.
September	Military coup d'état in Argentina. Argentine Navy shells a Soviet trawler. British Foreign Secretary visits Buenos Aires for talks on claim.
	Argentine civilians calling themselves "Condor Commandos" invade the Falklands in a hijacked airliner. Twenty Argentine symbolic "invaders" who land in the Falklands become national heroes. British send HMS *Puma* to Falklands. This was the penultimate U.K. naval response, the last of which would be in 1977.
	Britain's Ministry of Defence renounces carriers and landing of troops against sophisticated opposition outside the range of land-based air cover.
	From 1966 on, the U.K. demonstrates an increasing willingness to compromise on the Falklands (in contrast to Argentine Military Government belligerency) and an increasing reluctance to make naval shows of force in response. However, concessions are always on issues other than sovereignty, while no Government states or shows willingness to defend sovereignty.
1967	An organized Falklands lobby emerges.
1968	Chalfont mission to Buenos Aires and Falklands.
	London moves from focus on wishes of Islanders toward a focus on their interests.
1969	Argentina offers to consider lifting a ban on direct communications between the mainland and the Falklands.
1970	Talks begin in London between Argentina and Britain. Falkland Islands delegates included.
	Military coup d'état in Argentina. British naval presence reduced to visits by ice-patrol ship.
1971	
August	Britain and Argentina reach agreement on air and sea communications, postal services, educational and medical facilities for Falkland Islanders in Buenos Aires, and customs measures.
	The Iranian Navy seizes the strategically important islands of Greater and Lesser Tunb at the mouth of the Persian Gulf.

British inaction in face of Iran's seizure of islands in the Persian Gulf.

1974   G.A. Resolution 3160 again urges peaceful resolution to the Falklands dispute.

Vice-Admiral Juan José Lombardo (later CNO and Commander of Operations for the Falklands invasion) is said to have submitted a plan for invasion to President Peron.

British and Argentine agreement to allow trade between Argentina and the Islands and to allow an Argentine state company, Yacimientos y Petroliferos Fiscales, the monopoly rights to supply the Islanders with petroleum products.

Argentine press and opposition politicians demand invasion of Falklands.

China seizes the Paracel Islands in the South China Sea.

South Vietnam takes the Spratley Islands, retaken by the Vietnamese Liberation Navy in 1976.

Turkey invades and occupies Eastern Cyprus. World inaction in face of Turkish action.

1975   Falklands offshore gas and oil potential is rumored as a result of geological survey led by D. H. Griffeths of Birmingham University (U.K.) to be nine times greater than the reserves of the North Sea, which are bringing prosperity to Britain.

Indonesia invades and occupies East Timor.

Attempted military coup in Argentina.

1976   The OAS Inter-American Juridical Committee finds for Argentina on the question of Sovereignty on the Falkland Islands.

The Shackleton Report on the economic viability of the islands calls krill the world's largest untapped source of protein.

Military coup d'etat in Argentina. Argentina occupies Southern Thule. British response is silence.

Shackleton visits Falklands. Argentina initiates withdrawal of Ambassadors in protest against Shackleton visit. Argentine navy fires on British ship.

4 February   The Argentine destroyer *Almirante Storni* fires on and attempts to board the British research vessel Shackleton seventy miles north of Stanley and 400 miles off the Argentine coast. Argentina announces that it considers the Shackleton was in Argentine territorial waters (see *Times of London*, 6 February 1976).

February	Britain increase the Royal Marine contingent on the Falklands from twenty to thirty-seven troopers following attempted seizure of the scientific research ship Shackleton.
	Argentina establishes a *scientific base on Southern Thule* on the South Sandwich Islands. (Remains in place through 1982.)
	Argentina threatens the use of force during the Shackleton mission (as it would again the following year).
1977	Admiral Emilio Eduardo Massera advances a Falklands invasion plan drafted by (1982 Naval Commander-in-Chief) Jorge Anaya.
	Anglo-Argentine talks are resumed. Argentine Navy commissions translation of "Gunboat Diplomacy." Argentine Navy uses force to capture six Soviet trawlers and factory ship on high seas. Britain backs Chile against Argentina over Beagle Channel dispute.
	HMS *Dreadnought*, *Phoebe*, *Alacrity* and two auxilaries sent to South Atlantic.
July	Secret talks are held in Rome on the future of the Falkland Islands (see the *Times of London*, 14 July 1977).
December	The parties meet in New York to discuss Falklands.
1977–80	Britain and Argentina hold talks in London, New York, Brazil and Peru. (*The New York Times*, May 19, 1982)
1978	Argentina assembles a large military force and engages in a show of force threatening invasion of the Beagle Channel Islands. (A real operation with troops already on Chilean soil is cancelled when the U.S. arranges Papal mediation).
	Successful Argentine naval demonstration against Chile. Anglo-Argentine talks on Falklands adjourned.
10 May	Discussion of the Argentine scientific base on Southern Thule in the South Sandwich continues.
December	Argentina orders 4 Meko 360 frigates from Germany's Blohm & Voss shipyards.
1979	Constantino Sergio Davidoff signs contract to scrap whaling station on South Georgia with Edinburgh shipping company.
	Argentine ambassadors return to their posts following recall for consultations. Argentine Navy orders 14 Super Etendard aircraft from France with Exocet missiles.
1980	Lord Carrington confirms that the November 27 discussions took place but states that sovereignty will not be transferred to Argentina.
	Britain's Ridley fails to persuade Falkland Islanders of the need for concessions to Argentina.

Iran imposes her will on the U.S.A. in seizure of Tehran Embassy.

U.N. General Assembly supports independence for Belize in spite of Guatemalan claim.

Argentine pilots begin Super Etendard training in Brittany.

2 January	Council on Hemispheric Affairs calls Argentina the worst human rights violator for third year in row.
4 January	The 34th U.N. General Assembly's Regular Session resumes on deadlocked U.N. Security Council seat; ends 1/7 with election of Mexico on 155 ballot, 133–3–8, after Cuba and Colombia withdraw.
26 March	President's Special Representative for Nuclear Affairs Gerard C. Smith in Argentina for talks on nuclear policy, Soviet grain shipments, human rights.
15–17 May	Brazilian President Joao Baptista de Oliverira Figueiredo visits Argentine President Jorge Rafael Videla; they sign economic and nuclear cooperation accords.
Summer	During his first year at post, British Ambassador to Buenos Aires Anthony Williams raises the possibility of Argentine invasion of the Falklands in reporting to London.
24–25 July	Permanent Council of the Organization of American States (OAS) meets in Washington, adopts Resolution 308 (432/80) by a vote of (16–3–4) deploring Bolivia coup, asking Inter-American Commission on Human Rights to look into violations of same.
6 August	Argentine President Jorge Rafael Videla denies active Argentine participation.
3 October	Argentine Junta ends three-day impasse, chooses Army head Gen. Roberto Eduardo Viola to succeed Videla, March 1981.
8 October	Brazil frees its last political prisoner.
13 November	UNGA, by a vote of 111–24–5, elects Panama on 23d ballot to fill Jamaica's UNSC seat after Cuba and Costa Rica withdraw.
30 November	In first vote in seven years, Uruguayans overwhelmingly reject new constitution that would give military (which first took over in 1973) permanent control.
2 December	Idea of leaseback fails in British House of Commons.
24 December	Argentina rejects December 12 Papal plan for settling Beagle Islands dispute.

1981

28 January– 1 February	Peru-Ecuador border war erupts in Andes Cordillera del Condor area claimed by both sides. Argentina, Brazil, Chile

	and U.S., guarantors of 1942 Rio Protocol, meet in Brasilia, order cease-fire February 1.
2 February	Organization of American States (OAS) Foreign Ministers meet in emergency session in Washington. On February 9, the *New York Times* reports that resolution asks for cease-fire but leaves solution up to Rio guarantors.
February	Shell and Esso Argentina announce oil discoveries in the Magellan Straits.
	Further talks are held in New York; a British proposal for a freeze on sovereignty talks while both countries cooperate in economic development of the Falklands is rejected by Argentina.
8–13 February	Ninety-four nonaligned nations meet in New Delhi.
27 February	Argentina arrests 8 human-rights activists, seizes files on 6,000 missing persons.
16–17 March	Argentine President-designate, Gen. Roberto Eduardo Viola visits in Washington.
19 March	President Reagan asks U.S. Congress to lift ban on military aid to Argentina.
20 March	Former Argentine President Isabel Martinez de Peron (arrested March 24, 1976) given eight-year prison term; freed July 6; flies to Spain July 10.
29 March	Viola sworn in as Argentina's 38th President; succeeds Jorge Rafael Videla (named March 1976); presents 13-man Cabinet, including 7 civilians.
30 June	The British Foreign & Commonwealth Office (FCO) reviews policy options should the idea of Leaseback to the U.K. of the Islands by Argentina not be accepted. One clear possibility was noted to be Argentine military action.
	(Argentine services had indeed begun some specific planning on a contingency basis during June, apparently unknown to the Junta.)
8 July	A July 1 U.S. letter to Congress says President Reagan will back development loans to Argentina, Chile, Paraguay, and Uruguay based on State Department determination of ''significant'' human-rights improvement.
August	Argentine Foreign Ministry approves South Georgia scrap steel recovery.
September	(Argentine Foreign Minister Camilion meets with U.K.'s Lord Carrington and arrives at the assessment that a Falklands solution is not a priority in U.K. foreign policy.)
15 September–18 December	Belize elected 156th U.N. member on September 25.

20 September	British Honduras becomes independent as Belize with George C. Price as Prime Minister.
30 September	U.S. Senate in voice vote repeals Argentina military sales ban.
	Argentina talks delivery on the ARA *Granville*, third of the trio of "A–69" French-built frigates.
6 October	U.S. United Nations Ambassador Jeane J. Kirkpatrick sends private letter to 40 countries asking for explanation of "malicious" anti-U.S. stand in September 28 Nonaligned Foreign Ministers' communiqué.
14 October	New Falkland Islands Legislative Council elected.
1 November	Antigua becomes independent as Antigua and Barbuda under Prime Minister Vere Bird.
7 November	Over 100,000 people in Buenos Aires protest Military rule, lack of jobs.
20 November	Viola temporarily steps down because of heart trouble.
mid-November	Delivery is completed to Argentina of 5 Super Etendard aircraft with one Exocet missile each.
7 December	(Admiral Anaya takes delivery of 5 of the 14 Super Etendard aircraft.)
9 December	(The Argentine Service Chiefs decide that General Viola must go.)
15 December	U.N. Security Council ends deadlock begun October 27, chooses Javier Perez de Cuellar (Peru) to succeed Kurt Waldheim (Austria; elected 1971) as U.N. Secretary General for five-year term as of January 1982; approved in UNGA by acclamation, December 15.
December	Anaya and Galtieri discuss invasion.
18 December	Viola removed; Argentina Army Chief Gen. Leopoldo Galtieri names Social Minister Adm. Carlos Lacoste Interim President; Galtieri sworn in as President December 22.
21 December	Argentine businessman Constantino Davidoff makes scrap salvage survey on South Georgia.
29 December	Argentine Air Force Chief Brigadier General Lami Dozo is told of the decision to invade and poses no objection since the decision is still preliminary. The Chief of Staff of the Army is not informed at this juncture.
1982	
3 January	Argentine General Oswaldo Garcia of the V Corps is contacted, but not informed, of option of using force and Operations Chief of the Joint Staff is picked to be the Governor of occupied islands but not told of the plan. Admiral Lombardo

of the Navy is still the only non–Service Chief fully brought in on the planning at this point, though Garcia is told by Lombardo to begin developing the capability to operate jointly with the Navy. His Corps area being next to the largest naval base (Puerto Belgrano), he assumes his mission is Chile and begins work on vertical envelopement and command and control for his new crop of conscripts to arrive at the end of February. (Argentina releases some draftees on schedule.)

6 January	(The Junta firms up the option of using force if the February 27–29 New York talks are not productive. Press leaks report Anaya's plan to send a Military Ambassador to London.)
12 January	Invasion Planning cell is established with Plan Blue set for July 1982.
20 January	(Ambassador Ortiz de Rosas briefs Galtieri equating the British insistence on the wishes of the Islanders with delay.)
	(The invasion-planning group has its first meeting.)
	(Decision taken. The Argentine position is to be conveyed to the British Ambassador on 27 January with the request that an answer be accorded in the New York negotiations.)
	(D-Day for the Falklands (barring British negotiating concessions) is set at 9 July 1982, and later moved up to May 15.)
24 January	(*La Prensa* news article by Rouco says that the United States would acquiesce in military action against the Falklands and sketches out the idea that Argentina now has a firm schedule for recovering the Islands.)
27 January	(Argentine *bout de papier* containing proposal for a permanent working group on the Falklands is provided to the British Ambassador in Buenos Aires.)
February	
first week	(Argentine Foreign Minister Costa Mendez is told of the decision that invasion is the alternative to negotiating success.)
3 February	(British Ambassador Williams protests South Georgia visit in December of Argentine businessman Davidoff to assess the scrap operation.) Anaya now controlling the invasion decision.
12 February	The Latin America Weekly Report discloses that Galtieri has obtained the neutrality of Uruguay in event of a seizure of the Falklands.
15 February	(Military planning is completed. Argentine Ambassador Enrique Ros is briefed on the plan and sent to New York.)
23 February	(Argentine businessman Constantino Davidoff visits U.K. Embassy in Buenos Aires.) (Will visit again for final time 9 March to notify of departure for South Georgia.)

26–27 February	Britain and Argentina hold talks in New York.
28 February	(Both sides issue a positive joint statement at the conclusion of the New York talks.)
1 March	(The Junta repudiates Ros's statement in New York and, instead, states that Argentina will pursue the course which best suits its interests.)
2 March	A joint Anglo-Argentine statement describes the February 26–27 talks in New York as "cordial and positive."
	Argentine Foreign Minister Costa Mendez sends ultimatum on concessions to U.K., threatening to end negotiations. Unless there is a quick solution, Argentina threatens to choose a procedure which better suits its interests.
3 March	Richard Luce, British Minister at the negotiations, tells the House of Commons the talks were positive.
4 March	Announcement by the Argentine Government of democratization measures and multiparty system, per promises of December 1981.
8 March	U.S. Assistant Secretary of State for Inter-American Affairs Thomas Enders visits Buenos Aires.
9 March	Davidoff informs British Embassy in Buenos Aires of his departure for South Georgia.
11 March	The *Bahia Buen Suceso* is scheduled to sail with the scrap party.
	Argentine plane makes emergency landing at Stanley. (Some believe it may have been a familiarization and reconaissance disguised as emergency landing.)
12 March	The *Latin America Weekly Report* says Argentine President Leopoldo Galtieri, installed December 2, is considering a range of options on the Falklands, *including invasion.*
19 March	About 39–42 Argentine workers for a scrap-metal firm land at Leith Harbor on South Georgia to dismantle the old whaling station. They have White Cards but they are not stamped for entry by the United Kingdom. Some of the party raise the Argentine flag. Members of a 26-man British Antarctic Survey team station nearby ask them to lower the flag and get immigration clearance or leave.
20 March	(Galtieri informs Argentine Ambassador Eduardo Roca of the contingency military alternative.)
21 March	Argentine ship departs South Georgia, leaving the scrap-metal workers there.
23 March	Luce tells the House of Commons that Argentina claims Government knew nothing of South Georgia landing. Britain says it wants the remaining workers off the Island (but it has

only a 3,600-ton ice-breaker, HMS *Endurance*, in the vicinity). Luce commits HMG to defend the Falklands.

24 March   First British intelligence assessments indicate Argentine intent to invade in South Atlantic. Signals point to 1 April as date.

Ambassador Eduardo Roca arrives early to take over Argentine U.N. Mission.

25 March   British icebreaker HMS *Endurance* reports that Argentine vessel *Bahia Paraiso* at Leith Harbor on South Georgia flys the pennant of the Senior Officer of the Antarctic Squadron. She is operating 3 landing craft and a military helicopter. (Embarked are Special Forces Group for Plan Alfa under Navy Lt. Alfredo Astiz, whose lead element landed at 0100 hours.)

British government protests strongly but scrap workers stay.

(British nuclear sub HMS *Superb* departs for Falklands.)

26 March   *Noticias Argentinas* reports Argentine Government ordered the landing of provisions on St. Peter of South Georgia islands, to supply the group of Argentine citizens who have been there since Sunday. Also reports that the British Government has authorized the use of force to evict them. Spanish news service reports that the British Navy ship *Endurance* is near the Island with 12 Marines awaiting Admiralty orders.

(Invasion Plan Blue is advanced to April 1–3.)

News Service ANSA cable from London reports that the British Government has authorized the use of force as the ultimate resort in case the Argentine citizens refuse to leave the Island, according to a report by the *Daily Telegraph*.

Argentine Foreign Minister Nicanor Costa Mendez reports that the Government has ordered the Navy warship *Bahia Paraiso* to go to the area of South Georgia.

100 Argentine Marines of Alpha force under Capt. Alfredo Astiz at Leith Harbor join scrap-workers but are seen by Royal Marines. London says no counterattack.

British intelligence in Buenos Aires obtains top-secret Argentine plans to invade the Falklands, according to later reports from the *Times* and *Daily Telegraph* of London in dispatches from the Argentine capital. *Times* quotes an intelligence expert as saying the invasion plan is sent in code to the U.K. Foreign Office which chooses to ignore it in what newspaper calls a complete error of judgement.

27 March   Latin-Reuter reports: "The Buenos Aires newspaper *Clarin* today cited naval sources as saying that the [Argentine]

guided missile corvettes *Drummond* and *Grandville* had been sent to that area and added that there had been an increase in the activity at the naval bases at Mar del Plata and Belgrano.''

ARA *Granville* and *Drummond* are announced to be enroute South Georgia.

Argentina provides British a *bout de papier* proposing reactivation of talks.

28 March   (The Argentine fleet sails from Puerto Belgrano.)

28 March   U.S. Assistant Secretary of State Thomas Enders, fending off press queries about the Salvador elections, says there is a story brewing in the South Atlantic.

Argentina tells Britain it will not regularize or withdraw the scrap-metal workers and reiterates its claim to the Falklands.

29 March   Britain says it is still pursuing a diplomatic solution. (British nuclear-powered submarine, HMS *Superb*, has probably left for the Falklands between March 25–29.)

British Foreign Secretary Lord Carrington tells Parliament Argentine invasion has created a potentially dangerous situation.

Press says Soviet Union matches U.S. South Atlantic photographic satellites KH-ll and Big Bird with Cosmos 1345 and 1346 and that at least six more would be launched during the crisis.

30 March   U.S. offer to mediate South Georgia dispute rejected by Argentina as not addressing the whole Falklands/Malvinas question.

Headed by the aircraft carrier *25 de Mayo*, an Argentine naval force steams toward the islands. Two missile-carrying frigates arrive at South Georgia.

U.K. Joint Intelligence Committee notes five main ships of Argentine Navy have put to sea with troops embarked. South Atlantic forces told to expect invasion. Commander of the Argentine Super Etendard Squadron is ordered to ready and arm the Exocets (French technicians withdrawn).

31 March   British intelligence confirms that the Argentine Fleet is bound for the Falkland Islands (not South Georgia). Prime Minister Thatcher calls a crisis cabinet meeting and asks President Reagan to intervene with Argentine President Leopoldo Galtieri. Thatcher later says this was the first time she knew for sure an invasion was coming.

Thomas Enders tells U.S. Secretary of State Alexander Haig that the United States Government has had an assurance

from the Argentine Foreign Minister that the Argentines
were not contemplating any military action.

31 March/1 April   (Final Argentine military decision to issue "jump off order"
to invade the Falklands.)

31 March   Press reports in the United Kingdom disclose the deployment
of the submarine to the Falklands by the U.K.

1 April   Operation Rosario is put into play.

Argentine Foreign Minister Nichanor Costa Mendez declines
the offer of a special British emissary and informs the British
Ambassador of Buenos Aires that the diplomatic channel is
closed as a means of settling the Falklands dispute.

The United Kingdom calls for an urgent meeting of the Security Council concerning an imminent invasion by Argentina. The President of the Council issues a statement on
behalf of the Council urging restraint on both parties.

The Argentine government asks the Organization of American States to study the Argentine-British confrontation over
South Georgia Island.

(Earliest date of any combat effectiveness for new 1982 conscripts in Argentina's military draft.)

United Kingdom letter of April 1 states that the U.K. has
good reason to believe that Argentinian armed forces are
about to invade the Falkland Islands and asks for an immediate meeting of the U.N. Security Council.

Argentine letter of April 1 brings to the attention of the Security Council the situation of grave tension between Argentina and the United Kingdom resulting from differences over
the entry of Argentine employees of a private company into
South Georgia.

According to Argentine sources, U.S. Ambassador Harry
Schlaudeman meets with Galtieri.

Reagan reaches Galtieri, urging restraint. Having been put
off for almost 24 hours, he spends an hour on the costs of an
invasion and listening to Galtieri's catalogue of Argentina's
territorial case. Galtieri says that time has run out.

U.N. Secretary General Perez de Cuellar issues press statements appealing for restraint. He also meets with the Argentine and British U.N. Ambassadors. The United Kingdom
calls for an urgent meeting of the Security Council and announces that an Argentine invasion will likely take place on
April 2.

Statement of April 1 by the President of the Security Council
issued after consultation among members, expressing concern about the tension in the region of the Islands and calling

on the Governments of Argentina and the United Kingdom to exercise restraint and refrain from the use or threat of force. Included in the text is the United Nations Secretary-General's appeal for maximum restraint.

2 April
Two thousand Argentine Marines capture East Falkland with three casualties. British Governor Rex Hunt orders the 67 Royal Marines to surrender after three hours of resistance.

Argentina's President Leopoldo Galtieri announces that Argentine forces have landed on the Falklands to reestablish Argentine sovereignty. He says to cheering crowds that the Islands are no longer the Falklands, now they are the Malvinas.

The British Government announces the severing of diplomatic relations with Argentina. It also announces that a large naval task force is en route to the Falklands.

Argentine dinner in Washington for U.S. Ambassador to the U.N. Ambassador to the U.N. Jeane Kirkpatrick and other U.S. officials.

3 April
Argentine Marines capture the 22-man British South Georgia Royal Marine landing party and British Antarctic Survey team. The South Sandwich Islands have already had an Argentine station ashore since 1976.

Argentina states that its displacement of the United Kingdom in the Falklands deprives the United Kingdom of any legitimate claim in Antarctica.

The U.N. Security Council reconvenes on the Falklands, adopting Resolution 502 (1982) demanding the immediate cessation of hostilities, withdrawal of Argentine forces, and calling on both Governments to seek a diplomatic solution to the dispute. Resolution 502 brands the Argentine invasion a breach of peace. Panama casts the only vote against 502, with China, the USSR, Poland, and Spain abstaining.

Argentina announces it is breaking relations with Britain and orders British diplomats to leave Argentina.

4 April
Severe restrictions on 1,800 British inhabitants of the Islands implemented by Argentine military government.

5 April
A 36-ship task force sets off from Portsmouth, England, for the 8,000-mile trip to the Falklands. British Foreign Secretary Lord Carrington takes upon himself the humiliation for the intelligence failure in the assessment of Argentine military intentions and resigns along with Luce. Thatcher refuses to accept the resignation of Defense Secretary John Nott.

Costa Mendez requests support from the members of the Organization of American States in battle against what he calls British colonialism.

In a radio message, the British Government advises British subjects to leave Argentina because of the crisis.

6 April   U.K. Foreign Secretary Francis Pym sends Haig a message: "Her Majesty's Government is determined to secure the withdrawal of Argentine forces and the restoration of British administration by whatever means are necessary; the role of the United States would be critical." Haig "said he was thinking of some sort of mediation; he surmises that it might be possible to think of negotiating with the U.K. and the Argentines some mixed administration to run the islands" (essay by Sir Nicholas Henderson, *The Economist*, November 12, 1983, p. 32).

U.K. asks European Economic Community (EEC) for economic sanctions against Argentina.

Secretary of State Alexander M. Haig, Jr., begins an effort to find a peaceful solution. Haig meets separately with Argentine Ambassador Esteban A. Takacs and British Ambassador Sir Nicholas Henderson in an effort to open discussions on a solution to the crisis.

7 April   U.K. Defense Minister Nott announces a 200-mile maritime exclusion zone around the Falklands, to take effect on April 12. He says the British will shoot first at Argentine vessels trying to run the blockade.

France, West Germany, Belgium, and Austria impose sanctions banning the sales of arms and military equipment to Argentina. Switzerland, the Netherlands, and Britain had already done so.

President Reagan directs Haig to sound out the U.K. and Argentina on ways of avoiding a military confrontation.

Argentina, in a ceremony at Stanley, the capital, extends its civil rule over the Islands, and Brig. Gen. Mario Benjamin Menendez is inducted as Governor.

8 April   U.S. Secretary of State Alexander Haig begins diplomatic shuttle between London and Buenos Aires, which is eventually to prove fruitless. He meets for six hours with senior British officials, who reaffirm their demands that Argentina withdraw from the Islands and that the Falkland Islanders support any agreement.

9 April   Falkland Islands debate in the OAS is postponed until Haig can report on his efforts to resolve the dispute.

Haig flies to Argentina.

Argentine letter of 9 April drawing attention to a communication the United Kingdom had sent to Argentina via the Swiss embassy in Buenos Aires stating that it would establish a maritime exclusion zone around the Falkland Islands, and also incorporating a reply to that communication, which Argentina regarded as a notification of blockade and an act of aggression.

United Kingdom letter of April 9 stating that Argentina was reinforcing its forces in the Falkland Islands, following the invasion on 2 April, and that, in those circumstances, the United Kingdom would establish from 12 April a maritime exclusion zone around the Islands within a 200-nautical-mile radius, and that from that time any Argentine warships and naval auxiliaries found within that zone would be treated as hostile and were liable to be attacked by British forces.

10 April   The European Common Market (EEC) imposes economic sanctions banning all imports from Argentina for one month.

Secretary Haig holds talks with Argentine Foreign Minister Nicanor Costa Mendez and with President Galtieri.

11 April   Haig returns to London with a three-point proposal for a simultaneous pullback of the British Navy and withdrawal of Argentine forces; British recognition of Argentine sovereignty; and interim administration of the Islands by the United States, Britain, and Argentina.

United Kingdom letter of 11 April stating, among other things, that the content of the U.N. Council Resolution 502 left no doubt that it was Argentina that bore responsibility for the current breach of the peace in the region. (Resolution 502 does not explicitly so state.)

12 April   Two hundred-mile maritime exclusion zone (Total Exclusion Zone) goes into effect.

Haig begins second round in London.

U.S. Delegate to the U.N. Jeane J. Kirkpatrick expresses optimism that Secretary of State Alexander M. Haig's mission to Britain and Argentina could achieve diplomatic solution and avoid clash over Falkland Islands. Another Reagan Administration official says Kirkpatrick's assessment is based on the fact that Argentine leaders told Haig that everything related to the crisis was negotiable except Argentina's claim of sovereignty over Falklands.

Haig speaks with British officials for 11 hours, then says problems remain because Argentina unexpectedly withdrew an unspecified concession on sovereignty.

Argentine officials and foreign diplomats in Buenos Aires say they are not optimistic about prospects of negotiated settlement of Falkland Islands crisis.

Peru letter of 12 April to which was attached the text of a telegram its Minister for Foreign Affairs had sent to the Foreign Affairs Minister of Argentina, the Secretary of State for Foreign Affairs of the United Kingdom, and the United States Secretary of State in connection with the events taking place in the Malvinas. In his telegram, the Peruvian Minister proposed that the parties concerned establish a 72-hour truce pending the exercise of good offices (to be provided by the United States Government) in order to prevent an armed confrontation.

Argentine letter of 12 April stating, among other things, that it was prepared to withdraw its forces from the Islands on the condition that the United Kingdom cease hostilities and not attempt to use Security Council Resolution 502 as an instrument for justifying a return to the previous colonial situation, thereby disregarding Argentina's sovereign rights and the appeals and resolutions of the United Nations urging the end of all colonial situations.

13 April

Peru's proposal for a 72-hour truce around the Falklands is accepted by Argentina but not by Great Britain.

Mr Haig returns to Washington to brief the President.

In Washington, D.C., the OAS in Resolution 359 expresses its concern over the conflict between Britain and Argentina and offers "friendly cooperation" in the search for reconciliation.

According to press reports, U.S. Administration sources said that the United States was providing Britain with fuel for its ships and aircraft at Ascension, intelligence on the disposition of Argentine forces, weather information, and a satellite communications channel.

United Kingdom letter of 13 April stating that it welcomed any statement on Argentina's readiness to withdraw its armed forces from the Falkland Islands but also stating that the United Kingdom considered that Argentina was not in a position to impose conditions not approved by the Security Council in its resolution.

United Kingdom letter of 13 April transmitting a copy of the telegram sent by its Secretary of State for Foreign and Commonwealth Affairs to the Minister for Foreign Affairs of Peru stating that the British Government appreciated the interest shown by the Peruvian Government in supporting efforts for a diplomatic solution, and that it hoped that that Government would impress on the Government of Argentina the need to comply with its obligations under international law.

Argentine letter of 13 April stating, among other things, that it welcomed the proposal of Peru and would refrain from any action that might lead to armed confrontation; but also stating that the Argentine Government would have no other alternative but to respond to the aggression in exercise of its right to self-defense if the British Government carried out its threats and established the blockade around the Malvinas Archipelago.

Belgian letter of 13 April in the annex of which the ten member states of the European Economic Community other things, stated that they had decided to apply a total embargo on the export of arms and military equipment to Argentina and that they would also take the necessary measures to prohibit all imports of Argentine origin into the Community.

Peruvian letter of 13 April to which was attached the text of a message from the Peruvian Foreign Minister transmitted to the United Kingdom relating to the Peruvian proposal for a 72-hour truce in the conflict over the Malvinas.

14 April

Thatcher tells the Commons that Argentine troops must leave the Falklands and Argentina must not test the TEZ if talks are to continue.

U.N. Secretary General Javier Perez de Cuellar discloses that he has formed a United Nations Secretariat Working Group the Falklands but will not mediate until Haig's efforts have been exhausted.

British officials in London and Washington are not optimistic about the chances of Haig reaching a solution before the British flotilla reaches Falklands.

U.S. President Reagan calls Argentine President Galtieri to again urge flexibility and restraint.

Panamanian U.N. letter of 14 April reiterates its support for the effective exercise of Argentine territorial sovereignty over the Malvinas Islands, South Georgia, and the South Sandwich Malvinas Islands, and stated that it was indignant that the British Government has decided to open hostilities against the Argentine nation.

Venezuelan letter of 14 April transmitting the text of a statement on the Malvinas situation made by its Minister for Foreign Affairs.

President Reagan announces that the Soviet Union is providing Argentina with sensitive military intelligence to monitor British Fleet movements.

Two Argentine patrol boats reportedly evade the 200-mile TEZ British "blockade" and arrive in Port Stanley without incident.

15–17 April	Argentine Fleet puts to sea while the U.K. Task Force is at Ascension.
15 April	During Haig's visit to Buenos Aires on April 15, Argentines put forward a proposal that Haig, in transmitting it to Pym, says is *not* something that he could urge the British Government to accept.

Argentine President Galtieri telephones President Reagan to discuss the crisis; President Reagan expresses to Galtieri his personal desire for a peaceful resolution of the dispute.

Argentina's only aircraft carrier and most of the rest of its fleet reportedly put out to sea from port 800 miles north of the Falklands.

Britain is finding Argentina's view of negotiation one-sided: "Their idea for troop withdrawals would heavily favor Argentina. At the end of the process, for instance, the British fleet would have had to return to British ports, whereas the Argentines would be only a few hundred miles away. British administration would be reestablished to a far lesser degree than under Haig's idea and there would be a disproportionate representation of Argentines on the executive and legislative councils. The proposals opened up the possibility of an influx of Argentines into the islands. Finally, (the Argentine) text would exclude our return to the status quo ante and did not preserve the principle that the islanders should choose their own future." (Essay by Sir Nicholas Henderson, *The Economist*, November 12, 1983, p. 28.)

16 April	Argentine's letter of 16 April stating that the initiation of negotiations with the intercession of the United States Secretary of State demonstrated its determination to find a peaceful solution to the dispute, and consequently that the Argentine side could not be accused of noncompliance with U.N. Security Council Resolution 502.

British government requisitions an additional 25 ships for its Atlantic Task Force.

17 April	Argentines reject a Haig proposal for provisional three-party administration of the Islands. They say sovereignty is not negotiable.
18 April	British Special Boat Squadron (SBS) and Special Air Service (SAS) units are put ashore in the Falklands.

U.S. officials are optimistic about Secretary of State Alexander Haig's efforts to find diplomatic solution.

Andean Pact countries, including Peru, announce their intention to increase trade with Argentina because of the EEC ban.

19 April	Great Britain requisitions more ships and an additional 900 men for the Falklands Task Force.

Haig returns to Washington from Buenos Aires with Argentine approval of British participation in a temporary administration.

Argentina announces that it will seek to invoke an inter-American defense treaty, known as the Rio Pact, over the objections of the United States.

Haig and the Argentines work on a plan for joint Argentine-British administration of the Islands. Argentines insist on a guarantee of eventual sovereignty. British say the plan appears to be unacceptable because it does not guarantee self-determination to the Falkland Islanders.

(The Junta adds clause 8 to its proposal, demanding an Argentine Governor for the Falklands.)

Perez de Cuellar quietly informs Britain and Argentina that he is available and provides each with an outline of what the U.N. could offer.

United Kingdom letter of 19 April, in the annex to which it states appreciation for the concern of the Peruvian Government in achieving a peaceful resolution of the situation in the Falkland Islands, but states that only after withdrawal of the Argentine forces would the right conditions exist for a negotiated solution to the dispute.

Haig's mediation efforts have apparently failed.

20 April   U.K Prime Minister Margaret Thatcher tells Parliament that proposals from Argentina are unacceptable.

United Kingdom letter of 20 April states that it would continue to take whatever measures may be needed in exercise of its inherent right of self-defense in the face of Argentina's unlawful invasion of British territory and serious violation of the rights of the people of the Falkland Islands, practically all of whom were British nationality.

21 April   Galtieri visits the Falklands.

Britain draws up a three-step peace plan that includes joint withdrawal of Argentine and British troops followed by an interim British administration and then by negotiations on granting sovereignty to Argentina.

Military sources confirm that an Argentine transport plane was intercepted by a British Harrier jet when it passed close to the British Task Force.

OAS decides (18–0–3, U.S.) by adopting Resolution 360 to convene Organ of Consultation on April 26 to consider collective actions against Britain. Columbia and Trinidad and Tobago abstain. The United States does not participate in the vote.

O.A.S. telegram of 21 April from the Secretary-General of the Organization of American States transmitting the text of a resolution by which the Organization's Permanent Council decided to convene the 20 Meeting of Consultation of Ministers of Foreign Affairs to consider the grave situation that had arisen in the South Atlantic.

22 April

Francis Pym, the British Foreign Secretary, flies to Washington to meet with Alexander Haig.

A second Argentine aircraft is intercepted by British Harrier jets as it approaches the British fleet. No shots are fired.

23 April

Pym flies back to London with new U.S. proposals that he calls unsatisfactory. Britain rejects Argentina's demand that it be assured of sovereignty within a fixed time.

Warning issued to Argentine Navy that any ships encountering the British Task Force will be dealt with as hostile.

24 April

Foreign Secretary Sir Francis Pym states that the most recent Argentine peace proposals are unacceptable, and returns to London from Washington.

United Kingdom letter of 24 April incorporates the communication that was conveyed by its Government to Argentina on 23 April, specifically states that it wanted to clarify that any approach on the part of Argentine warships, including submarines, naval auxiliaries, or military aircraft that could amount to a threat to interfere with the mission of the British forces in the South Atlantic would encounter an appropriate response (nine days before the sinking of the *Belgrano*).

Argentine letter of 24 April states that the United Kingdom's communication of 23 April demonstrated that the United Kingdom was *not confining its threat of aggression to a specific zone*, but rather was *extending its warlike activities to the South Atlantic*, even against Argentine civil aircraft, in violation of the express provisions of a number of international instruments.

25 April

The Argentine Navy submarine *Sante Fe* is shelled and beached on South Georgia Island by Royal Navy helicopters, and South Georgia is recaptured by the SAS and Royal Marines in a two-hour battle. British Forces capture 190 prisoners. Prime Minister Thatcher and Defense Minister John Nott announce the recapture in London.

Foreign Minister Costa Mendez states that Great Britain and Argentina are technically at war. (Eight days before the sinking of the *Belgrano*.)

Costa Mendez arrives in Washington but refuses to meet Haig because Britain had just retaken South Georgia; he spends his time gathering support for the Argentine case at a forthcoming meeting of the Organization of American States.

Argentine letter of 25 April states that the United Kingdom's attack on South Georgia was carried out at a time when the negotiations with the participation of the United States Secretary of State were still open, and also states that Argentina considered that the new act of British aggression constituted a grave breach of international peace and security.

26 April

Prime Minister Thatcher warns Argentina that time available for negotiating a peaceful settlement draws short. Argentine withdrawal, self-determination for the Islanders, and at least temporary imposition of British administration are stated as minimum conditions. The full Alpha force of Argentine Marines is ashore on South Georgia.

Whitehall sources disclose that British forces are likely to be in action against Argentine occupation troops on the Falklands within 48 hours.

Haig tells OAS Foreign Ministers in Washington that the Falklands crisis should be solved within framework of UNSC Resolution 502 of April 3; on April 28, Ministers adopt resolution (17–0–4, U.S.) supporting Argentine claim to Islands and urging both sides to withdraw forces from the area.

The Argentines seemed worried about the Common Market's economic sanctions. If extended for a year, the European boycott could cost Argentina as much as $1 billion, about 13 percent of the country's total foreign trade the previous year. The European embargo will hamper Argentina's exports of beef, vegetable oil, and livestock feed. In addition, the European sanctions have complicated the country's hard-cash crisis: Bankers estimate that Argentina's foreign reserves have sunk to less than $2 billion.

Japanese letter of 26 April, in the annex to which its Minister for Foreign Affairs states that his Government strongly hoped that the parties to the dispute over the Malvinas Islands would continue their efforts for a peaceful resolution.

United Kingdom letter of 26 April states that in exercise of the inherent right of self-defense recognized by Article 51 of the United Nations Charter, the British forces reestablished British authority on South Georgia; and also stating that no amount of selective quotation from statements by British

Ministers could obscure the fact that it was Argentina that first used armed force in defiance of the U.N. Security Council's urgent call on 1 April.

Cuban letter of 26 April asks for the circulation of an attached communiqué issued by the Co-ordinating Bureau of the Non-Aligned Countries which express its grave concern over the developments in the region of the Malvinas Islands and requests the interested parties to actively seek a peaceful solution of their dispute and to refrain from any action that might endanger peace and security in the area.

27 April

The United States submits a detailed proposed memorandum of agreement to both parties. Major elements of the memorandum are cessation of hostilities, a 50 percent drawdown of forces within 7 days, total Argentine withdrawal within 15 days, the end of economic and financial sanctions, a three-country U.S.-U.K.-Argentine special interim authority each staffed by not more than 10 persons and accompanied by the country's flag; 2 Argentine representatives of the Argentine population with at least 1 Argentine on each council; restoration of movement, travel, and transport; and finally, negotiations on a definitive status and removal from the List of Non–Self-Governing Territories by December 31, 1982. Should the parties be unable to reach agreement by the end of the year, the United States is to undertake a six-month mediation.

The British Ministry of Defense issues a categorical denial that a small British force had landed on the Falkland Islands proper.

28 April

The OAS Foreign Ministers reaffirm in Resolution 28 majority support for Argentine sovereignty over the Falkland Islands. They ask that Britain and Argentina agree to a truce and withdraw their forces from the Falklands.

OAS letter of 28 April from the President of the Twentieth Meeting of Consultation of Ministers of Foreign Affairs of the OAS transmitting a resolution adopted in connection with the situation in the South Atlantic and which specifically urges the United Kingdom immediately to cease the hostilities it was carrying on within the security region defined by Article 4 of the Inter-American Treaty of Reciprocal Assistance, and to refrain from any act that might affect inter-American peace and security; urged Argentina likewise to refrain from taking any action that might exacerbate the situation; and also urged both Governments immediately to call a truce that would make it possible to resume and proceed normally with the negotiation aimed at a peaceful settlement of the conflict, taking into account the rights of sovereignty of

Argentina over the Malvinas Islands and the interests of the Islanders.

Britain declares total sea and air blockade for 200 miles around Islands, to come into force starting April 30.

Argentine letter of 28 April states that the decision by the United Kingdom to establish a total exclusion zone around the Falkland Islands involved a clear, illegitimate use of force, in violation of international law and of U.N. General Assembly resolution 3314 (XXIX) on the definition of aggression; and also states that the United Kingdom could not invoke the right of self-defense, since that provision might be applied only in order to avert an imminent and serious danger, and that it was, consequently, impossible to invoke the right of self-defense in islands situated 8,000 miles from British territory.

Argentina says the latest U.S. peace plan is under study. The plan stipulates that Argentine troops would leave the Islands, military threats from Britain would end, and there would be a brief administration by Britain before a joint administration and negotiations.

29 April   Letter from the Argentine Minister of Foreign Affairs to U.S. Secretary of State on Argentine views rejects U.S. proposals. (The Argentine view is that this letter did not term the U.S. proposals unacceptable but was directed at certain points including some changes that had been made in the document, and suggested other formulations.)

Argentina announces that the latest Haig proposal would not meet its objective of sovereignty.

Argentina announces its own exclusion zone along its mainland and for 200 miles around the Falklands.

The Soviet Government reportedly warns Britain that it will not tolerate any British interference with Soviet maritime trade in the South Atlantic.

30 April   Secretary Haig announces failure of his mediation effort, U.S. support for Great Britain in the Falklands dispute, and economic sanctions against Argentina following Argentine failure to accept U.S. proposals. Haig also announces that the United States will answer affirmatively requests for materiel support to the British military.

President Reagan accuses Argentina of armed aggression.

U.N. Secretary General Perez de Cuellar meets with Argentine Foreign Minister Costa Mendez in New York and gives him a framework for a solution.

British naval forces are reported to have set up positions to impose 200-mile air and sea blockade around the Falklands.

Soviet authorities officially deny that they have provided any military information to Argentina.

1 May   Vulcan bomber of the RAF (Royal Air Force), Harriers from the Task Force, and warships attack Argentine positions in the first of several softening-up actions. Over 80 Argentine casualties result.

British Foreign Secretary Pym meets with U.S. Secretary Haig and U.S. Secretary of Defense Caspar Weinberger to review political, military, and economic aspects of the crisis in the South Atlantic.

2 May   British submarine sinks Argentina's only cruiser, the *General Belgrano*, killing over 300 Argentine crewmen, one week after Costa Mendez's statement that a state of war exists upon British recapture of South Georgia and sinking of Argentine submarine *Sante Fe*. Peruvian peace making effort is aborted.

U.N. Secretary General shows Pym a U.N. proposal in New York.

Peru offers a simpler plan proposing cease-fire, a phased withdrawal of forces, interim administration of the Islands, and negotiations on sovereignty.

In Rome, Pope John Paul II asks for a peaceful solution to the Falklands crisis.

3 May   Argentina rejects seven-point peace proposal put forward by Peru's President Belaunde, calling the peace proposals similar to previous U.S. proposals. Belaunde continues his efforts.

Argentine communiqué describes the *Belgrano* sinking as a treacherous act of aggression in violation of the U.N. Charter and Resolution 502.

U.S. State Department expresses deep regret over the loss of life in the sinking of the *Belgrano*.

British helicopters reportedly sink one Argentine patrol vessel and damage a second.

Haig confers with Belaunde in the early morning about the peace plan. Argentina dispatches two ranking officials to Peru. Pym returns to London.

4 May   HMS *Sheffield* is set afire by an air-launched Exocet cruise missile of the Argentine Air Force; it later sinks. Twenty men are killed. A British Harrier jet is shot down and the pilot is lost.

Britain announces that the *Queen Elizabeth II* will transport 3,000 troops of the 5th Infantry Brigade to the South Atlantic.

Following the sinking of the *Belgrano,* British officials provide background to the press to the effect that there is no plan for an immediate full-scale invasion; that the plan is to deny naval and air contact and thereby isolate the garrison; and that the next move, presumably diplomatic, is up to Argentina. Defense Ministry speaks of British intention to tighten the screw on Argentina. Defense Minister Nott says *Belgrano* was a threat to his men and therefore it was correct that it was attacked. (Nott draws an implied distinction between attacks on Stanley as turning the screw and sinking the *Belgrano* as self-defense).

Ireland decides to seek a U.N. Security Council meeting to call for a cease-fire and to ask the EEC to end its economic sanctions. Irish Defense Minister says in reaction to the *Belgrano* sinking and attacks on Stanley that the U.K. is very much the aggressor now, and describes Ireland as assuming a neutral stance.

Britain makes a second attack on Port Stanley airfield.

Argentine Foreign Minister declares Argentina is ''willing to negotiate a peaceful solution'' through the U.N., and calls for a cease-fire.

United States authorizes all nonessential personnel and some Embassy dependents to leave Argentina temporarily.

U.S. House of Representatives adopts, by a voice vote, a resolution urging Argentina to withdraw from the Falklands and calling for full diplomatic support for Great Britain.

5 May

Argentina bans nonessential imports for 45 days and devalues the peso by 16.8 percent.

The United States and Peru present a new set of peace proposals to Britain and Argentina. Argentina rejects Peru's plan as not guaranteeing Argentine sovereignty. Argentina says it is willing to negotiate a peaceful solution through the United Nations.

British Foreign Secretary Pym admits that HMS *Sheffield* was hit with a probable loss of 30 men killed and 57 injured. He says the Government is working on an early cease-fire and the withdrawal of Argentine forces.

At Ireland's request, U.N. Security Council meets in an informal session to assess the situation in the South Atlantic. Ireland is seeking an immediate halt to the fighting and a negotiated settlement under U.N. auspices.

6 May	The Secretary General announces Argentine and U.K. agreement to U.N. settlement effort.
	HMG informs Parliament that it is willing to accept the Belaunde proposals.
	Britain replies positively to the Secretary General. The U.S.-Peruvian plan fails; Mr. Pym blames what he calls Argentine intransigence.
	Argentine Defense Minister Ameadeo Frugoli asserts that Argentine sovereignty over the Falklands must be recognized.
	British Defense Secretary John Nott says U.K. will never agree to cease-fire without "total withdrawal" of Argentine forces from Falklands.
7 May	Peru and the United States abandon their joint peace effort after it fails to gain Argentine approval. The U.K. extends the total exclusion zone to within 12 miles of the Argentine coast, de facto confining the Argentine Navy to coastal waters. (It in fact never left port after the sinking of the *Belgrano*.)
	Local elections in Britain reveal the strength of the Conservative Party.
	Britain announces that RAF Nimrods have been fitted with air-to-air refueling probes and will be deployed in the South Atlantic.
	The European Community defends its right to impose trade sanctions against Argentina, answering an Argentine complaint that the embargo violated the General Agreement on Tariffs and Trade (GATT).
8 May	The U.N. Secretary General begins indirect negotiations. He meets separately with Sir Anthony Parsons, Head of the British Mission to the United Nations, and Enrique Ros, Argentina's Deputy Foreign Minister.
9 May	Argentina admits that British aircraft attacked and captured an Argentine vessel (*Narwal*), which was reportedly engaged in surveillance activity.
	British warships bombard Argentine military installations surrounding Port Stanley and Darwin, after several days of quiet in the South Atlantic.
	News correspondents report that an Argentine helicopter (Puma) was shot down near Port Stanley.
10 May	Argentina drops its insistence that its sovereignty over Falklands be recognized before withdrawal of its troops from Islands.

Britain sets up an area of "controlled air space" (an exclusion zone) over Ascension Island, which will cover a 100-mile radius around the Island's Wideawake airfield.

British warships again bombard Argentine military targets around Port Stanley.

11 May   British warship hits Argentine supply ship in Falkland Sound. British control of the water between the two Islands signals effective blockade of the Argentine land forces and redefines nature of the war.

SAS advance party for the Pebble Island raid is put ashore on West Falkland.

12 May   Brazilian President Joao Baptista Figueiredo discusses Falklands crisis with President Reagan in Washington, D.C.

Two Argentine A–4 Skyhawk fighter-bombers are shot down.

13 May   President Galtieri softens the Argentine stance on sovereignty by telling British journalists that Argentine sovereignty is his objective but talks could extend over a reasonable time provided it is not another 149 years.

Prime Minister Thatcher tells the House of Commons that what she seeks is a peaceful solution, not a peaceful sell-out.

14 May   Twenty-two SAS regiment conducts a raid on the Argentine airfield on Pebble Island off the north coast of East Falkland. The commandos, landed by helicopter, carry out a night attack that reportedly destroys ammunition stores and 11 aircraft (mostly Pucara light-attack planes).

Argentine POWs from South Georgia are repatriated except for their Commanding Officer, Captain Alfredo Astiz, who is held for questioning by the French and Swedes concerning the murder of two French nuns and a Swedish national in 1977.

Three of a handful Argentine A–4s attacking the RNTF 30 miles north of the Falklands are destroyed by ship-to-air missiles from one of two British frigates equipped with the new Sea Wolf missile. Two ships sustain moderate but reparable damage.

After six consecutive days of talks with the U.N. Secretary General, negotiations are interrupted. Ambassador Anthony Parsons is called to London for consultations.

The Soviet Foreign Ministry in Moscow advises Sir Curtis Keeble, U.K. Ambassador to the Soviet Union, that it considers Britain's TEZ around the Falklands unlawful.

15 May	The Pebble Island raid demonstrates British capacity to strike on land, as the Task Force reaches 25,000 men on 100 ships.
	British Defense Ministry declares the destruction of Argentine planes and military installations in British raids on the Falklands.
15–16 May	Major Argentine newspapers report that the U.S. Ambassador to Buenos Aires, Harry W. Shlaudeman, is plotting with opposition leaders to overthrow the Junta. *The New York Times* characterizes these stories as clearly inspired, implying that the Argentine Government has fomented these accounts.
16 May	The British government decides on its final offer.
	Common Market countries defer until Monday the decision on removing sanctions against Argentina, which are scheduled to expire at midnight.
17 May	Ambassador Sir Anthony Parsons returns to New York and conveys to the U.N. Secretary General the draft interim agreement and a letter specifying that the Dependencies are not covered by that agreement. The Secretary General requests an Argentine reply within two days.
	EEC, except Ireland and Italy, extends its sanctions against Argentina for another week.
	North Atlantic Council Ministerial Meeting is held in Luxembourg, May 17–18. The Falklands situation is addressed in its final communiqué of May 18.
18 May	Equivocal Argentine reply.
	The *Canberra*, carrying 2,000 British troops, enters the war zone. Military analysts characterize its arrival as one of the last steps needed for invasion.
	Argentina asserts that the presence of British nuclear submarines in the South Atlantic is a violation of the nuclear nonproliferation treaty.
19 May	U.K. Ambassadors Anthony Parsons reminds the Secretary General of the 48-hour deadline for a firm Argentine reply. Late in the evening, the firm Argentine response reflects a hardening of the Argentine position and is judged tantamount to a rejection of the final British proposals.
	Secretary General Perez de Cuellar starts his negotiating day with hour-and-a-half session with Parsons on what Prime Minister Thatcher described as Argentina's discouraging response to British proposals.
	U.N. Secretary General Perez de Cuellar telephones the leaders of Argentina and Britain to appeal for more time to reach an accord.

Independent Television News reports that orders had already been issued to the British Task Force Commander, Rear Admiral John F. Woodward, to launch an invasion as soon as it is militarily feasible.

20 May   The Secretary General informs the President of the Security Council that his efforts do not offer the prospect of success at this time.

Prime Minister Thatcher speaks ill of the Argentine inclination for negotiating a peaceful solution, citing what she calls obduracy, delay, deception, and bad faith. She rejects U.N. appeal for more time to reach an accord.

British Task Force Commander ''Sandy'' Woodward is given the go-ahead to launch a series of landings and hit-and-run operations on the Falklands. (The Task Force was placed under active service conditions on May 18.)

21 May   British White Paper summarizes U.K. view of the negotiations for a peaceful settlement . . . a strong signed that diplomacy was exhausted.

British troops begin landing, supported by air and sea attacks on Argentine positions. The Task Force establishes a firm bridgehead at San Carlos Bay on East Falkland Island. HMS *Ardent* is sunk by Argentine air attack at a cost of 14 Argentine aircraft. As many as 1,000 troops initially land on the Islands.

U.N. Security Council President Ling Qing of China orders urgent closed-door consultations of the 15 member body to consider the collapse of the Falklands peace talks and new fighting in the South Atlantic. The Council decides during a 90-minute private meeting to convene an emergency public session at 2:30 P.M. EDT.

Argentine Government says Costa Mendez will fly to New York to ask the U.N. Security Council to call a truce.

22 May   Reinforcements for the British troops land on East Falkland Island. Britain says beachhead has widened to 10 miles and says 16 enemy planes have been shot down. London acknowledges that the frigate *Ardent* has been sunk.

At the Vatican, Pope John Paul II reiterates his calls for both countries to cease hostilities and resume negotiations.

23 May   HMS *Antelope* is crippled and later sinks at a cost of six Argentine aircraft.

Britain says it has downed 10 Argentine jets.

U.N. Secretary General is urged by Security Council speakers to renew his efforts to negotiate a peaceful settlement in the South Atlantic crisis.

Pope John Paul II calls for cessation of hostilities and resumption of negotiations.

Galtieri, responding to Vatican plea, offers cease-fire.

24 May   Air combat intensifies as seven Argentine aircraft are shot down.

Argentina acknowledges that the British have a 5.4 mile beachhead.

Excepting Ireland and Italy, the EEC extends economic sanctions against Argentina indefinitely.

The Brazilian Government presents a peace plan to the U.N. Security Council that includes provisions for an immediate cease-fire and a pull-back of forces by Britain and Argentina.

25 May   Two weeks after its mediation attempt, Peru announces that it will meet any and all military aid requests from Argentina.

Argentine Foreign Minister Costa Mendez requests a negotiated peace in the Falklands with the U.N.'s help.

The British begin to move land forces inland. Fierce Argentine air attacks on the British Task Force damage three frigates and a cargo ship. Britain says three Argentine Skyhawk jets have been shot down. HMS *Coventry* is sunk and the *Atlantic Conveyor* is hit and burned by an Exocet missile; 22 crewmen are killed.

U.S. Secretary of State Haig states his belief that the British will prevail early on in the Falklands war. The United States commences supplying Britain with war materiel.

According to a senior State Department Official, Israeli military equipment on an Equadorian cargo plane destined for Argentina is detained by Federal authorities in New York. An Israeli official denies that the cargo was destined for Argentina.

Prime Minister Thatcher rejects a cease-fire appeal by Pope John Paul II, stating that Argentina must first withdraw its troops from the Falklands.

26 May   By unanimous vote, the U.N. Security Council adopts Resolution 505 reaffirming Resolution 502 of April 3. The Resolution expresses "appreciation to the Secretary General" for his efforts to implement Resolution 502; requests the "Secretary General, on the basis of the present resolution, to undertake a renewed mission"; urges both parties "to cooperate fully" with the Secretary General, and requests the Secretary General "to enter into contact immediately with the parties with a view to negotiating mutually acceptable terms for a cease-fire, including, if necessary, arrangements for the dispatch of United Nations observers to monitor compliance with the terms of the cease-fire."

According to Argentine shipping and agricultural officials, the Soviet Union has postponed approximately one-half of its grain purchases.

British advance eastward on East Falkland on a two-pronged route.

Pope John Paul II announces that he will visit Argentina on June 11–12.

28 May   Argentine note from the Foreign Minister to the U.S. Secretary of State tacitly rejects the U.S. proposal of the previous month (27 April).

Second battalion of the Parachute Regiment takes Goose Green and Darwin in extended fighting. The 1,400-man garrison surrenders to 600 British paratroopers the next morning. Argentina denies British military claims of the recapture.

Pope John Paul II begins a six-day visit to Britain. He calls on the two nations at war in the Falklands to end the fighting.

29 May   Argentine President Galtieri suggests that Argentina may be forced to seek aid from the Soviet Union.

OAS Foreign Ministers, in voting 17–0 with 4 abstentions, denounce British action in the Falklands and U.S. aid to Britain.

30 May   British troops capture settlements of Douglas and Teal Inlet.

The British government denies Argentine reports that the British aircraft carrier *Invincible* was critically damaged by an Exocet missile.

31 May   Commando Royal Marines occupies Mount Kent.

British Defense Ministry reports that British troops are within 15 miles of Stanley, encircling the Argentine garrison.

During the mediation attempt of the U.N. Secretary General Perez de Cuellar, Argentine President Galtieri suggests that explicit recognition of Argentine sovereignty over the Islands need not be included in an agreement. He insists, however, on an interim administration designed apparently to produce Argentine control inevitably.

1 June One thousand four hundred Argentines are captured when British forces retake Darwin, Goose Green, Douglas, and Teal Inlet in their push toward Stanley.

Argentina is claiming that *Invincible* has been critically damaged by an Exocet.

2 June Argentine Foreign Minister Costa Mendez departs Argentina for the meeting of nonaligned countries in Havana.

British forces close in on and occupy positions within sight of Stanley via the west and southwest as well as troop landings.

Perez de Cuellar acknowledges failure to win cease-fire between U.K. and Argentina.

According to British journalist Jon Snow, British commandos have blown up five Super Etendard jets in an attack on mainland Argentine military bases the previous week. The report is denied by the British Defense Ministry.

3 June Crew members of a U.S. C–130 aircraft, which had landed in Buenos Aires, are arrested after taking photographs of the airport and several aircraft. They are released several hours later after turning over the film to Argentine officials.

According to Argentine and Brazilian sources, two Brazilian Mirages intercept a British Vulcan bomber outside Brazilian air space and force it to land at an airfield in Rio de Janeiro.

Argentine President Leopoldo Galtieri announces that Argentina will accept eventual aid from the Soviet Union or from any other country that will offer it.

4 June By a vote of 9–2 (United States and U.K.) with 4 abstentions, the U.N. Security Council calls for an immediate cease-fire in the Falkland Islands. Reporting a delay in communication, Ambassador Kirkpatrick discloses that the U.S. voted No but received new instructions to abstain just after the vote.

High Argentine military source denies that the Soviet Union is installing a radar system along the Argentine coast.

British forces given the "go-ahead" for the final offensive push against Port Stanley.

5 June U.N. Security Council fails to ratify a resolution calling for a cease-fire in the South Atlantic due to U.S. and British vetoes.

U.S. Chief Delegate to the U.N. Jeane Kirkpatrick, in saying she would have done better to abstain, regrets the use of the veto on the Security Council resolution of the previous day.

Argentina protests the alleged British use of Argentine POWs to find and defuse Argentine explosives in the Goose Green and Port Darwin areas.

6 June   British troops on the Falklands are reinforced by elements of the 5th Infantry Brigade, the first major troop reinforcement effort by the British.

7 June   British launch heavy artillery attack on Stanley.

President Reagan flies to Britain for talks with Prime Minister Thatcher on the Falklands issue.

8 June   Landing ships *Sir Tristam* and *Sir Galahad* are hit by Argentine aircraft fire, along with the frigate HMS *Plymouth*, inflicting heavy casualties on the first battalion of the Welsh Guards.

Britain claims 11 Argentine fighter planes have been shot down. Four British ships are damaged.

France announces that it would deliver purchased Exocet missiles to Peru only after the conclusion of hostilities in the South Atlantic.

British Defence Ministry announces that British forces are firmly established at Fitzroy settlement and Bluff Cove.

Although Galtieri later rejects the latest U.N. peace proposal, he states that Argentina is willing to agree to a simultaneous withdrawal of British and Argentine troops and to a temporary U.N. administration of the Malvinas Islands.

10 June   Argentina says its planes inflict ''heavy casualties'' on British in areas of Mount Kent west of Stanley and Fitzroy.

11/12 June   The British conduct a series of night attacks on the high ground west of Stanley. The three critical peaks of Mount Longdon, Two Sisters, and Mount Harriet are captured. HMS *Glamorgan* is hit by a cruise missile but not put out of action.

11 June   Pope John Paul II repeats his plea for peace in the Falklands upon arriving in Argentina. He is greeted by President Leopoldo Galtieri.

Britain says about 60 British troops have been killed and 120 wounded in the June 8 attacks on two British landing ships off Bluff Cove.

Argentine Foreign Minister Costa Mendez states that all options for a peaceful solution to the conflict have been exhausted.

12 June   British troops launch a major offensive at dawn against Argentine defensive positions to the West of Port Stanley. The British Ministry of Defence reports that their troops have

consolidated their positions on the high grounds within three miles of the capital, controlling Mt. Langdon, Two Sisters Hills, and Mt. Harriet.

British frigate H.M.S. *Glamorgan* comes under Argentine fire. A British Ministry of Defense spokesman reports that 9 men have been killed and 17 injured.

13/14 June

Argentina and Britain reportedly agree to an International Red Cross proposal that the 600 Islanders in Port Stanley be sheltered in a declared neutral zone.

Further British night attacks gain them Mount William and Wireless Ridge. Argentine troops abandon the last positions outside of Stanley. White flags begin to appear and Argentine Commander General Mario Menendez asks permission to discuss terms with the British.

14 June

British troops take three strategic hills two-to-three miles from Stanley, and force a large Argentine retreat.

In light of British advances to within Port Stanley city limits and breakdown of Argentine defenses, Argentine Government authorizes Malvinas Commander General Mario Menendez to hold talks with British Forces Commander Major General Jeremy Moore. De facto cease-fire established.

Argentine troops in the Falkland Islands render their unconditional surrender to British forces at 10:59 P.M. local time after negotiating surrender terms with British Falkland Islands Commander Brigadier John Waters. Fourteen thousand eight hundred Argentine troops taken prisoner.

Cease-fire declared by Argentine military command.

15 June

Prime Minister Thatcher rejects any participation in the future by Argentina or the U.N. in administration of the Falklands.

Argentine troops surrender to British forces on the Falklands.

Angry Argentine mobs gather in the streets and around the Presidential palace demanding President Galtieri's ouster. Police fire tear gas into the crowds.

Britain warns Argentina that it will hold up the release of some high-ranking Argentine prisoners of war until the Argentine Government agrees to a blanket declaration that all hostilities in the ten-week war have ended.

17 June

President Leopoldo Galtieri of Argentina steps down as President and Commander in Chief of the Army, and as a member of the Junta. The Cabinet also resigns. Major General Cristino Nicolaides replaces Galtieri as Army Commander and member of the Junta. Major General Alfredo Oscar Saint Jean is temporarily named President.

18 June	Agreement between Argentina and Britain over repatriation of most of the Argentine prisoners held on the Falklands.
	U.K. Foreign Secretary Francis Pym says Argentina must declare it has ceased to wage war against Britain before 1,000 Argentine *officers* captured by the British will be returned.
	Argentina terms the truce with Britain precarious while British troops occupy Falklands and continue TEZ and economic sanctions.
20 June	Argentine forces on Southern Thule in the South Sandwich group surrender to the British. The Argentine presence maintained since 1977 is dislodged.
	While meeting in Luxembourg, EEC Foreign Ministers lift Common Market economic sanctions against Argentina.
22 June	Major General Reynaldo Benito Antonio Bignone is named President of Argentina by the Argentine Army. He assume the office on July 1. The Army promises restoration of civilian rule by early 1984. In protesting the appointment of a military man to the Presidency, an Air Force General and Navy Admiral resign from the ruling military body.
23 June	Prime Minister Thatcher confers in Washington, D.C., with President Reagan on the Falklands crisis.
24 June	According to Argentina Foreign Minister Costa Mendez, the decision to declare an end to hostilities will rest with Argentine President-designate Reynaldo Bignone.
25 June	Argentina's six-year ban on political activity is set aside after President-designate Bignone meets with political leaders of 14 different political parties.
	U.S. Secretary of State Haig resigns his position because of differences with President Reagan over foreign policy. George Shultz, former Treasury Secretary, is appointed to the post.
26 June	Sir Rex Hunt, British Governor of the Falklands, returns to Stanley.
1 July	Reynaldo Bignone, in succeeding Leopoldo Galtieri as President, promises to restore democracy to Argentina by March 1984.
6 July	Argentine peso devalued 22 percent for trade. It is floated for other transactions. Credit controls implemented.
	British Armed Forces Minister Peter Blaker tells Parliament that British losses in the Falklands war amounted to 255 dead and 777 wounded.
12 July	British Foreign Office announces an end to the Falklands War. Argentine prisoners of war (593) still held by the Brit-

ish will be returned to Argentina. Argentine Foreign Minister Juan Aguirre Lanari expresses his appreciation for Britain's decision but says that a formal cease-fire has not been declared and that only "a de facto cessation of hostilities" is in effect.

U.S. economic sanctions imposed on Argentina at the outbreak of the Falklands war rescinded by President Reagan. Ban on military sales remains in effect.

22 July	Parliament learns from Prime Minister Thatcher that Argentina has been asked to not to violate a 150-mile protective zone around the Falklands.
26 July	Argentine Army removes from duty those senior commanders responsible for the Falklands campaign.
2 August	United Kingdom opposes Reagan Administration embargo against providing U.S. technology to the Soviet Union for use in constructing a natural gas pipeline from Siberia to Western Europe. This action follows similar moves by France and Italy.
5 August	After being criticized for proposing the formation of a political party centered around the Military, General Basilio Lami Dozo, a former Junta member, resigns from the Air Force.
10 August	France is the first country in the Common Market to announce an end to the embargo on the sale of arms to Argentina.
12 August	Three Argentine fishing vessels are ordered by the British Navy to leave the restricted zone around the Falklands.
13 August	Continued war with Britain is supported by some 2,000 people gathered at a rally in Buenos Aires.
24 August	Economics Minister José Maria Dagnino Pastore and Central Bank President Domingo Caballo resign.
25 August	Argentine Government announces annual inflation rate of 500 percent.
10 September	Admiral Jorge Isaac Anaya of the Navy and Brigadier Jorge Hughes of the Air Force resume their involvement with the government of President Bignone.
14 September	Financial sanctions implemented against Argentina during the Falklands War are rescinded. Though trade embargo is maintained, $1 billion in Argentine assets frozen by the British are released.
15 September	Argentina extends 1972 nonaggression treaty with Chile in a ceremony attended by Argentine Ambassador Carlos Ortiz de Rozas.

18 September	Argentina institutes Prohibition on the sale of beef in restaurants twice a week, along with establishment of price ceilings on milk and bread and a planned rationing system for fuel are announced.
22 September	Approximately 20,000 people gather in Buenos Aires to protest low wages and an estimated annual inflation rate of 450 percent.
24 September	New Argentine Ambassador to the U.S. Lucio Garcia del Solar of Argentina presents his credentials to President Reagan.
10 October	In La Paz, Bolivia's Congress reelects Hernan Siles Zuazo for President, bringing a return to civiliam government to that country. Mr. Siles Zuazon had already been elected in 1980 but was prevented from taking office by a military coup.
19 October	U.N. General Assembly votes 104–50 to elect Nicaragua to the Latin American seat on the Security Council.
	United Kingdom signs agreement extending the Polaris sales agreement of April 6, 1963 (TIAS 5313), to cover the sale of Trident II weapon system. Effected by exchange of notes at Washington October 19, 1982. Entered into force October 19, 1982. Superseded amendment of September 30, 1980.
26 October	Prime Minister Thatcher informs the House of Commons that Britain expended approximately $1.19 billion in the Falklands War.
27 October	Argentine Government, in an agreement with the IMF (International Monetary Fund), announces its intention to cut government spending in order to receive a $2 billion loan from the institution and thereby prevent default on the country's $40 billion foreign debt.
4 November	UNGA adopts Argentine Resolution 37/9 (90 [United States]–12-[UK] 52) calling for negotiations on Falklands sovereignty; U.K. denounces resolution as a charade inspired by Argentina.
15 November	Brazilians vote in free municipal, legislative, and gubernatorial elections for the first time in 17 years.
	Secretary Shultz heads U.S. delegation to the 12th regular session of the General Assembly of the Organization of American States held in Washington, D.C., November 15–20. On November 18, the General Committee approves a draft resolution expressing support for U.N. General Assembly Resolution 37/9 of November 4 and calling for negotiations on the sovereignty dispute over the Falkland Islands.

30 November   President Reagan makes an official working visit to Latin
                            America November 30-December 4 to hold bilaterals with
                            heads of state. The President visits Brazil November 30-De-
                            cember 3; Columbia December 3; Costa Rica December 3–4;
                            and Honduras December 4. While in Costa Rica, the Presi-
                            dent meets with Salvadoran President Alvaro Magana and
                            with Guatemalan President Brigadier General Jose Rios
                            Montt while in Honduras.

13 December   Supplemental arrangement relating to the agreement of Feb-
                            ruary 25, 1976 (TIAS 8230) concerning a U.S. naval support
                            facility on Diego Garcia, British Indian Ocean Territory is
                            signed at Washington, D.C. Entered into force December
                            13, 1982.

                            Britain begins infrastructure improvements in the Falklands
                            which will approach $ U.S. 2 billion. A major military pres-
                            ence is added to the Islands.

                            Argentina begins a rearmament which will include SA–7
                            Grail Surface to Air Missiles, Type 209 submarines, Type
                            TR–1700 submarines, MEKO 360 destroyers, mm 40 ship-
                            mounted Exocet missiles, Maritime patrol aircraft, Mirage
                            3C fighters, Airborne Warning and Control Aircraft, its own
                            IA–63 fighters, C–212 transports, and communications gear
                            for joint operations.

Documents

UNITED NATIONS RESOLUTIONS AND DECISIONS

1. GA Resolution 1514 (XV), December 14,1960
   (Declaration on the granting of independence to colonial countries and peoples)
2. GA Resolution 2065 (XX), December 16,1965
   (Question of the Falkland Islands—Malvinas)
3. GA Resolution 3160 (XXVIII), December 14,1973
   (Question of the Falkland Islands—Malvinas)
4. GA Resolution 31/49, December 1,1976
   (Question of the Falkland Islands—Malvinas)
5. SC Resolution 502 (1982), April 3,1982
6. SC Resolution 505 (1982), May 26,1982
7. GA Resolution 37/9, November 9,1982

COMMUNIQUÉS OF THE MOVEMENT OF NON-ALIGNED COUNTRIES

8. Lima,1975
9. Columbia,1976
10. New Delhi,1977
11. Havana,1978
12. Belgrade,1978

13. Colombo,1979

14. Havana,1979

15. New Delhi,1981

16. New York,1981

17. Havana,1982

18. New York,1982

19. Managua,1983

20. New Delhi,1983

PROPOSALS AND TEXTS BY THE PARTIES AND MEDIATORS

21. U.S. Proposals, April 27, 1982

22. Argentine Note of, May 28, 1982
        and Letter of, April 29, 1982

23. Peru-U.S. Proposal, May 5, 1982

24. British Government Document Annex—Falkland Islands Draft Interim Agreement,
        May 21,1982

25. Argentine Diplomatic Note to U.S. Department of State, May 26, 1982

NOTES

PREFACE

Falkland Islands is the English-language geographic term for the two principal and several outlying islands. The use of the English-language term throughout implies no judgment on sovereignty. The original name was Les Isles Malouines, after the native St. Malo of the first settlers and that remains the French-language geographic term. The Spanish Malvinas is sometimes used when discussing the islands as a political idea and component of National Honor to recall the power of the irredentist feeling for the islands in Argentina. Similarly, the occasional use of the outmoded term Kelper to describe Falkland Islanders is deliberate and affectionate, reminding the reader that, soldiers and contractors aside, this is a society and a culture not just a population. This is quite a separate question from the points of the two sides touching on self-determination vs. decolonization, indigenous rights vs. settler usurpation. The island families who are Kelpers go back further in their land and way of life than most Americans or Argentines do in theirs.

I

1. The General Assembly has taken U.N. authority over Namibia back from the "trustee," South Africa, and may well decide to keep any future trust under its direct, majoritarian supervision. South Africa never turned its mandate into a trusteeship.

2. The "assumption of change" dictates that it must be by the success or failure of radical action. States using ethnic unity as grounds for irredentism must watch for counterarguments suggesting their incorporation into the ethnically related neighbor.

3. Andorra is a co-principality of the President of France and the Bishop of Urgel, Spain.

4. Thomas Franck and Paul Hoffman, "The Right of Self-Determination in Very Small Places," *NYU Journal of International Law and Politics* (1976): 384.

5. Ibid.

6. The one assessed property of territoriality as the rule of the modern political system that is more frequently violated than self-determination is that the political unit must be internally structured by an identifiable dominance hierarchy. (See, for example, Edward Soja, "The Political Organization of Space," Commission on College Geography, Resource Paper 8, 1971.) The number of groups worldwide who would change and usually replace their internal dominance hierarchy are another major threat to world order. Their claims within the nation-state are now often and in some cases exclusively pursued by armed violence and terrorism beyond the borders of which they claim to be legitimate masters.

7. As did East Prussia from 1919 to 1939. See Honore M. Catudal, Jr., *The Enclave Problem of Western Europe* (Montgomery: University of Alabama Press, 1979). States within states are rare. Normally their status is de jure or de facto subordinate, defining negatively what sovereignty really means. Italy contains the Vatican and San Marino. In contrast, France has Monaco only on its coast, but Andorra (jointly administered with Spain) is *contained,* as is the other unique situation of Llivia, which is on Spanish soil. South Africa completely surrounds Lesotho.

8. Catudal, *The Enclave Problem.*

9. Nevassa: The United States and Haiti contest title to the Caribbean island of Nevassa. Talks have been suspended since 1979. South Tyrol: Northern Italy includes the region of South Tyrol that is also claimed by Austria. Austria is not actively pursuing the matter.

10. Catudal, *The Enclave Problem,* p. 84.

11. James Cable, "Who Was Surprised in the Falklands, and Why?" *The Economist.*

12. Paul Calvert, "Guatemala and Belize," *Contemporary Review* (January 1976): 7.

13. Calvert, "Guatemala and Belize," p. 9.

14. Paula Herman, "British Honduras: A Question of Viability," *World Affairs* (Summer 1975): 61.

15. Franck and Hoffman, "The Right of Self-Determination in Very Small Places," p. 343. See pages 369–71 for an interesting synthesis of Spanish Sahara, Eastern Timor, Djibouti, and Belize, and clause 6 of 1514, the "grandfather clause," to the effect that self-determination may not be used to interfere with the territorial integrity of states.

16. "Assembly Reaffirms Right of People of East Timor to Self-Determination," *UN Monthly Chronicle* (January 1982): 19.

17. Erlich Haggai, *The Struggle over Eritrea: 1962–1978* (Stanford: Hoover Institution Press, 1983), p. 1.

18. Ibid., p. 6.

19. Ibid.

20. Ibid., p. 8.

21. "Guyana's Oil Is Fueling a Territorial Dispute," *Business Week,* May 3, 1982, p. 34.

22. *New York Times,* 17, June 1984.

23. Peter Welsley-Smith, *Unequal Treaty 1898–1997* (Oxford: Oxford University Press, 1980), p. 164.

24. Dori Jones and Harold Ellithorpe, "Thatcher Seeks a Future for Hong Kong after 1997," *Business Week,* 19, July 1982, p. 80.

25. Robert Kaylor, "How Bustling Hong Kong Copes with Uncertainty," *U.S. News and World Report,* 27 June 1983, p. 45.

26. OAU Assembly Resolution AHG/Res. 17 (I), 17–21 July 1964.

27. U.N. Document A/C.4/SR.2175, Fourth Committee, November 27, 1975, p. 15 (from Franck and Hoffman, "The Right of Self-Determination in Very Small Places," p. 342).

II

1. Indeed, the very notion in international law that discovery conveys sovereignty was questioned by the foremost American jurist on the subject of Falklands sovereignty, Julius Gobel, in his "The Struggle for the Falkland Islands" (1927): "the doctrine that the mere discovery of a new land can give rights of sovereignty . . . is baseless in law and, in fact, entirely at variance with the principles of Roman law upon which, through the efforts of Spain, the international law relating to the acquisition of sovereignty was founded. The author trusts that these results will once and for all put an end to the frivolous and uncritical acceptance by law writers of the idea that discovery can give any shadow of right, and that they will move historians to abandon the fantastic picture of Spain seeking to exclude the rest of Europe from the New World by setting up merely a right by discovery to regions which she did not in fact control." (Page xxix) The enthusiasm for discovery persists in legal and political thinking. It must be allowed that Spain kept all the options she could and worked assiduously to keep England out of South America. It might well be tempered by doctrine paralleling that of blockade or quarantine: one cannot proclaim what one cannot enforce.

2. H.S. Ferns, *Britain and Argentina in the Nineteenth Century,* p. 232.

3. As if to act out the problem with political gestures aimed at securing good will, Ortiz de Rosas alienated the Islanders by using the "hearts and minds" phraseology in an interview widely circulated in the islands in 1981.

4. Political retrenchment can also be dated from a 1966 watershed.

5. House of Commons *Official Report,* March 26, 1968 and March 28, 1968.

6. Hastings and Jenkins, *Battle for the Falklands,* pp. 28–29.

7. Falkland Islands Review, 14–15.

8. Some of whom would ironically be temporarily disenfranchised by changes in the Nationalities Act.

9. *The Economist,* June 19, 1982, p. 37.

10. A side effect of drawing a line on who (in principled consistency) in the Nationality Act was British by virtue of birth in Britain or of British parentage.

11. Galtieri quoted verbatim (author's translation) in purported testimony before the Rattenbach Commission in the Buenos Aires . Iy *Clarin,* 8 December 1983.

12. Hastings and Jenkins, *Battle for the Falklands,* pp. 56–57.

13. Official Report, House of Commons, 23 March 1982, Col. 799.

14. Lord Franks, The Franks Report (Report of a Committee of Privy Counselors, London, HMSO, presented to the Parliament by the Prime Minister, January 1983), paragraphs 333–334.

15. King, *Falklands Experience,* p. 2.

16. *La Prensa,* 24 January, p. 1.

17. David E. King, *The Falklands Experience*, unpublished thesis, St. John's College, Cambridge University, June 1984.

18. The Falklands was ironically not an instance of a significant trend which Father Campbell has diagnosed: that of crisis inflation. Without a major calamity in the last two generations in the West, governments have been accustomed to inflate the dimensions and consequences of crisis and therefore the credit which they obtain for solving them. This allows them to govern with smoke and mirrors and constitutes an important abuse of the public trust in Western governments. (Colin Campbell, S.J., Inauguration of the Martin Chair in Philosophy and Politics, February 2, 1984, Georgetown University).

19. Uruguayan naval units may have had hints of the jump-off state of readiness of the Argentine fleet and Marine infantry troops during their bilateral maneuvers the previous week with the Argentine Navy.

20. Colin Campbell, S.J., Lecture upon inauguration of the Martin Chair in Philosophy & Politics, Georgetown University, February 2, 1984.

21. Argentina attacked when the Marine garrison was augmented by a hold-over of the rotating contingents, i.e., at double strength. Thus their presence was doubled, then reduced by putting some Marines aboard *Endurance* to supplement her landing team. The absence of the Royal Naval vessel was likely more telling for Argentine planning which in principle aspired to a bloodless "moral" victory. The absence of some of the Marines thus gives no credence to the Prime Minister's assertion in a February letter that the Royal Marines were "sufficient deterrent against any possible aggression."

III

1. Ship information IISS, *The Military Balance*, 1981–82.

2. Unless, that is, one can develop an Argentine perspective of the question as in the working hypothesis entitled Plan B, which we shall explore below.

3. Witness the fact that no British Army regulars served in Africa between WW I and the Mau Mau uprising in Kenya.

4. Article 3 of the Rio Treaty states that

The High Contracting Parties agree that an armed attack by any State against an American State shall be considered as an attack against all the American States and, consequently, each one of the said Contracting Parties undertake to assist in meeting the attack in the exercise of the inherent right of individual or collective self-defense recognized by Article 51 of the Charter of the United Nations.

5. Indeed, for the purposes of the Falkland Islands in the South Atlantic, we enjoy no such alliance with Great Britain. The North Atlantic Treaty specifically excludes areas below the Tropic of Cancer from the treaty area, and makes exception when discussing national territory for the overseas territories of alliance partners that lie beyond the alliance area. If the special relationship implies support or other non-NATO obligations, these are a matter of bilateral contract or understanding.

6. The proposed sale, in 1937, of U.S. destroyers to Brazil highlights the sense of naval rivalry. The Argentine reaction was strong enough to force withdrawal of the offer. U.S. responsiveness somewhat helped the pro-Western faction, as well as the government of Robert Ortiz and his foreign minister Cantilo.

7. Joseph S. Tulchin in "Two to Tango," *Foreign Service Journal*, October 1982, p. 24.

8. Leslie H. Gelb, *The New York Times*, April, 1983.

9. See Richard L. Jackson, *The Non-aligned, the U.N. and the Superpowers* (New York: Praeger Publishers, 1983), pp. 48–49.

10. See Documents in appendix on nonaligned positions on the Falklands.

11. Oscar Raul Cardosa, Ricardo Kirschbaum, and Eduardo van der Kooy, *Malvinas: The Secret Plot*, unpublished.

12. Madrid EFE (the Spanish Press Service) in Spanish, 15 September 1983.

13. R. Rose and G. Peters, *Can Government Go Bankrupt?* (New York: Basic Books, 1978), p. 23.

14. *Samuel P. Huntington; American Politics: The Promise of Disharmony* (Cambridge, Mass.: Harvard University Press, 1982).

15. A. O. Hirschman, *Shifting Involvements: Private Interest and Public Action* (Princeton: Princeton University Press, 1982).

16. In the prescriptions for reestablishing governmental authority, Huntington argues for limiting political participation and political (distributive) claims.

17. D. Sanders, *Patterns of Political Instability* (London: Macmillan, 1981), p. 6 and *passim*.

18. See the work of Ekkart Zimmermann of the Hochschule der Bundeswehr, Munich, particularly ''Pitfalls and Promises in the Study of Crises and Crisis Outcomes in Liberal Democracies: Towards a New Approach,'' manuscript courtesy of the author.

19. G. B. Powell, *Contemporary Democracies: Participation, Stability, and Violence* (Cambridge, Mass.: Harvard University Press, 1982).

20. It is likely that Argentina did not have confidence in its ability to issue a tamper-proof recall order. If the field commander is not sure of the authenticity of a recall, he ought to assume it to be disinformation.

21. Alexander M. Haig, Jr., *Caveat: Realism, Reagan, and Foreign Policy* (New York: Macmillan Publishing Company, 1984), p. 265.

22. Statement to the Subcommittee on Inter-American Affairs, House Foreign Affairs Committee, August 5, 1982.

IV

1. The analogy if not the full outrage was evoked as well for the U.S. mediator:

The junta, displaying a pattern of behavior typical of many militarized, authoritarian, xenophobic regimes, thought it could get away with [invasion] because Britain was weak and the United States was corrupt. Adolf Hitler and the militarists of imperial Japan had made precisely the same miscalculation about the democracies in the 1930s. (Haig, *Caveat*, p. 267.)

2. The *Argentine perspective on March 1982:* Davidoff had British Embassy (Buenos Aires) permission for his scrap mission and had indeed asked to charter *Endurance*. Thus is was British Governor Rex Hunt who complicated the third Davidoff trip in a chartered vessel, of which he was aware. Davidoff asked the Embassy for permission for March 9. An officer of the Embassy flew to Stanley on March 10 and told the Governor the next day. Hunt then ordered the *Endurance* out of South Georgia before the arrival of the scrap workers and she left the islands on the 17th, the workers arriving on the 18th and their ship departed the next day. *Endurance* returned to Stanley, picked up Royal Marines and departed on the 20th (against the advice of the Foreign office, according to the Franks report). Thus the British created the South Georgia crisis by ignoring their own procedures of approval and granting of White Card documents.

3. Henderson, "American and the Falklands: Case Study in the Behaviour of an Ally," *The Economist,* November 12, 1983, p. 18. Argentina says it was told March 21 by the Foreign Office that no military personnel had disembarked at South Georgia and the FCO regretted any fuss. Argentina was then told the next day that *Endurance* would hold at Gritviken while Parliament was informed, then told the next day that *Endurance* would proceed with the evacuation of the workers due to emotions in Parliament. Upon that notification, Argentina ordered the *Bahia Paraiso* to protect the workers. Thus to the Argentines, the March 30 British declarations are a direct consequence of the Parliamentary debates of March 23/24 and not of the South Georgia landing. They note that the British submarine *Superb* was dispatched on March 25.

4. Henderson, "America and the Falklands." Enders recollects that the assurance was less categorical. This is also the Argentine view: The Argentine fleet mobilized March 28 had been prepared on a "normal" contingency basis at the beginning of 1982. That contingency was felt necessary because the 1981 Island Council elections and December Parliamentary debates in London foretold in their estimation the possibility of total British intransigence and the effective end of talks in 1982, which they judged unacceptable.

5. It is the Argentine view that had the U.S. been willing to mediate in the same terms on March 30 or April 1, their "recovery" of the islands would not have been necessary.

6. Henderson, "America and the Falklands." Participation in the interim administration was unspecified but the U.S. certainly had itself in mind.

7. Haig, *Caveat,* p. 271.

8. Ibid., p. 280. Argentine diplomats question whether the Argentine Ambassador was so instructed by this time. Costa Mendez was dispatched to Washington on April 6.

9. Argentina's perspective is that it did not decline but rather asked Washington to detain the British ships headed its way and mediate the dispute based on U.N. Decolonization Resolutions. They say that the United States did not reply until April 1 and the answer was unclear, simply repeating the U.S. wording of March 30. Argentina again asked for its kind of halt to the fleet with Decolonization-based mediation. The answer in a phone call from President Reagan came two hours after their "fail-safe" point at which the invasion fleet could not be recalled.

10. Haig, *Caveat,* p. 266. The Argentine Foreign Minister did not get this message of high principle in his talks with Haig April 6–14.

11. Chancellor Costa Mendez is now of the view that Argentina should perhaps have accepted President Reagan's offer of Vice-President Bush (who was then in China) as a mediator. Another principal Argentine diplomat is indeed of the opinion that his government erred fundamentally in not instantly accepting the offer of President Reagan in his phone call to send Vice-President Bush, with his diplomatic experience and U.N. background on the issue, to mediate. (For all the later accusations of British bad faith for fighting while negotiations were underway, Argentina could then have undertaken its act of force with a claim that it was only implementing what it understood the United States to be arranging politically.)

12. Haig, *Caveat,* p. 270.

13. Ibid.

14. Ibid., pp. 270–71. Argentina dates the talks from April 6 following the OAS meeting.

15. Argentine officials state that Haig did not convey this to Argentina.

16. One U.S. diplomat, perhaps the best student and friend of the United Kingdom,

feels that Britain began to take action without benefit of a coherent strategy. This may reflect the extent to which the parallel implementation of diplomacy and the possible use of force are axiomatic in Western geopolitical thinking: One just starts talking and moving forces toward the crisis point, assuming they are mutually compatible and indeed mutually reinforcing tools for crisis management. The naval and ground commanders called the extended time taken by the Task Force to steam to the crisis point a "period of military preparation, and time for the politicos to try to resolve the issue." The tandem approach is apparently as natural to their thinking as to that of statesmen and diplomats. (See Woodward and Moore in *Journal of the Institute for Defense Studies*, March 1983, p. 20). Admiral Sir Terence Lewin has stated firmly however that there were no political "holds" on the progress of the task force.

17. Henderson, "America and the Falklands," p. 31.

18. Henderson, "America at the Falklands," p. 31.

19. *Boston Globe*, 2 March 1983, p. 1.

20. Henderson, "America and the Falklands," p. 32.

21. Neither *within* the "Latino Lobby" nor within the Executive Branch as a whole did this view hold final sway. The same would hold true on the Hill: Sir Nicholas Henderson concludes that "in the United States Congress the influence of the Latin Lobby proved to be slight." ("America and the Falklands," p. 31). Even his country's opponents on Northern Ireland policy, Senators Ted Kennedy and Daniel Patrick Moynihan and Speaker O'Neill voiced support on the question of the Falklands. Indeed, one member of the Senate Foreign Relations Committee brushed aside the Ambassador's points on self-determination to say that U.S. support stemmed purely from the special relationship: America would help Britain because it is Britain. U.S. values, however, were not completely parallel to British values in one major policy area. Colonialism had been dismantled with U.S. encouragement. Henderson's diplomatic antennae picked up both an aversion to a military dictatorship and "lingering inhibitions about continued colonial rule in the Falklands," p. 31. Principle and partiality, however, carried the day, and the Senate and House passed resolutions favoring the British cause. The range and import of U.S. legislation on the Falklands was politically instructive:

H. Con. Res. 328 (Bingham, Seiberling, Pritchard, Findley, Fascell, Solarz, Wolpe): Urged referral of the issue of sovereignty over the Falkland Islands to the International Court of Justice; introduced May 5, 1982; referred to the Committee on Foreign Affairs.

H. Res. 441 (Solarz): Called for Argentina to comply with U.N. Security Council Resolution 502, and for the United States to provide full diplomatic support for Great Britain if efforts to resolve the dispute peaceably should fail. Introduced April 28, 1982; referred to the Committee on Foreign Affairs. Resolution; passed the full House on May 4, 1982.

S. Res. 364 (Pressler): Expressed the support of the efforts of the United Kingdom to reclaim the territory of the Falkland Islands. Introduced April 19, 1982; referred to the Committee on Foreign Relations.

S. Res. 368 (Moynihan): Called for a sense of the Senate that unless Argentina promptly withdrew its forces from the Falkland Islands, the United States should embargo trade between itself and Argentina. Introduced April 21, 1982; ordered held at the desk.

S. Res. 382 (Biden): Resolved that the United States not stand neutral and recognize Britain's right to self-defense to achieve full withdrawal of Argentine forces from the Falkland Islands. Introduced April 24, 1982; called up by unanimous consent. Passed the Senate 78–1 (with 20 not voting) April 29.

(Precce, Charlotte P., Bert Cooper and Nina Serafino, "The Falkland/Malvinas Crisis," Washington: Congressional Research Service, ms. p. 18)

22. The Argentine view is that their goal at this point was simply to stop the British fleet and obtain serious negotiations for both parties with their presence on the island, with the United States or U.N. guaranteeing the process and agreement. Both in March and April Argentina felt it had to focus the United States on the situation to get the U.K. to negotiate seriously, not to gain sovereignty but to get a serious hearing. In this non-conspiratorial scenario, the Galtieri government did not wish to intervene until after the South Georgia incident. (This is separable in Argentine thinking from the facts that the Navy and the Buzo Tactico had been months in training.)

23. Henderson, "America and the Falklands." Argentine leadership conversely found the American Secretary of State without finesse, unwilling to tell them about the United Kingdom except in terms of military menace, and unskilled or unwilling as a true negotiator. They believe he concocted the irrationality leitmotif after Argentina successfully reconvened the OAS. As regards concessions, Argentine officials note that as of the April 18 and May 13 they were prepared to omit sovereignty as a precondition and to negotiate without prejudging the outcome.

24. Ibid., p. 33.

25. The British War Cabinet had, for example, declared a Total Exclusion Zone (TEZ) of 200 miles around the Falklands while Haig was en route from Washington. Such blockades being a legal matter of ability to enforce, the implication was that British submarines would be on station when the TEZ came into effect on April 12. Unless Northwood were waiting for *more* resources on the spot, the presence of one British hunter-killer *hinted at* by the Prime Minister would have allowed the declaration of a preemptive TEZ before the Argentine invasion.

26. James Reston in the *New York Times*, 11 April, 1982, IV, p. 17, col. 5. Argentine leaders read the timing of British escalations as coordinated with Haig's missions and major decisions, right from his choosing initial consultations with the British followed by remarks about being impressed with British determination. That led directly to the assembly of crowds at the Casa Rosada. They were stunned that the first Exclusion Zone on April 8 was declared during his visit. They saw collusion in the fact that the attack on South Georgia came two days before Argentina received its copy of the U.S. proposals and five before the U.S. withdrawal from mediation.

27. *New York Times*, 12 April 1982, I, p. 10, col. 4.

28. Henderson, "America and the Falklands," p. 32.

29. Haig, *Caveat*, p. 272.

30. Ibid.

31. Ibid., p. 273.

32. Ibid., pp. 273–74.

33. Ibid., p. 276.

34. Ibid., p. 274.

35. Haig, in *Time*, 9 April 1984, p. 60.

36. Haig, *Caveat*, p. 281. The Argentine recollection is that at this point the negotiations were conducted in two parallel teams, one of principals and one at the working level. The working level Argentines do not recollect conveying a feeling that their time was short.

37. Ibid., p. 282

38. Ibid.

39. Jack Anderson transcript quoted in *Newsweek*, 26 April 1982, p. 41.

40. Haig quotes Galtieri's reaction as: "The British won't fight." (*Time*, 9 April 1984).

41. Transcript of a Reagan-Haig conversation, *Washington Post*, April 21, 1982.

42. *New York Times*, 11 April 1982, IV, p. 17, col. 5.

43. *New York Times*, 12 April 1982, I, p. 10, col. 4.

44. Ibid., p. 1, col. 4.

45. *New York Times*, 19 May 1982, p. 4.

46. On April 12, Argentina accepted the Peruvian proposal of a 72-hour truce. Argentina stated that it would await a British response, but Argentine officials tacitly acknowledged that cease-fires and negotiations benefitted Argentina, given her occupation of the Falkland Islands.

47. Argentine negotiators feel much of their "new" position had been made clear in the "parallel talks" of April 10.

48. Hastings and Jenkins, *Battle for the Falklands*, p. 110.

49. Haig, *Caveat*, p. 284.

50. Ibid., p. 285.

51. *New York Times*, 15 April 1982, I, p. 1, col. 6.

52. Haig, *Caveat*, pp. 284–85.

53. See, for example, "Falklands Reconnaissance Improved by Soviet Union," *Aviation Week and Space Technology*, May 24, 1982, p. 20.

54. *Time*, April 9, 1984, p. 61. Argentine sources state that the information provided was that the fleet left Ascension on April 16.

55. *Time*, April 9, 1984, p. 60.

56. Haig, *Caveat*, p. 286. Guaranteed completion appears contradictory to point 3 of the British priorities, unless of course the outcome of the negotiation referred to was not guaranteed to be Argentine sovereignty. However, if in fact Argentine sovereignty was not guaranteed in this latter package, why should Haig have found it inconceivable for Argentina to reject these terms? The Argentine priority was firmness of the outcome over timing, though invasion or military defense was preferable to a long delay. Some Argentine participants claim Haig never presented British points to them. Perhaps the points of the counter-draft were conveyed orally and seemed to be a thing proposal.

57. Haig, *Caveat*, p. 286.

58. Ibid.

59. Ibid., p. 287.

60. *New York Times*, 18 April 1982, p. 18.

61. *New York Times*, 18 April 1982, p. 18.

62. Haig, *Caveat*, p. 289.

63. Ibid.

64. *New York Times*, April 20, 1982, Section I, page 17, column 1.

65. Haig, *Caveat*, p. 290. Such as Argentine position was really more reflective of April 10 than April 19 in the Argentine view, but this demonstrates how little they had conveyed the flexibility they felt to the mediator.

66. *Time*, 9 April 1984, p. 61.

67. *New York Times*, 25 April 1982, I, p. 1, col. 4.

68. Haig, *Caveat*, p. 290.

69. Ibid.

70. Ibid.

71. *New York Times*, 26 April 1982, I, p. 1, col. 4.

72. *Washington Post*, 28 April 1982, I, p. 25, col. 4.

73. *Time*, 9 April 1984, p. 61.

74. Haig, *Caveat*, p. 292.

75. *New York Times*, April 30, 1982, I, p. 9, col. 1.

76. *New York Times*, April 30, 1982, I, p. 1, col. 1.

77. Haig, *Caveat*, p. 293.

78. Henderson, "America and the Falklands," p. 34.

79. And to a lesser degree, the British.

80. Victoria Gamba, interview by the author, Buenos Aires, November 1983.

81. Haig, in *Time*, 9 April 1984, p. 60.

82. Ibid.

83. Haig, *Caveat*, p. 270.

84. Ibid.

85. Ibid., p. 271.

86. Ibid.

87. Air supply of some type continued until surrender. The actual question is dependable, high-volume logistics.

88. Haig, *Caveat*, p. 293.

V

1. Domingo Da-Fieno, conference moderated by the Author at Foreign Service Institute, June 21, 1984; since transcribed at pp. 78–81 of Diane B. Bendahmane and John W. McDonald, eds., *Perspectives on Negotiation* (Washington: GPO, 1986).

2. Tam Dalyell, quoting Peter Snow, in the *New Statesman*, May 1983.

3. Counsellor Da-Fieno puts Galtieri's call at "the early hours of Sunday, May 2," but Belaunde Terry says the acceptance was not in time for the 10:00 Haig-Pym meeting as originally planned, and the debate was certainly a lengthy one. Da Fieno states that U.S. Ambassador Ortiz was informed of Galtieri's acceptance in principle. See Bendahmane and McDonald, eds., *Perspectives on Negotiation*, p. 80.

4. Rice, Desmond and Arthur Gavshon, *The Sinking of the Belgrano* (London: Secker and Warburg, 1984) state that Costa Mendez says he cannot believe that Haig or Pym did not immediately inform Thatcher; an Argentine military officer says Peru was discussing everything with Haig, and Haig was affirming that Pym was with him in his office and fully informed of the morning conversations. However, this military source also says that the acceptance in principle to be confirmed by 8:00 was passed during the last Argentine conversation with President Belaunde on 2 May at mid-day when he transmitted it to Washington. Argentina in effect sent a final message and closed down transmission. To what degree the proposal was accepted only *in principle* is conveyed by the wording of Galtieri, in the second and supposedly final confirmation of acceptance in principle: "I have studied your plan. I think it is feasible." (Rice and Gavshon, *The Sinking of the Belgrano*, p. 164.) There was a constant *assumption* of engagement: The Peruvian Foreign Minister believed that whatever Haig accepted was all right with Pym and whatever was right with Pym had been cleared with London.

5. Haig, *Caveat*, pp. 293–94.

6. Armada de la Republica Argentina: Navy of the Argentine Republic, a preface equivalent to United States Ship (USS) or Her Majesty's Ship (HMS).

7. Three hundred and sixty eight of the crew of *Belgrano* perished, over one-third of Argentina's casualties.

8. Hastings and Jenkins understand that Anaya "encouraged the junta to reject Belaunde not once this week but twice, and then to reject [Perez] de Cuellar as well" (p. 167).

9. *New York Times,* 24 April, 1982, p. 5. One's view of what applied beyond the TEZ depended on one's view of the relations between the two countries and thus between their armed forces by May 2. While the peacemakers were still at work, the two navies had been at war in real terms since the recapture of South Georgia (including the sinking of the submarine ARA *Santa Fe)* the week before.

10. Ibid.

11. That indeed is the more charitable of several critical views of the elements of the failure of the Peruvian mediation. To gain an understanding of the complexity of the Falklands diplomacy of the weekend of May 1–2, 1982, one must examine in detail not only official Argentine and British perceptions but also internal criticism such as that of Argentina's Rattenbach Commission, and on the British side the theses of the Honorable Tam Dalyell, Labor member of Parliament for Linlithgow, in his publications and extended parliamentary questioning of the official British positions; and Desmond Rice and Arthur Gavshon in their *The Sinking of the Belgrano* (London: Secker & Warburg, 1984); as well as Mr. Gavshon's ongoing investigation. Their questioning is incisive. Some of the questions are unanswered, and some unanswerable. Whether or not one accepts their framing of the questions or their answers, they help sharpen analysis of diplomatic method in what this analysis judges to be Round I of the Peruvian mediation. I shall for brevity take the alternative views they express as a "Team B" view. While I have taken the more interesting questions they raise in my own form and order, as well as posing other directions of inquiry, I hope that the synthesis does their assertions no injustice. Like theirs, this is an *ongoing* investigation of a sensitive and difficult subject matter. They have been generous with their time and knowledge, and our differences are honest ones which may yet be narrowed or resolved.

12. Henderson, "American and the Falklands, p. 35.

13. "Falkland Islands: An End to Diplomacy, A Start to War."*Economist,* May 22, 1982, p. 19; and Nossiter, Bernard. "Pym Uninterested Any U.N. Efforts Now." New York Times,4 May 1982, P. 1.

14. For an excellent account of Argentine capacities and operations, see Robert L. Scheina, "The Malvinas Campaign." US Naval Institute Proceedings, Naval Review 1983, December 1983, pp. 93–106.

15. Admiral John ("Sandy") Woodward, cited in Hansard, "Written Answers to Questions for April 13, 1984," London: HPO, 1984.

16. Haig's memoir has the *Belgrano* Exocet-armed (*Caveat,* p. 293). Argentine officers say there were no Exocets with the *Belgrano* task force. It clearly seemed probable to the Royal Navy that the escorts were so armed and *Belgrano* not. In any case the Royal Navy had to assume the Escorts were so armed but could not count on the *Belgrano* not being armed with missiles. In one of the more sad ironies of the collapse of the Peruvian effort, the presumption of Exocets aboard *Belgrano* (logical given Argentine capabilities like the jury-rigged truck-mounted Exocet on the Islands, which hit HMS *Glamorgan)*

may have been created by rumored dummy launching boxes once rigged to intimidate Chile.

17. Team B: two separate orders countermanded the orders and sent the task group back to State Island at the tip of South America,and this order was intercepted by the AD417 equipment aboard the British Nimrod aircraft and by U.S. facilities.

18. Team B: The pincer movement was cancelled at 2,000 hours. The pincer movement may never have been an operations order at all. *It was only a professionally responsible assumption by the British Commander.* If the specific order to close on and attack the carrier group located late Saturday night was cancelled, then why was the *25 de May* searching for the British? Her S–2 aircraft found the British carrier group at 2330 hours and the Argentines closed their distance to 180 from 350 miles, but could not launch at dawn. It is more probable that only on Sunday, May 2, was that attack called off, and then the first Exocet attack was mounted. It too aborted. There was then a withdrawal of the Argentine fleet in the north but not visibly of the *Belgrano* (she was simply on her homeward tack of her patrol zone) and certainly no unilateral Argentine cease-fire or armistice. The *Belgrano* group in the south had only the general "find and destroy" order.

19. *Conqueror,* for example, dove to 500 feet when attacked following her torpedoing of the *General Belgrano.* The shallows of the bank are 150 feet.

20. It is not in the public domain whether *Conqueror's* orders or rules of engagement included the escorting Exocet-armed destroyers. One was struck by a torpedo from *Conqueror* which did not explode. In their tight, parallel formation, the three ships might all have been intended targets. Prudence demands only one for the capital ship if one wishes to damage her. Prudence would argue for also damaging the escorts with their significant antisubmarine warfare capability.

21. Lord Sir Terence Lewin, however, has made the hypothetical statement that had he known of the Peruvian peace plan he would not have sent the order to sink the *Belgrano;* in an unpublished interview with Arthur Gavshon, Ms. Cortez and Mr. Gavshon.

22. Team B: the U.S. Secretary of State has said that on Saturday there was British enthusiasm for the Peruvian plan and thus there may have been an opportunity for a breakthrough. Haig started too late on Saturday to have had this reaction from anyone but Francis Pym, who denies a Saturday contact with the U.S. Secretary of State. Team B also contends that Secretary Haig believes he was in touch with Pym on the evening of Saturday, May 1, after Pym arrived in Washington. Dalyall: "Haig was up all the Saturday night on the phone with the Peruvian negotiations. Pym, his staff, and the British Embassy knew full well what Haig was doing and they did not fail in their duty to tell Chequers." (p. 91) As of Saturday there was little for Britain to be enthusiastic about, and, were there a British reaction, it does not seem to have been phoned to Belaunde even though he was up past midnight Washington time.

23. Haig, *Caveat,* p. 293. The Secretary also seems to attribute clearance with the U.K. to Belaunde. He refers to Belaunde reducing the Proposal to five points, presenting them to both sides and gaining acceptance in principle.

24. Francis Pym "Francis Pym Replies," Letters to the Editor, *London Daily Mirror,* 20 May 1983.

25. Ibid.

26. Ibid.

27. Ibid.

28. Ibid.

29. Answers by the Foreign and Commonwealth Secretary to M. P. Tam Dalyell's questions in U.K. Foreign Office, *Official Report* 56, columns 1260–1261.

30. Francis Pym, "Francis Pym Replies," Letters to the Editor, *London Daily Mirror*, 20 May 1983.

31. Ibid.

32. Haig, *Caveat*, p. 293. Team B sees this as a clash of U.S. and U.K. views on the morning's events. Haig's negotiation was apparently (until Pym's arrival at the U.S. Department of State at 10:00) on behalf of rather than *with* Great Britain. With Haig's outlining the Peruvian plan to Pym, it is not yet clear that Britain felt itself engaged. The mediator clearly felt that the parties were engaged in a dialogue. There is evidence that Haig felt he was indeed authorized by Pym to pursue specific language with Argentina through Peru.

33. Henderson, "America and the Falklands." p. 36.

34. Ibid., p. 36.

35. Team B: The British Embassy and thus the Prime Minister knew from noon Saturday of the Peruvian initiative. (If the Peruvian impression that they kept the British Embassy in Lima fully informed of the plan throughout Saturday is accurate, Embassy Lima did or should have told London on Saturday of a peace process. The kind of close relationship that is the stock-in-trade of long-term, serious professional diplomacy is cited: British Ambassador Charles Wallace's wife had been a friend of Peruvian President Belaunde Terry when he was in political exile in Spain.) It is concluded that the Prime Minister thus knew via her post in Lima by at least noon in Peru (6:00 A.M. Saturday in England) of the Peruvian effort, chose to ignore the chance for peace, and pursued the pure military humiliation of Argentina in order to better her administration's political image. According to Team B, Peruvian Foreign Minister Xavier Arias Stella said that he kept British Ambassador Wallace "informed by telephone of every step of our attempts" from Saturday, May 1, at 12:30 P.M Lima time. Peruvian President Belaunde, he says, confirmed this personally, as did Dr. Manuel Ulloa, the Prime Minister of Peru. (The problem: there was no initiative as on noon Saturday, and would not be for some 12 hours. Peru offered no plan or proposal to Wallace at any point. The Ambassador's recollection is that he first heard of the Peruvian proposals Sunday evening at 6:30.) Haig clearly thought he had something to offer Pym. Pym left that impression (despite his cool reaction, which was several times reiterated) by leaving Haig with "negotiating instructions" in an open-ended mandate.

36. As reconstructed from multiple sources, including interviews.

37. Henderson, "America and the Falklands," p. 36.

38. The torpedo used is of World War II design. U.S. intelligence assets do not seem to have been relocated at the time of the sinking of the *Belgrano*. If British subs were in the area on patrol before the Argentine fleet ventured out into the area, they could have known from intercepts which units were on patrol in their areas.

39. The Team B view would be that diplomacy was only a cover for the deployment of force.

40. Rattenbach Report, para. 634.

41. Ibid, para. 614.

42. Haig's memoir has the whole peace effort (or the second rather than the first Peruvian Round) aborted by the loss of the *General Belgrano* (*Caveat*, p. 243). He is also at odds with this investigation in claiming that the captain of *Conqueror* acted on

standing orders rather than a specific instruction of the War Cabinet authorizing a sinking outside the TEZ.

43. Thomas Enders, p. 3. Testimony before the House Subcommittee on Interamerican Affairs, August 5, 1982. Annex on Legal Aspects, p. 3. Washington: VSGPO, 1982.

44. The British Cabinet reacted to first blood by warily indicating some interest in further diplomacy—rather the opposite of the Argentine reaction.

45. House of Commons minutes of the proceedings of the Foreign Affairs Committee, session 1982–83 (London; HMSO, 11 May 1983), Draft, Chairman's report on a policy for the Falkland Islands, Section 3, paragraph 11.

46. Costa Mendez maintains that the British answer of May 5 was not officially sent to Argentina but only conveyed by phone. He feels that the Peruvian paper of May 1 was accepted by Galtieri. Costa Mendez also recalls a Peruvian paper of 21 May which was "also" accepted by Galtieri and this acceptance conveyed to Belaunde by telephone on 22 May. The General was then in the south. The British, he says, never answered. (They had landed in the Falklands.)

47. The new "toy" sadly made terms which were unobtainable in the era of bilateral negotiations seem undesirable now.

VI

1. Haig, *Caveat*, p. 25.

2. Security Council Statement SC/4401 of 5 May 1982. New York: United Nations, 1982.

3. *New York Times*, May 11, 1982, p. A1. The official U.N. statement of 10 May called the U.N. mediation a "procedural mechanism to deal with the immediate crisis under Article 40 of the United Nations Charter, which provides for preliminary measures which do not prejudice the rights, or positions, or the claims of the parties involved."

4. Hastings & Jenkins, *The Battle for the Falklands*, pp. 28–29.

5. *New York Times*, May 12, 1982, p. A1.

6. Sir Anthony Parsons. "The Falklands Crisis in the United Nations." *International Affairs*, Spring 1983, p. 170.

7. As events would have it, the proposal was made less than one month before a final British military victory.

8. Draft Interim Agreement. British White Paper of May 21, in US Department of State, "The South Atlantic Crisis: Background, Consequences, Documentation." Washington: GPO, 1982, A, p. 12.

9. Ibid.

10. *New York Times*, May 19, 1982, p. 1.

11. *New York Times*, May 20, 1982, p. 1.

12. This was the Argentine view because Argentina had no superpower backer. It saw Britain's toughness backed up by that of a U.S. administration anxious to efface the perceived ineffectiveness of the Carter Administration.

13. U.N. Secretariat Document S/15099 of 21 May, 1982, p. 1.

14. Anthony Parsons. "The Falklands Crisis in the United Nations." *International Affairs*, Spring 1983, p. 175.

15. Unfortunately, this was hinted at *during* the Perez de Cuellar talks. Washington looked askance at the U.N.'s coincidence with the Peruvian effort, as Turtle Bay had Washington's shuttle, and it ironically stated and acted out its assessment so as to undercut

the United Nations in its early stages. Press spokesmen and private emissaries alike kept the U.S. hand in.

16. Remarks on entering U.N. Headquarters, May 26, 1982. (U.N. Public Affairs Office, Press release for 26 May 1982.)

17. On June 15, 1982, Prime Minister Thatcher rejected any future participation in island affairs by the United Nations or Argentina. Each fall the General Assembly passes a resolution on the question of the Falkland/Malvinas Islands. Argentina continues a very active U.N. diplomacy, in conjunction with 20 nations of the Latin American group (GRULA), in the General Assembly context.

VII

1. The text of the January 27 Argentine *bout de papier* entitled "The Argentine Position" can be found in Cardozo, Kirschbaum and Van der Kooy, *Malvinas, La Trama Secreta*. Buenos Aires: Editorial Planeta Argentina, 1983, at pp. 323–5.

2. Submitted to Secretary Haig late that afternoon in Buenos Aires; see Oscar Raul Cardozo, Ricardo Kirschbaum and Eduardo Van der Kooy, *Malvinas, La Trama Secreta*, pp. 327–29.

3. See U.S. Department of State, *The South Atlantic Crisis: Background, Consequences, Documentation* (Washington: GPO, 1982), pp. 8–9.

4. U.S. Department of State, *The South Atlantic Crisis: Background, Consequences, Documentation*, p. 10.

5. Ibid.

6. Cardozo, Kirschbaum and Van der Kooy, *Malvinas, La Trama Secreta*, pp. 342–43.

7. For the original in English see U.S. Department of State, *The South Atlantic Crisis: Background, Consequences, Documentation*, pp. 12–13. For Spanish working copy as used by the U.N and Argentina, see Cardozo, Kirschbaum and Van der Kooy, *Malvinas, La Trama Secreta*, pp. 352–54.

8. Cardozo, Kirschbaum and Van der Kooy, *Malvinas, La Trama Secreta*. pp. 355–57.

9. U.S. Department of State, *The South Atlantic Crisis: Background, Consequences, Documentation*, pp. 10–12.

10. U.S. Department of State, *The South Atlantic Crisis: Background, Consequences, Documentation*, p. 13.

11. U.S. Statements of April 30 by President Ronald Reagan and Secretary of State Alexander Haig, *New York Times*, May 1, 1982, page 1 column 6. Haig's Full text in Desmond Rice and Arthur Gavshon on. *The Sinking of the Belgrano*. (London: Seckert Warburg, 1984.) p. 195–96. In these key statements, the U.S. leadership effectively ended U.S. neutrality on the subject of the forceful occupation of the Falkland Islands.

12. *New York Times*, March 2, 1988, p. 1. (Spanish original in Cardozo, Kirschbaum and Van der Kooy, *Malvinas, La Trama Secreta*, p. 54.)

13. U.S. Statement of April 30 by Secretary of State Alexander Haig, in Rice and Gavshon, *The Sinking of the Belgrano*, p. 195.

14. For some interesting rethinking of military organization, see James Brown and Michael J. Collins, *Military Ethics and Professionalism* (Washington, D.C.: National Defense University, National Security Essay Series 81–82), p. 70.

15. Speech at the Cosmos Club, Washington, D.C., September 14, 1983.

16. Hugh Trevor-Roper, *New York Times,* 29 May, 1982.

17. I am indebted for the idea of perceived "pain" to Dr. William Zartman, Analysis Group Meeting, Foreign Service Institute, Rosslyn, Virginia, June 26, 1984.

18. Argentine public policy is that a second switch-over occurred with the sinking of the *Belgrano*.

19. This last principle is not *necessarily* important to a middle power of world reach, though it was to Britain.

VIII

1. Dr. Gary Wynia, "The Argentine Military," Symposium on the Military and Democracy in Latin America, Center for the Study of Foreign Affairs, Foreign Service Institute, Washington, D.C., December 5, 1983.

2. The theme, derived from the author's interviews in the Falklands, is that prior to the war the Islanders and the Argentines were moving towards an accommodation, no matter how unenthusiastically, and that the war destroyed this motion. This firm conclusion does not seem to be the thesis generally held in the literature on the Falklands, which rather maintains that antipathy between Kelper and Argentine was old and constant, although certainly heightened because of the war. A sample of this thinking is that the Kelpers, who were "never supportive of any kind of settlement which introduced Argentine sovereignty, are even more negatively disposed toward Buenos Aires than before the conflict" (Gerald W. Hopple, "Intelligence and Warning Lessons," in Bruce Watson and Peter M. Dunn, eds., *Military Lessons of the Falkland Islands War: Views from the United States* [Boulder, Co.: Westview Press, 1984] p. 111). In an even more extreme statement, it has been the notion that the Argentine position on sovereignty had right on its side, and that it was "the stubbornness of the islanders" and their "marked antipathy to Argentina" that caused an impasse (Laurence Freedman, "The War of the Falkland Islands, 1982," *Foreign Affairs* 61 [Fall 1982]: 197.)

The difference lies in the distinction between "political" antipathy and "cultural" antipathy. Unification against any Argentine role in their *political* lives, based on occupation and isolation, is more recent, pronounced, and articulable a political phenomenon than any latent cultural antipathy. Political and leadership questions are part of the same dialogue as thinking about the invasion and future political status. They therefore share vocabulary and analytical frameworks (whether formal or unconscious). It was Argentine governance of the Argentines and the Kelpers that was disillusioning even with the allowance made for hostilities. Culturally, on the interpersonal level, common values and behavioral norms prevailed. If not always parallel (the courtesy of the hispanic *caballero* combined with that of the military officer struck the Kelpers as "Prussian"), it was nonetheless understandable and appreciated.

3. Clearly the potential of this idea was diminished by its unilateral proposal by the Argentine Foreign Minister in Caracas in late 1983. Its validity is not reduced, only its political appeal and "neutrality." Should Argentina pursue U.N. Forces as "recognition" of its claims, it will attain neither. In the coming century, the idea may appeal to a British government whose alternative is again a merely token British force.

Selected Bibliography

BOOKS

Alfonsin, Raul. *Ahora: Mi Propuesta Politica*. Buenos Aires: Editorial Planeta S.A.I.C., 1983.

Barnet, Richard J. *Roots of War*. New York: Penguin Books, 1971.

Benedict, B., ed. *Problems of Smaller Territories*. London: Athlone Press, 1967.

Betts, Richard K. *Surprise Attack*. Washington, D.C.: Brookings Institution, 1982.

Braybrook, Roy. *Battle for the Falklands (3)—Air Forces*. London: Osprey Publishing, 1982.

Caillet-Bois, Capt. de Fragata Teodoro. *Historia Naval Argentina*. Buenos Aires: Emece Editores, 1951.

Canetti, Elias. *Crowds and Power*. New York: Continuum Publishing Corporation, 1962.

Cantori, Louis, and Steven Spiegel. *The International Politics of Regions*. New Jersey: Prentice-Hall, 1970.

Cardoso, O. R., R. Kirschbaum, and G. Van der Koog. *Malvinas: La Trama Secreta*. Buenos Aires: Editorial Planeta Argentina, 1983.

Catudal, Honore M., Jr. *The Exclave Problem of Western Europe*. University, Alabama: University of Alabama Press, 1979.

Cawkell, Mary. *The Falkland Story, 1592–1982*. Oswestry: Anthony Nelson, 1983.

Cockburn, A. *War in the Falklands*. New York: Riverrun, 1982.

Coffin, Royce A. *The Negotiator: A Manual for Winners*. New York: Barnes and Noble, 1976.

Coll, Alberto R., and Anthony C. Arend, eds. *The Falklands War: Lessons for Strategy, Diplomacy and International Law*. London: Allen and Unwin, 1985.

Conil Paz, Alberto. *Argentina's Foreign Policy 1930–1962*. Notre Dame: University of Notre Dame Press, 1966.

Consejo Argentino para las Relaciones Internacionales. *Malvinas, Georgias y Sandwich del Sur: Diplomacia Argentina en las Naciones Unidas 1945–1981*. Buenos Aires: C.A.R.I., 1982.

Cox, Kevin, David Reynolds, and Stein Rokkar, eds. *Locational Approaches to Power and Conflict*. New York: John Wiley and Sons, 1974.

Craig, Gordon A., and Alexander L. George. *Force and Statecraft*. New York: Oxford University Press, 1983.

Dalyell, T. *One Man's Falklands*. London: Cecil Woolf, 1982.

———. *Thatcher's Torpedo*. London: Cecil Woolf, 1983.

del Carril, Bonifacio. *La Cuestion de las Malvinas*. Buenos Aires: Emece Editores, 1983.

de Molina, Alfredo Diaz. *Las Islas Malvinas y una Nueva Diplomacia*. Buenos Aires: Libreria Editorial Platero S.R.L., 1976.

DeSmith, S. A. *Microstates and Micronesia: Problems of America's Pacific Islands and Other Minute Territories*. New York: New York University Press, 1970.

Destefani, Laurio H. *The Malvinas, the South Georgias and the South Sandwich Islands, the Conflict with Britain*. Buenos Aires: Edipress, 1982.

Dobson, C., J. Miller, and R. Payne. *The Falklands Conflict*. London: Coronet Books, 1982.

Ecuador, Ministry of Foreign Relations. *El Problema Territorial Ecuatoriano-Peruano*. Quito: Government of Ecuador, 1981.

Eddy, P., M. Linklater, and P. Gillman. *The Falklands War*. London: Sphere Books, 1982.

English, Adrian, and Anthony Watts. *Battle for the Falklands (2)—Naval Forces:* London: Osprey Publishing, 1982.

Erlich, Haggai. *The Struggle over Eritrea: 1962–1978*. Stanford: Hoover Institution Press, 1983.

Escott, T. H. S. *The Story of British Diplomacy*. Philadelphia: George W. Jacobs and Co., 1908.

Ferns, H. S. *Britain and Argentina in the 19th Century*. Oxford: OUP, 1960.

Fitzgibbon, Russel H., ed. *Global Politics*. Berkeley: University of California Press, 1944.

Fowler, William. *Battle for the Falklands (1)—Land Forces*. London: Osprey Publishing, 1982.

Fraga, Jorge Alberto. *Las Islas Malvinas: Sintesis del Problema*. Buenos Aires: Instituto de las Islas Malvinas y Tierras Australes Argentinas, 1980.

Garcia Lupo, Rogelio. *Diplomacia Secreta y Rendicion Incondicional*. Madrid: Editorial Legasa, 1983.

George, James L., ed. *Problems of Sea Power as We Approach the Twenty-First Century*. Washington, D.C.: American Enterprise Institute for Public Policy Research, 1978.

Geraghty, Tony. *Who Dares Wins*. Glasgow: William Collins Sons & Co., 1980.

Goebel, Julius. *The Struggle for the Falkland Islands: A Study in Legal and Diplomatic History*. New Haven: Yale University Press, 1927.

Grant, C. H. *The Making of Modern Belize*. Cambridge: Cambridge University Press, 1976.

Gutierrez, Pedro Rafael. *Las Malvinas: Provincia Argentina*. San Jose, Costa Rica: Ediciones Lena, 1982.

Haig, Alexander M., Jr. *Caveat: Realism, Reagan, and Foreign Policy*. New York: Macmillan Publishing Company, 1984.

Hall, Ron, ed. *War in the Falklands*. London: Weidenfeld and Nicolson, 1982.

Han, Henry Hyunwook. *Terrorism, Political Violence and World Order*. New York: University Press of America, 1984.

Hanrahan, B., and R. Fox. *I Counted Them All Out and I Counted Them All Back*. London: B.O.C., 1982.

Hastings, M., and S. Jenkins. *Battle for the Falklands*. London: Michael Joseph, 1983.

Hernandez, Pablo J., and Horacio Chitarroni. *Malvinas: Clave Geopolitica*. Buenos Aires: Ediciones Castaneda, 1977.

Hoffman, Fritz L., and Olga Mingo. *Sovereignty in Dispute: The Falklands/Malvinas, 1943–1982*. London: Westview Press, 1984.

Jackson, Richard L. *The Non-Aligned: The U.N. and the Superpowers*. New York: Praeger Publishers, 1983.

Kanaf, Leo. *La Batalla de las Malvinas*. Buenos Aires: Tribuna Abierta, 1982.

Kidron, Michael, and Dan Smith. *The War Atlas*. New York: Simon & Schuster, 1983.

Kon, Daniel. *Los Chicos de la Guerra*. Buenos Aires: Editorial Galerna, 1982.

Laffin, J. *Fight for the Falkland Islands*. London: St. Martin, 1982.

Latin American Bureau. *Falklands/Malvinas: Whose Crisis?* London: Latin American Bureau, 1982.

Laver, Michael. *Playing Politics*. New York: Penguin Books, 1979.

McMahon, Matthew M. *Conquest and Modern International Law*. Washington, D.C.: Catholic University of America Press, 1940.

Manley, Robert H. *Guyana Emergent*. Cambridge: Schenkman Publishing Co., 1979.

Milne, R. S. *Politics in Ethnically Bipolar States*. London: University of British Colombia Press, 1981.

Montenegro, Nestor J., and Eduardo Aliverti. *Los Nombres de la Derrota*. Buenos Aires: Nemont Ediciones, 1982.

Ofuatey-Kodjoe, W. *The Principle of Self-Determination in International Law*. New York: Neller Publishing Co., 1977.

Page, Joseph A. *Peron*. New York: Random House, 1983.

Paxton, John, ed. *The Statesman's Yearbook*. New York: St. Martin's Press, 1983–1984.

Perl, Raphael. *The Falkland Islands Dispute in International Law and Politics*. London: Oceana Publications, 1983.

Perrett, Bryan. *Weapons of the Falklands Conflict*. Poole: Blandford Press, 1982.

Preiswerk, Roy, ed. *Documents on International Relations in the Caribbean*. St. Augustine Florida: Institute of International Relations and Rio Piedras Puerto Rico: Institute of Caribbean Studies, 1970.

Price, David Lynn. *The Western Sahara*. The Washington Papers, Volume 7. Beverly Hills: Sage Publications, 1979.

Quigg, Philip W. *A Pole Apart*. New York: McGraw-Hill Book Co., 1983.

Raiffa, Howard. *The Art and Science of Negotiation*. Cambridge, Mass.: Harvard University Press, 1982.

Rapaport, Jacques, Ernest Muteba, and Joseph Thcrattil. *Small States and Territories: Status and Problems*. A UNITAR Study. New York: Arno Press, 1971.

Reginald, R., and J. M. Elliot. *Tempest in a Teapot: The Falkland Islands War*. London: Borgo Press, 1982.

Rice, Desmond, and Arthur Gavshon. *The Sinking of the Belgrano*. London: Secker & Warburg, 1984.

Schonfeld, Manfred. *La Guerra Austral*. Buenos Aires: Desafios Editores, 1982.

Skidmore, Thomas E., and Peter H. Smith. *Modern Latin America*. New York: Oxford University Press, 1984.

Soja, Edward. *The Political Organization of Space*. Resource paper no. 8. Commission
    on College Geography, 1971.
Storni, Segundo R. *Intereses Argentinos en el Mar*. Buenos Aires: Instituto de Publi-
    caciones Navales, 1967.
Strange, Ian J. *The Falkland Islands*. North Pomfret, Vt.: David & Charles, 1983.
The *Sunday Times* Insight Team. *The Falkland War*. London: Sphere Books, 1982.
Viola, Oscar Luis. *La Derrota Diplomatica y Militar de la Republica Argentina en la
    Guerra de las Islas Malvinas*. Buenos Aires: Tinta Nueva, 1983.
Wemyss, Martin La Touche. *75 Days of Conflict*. London: Confex, 1982.
Wesley-Smith, Peter. *Unequal Treaty 1898–1997*. Oxford: Oxford University Press,
    1980.

OCCASIONAL PAPERS

The Argentine Report. Washington, D.C.: Southern Cone Publishing & Advisory Ser-
    vices, Inc., April 1984.
Barker, Nicholas. Manuscript on the Future of the South Atlantic. Churchill College,
    Cambridge University, June 1984.
Burns, Robert Andrew. "Diplomacy, War and Parliamentary Democracy: Further Lessons
    from the Falklands or Advice from Academe." Harvard University, June 1983.
Burton, John W. "The History and Present State of Conflict Resolution." Paper presented
    to the first meeting of the Council for the Facilitation of International Conflict
    Resolution. University of Maryland, June 18, 1984.
Campbell, Colin. "In Search of Executive Harmony: Cabinet Government and the U.S.
    Presidency—the Experiences of Carter and Reagan." Paper presented at the annual
    meeting of the American Political Science Association, 1983.
Dominguez, Jorge I. "U.S.-Argentine Relations: Some Reflections." Center for Inter-
    national Affairs, Harvard University, 1983.
Falcoff, Mark. "Argentina, the United States, and Hemispheric Security: Bringing Two
    Worlds Closer Together." Paper presented at the second Argentine-American
    Forum, 1983, Wye Plantation, Md.
Ford, John, and L. Ronald Scheman. "The Role of Regional International Organization
    in Mediation and Settlement of Disputes: The OAS Experience." Xeroxed man-
    uscript courtesy of the author.
Gamba, Virginia. "La Cuestion y La Crisis." August 30, 1983.
Gaunt, Robert. "The Use of Maritime Power in the South Atlantic Conflict."
Gompert, David C. "Lessons of the Falklands War." Paper presented to the John Bassett
    Moore Society of International Law, 1982.
Grondona, Mariano. "Schism in the West." Paper presented at the Argentine-American
    Forum, 1983, Wye Plantation, Md.
Haig, Alexander. "The Prospects for Peace in the South Atlantic." Washington, D.C.:
    U.S. Department of State, May 1982.
International Studies Association. *International Problem Solving Organization*. A Pro-
    posal submitted by John Burton to a meeting of associates held at the 24th Annual
    Convention of the International Studies Association held in Mexico City, April
    5–9, 1983.
King, David E. "The Falklands Experience." St. John's College, Cambridge University,
    June 1984.

Lopez, Carlos. "Maritime Perspectives in the Southern Cone: A South American View."

McGee, Gale. "Some Personal Observations on the OAS and the Falklands."

Menaul, Air Vice Marshal Stewart W. B. "Lessons from the Falklands Campaign."

Musich, Arnaldo T. "Argentina and the United States Relations." Paper presented at
    the second Argentine-United States Forum, Wye Plantation, Maryland 1983.

Shoyer, Andrew W. "Toward a Solution to the Falklands (Malvinas) Dispute". December
    5, 1983. Georgetown University School of Foreign Service.

Wedge, Bryant. "Problems Solving Procedures." Letter to Argentine Ambassador Es-
    teban Takacs of May 21, 1982. Xerox. Fairfax, Virginia: Center for Conflict
    Resolution, George Mason University, 1982.

OFFICIAL PUBLICATIONS

United Kingdom, Foreign and Commonwealth Office. *Britain and Its People: An Outline*.
    London: Her Majesty's Stationery Office (HMSO) February 1983.

Britain and the Falkland Crisis—a Documentary Record. COI Publication No. 192/RP/
    82. Washington, D.C., 1982.

Conference on the Anglo-Argentine War of 1982. *Lessons of the South Atlantic War*.
    Proceedings. London: mss, 1984.

Falkland Islands United Kingdom. Parliament. Appendices to the Minutes of Evidence,
    Session 1982–1983. London: Her Majesty's Stationery Office, May 1983.

United Kingdom. House of Commons. *Falkland Islands*. Minutes of Evidence for 3, 4,
    7 February 1983, Foreign Affairs Committee Session 1982–83. London: Her
    Majesty's Stationery Office, February 1983.

United Kingdom. Foreign and Commonwealth Office. *The Falkland Islands and De-
    pendencies*. London: Her Majesty's Stationery Office, April 1982.

United Kingdom. Foreign and Commonwealth Office. *The Falklands: The Facts*. London:
    Her Majesty's Stationery Office, December 1982.

Franks, Lord Joseph. *Falkland Islands Review*. London: HMSO, 1982.

Government of Argentina. Ministry of Defense. *Documento Final de la Junta Militar
    Sobre La Guerra Contra la Subersion y el Terrorismo*. Xeroxed manuscript.
    Buenos Aires: 1983.

Kirkpatrick, Jeane J. Testimony before the House Appropriations Committee, Foreign
    Operations Subcommittee, May 4, 1982.

Laue, James H. on S.564, Testimony on the U.S. Academy of Peace Act before the
    Subcommittee on Education, Arts, and Humanities of the Committee on Labor
    and Human Resources of the U.S. Senate, March 16, 1983.

Minutes of Evidence. Taken before the Foreign Affairs Committee, June 20, 1984.
    London: HMSO; 1984.

Minutes of Evidence: Falkland Islands. Wednesday, 21 March 1984; Monday, 21 Feb-
    ruary 1983; Monday, 24 January 1983; Monday, 6 December 1982; Monday, 15
    November 1982. London: HMSO.

Minutes to the Proceedings of the Foreign Affairs Committee. Session 1982–83. London:
    Her Majesty's Stationery Office, May 1983.

Organization of American States. *Annual Report of the Secretary General 1981–1982*.
    Washington, D.C.: OAS, 1982.

Organization of American States. *Annual Report of the Secretary General 1982–1983*. OAS, Washington, D.C., 1983.

Preece, Charlotte P., Bert Cooper, and Nina Serafino. *The Falkland/Malvinas Islands Crisis*. Washington, D.C.: Congressional Research Service, 1982.

Roberts, Brad. *The Military Implications of the Falklands/Malvinas Islands Conflict*. Washington, D.C.: Congressional Research Service August 17, 1982.

U.N. Security Council Documents from S/14940 to S/15575 selectively. Exact documents and a synopsis of each document can be found under "Falklands" at the U.N. Woodrow Wilson Library desk.

U.N. Verbatim Records. Documents No. S/PV 2345, 2346, 2349, 2350, 2359, 2360, 2362, 2363, 2364, 2366, 2368, 2371, 2372, 2373. Congressional Research Service, August 17, 1982.

United States Department of State. *La Crisis del Atlantico del Sur: Antecedents, Consecuencias, Documentacion*. Washington, D.C.: Servicio de Informacion de los Estados Unidos de America, 1982.

Shackleton, Lord. *Falkland Islands Economic Study 1982*. London: HMSO, 1982.

United Kingdom. House of Commons Defense Committee. *The Future Defense of the Falkland Islands*. Third Report, session 1982–1983. London: Her Majesty's Stationery Office, May 1983.

United Kingdom, House of Commons Defense Committee. *The Handling of Press and Public Information during the Falklands Conflict*. First report. London: Her Majesty's Stationery Office, 8 December 1982.

United Kingdom. Foreign and Commonwealth Office. *The Falkland Islands—Early History*. Background Brief. London: Foreign and Commonwealth Office, May 1983.

United Kingdom. *Falkland Islands Economic Study 1982*. London: Her Majesty's Stationary Office. Presented to Parliament, September 1982.

United Kingdom. Prime Minister. "Report of a Committee of Privy Counselors." *Falkland Islands Review*. London: Her Majesty's Stationery Office. Presented to Parliament, January 1983.

United Kingdom. Secretary of State for Defense. *The Falklands Campaign: The Lessons*. London: Her Majesty's Stationery Office. Presented to Parliament, December 1982.

United States. Department of State. *Conventional Arms Transfers in the Third World, 1972–83*. Washington, D.C.: U.S. Department of State, August 1982.

United States Department of State, Bureau of Public Affairs. *The South Atlantic Crisis: Background, Consequences, Documentation*. Washington, D.C.: Bureau of Public Affairs, U.S. Department of State, August 1982.

PERIODICALS

Alisky, Mervin. "Latin Reactions to the Falklands." *Wall Street Journal*, June 2, 1982, p. 2.

"America and the Falklands." *The Economist*. November 12, 1982, pp. 13–31.

"America's Falklands War." *The Economist*, March 3, 1984, 29–31.

"Argentina Began It All with Force?" Interview with Jeane Kirkpatrick. *Newsweek*, May 17, 1982, pp. 34–35.

Arma Y Geoestrategia 2, no. 6 (May 1983).

"Assembly Reaffirms Right of People of East Timor to Self-Determination." *UN Monthly Chronicle*, January 1982, 19–20.

"Britain's Foreign Office." *The Economist*, November 27, 1982, 19–26.

Brooks, Roger A. "U.N. Peace Keeping: An Empty Mandate." *Backgrounder*, April 20, 1983.

Calvert, Peter. "Guatemala and Belize." *Contemporary Review*, January 1976, 7–12.

———. "Sovereignty and the Falklands Crisis. *International Affairs*, 1983, pp. 22–32.

Connell-Smith, Gordon. "The OAS and the Falklands Conflict." *World Today*, September 1982, pp. 48–63.

Crick, Bernard. "The Curse of Sovereignty." *The New Statesman*, May 14, 1982, 6–7.

"Del Mar." *Organo del Instituto Browniano*, no. 118, Enero-Junio 1982.

Dunnett, Denzil. "Self-determination and the Falklands." *International Affairs*, 1983, pp. 64–81.

The Economist. April 3–June 26, 1982; July 10, 1982.

Henderson, Nicholas. "America and the Falklands: Case Study in the Behaviour of an Ally." *The Economist*, November 12, 1983, pp. 31–38.

International Relations (London) 7, no. 4 (November 1982).

Irving, Edmund. "Does Withdrawal of Endurance Signal a Falkland Islands Desertion?" *The Geographical Magazine*, January 1982.

"The Junta's Wrigglings." *The Economist*, May 15, 1982, pp. 21–22.

Kaylor, Robert. "How Bustling Hong Kong Copes with Uncertainty." *US News and World Report*, June 27, 1983, 45.

Makin, Guillermo A. "Argentine Approaches to the Falklands/Malvinas: Was the Resort to Violence Foreseeable?" *International Affairs*, 1983.

Metford, J. C. J. "Falklands or Malvinas? The Background to the Dispute." *International Affairs*, Summer 1983, 463–81.

Millennium: Journal of International Studies, 12, no. 1 (Spring 1983).

Moore, John Norton. "The Inter-American System Snarls in Falklands War." *American Journal of International Law*, October 1982.

Murguizur Carlos, Juan. "The South Atlantic Conflict: an Argentinian Point of View." *International Defense Review*, 1983.

Newsweek, April–June 1982.

Parsons, Anthony. "The Falklands Crisis in the United Nations, 31 March–14 June 1982." *International Affairs*, Spring 1983, pp. 169–78.

Patterson, B. "The Plight of East Timor." *America*, November 12, 1983, 288–90.

Peace and Change: A Journal of Peace Research 8, no. 2/3, *Conference on Peace Research in History and the Consortium on Peace Research, Education and Development*, Summer 1982.

"Playing Tough." *The Economist*, June 16, 1984.

Purcell, Susan Kaufman. "War and Debt in South America. *Foreign Affairs*, 61, no. 3 (1982): p. 660–74.

Scheina, Robert L. "The Malvinas Campaign." Naval Institute, *Proceedings/Naval Review*, December 1983.

Time Magazine. April 12–June 5, 1982.

Turner, Stansfield. "The Unobvious Lessons of the Falklands War." U.S. Naval Institute *Proceedings*, April 1983.

U.S. Naval Institute. *Proceedings* 109; no. 9; September 1983.

———. *Proceedings* 109; no 12; December 1983.

U.S. News and World Report. April 19–June 7; 1982.

Van Sant Hall, Marshall. "Argentine Policy Motivations" in the Falklands War and the
    Aftermath." *Naval War College Review,* November–December, 1983.

Wallace, William. "How Frank was Franks?" *International Affairs,* 1983.

"Whale of a Tale." *The Economist,* June 23, 1984.

"Why U.N. Couldn't Keep the Peace—and Why It May Yet Succeed." *U.S. News and
    World Report,* May 31, 1982.

Willenson, Kim. "The Beagle War." *Newsweek,* November 13, 1978, 88.

Williams, Phil. "Miscalculation, Crisis Management and the Falklands Conflict." *World
    Today,* April 1983, 144–49.

The World Today (Royal Institute of International Affairs). 38, no. 5 (May 1982), P. 161–
    65.

———. 38, no. 6 (June 1982), P. 203–7.

———. 38, no. 9 (September 1982), P. 327–47.

Yanzhorn, Guan. "Argentina's Diplomatic Victory." *Beijing Review,* November 15,
    1982, 9–10.

INDEX

acts of domination, by British, 39

Alexander VI (Pope), Spanish-Portuguese Treaty of Tordesillas, 37–38

Allara, Gualter, 56

Anaya, Jorge, 125

Antarctica, economics of joint undertakings, 290

Arauz Castex, Manuel, 53

Argentina: Acts of Domination, 39; British Task Force actions against, 236–47; Buenos Aires invasion by Great Britain, 40–41; Buenos Aires mediation meetings, 114–17; crisis management efforts, 73–98; diplomacy as Falklands foreign policy, 259–60; diplomatic efforts, 44–54; early diplomacy efforts, 44–46; Falklands seizure, 101–10; following Falklands crisis, 257–90; "Fortress Falklands" reaction, 258–59; joint occupation evaluation, 277–78; joint sovereignty evaluation, 278; joint undertakings with Great Britain, 287–90; joint use evaluation, 277; Kelpers in, 264–72; law and power rules, 252–53; lease-back compromise, 276; London mediation efforts, 116–19; mediation assessment following Falklands crisis, 272–75; military action by Great Britain in 1966, 49; nonaligned nations and, 82–83; normalization efforts by Great Britain, 226–27; partition issues, 276–77; Perez de Cuellar mediation, 234; Peruvian initiatives and, 151; Plan B dissolution, 261–63; postwar negotiations with Great Britain, 46–56; Puerto Soledad conflict with United States, 41; rearmament of, 260–61; at Rome Postal Convention (1908), 42; Rosas government, 42; Southern Thule occupation, 55–56; sovereignty issues with Great Britain, 49–52; sovereignty negotiations, 230–36; sovereignty proposals evaluated, 279–80; special interests of, 281–83; trusteeship following Falklands crisis, 278; U. N. guarantor troops, 286–87; U.S. mediation in Falklands crisis and, 99–148; U.S. military disengagement proposals, 219–21; U.S. relations, 78–

81; Washington mediation efforts,
120–21. *See also* Falklands crisis
arms supplies, to Argentina, 260–61

Beagle Channel, territorial dispute over,
19–20, 57
Belize, territorial dispute over, 20–21
Brazil, arms supplies to Argentina, 260–
61
British Task Force: combat effectiveness
of, 240–41; command of, 242–43;
deterrence, 243–44; flexibility of, 241–
42; military actions by, 236–47;
restraint of, 241
brushfire war, and Falklands crisis, 1–3
Buenos Aires: round two mediation, 123–
30; sovereignty, 41
Byron, Commodore John, 39

Callaghan, James, 53
Carrington (Lord), 105
Chalfont (Lord), 50
Chile, Beagle Channel dispute, 57
combat effectiveness, by British Task
Force, 240–41
Committee of the Twenty-Four (C–24),
48
Common Market, NATO (North Atlantic
Treaty Organization) and, 247–48
Contact Group, Peruvian proposal and,
221–22
Cortazzi, Hugh, 56
Costa Mendez, Nicanor, 104, 117–18;
military disengagement proposals, 219–
21; in round two Buenos Aires
mediations, 124–30; Special Interim
Authority (SIA) proposed, 227
culture, politics and, 266

decolonization: objects of, 233; U.N.
activities, 6–10; visiting missions,
284–85
deterrence, by British Task Force, 243–
44
diplomacy: following Falklands crisis,
259–60; Haig's role in U.S.
diplomacy, 107–21; mediation
assessment following Falklands crisis,

272–75; Peruvian initiatives, 151–86;
postwar efforts by Argentina, 44–46;
practical politics and, 280–81; U.S.
efforts in Falklands crisis, 99–148

East Timor, territorial dispute over, 21
economics of joint undertakings, 287–90
EEC (European Economic Community),
NATO and, 247–48
Eritrea, territorial dispute over, 22
The Essequibo, territorial dispute over,
22–23

Falklands: discovery of, 37–38; following
Falklands crisis, 257–90; geography of,
44–46; Great Britain and, 41–44;
invasion analysis, 58–71; Kelpers
following conflict, 264–72; lobby, 57–
61; population and demographics, 57–
58; sovereignty of, 37–44; U.N.
military observers in, 283–84
Falklands crisis: British honor and, 111–
14; British Task Force actions, 236–47;
Buenos Aires meetings, 120–32;
contexts of, 1–36; crisis management
efforts, 73–98; EEC (European
Economic Community) and, 247–48;
Haig's role in U.S. diplomacy, 107–
21; interim administration, 227–28;
joint use/occupation/sovereignty
evaluation, 277–78; lessons learned
from, 244–46; military disengagement
proposals, 219–24; National Honor
versus National Interest, 3–6; NATO
implications, 246–47; negotiations
overview, 218–36; 1977 signals, 56–
57; nonaligned nations and, 82–83;
nonaligned resolutions on Falklands,
10–14; normalization efforts, 226–27;
origins of, 37–71; Peruvian initiatives,
151–86; Plan B dissolution, 261–63;
Port Stanley hijacking, 49; restraint of
British military, 241; sovereignty
negotiations, 230–36; Suez syndrome
and, 250–51; trusteeship following,
278; U.N. decolonization activities, 6–
10; U.N. guarantor troops, 286–87;
U.N. mediation efforts in New York,

195–215; U.S. mediation efforts, 99–
148. *See also* brushfire war
Falklands Island Company (FIC), 265
fisheries, joint undertakings, 288–89
"Five Points," Haig proposal, 125–29
France: arms supplies to Argentina, 260–
61; colonization of Falklands, 40
free association, evaluation of proposal
for, 278–79

Galtieri, Leopoldo, 114–19
General Assembly Resolution 2065,
48
Germany, arms supplies to Argentina,
260–61
Gibraltar, territorial dispute over,
23–25
Goa, territorial dispute over, 17–19
Great Britain: blockade effect, 116–19;
British Task Force actions, 236–47;
Buenos Aires invasion, 40–41; crisis
management efforts, 73–98; effects of
victory on, 263–64; Falklands crisis of
1770 response, 249–50; Falklands
seizure response, 103–9; following
Falklands crisis, 257–90; Haig's role in
U.S. diplomatic efforts, 109–19; Heath
government, 46; Interim Draft
Agreement Counteroffer of May 17,
234; joint undertakings with Argentina,
287–90; lease-back compromise, 276;
military action in 1966, 49;
normalization efforts, 226–27; Peruvian
initiatives and, 151–86; Port Egmont
settlement, 38–39; postwar negotiations
with Argentina, 46–56; pre–World War
II Falklands claims and conflicts, 41–
44; Resolution 502 and, 222–25; Rosas
government and, 42; Shackleton
survey, 53; sovereignty negotiations,
230–36; special interests of, 283–87;
Suez syndrome, 250–51; U.N.
guarantor troops and, 286–87; U.S.
military disengagement proposals, 219–
21; Washington mediation efforts,
120–21; Wilson government, 46–47
Grytviken, 42–44

Haig, Alexander, 99, 104; Buenos Aires
meetings, 114–17; "five points," 125–
29; military disengagement proposals,
219–21; Peruvian initiatives
considered, 152–77; role of in
Falklands crisis mediation, 107–21
Heath government, Falklands negotiations
with Argentina, 46
Henderson, Sir Nicholas, 108
Hong Kong, territorial dispute over, 25–
28

independence, evaluation of proposal for,
279
interim administration, views of,
227–28
Interim Draft Agreement Counteroffer
of May 17, 234
Israel, arms supplies to Argentina, 260–
61

Jewett, David, 39
joint undertakings, 287–90
Junta: endgame strategies, 236–39; "none
for five," 76, 255; sovereignty
negotiations and, 230–36; U.S.
negotiations with Haig, 114–21. *See
also* Argentina

Kelpers: Falklands crisis and, 46–54;
following Falklands crisis, 264–72;
Peruvian initiatives and, 151;
plebiscite, 47
krill, joint undertakings, 288–89

Lami-Dozo, Basilio, 125
law, power and in modern world,
252–53
lease-back, evaluation of, 276
London, mediation efforts in, 116–19
Lord North, Falklands crisis of 1770
response, 249
Luce, Richard, sovereignty negotiations,
230–36

Malvinas Islands. *See* Falklands
marine biology, joint undertakings, 288–
89

mediation: assessment of, following
  Falklands crisis, 272–75; differing
  agendas, 101–3; "five points," 125–
  29; impasse in, 130–32; joint use/
  occupation/sovereignty evaluation,
  277–78; lease-back compromise, 276;
  in London, 116–19; mediation efforts
  following April 2 announcement, 103–
  10; partition issues, 276–77; Peruvian
  initiatives, 151–86; settlement
  possibilities, 100–101; U.N. efforts in
  New York, 195–215; U.S. efforts in
  Falklands crisis, 99–148; Washington
  round one, 120–22; Washington round
  two, 132–35
military action: Beagle Channel dispute,
  57; British retrenchment of 1966, 49;
  Shackleton incident, 55
military actions, of British Task Force,
  236–47
Moreno, Manual, 42

National Honor: versus National Interest,
  3–6; new vision of, 282–83; redefining
  following Falklands crisis, 282–83;
  timing and, 253–55
National Interest, versus National Honor,
  3–6
NATO (North Atlantic Treaty
  Organization): EEC (European
  Economic Community) and, 247–48;
  implications of Falklands crisis, 246–
  47; Suez syndrome and, 250–51
negotiations: endgame strategies, 236–39;
  Interim Draft Agreement Counteroffer
  of May 17, 234; overview of elements,
  218–36; Perez de Cuellar mediation,
  234; sovereignty issues with Great
  Britain and Argentina, 49–52;
  sovereignty negotiations, 230–36
neutralization: evaluation of proposal for,
  279
nonaligned movement, Falklands
  resolutions, 10–14
nonaligned nations, Falklands crisis and,
  82–83
"none for five": definition of, 76;
  principle of, 255

Nootka Sound-St. Lawrence accord
  (1790), 39
normalization, efforts toward, 226–27
Nott, John, 104, 117

OAS. See Organization of American
  States (OAS)
oil exploration, joint undertakings,
  288
Organization of American States (OAS):
  in Falklands crisis mediation, 106–7;
  following Falklands crisis, 284–85
Ortiz de Rosas (Argentine Ambassador),
  48–49, 152

partition, evaluation of, 276–77
Perez de Cuellar, Javier, 99; mediation
  efforts, 234; Peruvian attempt and,
  156
Peru: British perceptions of mediation
  efforts, 159–60; initiatives of, 151–86;
  Team B thesis, 167–77
Plan B, dissolution of, 261–63
politics, culture as influence on, 266
Port Egmont settlement, 38–39
Port Louis/Puerto Soledad settlement,
  40
Port Stanley hijacking, 49
Portugal, discovery of Falklands,
  37–39
power: in law and the modern world,
  252–53
public policy, in Falklands crisis,
  244–46
public reaction, National Honor and,
  85–86
Pym, Francis, 104; in Peruvian
  initiatives, 151–73

Reagan, Ronald: in Falklands crisis
  mediation, 107; Peruvian initiatives
  considered, 152–77
Resolution 502 (U.N.), Haig's use of in
  mediation efforts, 117, 220–24
Rio Treaty Conference (1947), 43
Rome Postal Convention (1908), 42

Ros, Enrique: Peruvian attempt and, 156; sovereignty negotiations, 230–36

Rowlands, Ted, 54, 57

Sahara, territorial dispute over, 28–30

Saint Malo, 40

San Carlos settlement, British landing at, 237

Saunders Island, British possession of, 39–40

science, research, and economics of joint undertakings, 290

Shackleton survey, 53

Shlaudeman, Harry, 105

Southern Thule, occupation of, 55–56

South Georgia: British military action in, 222–27; strategic importance of, 42–43. See also Falklands crisis

South Sandwich Islands, 43; in Falklands crisis, 225–26

sovereignty: evaluation of proposal for, 279–80; of Falklands, 37–44; redefining of, 282

sovereignty negotiations, 230–36

Spain: discovery of Falklands, 37–39; Falklands crisis of 1770 response, 249–50

Spanish-Portuguese Treaty of Tordesillas, 37–38

Spanish Sahara, territorial dispute over, 28–30

Special Interim Authority (SIA), formation of, 227

Stella, Arias, 185

Stewart, Michael, 48

Suez syndrome, 250–51

superweapons, 245

territorial disputes, 17–30; Beagle Channel, 19–20, 57; Belize, 20–21; deterrence of military actions during, 243–44; East Timor, 21; Eritrea, 22; The Essequibo, 22–23; Gibraltar, 23–25; Goa, 17–19; Hong Kong, 25–28; in Latin America, 105–6; lessons learned from, 244–46; mediation assessment following Falklands crisis, 272–75; perceptions of territory, 14–

17; Suez syndrome and, 250–51; U.S. role in, 105–6; Western Sahara, 28–30. See also Falklands crisis

territory: perceptions of, 14–17; redefinition of value, 251–52. See also territorial disputes

Terry, Fernando Belaunde, 99; Peruvian initiatives, 151–86

Thatcher, Margaret, 112; London mediation efforts, 116–19; Washington mediation efforts, 120–21

third–party mediation: in Falklands dispute, 99–148. See also Falklands crisis; mediation; United States

Third World, implications of Falklands crisis for, 247–55

Treaty of Friendship (1825), 39

Treaty of Madrid (1670), 38

Treaty of Tordesillas (1494), 37–38

Treaty of Utrecht (1713), 38

trusteeship, elements of, 278

United Nations: Article 73 compliance by Great Britain, 229–30; decolonization activities, 6–10; decolonization visiting missions, 284–85; Falklands seizure response, 103–9; General Assembly Resolution 2065, 48; guarantor troops, 286–87; Interim Draft Agreement Counteroffer of May 17, 234; mediation assessment following Falklands crisis, 272–75; mediation attempts in Falklands crisis, 99–148; mediation efforts in New York, 195–215; military observers, 283–84; Resolution 31/49, 55; Resolution 502, 219–21; trusteeship following Falklands crisis, 278

United States: Argentine relations, 78–81; mediation assessment following Falklands crisis, 272–75; mediation role in Falklands crisis, 99–148; Peruvian initiatives and, 151; Puerto Soledad conflict, 41; Reagan's call to U.N., 232–33; round two mediation in Buenos Aires, 123–30; Special Interim Authority (SIA) proposed, 227;

Washington mediation efforts, 120–21,
132–35. *See also* United States

Vernet, Louis, 41
Videla, Jorge, 81
Vignes (Argentine foreign minister),
52

Walters, General Vernon, 115
Western Sahara, territorial dispute over,
28–30
Wilson government, Falklands
negotiations with Argentina, 46
World War I, British-German clash off
Falklands, 43

ABOUT THE AUTHOR

DOUGLAS KINNEY is a foreign affairs specialist with interests in risk assessment and negotiation. Mr. Kinney was educated at Milton Academy, Harvard College, and Harvard University's Kennedy School of Government. His experience in public and foreign policy encompasses economic development, European and Latin American affairs, multilateral diplomacy, politico-military affairs, and crisis management.

In economic development, Mr. Kinney has done computer modeling of America's future patterns of international trade; consulted for the Tennessee Valley Authority (TVA) on political and public service redistricting; and served in the first Peace Corps program in Upper Volta, specializing in rural water supply.

In European and Latin American affairs, Mr. Kinney has served abroad in the American Embassies in Mexico City and Rome, as well as on Delegations to Brussels and Geneva. His latest overseas post was as Deputy Political Counselor in Caracas, Venezuela. In the Department of State, he has worked on both Latin American and European affairs. He served as Chairman of the Open Forum in the Policy Planning Staff, and in Henry Kissinger's Executive Secretariat, including travel with the President or the Secretary of State to some 18 countries. Mr. Kinney's working languages are French, Italian, and Spanish.

In multilateral diplomacy, he has served in the Office of United Nations Political Affairs on the Middle East and United Nations Peacekeeping Forces, where he sketched out the first non-UN peacekeeping force for the Sinai, today the Multilateral Force and Observers (MFO). Mr. Kinney also served at the U.S. Mission to the United Nations in New York as Latin America advisor to Ambassador Jeane Kirkpatrick and Deputy United States Representative to the Trusteeship Council.

In politico-military affairs, Mr. Kinney has served in the Office of NATO Affairs. He was Chairman of the Interagency Group on Civil Emergency Planning (CEP), and has also served on U.S. Delegations to NATO on force planning and beddown of Cruise and Pershing II missiles. Mr. Kinney is a graduate of the National War College. He has served in the Office of Theater Military Policy, Bureau of Politico-Military Affairs; as Political Adviser for Joint Chiefs strategic games and field exercises of the Atlantic Command; and as Adviser on Intermediate-Range Nuclear Forces (INF) on the U.S. Delegation to the Nuclear & Space Arms Talks (NST) at Geneva which led to the 1988 INF Treaty with the Soviet Union.

Mr. Kinney has worked on crisis management of disasters, civil disorder, kidnappings, and skyjackings and the negotiation/mediation of political crises. He has contributed to MIT's CASCON computer detabase on political crises; the Foreign Service Institute's Perspectives on Negotiation seminars; Harvard's crisis case studies series; A.R. Coll & A.C. Arend's *The Falklands War: Lessons for Strategy, Diplomacy and International Law*; and C.R. Mitchell & K. Webb's *New Approaches to International Mediation* (Westport, CT: Greenwood Press, 1988). Mr. Kenney was the recipient of a Una Chapman Cox Fellowship, served as an Associate of the Institute for the Study of Diplomacy at Georgetown University, and has taught negotiation at Georgetown's School of Foreign Service.